Why Privacy Matters

Why Privacy Matters

NEIL RICHARDS

OXFORD
UNIVERSITY PRESS

OXFORD
UNIVERSITY PRESS

Oxford University Press is a department of the University of Oxford. It furthers the University's objective of excellence in research, scholarship, and education by publishing worldwide. Oxford is a registered trade mark of Oxford University Press in the UK and certain other countries.

Published in the United States of America by Oxford University Press
198 Madison Avenue, New York, NY 10016, United States of America.

CIP data is on file at the Library of Congress

ISBN 978-0-19-093904-5

DOI: 10.1093/oso/9780190939045.001.0001

Printed by Integrated Books International, United States of America

For Fiona and Declan

Contents

Introduction

The Privacy Conversation

Privacy is dead. There should be no doubt whatsoever about that. We live in a society that constantly generates vast quantities of human information—information about you, me, and everyone we know. This information is in turn tracked, screened, and sorted by corporations and governments and shared exponentially to others. Ad networks monitor our web-surfing to send us "more relevant" ads. The National Security Agency screens our email activity for signs of radicalism. Schools track student sleep and activity patterns; CCTV cameras watch every street corner and traffic light; and drones have appeared in our skies. Vast databases of human information are assembled for purposes of "training" artificial intelligence programs designed to predict everything from traffic patterns and virus contagion to the location of undocumented migrants. We spy on the activities of loved ones, whether though "Find My Friends" or by tracking everything they do and say with their cell phones. We're even tracking ourselves, using personal electronics like Apple watches, Fitbits, and other gadgets that have made the "quantified self" a realistic possibility.

Privacy's death has fittingly been a public one. Commentators and scholars have bemoaned the Death of Privacy at length. One 2017 *New York Times* article suggested that massive data breaches like the one suffered by credit broker Equifax signal "the end of privacy."[1] Such statements are treading well-worn ground. At the launch of Sun Microsystems' Jini technology in January 1999, Sun CEO Scott McNealy famously declared, "You have zero privacy anyway. Get over it."[2] McNealy's outburst made headlines at the time, and it continues to be quoted today by technologists, journalists, and academics, even as Jini (and Sun itself) have faded over the horizon of our memories. Many others agree. At a Federal Trade Commission event in 2013, Vint Cerf, a leading figure in the creation of the internet and Google's "chief internet evangelist," suggested that privacy might be a historical anomaly.[3] Pulitzer Prize-winning journalist Thomas Friedman infamously declared in 2014 that "privacy is over."[4] Facebook founder Mark Zuckerberg was more blunt, declaring in his peculiar and self-serving way that privacy was no longer a "social norm."[5] To repeat: privacy is dead, or at a minimum, it is dying.

That's the conventional wisdom, anyway. It's something I hear a lot. In fact, it's part of a conversation I've had so many times that I've started calling it just "The Privacy Conversation." I've had The Privacy Conversation with my colleagues and students, with taxi drivers and waiters, with barbers and bartenders. I've had it with family and friends, and I've had it with people I've met in line at airports and baseball stadiums while we waited to go through privacy-invasive metal detectors. I have The Privacy Conversation about once a week, and it goes something like this.

I'll be chatting with someone—usually someone I've just met—and they'll ask me what I do. "I'm a law professor," I explain, and then they'll ask what kind of law I teach. Before the words "privacy law" even pass my lips, I know what's coming. There's going to be a pause, and they're going to say one of two things. Sometimes they'll jokingly say something like "Well, you must be very busy then!" But other times, the more interesting times, something else happens. They'll say something like "Well, there is no privacy anymore, is there?" And then there's another pause and a funny noise. It sounds a bit like a cough and a bit like a laugh, but it's more of a sad sound than a happy sound. It's a wistful sound, as if they are lamenting the Death of Privacy, lamenting the end of something they hardly appreciated before it was gone.

Then it's my turn to talk. (Though it's hard for a law professor, I try to be brief.) I explain that "Privacy Is Dead" is a myth, and a self-serving one at that, put forth by companies and governments that have lots to gain if our belief in privacy is lost. The Privacy Is Dead idea is false on its own terms. Our technologies collect lots of personal information, but lots of things are still private. We still wear clothes to cover our naked bodies; we still lock the doors to our homes (and our bedrooms and our bathrooms); we still keep secrets; and we still care about privacy. Besides, it's just not the case that all digital information is known to everyone. We might talk about our information being "out there," but most information exists in the vast intermediate spaces between being wholly private and wholly public.

More important, this Privacy Is Dead talk masks the real interests at stake: control of our digital society. We live in a society in which information is power, and "privacy" is the word we use to talk about the struggles over personal information, personal power, and personal control. If we think of it this way, privacy is very much alive—but very much hanging in the balance.

We use privacy talk to try to come to grips with the tremendous changes in our society wrought by technologies running on human information, as well as our own places in that society. The rules for the collection and use of our information aren't settled yet. But ordinary people are disempowered. Most of us lack sufficient knowledge about the technologies and the dense privacy policies and similar legal agreements that control ever more important parts of our lives. And even if we knew more, most of us would still lack the power or technical skills to do anything about it. That's why many of us feel that our privacy—our ability to have a say over our human information—is slipping away, running through our fingers like so many fine grains of sand.

At the same time, the flow of our human information has become one of the most important building blocks of our increasingly digital society. It's become a cliché in the technology community to call personal data—your data—"the new oil."[6] From this perspective, human information is the fuel of the information economy: just as the Industrial Age's engines (cars, planes, and factories) ran on oil, so too do the Information Age's engines (social networks, GPS navigation software, and ad-targeting algorithms) run on data. It follows, insist the "new oil" evangelists, that access to human information is as essential to our information economy as access to oil was to our industrial economy. From this perspective, the processing of human information is inevitable, and privacy is just another old-fashioned, outdated concept that stands in the way of Progress.

I disagree: privacy isn't dead, nor should it be. But privacy is up for grabs. Our conversations about privacy are just the lively battleground over this "new oil" of personal information. They are fights over social power because information is power, and in any society, information about the people in it confers social power.

Viewed from this perspective, privacy matters. How we talk about privacy matters. And how we think about privacy matters. Privacy is about more than just keeping human information unknown or unknowable. It's certainly more than the ability of individuals to "control" access to that information. Put simply, privacy is about power. Privacy is about the rules governing the extent to which human information is detected, collected, used, shared, and stored and how those activities can be used to affect our lives. It's not just about who knows what about us, but about what rules apply to what they know. Thus, a "secret" is still a secret once it is shared with a confidant, and we still continue to care about what we share. Similarly, our data can remain private even when we share it with companies. After all, their "privacy policies" detail not just what information is collected about us but what the company will (and won't) do with that information. In an age of data, privacy rules are the rules that govern the flows of human information—the information about our beliefs, our aspirations, and every moment of our lives.

The battle for privacy isn't over. As we'll see, it's a battle that has been raging in one form or another for almost 150 years. If anything, it's a battle that's just beginning as more kinds of human information are collected and assembled, from internet reading and viewing habits to smartphone location data, and from Fitbit activity and sleep pattern data to the unique genetic codes locked inside our cells. But if we accept the fatalist myth that Privacy Is Dead (or its self-serving cousin, that "data is the new oil"), if we think about privacy as outdated or impossible, if we think about our information as inevitably "out there" and beyond human or social control, we will have given up. This fatalist view of privacy is irresponsible, and it's destructive. We should not cede our power and responsibility to help set reasonable rules for the collection, use, storage, and sharing of our human data. If we do give up, our digital revolution will have few rules governing information. In such an anarchic society, as in any anarchy, only the powerful will prosper, while the digitally disempowered will become even more so.[7]

Because privacy is up for grabs, we need to better explain what it is and what it can do for us. We need to identify when we must protect against the collection or exploitation of personal data, and when we should let the data flow. The "new oil" way of thinking about privacy is problematic, but even on its own terms it doesn't prove that privacy is dead. Just as we did with the "old oil" of petroleum, we need to know when human information should be produced and how (and in whose interests) its power should be harnessed. We need to know how to protect against the equivalent of oil spills, air pollution, and potentially cataclysmic climate change. We are of course still dealing with many of these Industrial Age problems many decades later, but at least we have a sense of what they are. When it comes to the Information Revolution, though, we are only just starting to ask the right questions rather than developing good answers to those questions. We need to spark and engage in a sustained and meaningful discussion about Why Privacy Matters, and we need to engage the public, because the future of privacy is the future of our society. Such questions are simply too important to be left to academics, technologists, and lawyers, and especially too important to be left to government security services or the companies making vast fortunes from our data.

This book is a longer form of what I say when I have The Privacy Conversation. It's my contribution to the debate we must continue to have about privacy, data, and the rules undergirding the infrastructure of our digital society. At its most basic, this book explains what privacy is and why we should care about it. My argument is simple: we need to put the misleading story of the Death of Privacy to one side, and we need to think more clearly about how technologies of human data can both make our lives better and make them worse. As with so many human inventions, we need to craft reasonable rules and protections so that we can maximize the good things about these technologies and minimize the bad things. And those rules should, first and foremost, serve human values that make our lives better, both as individuals and as members of society.

Right now, when we talk about these issues in the United States, in Europe, in Britain, or anywhere else, it can seem like the deck is stacked against privacy. Calls for privacy regulation are met with arguments that privacy rules get in the way of other good things, like "security"—the prevention of crime, fraud, or terrorism. Others argue that privacy can threaten "innovation," that magical term from Silicon Valley's PR departments evoking a religious faith in Progress toward a technological utopia. Security and innovation can both be very good things, but privacy can be a very good thing, too. Unlike security or innovation, though, privacy often gets marginalized, seen as a backward or old-fashioned value, or maybe just something vague and poorly understood.

In this book, I will show that privacy is neither backward nor old-fashioned; in fact, I will show how a meaningful measure of privacy is essential to any digital society that reasonable humans would want to live in. But privacy is poorly understood; it can mean many things, and people talking about privacy often talk at cross purposes to one other. Hence this book, in which I'll try to help us understand privacy better. I'll explain what privacy is and what it isn't. I will show what privacy can do for us, why privacy matters, and how privacy will continue to matter far into the digital future. Along the way, I'll also show that it's not only "privacy" that we talk about in vague and sloppy ways; we also talk about "innovation" and "security" that way, too. We need to be clearer about what we mean when we use these words, especially if we want to build a digital future that is innovative and secure and has reasonable and fair rules regulating human information. If we're clear about why we're protecting human information, then we can make intelligent decisions that guide our human information policy. And only then can we properly make some of the inevitable trade-offs between and among privacy, security, and innovation.

So why does privacy matter? What are we trying to protect when we talk about privacy protection through law, technologies like encryption, or social and ethical norms? Put simply, privacy matters because it helps us to develop our identities, it allows us to exercise political freedom and it protects us as consumers. But to begin with, it's important to understand that privacy protections shouldn't be absolute; we need to have a mix of rules that keep things private and rules that allow information to flow, whether that information is facts reported by a free press or personal data deployed to make our lives better (something that certainly does happen, though far less often than Silicon Valley might have you believe). We shouldn't want perfect security—perfect security is not only impossible, but down that path lies both enormous inconvenience as well as the specter of a pervasive police state. Nor should we want unfettered innovation of everything in society. Criminals and terrorists can be innovative; companies and foreign governments that disrupt our democratic processes are too. The iPhone was an innovation; so too were nerve toxins, nuclear weapons, and attempts to manipulate recent U.S. elections by Russia and Cambridge Analytica. Similarly, privacy shouldn't be seen as something that is always a good thing in and of itself. As a philosopher might put it, privacy isn't an *intrinsic good* but an *instrumental value*. Privacy shouldn't be thought of as an end in itself. Instead we should think of it as something we want because it enables other valuable opportunities, states of well-being, and human values that we can talk about without referring to the vague word "privacy." In this book I'll show how privacy can promote and safeguard lots of things that any decent society should care about. There are many of them, but I'll focus on the three I think are particularly important: identity, freedom, and protection.

Let me say a little bit about these three instrumental privacy values before we go any further. Privacy rules can promote *identity* formation because privacy can help us to figure out who we are and what we believe, by ourselves and with our intimates and confidants. In my previous book, *Intellectual Privacy*, I argued that a special kind of privacy (the intellectual privacy of the title) is necessary in a democracy because it allows us to develop our political beliefs free from the skewing effects of being watched, monitored, and judged.[8] Intellectual privacy secures the intellectual freedom to figure out what we believe about the world and our place in it. Intellectual privacy is essential to the development of our identities, but it is not the only kind of privacy that matters to our identities. The same kinds of privacy protections that can allow us to develop our political and religious beliefs can also help us figure out who we are more generally. Privacy grants us the space to engage in self-examination and the space to play, by ourselves and with others, to work out who we are as human beings. Privacy even gives us the space to have multiple, sometimes conflicting identities. Some privacy skeptics, such as Judge Richard Posner and Mark Zuckerberg, have argued that privacy just lets us be dishonest about who we really are. I will show instead that most identity play of this sort is not dishonest. On the contrary, identity play is an essential part of being human. And privacy makes the development of a person's *identity*, and thus being human, possible.

Privacy matters for a second reason as well: it safeguards democratic *freedom*. For centuries, Western legal and political culture has been deeply suspicious about the power of government. The lengthy debate produced by Edward Snowden's revelations about the American surveillance state reignited age-old questions of how much government surveillance is appropriate in a democratic society, as well as who should watch the watchers. Government officials calling for inroads into privacy across the digitized, democratic world have argued that increased surveillance of our lives is the price we must pay for liberty and safety. I will show instead that the conflict between privacy and security has been overblown and that security-minded government officials have both overstated the need for surveillance and understated the costs of fine-grained government monitoring in our lives. While we will sometimes need to reconcile conflicts between privacy and security, privacy protections will remain necessary if we want political freedom against the power of the state. In fact, not only does mass surveillance make us less free, but it can actually make us less safe as well. A surveillance apparatus focused on ineffective bulk surveillance of everyone's data must trade off the costs of that surveillance against more effective means of doing its job. At the same time, a surveillance agency that knows everything about everyone (and every politician) can represent a clear and present danger to democratic government, for instance, by blackmailing politicians or rigging elections. This is a very real threat, as the people of South Korea learned to their shock in the summer of 2017, when they discovered that their own security services had tried to rig their elections in favor of a preferred candidate.[9] Privacy thus enables democratic *freedom* and protects us as citizens of free, self-governing societies.

Along the same lines, privacy can give us *protection* as well, whether as consumers or employees. In an information society, information is social power. From this perspective, the debates over digital privacy are really just debates about how power will be allocated in an information society and how much power the humans in that society will get as consumers or citizens. Many of those calling so loudly for the Death of Privacy are really seeking its demise so that they can line their own pockets. Those companies have deeply vested interests in using information about people to observe them, make inferences about them, and control them. This control can range from marketers trying to influence consumer preferences to companies using personal data to sort and discriminate, political candidates using personal data to deliver finely targeted personalized propaganda, and employers trying to cut down on employees' healthcare costs by discriminating against the disabled. Such data-driven tactics of sorting and persuasion can undermine the ability of individuals to make authentic or even rational choices, and they can deny the kinds of equal opportunities we traditionally say we believe in. In an economy that exploits personal data, the battles over privacy will ultimately determine the allocation of power in our economy and our society as a whole. In the twentieth century, governments around the world developed consumer protection laws to address the power asymmetries caused by the industrial economy. Today we need a new set of consumer protection rules to guard against the power asymmetries and unchecked abuses of the information economy to protect consumers as they actually are, not as rhetoric or economic theory would like them to be. Protecting consumers in this way requires us to recognize them as something I call the "situated consumer."

If we get them right, consumer protection rules can also promote trust—trust in our digital society as well as trust in the information relationships that have become the essential building blocks of that society. Think, for a moment, about the most important relationships in your life. These might well include your relationships with your spouse or partner, your family and close friends, your doctor, and digital intermediaries providing access to technologies that let you live your modern life. Each of these relationships can last for decades. Critically, in each of these relationships, sensitive or even intimate information flows between you and others. Think about the secrets we share with lovers and family members or confide in our doctors (even those we may have just met). Now think about the information that we share as customers of digital services: records held by search engines of every*thing* we want to know, records held by internet service providers of every*thing* we read, records held by social networks of every*one* we know, and records held by GPS services of every*where* we go. In our world of mobile communications, a single company such as Google could have access to all of this data at once. Google runs the leading search engine, it runs internet service in whole cities, it runs social networks, and it runs the popular Google Maps GPS service. But do you trust it? Should you?

In each of these relationships with loved ones, doctors, and tech giants, an attention to privacy—the rules governing shared information—is essential for them to function. This is particularly the case for our relationships with tech companies, who serve as our "digital intermediaries." If we don't trust our digital intermediaries, we'll be less likely to share our information with them, which can make them (and us) worse off. In sharp contrast, when there is meaningful trust between humans and their intermediaries, sustainable relationships can flourish. When these relationships flourish, information flows in a state of trust, and both the companies and their customers (you and me) are better off. Information rules are necessary to build the trust that is necessary for these relationships (and in the aggregate, society itself) to function and to flourish. In other words, a sustainable and ethical digital society will depend on the trust that is safeguarded by the rules protecting our privacy. In these ways, privacy rules promoting consumer protection can *protect* us as *situated consumers* and members of society.

Taken together, the three privacy values I offer enable us to act in the various roles we play in society. Identity allows us to be thinking, self-defining humans; freedom lets us be citizens; and protection safeguards our roles as situated consumers and workers, allowing us, as members of society, to trust and rely on other people so that we can live our lives and hopefully build a better future together.

This, then, is the basic argument I want to make. Privacy isn't dead or dying. On the contrary, privacy will become increasingly important as our digital revolution continues to charge ever further ahead. If we want to build a digital society consistent with our hard-won social values—a society that is fair, just, equitable, free, and sustainable—then a meaningful commitment to privacy must continue to be a part of that society. Privacy matters, and it will continue to matter, not just because privacy is a proxy for social power but because good privacy rules promote the essential human values of identity, freedom, and protection. If we want to retain our traditional commitments to these hard-won, precious, and sometimes fragile values, we need privacy rules to protect, safeguard, and encourage them. This book explains why and how we should do that.

The questions that prompt this book are thus What is privacy? and Why does it matter in our digital world? These are questions that everyone *should* care about, and they are questions that in my experience almost everyone *does* care about, regardless of where they live, what they do for a living, or how long they went to school. Because these questions matter—because privacy matters—I've tried to write the book in a way that is as clear and accessible as possible. All too often, I've found, scholars who have something important to say camouflage the power of their ideas under a cloud of academic jargon, whether they mean to or not. But make no mistake: while I've tried to be clear, underneath the hood of my argument is a lot of serious academic scholarship by me, my coauthors, and, most important, by other members of the large and growing privacy law community around the world. This work builds on and connects their hard work and insights, and it would not have been possible to write without their many, many contributions. I encourage both specialists and students of privacy law to dig into the end notes both to check my work and for further reading in this fascinating and important area.*

Finally, let me say a little about the structure of this book (and my argument) before we begin. The book is divided into two parts. Part 1 consists of the first three chapters. They are about the ways we should (and shouldn't) think and talk about privacy. Chapter 1, "What Privacy Is," explains what I mean when I talk about "privacy" in this book and offers a provisional definition of privacy as "the degree to which human information is neither known nor used." Chapter 2, "A Theory of Privacy as Rules," makes the argument that we should think about privacy as the rules governing human information in our society, rules that serve specific values rather than vague notions of privacy or individual control over embarrassing information. The first two chapters offer a fairly broad definition of privacy, so chapter 3, "What Privacy Isn't," clarifies my argument by explaining and debunking a series of misconceptions about privacy and refining our understanding of privacy so that it can do good work in our society to promote important human values. Part 2, chapters 4 through 6, explains further the three most

---

* There are also a few footnotes like this one, which offer additions to the main argument that are more substantive—and interesting—than lists of academic citations, like the story in part 1 of Taylor Swift's use of facial recognition technology.

important human values I think our privacy rules should serve: identity, freedom, and protection. In contrast to much of the fatalism around Death of Privacy talk, the book concludes on a note of hope, arguing that we can and should begin to think about privacy as a fundamental right on par with the other fundamental rights we cherish.

PART 1

HOW TO THINK ABOUT PRIVACY

Privacy is everywhere you look. Open your phone, and you might see emails from companies telling you about their data practices; maybe they've changed their privacy policy, or maybe they are sending you an update about those practices because the law requires them to do so. A few minutes later, you might have to click "I agree" to another company's privacy notice to use their app, or a website might require you to agree to their use of software cookies if you want to read an article.[1] Open any newspaper or news website and you will undoubtedly see privacy stories. It might be a grocery store, credit card company, or credit bureau that has suffered a data breach. It might be a company that has inadvisably added a microphone, a camera, or a GPS chip to a speaker, a doorbell, or a doll without thinking through the consequences.[2] It might be about one of Facebook's ongoing privacy struggles. You could imagine any one of a number of examples here, whether it's their privacy practices in general or the ones stemming from their relationship with the election-warping data broker Cambridge Analytica.[3] It might be about the U.S. government's partnership with the data broker Palantir to identify undocumented immigrants for midnight roundups by ICE agents.[4] Or it might be about facial recognition technologies deployed by governments,* or by Taylor Swift,† or by sports teams.‡ Or any one of dozens of other issues.

Other times, privacy is lurking just beneath the surface. If you apply to a school, for a job, or for a promotion, information about you—even information you might not know about—is increasingly being used by schools and companies to make these sorts of consequential decisions.[5] If you search for something on Google, scan your Twitter or Facebook feed, or look at your YouTube home page, you're seeing links and posts tailored to you, based on the analysis of the often vast amounts of data that the platforms know about you.[6] And then there are the ads. Advertising is ubiquitous in the digital environment, and frequently it is "targeted," selected by the algorithm based upon what is known about you. This information is often substantial and sensitive, including your location, gender, race, age, political preferences, sexuality, and a partial transcript of everything you browse or read on your device.[7] You're not just looking at the ad; all too often, the ad is looking right back at you. And it's taking notes.

Our digital society constantly faces issues involving the use of human information. In the English-speaking world, at least, most of the time we use

---

* Consider Sweden, where a "high school in Skellefteå conducted a pilot program . . . where the attendance of 22 students over a period of three weeks was taken with the help of facial recognition technology." Adam Smith, *Sweden Gets First GDPR Fine After Facial Recognition Used in School*, PC MAGAZINE, Aug. 27, 2019. Consider China, where "a vast surveillance apparatus . . . of millions of cameras equipped with facial recognition technology" is being marketed to other sovereign nations and their "data [is] being siphoned back to China." Arjun Kharpal, *China's Surveillance Tech Is Spreading Globally, Raising Concerns About Beijing's Influence*, CNBC, Oct. 8 2019. Or consider the United States, where "[r]oughly one in two American adults has their photos searched by the US government using facial recognition." Shirin Ghaffary & Rani Molla, *Here's Where the US Government Is Using Facial Recognition Technology to Surveil Americans*, Vox, July 18, 2019. For a thoughtful examination of the issues surrounding facial recognition by two prominent scholars, see Evan Selinger & Woodrow Hartzog, *What Happens When Employers Can Read Your Facial Expressions*, N.Y. TIMES, Oct. 17, 2019.

† No, really. *Rolling Stone* magazine reported in December 2018 that Swift has been deploying state-of-the-art facial recognition systems to identify potential stalkers in attendance at her shows. Swift's surveillance system worked like this: A technology company set up a flashy kiosk with a video playing rehearsal clips of Swift, and the system took photos of every unwitting fan who stared at the screen. These images were then cross-referenced against a list of "hundreds of the pop star's known stalkers." Steve Knopper, *Why Taylor Swift Is Using Facial Recognition at Concerts*, ROLLING STONE, Dec. 13, 2018.

‡ No, really. In 2019, numerous news outlets reported that the English football team Manchester City had been trialing the use of facial recognition cameras to improve the speed with which they could admit fans to matches at their Etihad stadium. David Collins, *Manchester City Tries Facial Recognition to Beat Football Queues*, THE TIMES, Aug. 18, 2019. Both the Taylor Swift and Manchester City projects were enabled by Blink Identity, a Texas-based company in which Ticketmaster has invested and which has also spent most of the past decade building a massive facial-recognition database for the U.S. Department of Defense in the Middle East. Maya Wolfe-Robinson, *Manchester City Warned Against Using Facial Recognition on Fans*, THE GUARDIAN, Aug. 18, 2019.

the word "privacy" to talk about them.[§] Occasionally, we see other terms being used; we might use the word "confidentiality" or "secrecy." You might even see these issues talked about in terms of "data protection," particularly if you are a lawyer or in Europe. In general, though, when we talk about these issues, we use some variation on the word "privacy." The problem is that no one—not the general public, not policymakers, nor even scholars—can quite agree on what precisely we mean by "privacy." It doesn't take a great leap of logic to recognize that this is a problem. If we can't agree on what we mean by privacy—much less on why it's important—then it will be almost impossible to talk about, work on, and solve these problems of human information in a principled and productive way. Part 1 takes this problem head-on, offering a way to think about privacy as about the rules that govern our human information. It also debunks some of the seductive but pernicious myths that pervade privacy discussions in the courts, among academics, and in public debate.

[§] To be clear, when I say "we" here, and throughout this book, I mean the general public, scholars, journalists, and politicians.

1

What Privacy Is

Privacy's Definitional Problem

It's customary at the beginning of a book about privacy to explain that even though privacy threats and privacy talk seem to be everywhere in our modern digital society, we lack a settled definition of what privacy is. Is privacy the amount of information that is known about people? If so, then privacy seems to be very much under threat. Or maybe privacy is about reasonable expectations against government surveillance, or our right to make fundamental decisions, the two ways American constitutional law defines "privacy."[1] Maybe it's about controlling how our information is handled,[2] or managing the flow of information in ways that are sensitive to social context,[3] or protecting against data breaches,[4] or eavesdropping,[5] or about intimacy,[6] or protecting our feelings from psychological injury, or the "right to be let alone"[7] (whatever that means).[**]

Privacy isn't just an Anglo-American idea, of course. Other cultures have their own conceptions of privacy. European law is a good example of this; in fact, European constitutional law has *two* separate rights to privacy, though neither is expressly called "privacy." These rights come from the foundational idea in European constitutional law that our most important human right is

---

[**] I'm being slightly facetious here. "The Right to Be Let Alone" famously entered the American privacy conversation with the publication of Warren and Brandeis's germinal article "The Right to Privacy," 4 Harv. L. Rev. 193 (1890). Warren and Brandeis appear to have borrowed the term from Thomas Cooley's influential treatise on torts. Neil M. Richards & Daniel J. Solove, *Privacy's Other Path: Recovering the Law of Confidentiality*, 96 Geo. L. J. 123, 129–30 (2006). "The Right to Be Let Alone," along with the right to an "inviolate personality," were Warren and Brandeis's attempts to describe what they meant by "the Right to Privacy" they were calling for in their article. Nevertheless, despite the attempts by literally dozens of historians and legal scholars (including this author), it remains unclear to this day precisely what they meant. The best reading of both Warren and Brandeis and the vast academic literature their article generated, I think, is that it sought to protect people (especially elites) against the emotional harm caused by new press practices of gossip columns and nonconsensual photography. It targeted the press for publishing true facts that inquiring minds wanted to know, and it relied on judges to police the (gendered) line between what was a fit matter for public debate and what was not the public's business. Neil Richards, Intellectual Privacy 21 (2015). Most significant, however, Warren and Brandeis gave a more important name to these issues than "the Right to Be Let Alone," by calling it, as they did in their article's title, "The Right to Privacy."

our dignity. In fact, one way to think about European privacy rights is as protection against different violations of our human dignity. The EU Charter of Fundamental Rights operates as Europe's equivalent to the American Bill of Rights, though it is much younger and is not quite as famous.[8] Article 7 of the EU Charter protects "private and family life" and mandates that "[e]veryone has the right to respect for his or her private and family life, home and communications." By contrast, Article 8 of the Charter is about what Europeans call "data protection" and states that "[e]veryone has the right to the protection of personal data concerning him or her." These rights are related but distinct in the sense that "[d]ata protection focuses on whether data is used fairly and with due process while privacy preserves the Athenian ideal of private life"[9]—the idea that citizens need places and relationships in which they can withdraw from participation in the public sphere of politics and commerce. Europe's new General Data Protection Regulation (GDPR) seeks to protect these rights in practice, and it has been highly influential in advancing these twin ideas of privacy (especially data protection) across the world.[10]

That's a lot of definitions, and believe it or not, it's just the tip of the iceberg of privacy definitions offered by lawyers, philosophers, sociologists, journalists, and others. Privacy scholar Daniel Solove puts it well when he argues that "privacy is a concept in disarray."[11] Solove confesses that he started working on his book *Understanding Privacy* hoping to offer his own comprehensive definition of privacy, but after a vast amount of research, he gave up, explaining frankly:

> [A]fter delving into the question, I was humbled by it. I could not reach a satisfactory answer. This struggle ultimately made me realize that privacy is a plurality of different things and that the quest for a single essence of privacy leads to a dead end. There is no overarching conception of privacy—it must be mapped like terrain, by painstakingly studying the landscape.[12]

Solove's topographic map of privacy ultimately found sixteen such "different things" that he divided into four categories: (1) information collection (surveillance and interrogation); (2) information processing (aggregation, identification, insecurity, secondary use, and exclusion); (3) information dissemination (breach of confidentiality, disclosure, exposure, increased accessibility, blackmail, appropriation, and distortion); and (4) invasion (intrusion and decisional interference).[13]

That's a lot as well. Solove's book is one of the leading books on privacy theory to date; it is nuanced and it is erudite. But his sixteen categories are more than most people can hold in their heads at any one time. (I must confess that I had to look some of them up again.) In addition, as Ryan Calo has pointed out, because Solove's categories are socially recognized, they lack a unifying principle. They lack the ability to say that something new is a privacy issue for the first time, as the theory seems to require us to wait for recognition by social consensus. And they lack the ability to say something is *not* a privacy issue and is better understood as part of something else.[14] Nevertheless, Solove has a point that it's likely futile for us to try to come up with a definition of privacy that is both broad enough to cover all of the many problems we might think of as privacy problems and also narrow enough to be useful in dealing with those problems. What is more, as technology and our social norms continue to evolve, it will certainly be futile to spend our time arguing about the most precise definition of privacy while problems continue to mount and while companies and governments march ahead with new projects fueled by human information. If privacy can mean lots of things, then its vagueness can provide cover to companies and government officials to give lip service to whichever definition of privacy suits them, while they just go ahead and do what they wanted to with our human information all along.[15]

That's a depressing thought. However, it's not all bad news. The good news is that we don't actually need a precise, universally accepted definition of privacy. Lots of things we care about lack precise definitions, but we still manage to protect them anyway. It is hard to define ideas, and our most important ideas are often the hardest ones to define. This is a common problem in law. Take the notion of *equality* clearly protected by the constitutions of most democratic societies, and in the United States by the Fourteenth Amendment to the Constitution. "Equality" can mean many different things. In the United States, it can mean equality of opportunity,[16] equality of outcomes,[17] nondiscrimination by the government,[18] government recognition and repair of racial disparities,[19] and an intentional government "blindness" to race, among other things.[20] When these values clash, such as in cases involving affirmative action in college admissions, the idea of "equality" can seem to produce more chaos than clarity.[21] Does our commitment to equality demand, for example, that the government treat everyone "equally" without reference to their race, even though good evidence exists that many racial minorities suffer systematic disadvantages in everything from access to nutrition and healthcare to bias in school discipline and standardized tests?[22] On the other hand, does equality demand that where race and material inequality are related, the government can (or must) take race into account in order to treat people "equally," even when this gives the government the dangerous power to treat people differently on the basis of race? Both of these are among a number of facially plausible interpretations of the "equal protection of the laws" guaranteed by the Fourteenth Amendment. This is a hard question to answer.

I'm sure you have your own views on these questions (I have mine), but the point is that we often differ on these questions because we have different definitions of "equality," even though at the same time we likely agree that equality is essential to any just and fair society. I don't mean to suggest here that equality is incoherent or unimportant. On the contrary, the equality of human beings is one of our most important values, and it is one we must protect doggedly, carefully, and with attention to the human consequences of legal rules in practice. Protection of equality is particularly important at this point in history when certain politicians have, once again, begun to mask agendas of autocracy, division, and xenophobia in the rhetoric of populism and grievance. The conversations we have over shared values like equality are some of the most important conversations we have as a society. But my point here is a simple one: even an idea as universally accepted as equality has proven hard to define clearly. We can agree that equality is essential to a good society even when we disagree about what equality means and why we value it.

If we dig a little deeper, we can see that many other important values resist precise definition. Take freedom of expression, a value almost universally shared as important and robustly protected by law all over the world. In the United States, the First Amendment's protection of "freedom of speech, and of the press" is probably its most important constitutional value, similar to the way human dignity is the most important value in Europe.[23] Yet even something as well protected as free expression lacks a precise definition. Europeans and Americans have well-documented disagreements about the justification and scope of free expression, which is why Holocaust denial is a crime in Germany, and why it receives the highest level of protection as political speech in the United States.[24] But even Americans can't agree on why free speech matters. American courts robustly protect free expression, but they lack a single explanation for why it is such a critical value. Instead, there are at least three main justifications for why free expression should get special protection (the search for truth, democratic self-government, and human autonomy), no single one of which explains most of the cases.[25] If you want to get really depressed about the difficulties of definition, consider obscenity law, which to this day remains haunted by Justice Potter Stewart's frustration at the U.S. Supreme Court's inability to define obscene movies separately from nonobscene ones with his famous declaration, "I shall not today attempt further to define the kinds of material I understand to be embraced within that shorthand description; and perhaps I could never succeed in intelligibly doing so. But *I know it when I see it*, and the motion picture involved in this case is not that."[26] Nevertheless, the fact that courts can't articulate a single justification for free expression and have failed to define obscenity hasn't prevented American courts from giving First Amendment claims an extraordinary level of special protection.[27] Similarly, while federal obscenity prosecutions not involving child pornography have been on the decline in recent years, the U.S. Department of Justice continues to have a criminal enforcement section dedicated to both "protecting children from sexual exploitation and prohibiting the distribution of obscenity," even though no one knows what obscenity means now that Justice Stewart is no longer with us.[28]

A Working Definition of Privacy

Let's return to privacy, perhaps chastened a bit by the difficulties of definitions. It is hard to define privacy, but it's hard to define lots of things we care about. Critically, though, this fact doesn't stop us from *talking about them*, and it doesn't stop us from trying *to protect them*. It's my argument in this book that privacy matters and we should try to protect it. But in order to protect something, we still need some sense of what we're talking about, even as we acknowledge that privacy, like equality, can be conceptualized in different ways and at different levels of abstraction. I won't subject you to a book on privacy in which the author throws up his hands in resignation like Justice Stewart. So what should we do? Let's try for a working definition. We would want this definition to be clear enough for ordinary people and policymakers to understand, but one that relies on the most persuasive academic thinking and research on privacy. We would want it to be clear without being glib, and sophisticated without being bewildering. Aware that definitions are tricky, let me offer such a working definition of privacy so we can at least be on the same page about what we are talking about in this book:

Privacy is the degree to which human information is neither known nor used.

My goal in offering this definition is not to suggest that this is the only definition of privacy, or that it is even the best definition of privacy for all purposes.
Instead, I'm proposing it as the best way of capturing the problems at the core
of this book: the human information technologies that are revolutionizing
our society and that are most often pointed to as evidence of the Death of
Privacy. It's a way for us to be clear about what we're talking about as well as
what we are not talking about. To this end, four elements of my working definition deserve brief additional explanation:

To reorder things for a moment, privacy is:

(1) *information* about
(2) *humans* that is
(3) *used as well as known* and is
(4) a matter of *degree*.

1. Information. First and foremost, it's important to understand that my
definition is about *information*. When I talk about privacy in this book, I am
thinking primarily in terms of other people and entities learning, knowing,
or using information. I'm talking about what lawyers and law professors
call "information privacy." In fact, the standard privacy law course in law
schools—including the one I teach every year at Washington University—
is usually called something like Information Privacy Law. Of course, when
we talk about privacy in ordinary conversations, information privacy isn't
always what we mean, nor, as we've seen, is it the only way that we might define privacy. If someone bursts into your bathroom while you are taking a
shower or blasts loud music into your home when you're trying to sleep, we
would almost certainly talk about an invasion of your privacy—your ability
to enjoy that space—that has occurred. For this reason, academics would
call this an invasion of *spatial privacy.*[29] Sometimes invasions of spatial privacy also involve the collection of information; in our two examples, the loud
music doesn't collect information, but the bathroom intruder might ("So
that's what you look like wet and naked!"). But even in the shower and loud
music cases, most of the time we would still be more concerned about the
disruption of our ability to use the space to shower or sleep in peace than the
collection of any information that might have been incidentally collected at
the same time.

Sometimes when we talk in terms of privacy, we might be talking about the "right to privacy" that the U.S. Supreme Court has held to be protected by the Constitution and that includes rights to make fundamental decisions about major life choices, such as whether or not to have children. This notion of privacy includes the controversial right to an abortion protected by *Roe v. Wade* and later cases.[30] Constitutional lawyers would call this kind of privacy *decisional privacy*. In these cases, what's at stake is the ability of the person to make important decisions about their lives and their bodies, protecting that right against interests that the government might have. Here, too, information remains important to decisional privacy. For example, *Planned Parenthood v. Casey*, the 1992 case that largely upheld *Roe*, involved a number of issues of information about pregnancy and abortion—for example, whether a married woman had to notify her husband before getting an abortion and whether state record-keeping provisions about abortion services were constitutional.[31] Human information is often essential to human autonomy, but what's important to take from this now is that the reproductive "right to privacy" cases are at their core primarily about the autonomy interest in making important life decisions rather than the collection or use of information.

Instead of spatial or decisional privacy, this book is about *information privacy*. When I talk about "privacy" here, I'm going to use that term as a shorthand to mean informational privacy rather than decisional, spatial, bodily, or some other kind of privacy. Without a doubt, these other kinds of privacy are important ones that the law should safeguard, but I am particularly interested in information privacy because information privacy is particularly important at this point in human history. As we start the third decade of the twenty-first century, we find ourselves in the midst of an information revolution that is transforming human civilization. These transformations are every bit as marvelous and as menacing as the transformations of the Industrial Revolution of the nineteenth and twentieth centuries. In that previous revolution, companies and governments exploited industrial technologies to produce a civilization almost unrecognizable from the one it replaced. Much of what the Industrial Revolution produced was literally marvelous: new transportation technologies, ranging from railways and cars to airplanes and spacecraft; new communications technologies, such as the telegraph, the telephone, radio, and television; new forms of production of goods available at vastly lower prices; and new jobs, including forklift operator, advertising executive, factory worker, and nutritionist.

At the same time, much of what the Industrial Revolution produced was terrifying, in ways that disrupted stable societies and came to threaten the very survival of our species on Earth. Mass media enabled democratic self-government as we recognize it today, but it also enabled the rise of demagoguery and fascism. The twentieth century produced unprecedented technological breakthroughs, but it was marked by warfare, genocide, and a threat of nuclear annihilation that cast a dark shadow over all civilization. The new industrial technologies produced goods that made our lives better, while also leading to pollution and the acceleration of potentially catastrophic climate change. Information technologies are the hallmark of our information revolution, and they promise benefits and threats every bit as marvelous and terrifying as those of the Industrial Revolution. This is why a focus on information privacy is so important at this point in human history, a theme I will return to throughout Part 2. And it's why I'm focusing on information privacy in this book.

2. *Human* **information.**   Privacy isn't just about any kind of information; it's about *human* information, which is information about human beings like you and me. Lots of legal definitions of privacy from around the world talk in technical terms of such things as "personal information" or "personal data."[32] For instance, the Video Privacy Protection Act of 1988 was passed by the U.S. Congress after a journalist obtained Supreme Court nominee Robert Bork's movie rental history and threatened to do the same to other government officials. This law covers "personally identifiable information" (which it defines as "information which identifies a person") held by companies that sell or rent videos.[33] By contrast, Europe's GDPR applies to "personal data," which it defines as "any information relating to an identified or identifiable natural person."[34]

Legal definitions like "personally identifiable information" or "personal data" are important, but because they have to do technical work in the legal system, they can be dry. (Other, analogous legal definitions can be even more obscure, like "Record" in the federal Privacy Act of 1974, or "Protected Health Information" in HIPAA, the leading health privacy law in the United States).[††] I believe it is much better to talk about "*human* information" when

---

[††] Privacy Act of 1974, 5 U.S.C. § 552a(a)(4) (2006) ("the term 'record' means any item, collection, or grouping of information about an individual that is maintained by an agency, including, but not limited to, his education, financial transactions, medical history, and criminal or employment history and that contains his name, or the identifying number, symbol, or other identifying particular assigned to the individual, such as a finger or voice print or a photograph[.]"); HIPAA Privacy Rule, 45 CFR § 160.103 (HIPAA's definition of "Protected Health Information" is "individually identifiable

we talk about privacy because that refers us back to the human beings whose information is being used in some of the technologies that are the hallmark of the digital age. When these technologies fueled by human information are deployed by companies and governments, they are often used to predict or change the behavior of human beings.[35] For example, so-called behavioral-targeting advertising algorithms use detailed information about your race, gender, sexual orientation, wealth, reading habits, and interests to "target" ads to you (your mind is the "target") so that you will buy certain products and not others.[36] Facebook uses both its subscribers and their information for experiments testing a wide variety of interfaces and other design features on those people to make sure its service is as engaging (some would say as "addictive") as possible.[37]

The addictiveness of social media and other platform interfaces creates opportunities for serious mischief. In one infamous study, Facebook worked with data scientists from Cornell University to test whether they could tweak the number of happy or sad posts users saw in their News Feeds to make those Facebook users happy or sad—something they called "emotional contagion."[38] Facebook found that emotional contagion was possible, just as it found it possible in another experiment to manipulate News Feeds to increase or decrease the likelihood that Facebook users would vote in an election.[39] Most disturbing, the British data company Cambridge Analytica used detailed psychographic profiles of potential voters derived from Facebook data to nudge the 2016 Brexit referendum on British membership in the European Union in favor of "Leave" and the 2016 U.S. presidential election in favor of the Republican candidate, Donald Trump.[40] These technologies can be deployed by other actors, such as the use by schools in the United States of surveillance software to predict—and hopefully deter—school shootings committed by their own students.[41] We will return to the ethics of these examples later, but the important point for now is that human information is being used to predict and influence (and some would say control) the behavior of human beings. Companies and governments with the right kinds of data and the right kinds of access to your attention can use these technologies to influence you, so that you are made to (in the words of a famous episode of

health information . . . that is: (i) Transmitted by electronic media; (ii) Maintained in electronic media; or (iii) Transmitted or maintained in any other form or medium" but excludes "individually identifiable health information: (i) In education records . . . (ii) In records described at 20 U.S.C. 1232g(a)(4)(B)(iv); (iii) In employment records held by a covered entity in its role as employer; and (iv) Regarding a person who has been deceased for more than 50 years.") (punctuation and subsection marks clarified for clearer reading).

the television program *Black Mirror*) "shut up and dance."[42] Talking in antiseptic terms like "data" or even "personal data" (or "users" or even "Facebook users") distances us from what's really at stake in discussions of privacy. What's at stake are human beings (including you and me), and how power is exerted over those human beings in various ways.

Talking about privacy in terms of *human* information also highlights the importance of the *human values* that I believe the rules governing human information should serve. When data scientists talk about values, they could mean the values that make up the data (i.e., the actual numbers in the database). Alternatively, they could mean the economic value that a certain amount of data has; after all, unimaginably large fortunes have been made by the founders and funders of data companies, from Amazon and Google and Facebook on down. But I mean something else here by values. When we talk about human information, and when we talk about the privacy rules that should govern information, we should also be talking about the human values we want to promote through those rules. This book is precisely about these kinds of values that should animate our discussions of human information—not how big it is or how much it is worth, but whether our privacy rules promote things we care about like identity, freedom, and protection. The values in the code might be powerful, and the value of the code might be lucrative, but we also have to recognize the importance of the *human values* built into the design of our human information technologies.[43]

3. Information that is *known* or *used*.   The third dimension of my definition is that it includes not just information that is known but also (and crucially) information that is used. This is a really important distinction, because coming to terms with the problems of human information requires us to focus on the *knowing and subsequent using* of that information. It requires looking at information broadly, at what the GDPR calls the "processing" of personal information (basically anything you might do with data) or what information lawyers and data scientists call the "life cycle" of data (basically looking at data from its collection/birth to its deletion/death).[44] This means we should think about human information not just at the time that it is collected and thus known but in terms of how it is used—its detection, collection, collation, correction, consultation, combination, adaptation, alteration, organization, transformation, transmission, recording, retrieval, analysis, storage, structuring, encryption, decryption, disclosure, deletion, destruction, and erasure—for a start.

My goal is to be inclusive in thinking about information and privacy so that we don't leave out of our definition important ways human information can be used. All too often, though, popular and legal conversations about privacy seem to stop at the moment our human information is collected. Solove has termed this the "secrecy paradigm"—the idea that privacy is only about keeping things hidden, and that information exposed to another person ceases to be private. This is the common trope in the way we talk about privacy, "that privacy is often represented visually by a roving eye, an open keyhole, or a person peeking through Venetian blinds."[45]

The secrecy paradigm echoes throughout American law as well. Under the Fourth Amendment, if you voluntarily give information to a third party, you may lose any "reasonable expectation of privacy" against the police in that information.[46] Thus, when mobster Jimmy Hoffa confessed to a police informant he had invited to his hotel suite his intention to bribe jurors in a criminal case, the U.S. Supreme Court ruled that his misplaced confidence in the informant did not protect him.[47] In another famous case, federal agents successfully obtained the bank records of Georgia bootlegger Mitch Miller without a search warrant on the grounds that he had lost any expectation of privacy in them when he shared them with the bank.[48] More recent cases involving emails and cell phone location information have rejected the strong form of the government's argument that the "third-party doctrine" applies to all data shared under any circumstances, but it shows the power of the secrecy paradigm that these cases were even debatable before they were decided.[49]

The secrecy paradigm is, of course, deeply flawed. As an initial matter, it's flawed at the level of ordinary language. Let's say there is a fact about me that only I know; it could be something naughty that I have done, something weird I believe, or some fact only I know (like the password to my home security system). Under typical English-language usage, we'd call this fact a secret. Now let's say I confide in another person and tell them my secret. I might tell my naughty deed to my lawyer, therapist, or priest. I might tell my weird belief to my wife. I might give my home security password to my friend Tom so that he can stream music or check his email while he zealously waters our house plants when we go on vacation. Guess what? In each of these cases, we'd still call the shared fact a secret. Privacy works the same way. In ordinary usage, we'd call information about us that no one else knows "private." When that information is collected by an app or website, it is governed by a "privacy policy." In most cases, privacy policies describe the information a company collects, how they use it, and when they will (and will not) disclose that information to others. In other words, privacy policies are about both the collection and the use of human information. Consider Google's privacy policy, which begins with the statement "When you use our services, you're trusting us with your information. We understand this is a big responsibility and work hard to protect your information and put you in control."[50] Google's privacy policy goes on to describe the range of "your information" that it collects, what it does with "your information," the choices it gives regarding that information, the ways it protects the information, and the broad but limited circumstances under which it discloses the information.[51]

Privacy policies have many flaws as a tool of human information governance. These flaws have been well documented by scholars,[52] journalists,[53] and even policymakers,[54] and I'll have much more to say about them in chapters 3 and 6. But the important point for now is that they show how our ordinary, everyday use of the term "privacy" itself transcends the secrecy paradigm. Just as a "secret" doesn't stop being a secret when you confide it to another person, "privacy" doesn't end when human information is collected, and it can extend to the ways in which that information is used and even disclosed. When we talk about privacy, it's important to reject the stilted and unrealistic view that privacy (at least its protections) should end when information is shared. In some respects, in our information society, the interesting privacy questions only *begin* once information is known by another. This is why our law has imposed duties of confidentiality—in some cases for centuries—on a wide variety of actors, including doctors, lawyers, accountants, and those who agree to be bound by a contract of nondisclosure.[55] It's why the privacy theorist Helen Nissenbaum argues that when we think about privacy, it's best to focus on whether the flow of information is appropriate in a particular context.[56] And it's why a whole host of privacy laws passed around the world since the 1970s govern the collection, use, security, and disclosure of information. These laws usually embody a set of principles called the Fair Information Practices, or FIPs. The FIPs were created in 1973 by a highly influential report of a U.S. government advisory committee, chaired by Willis Ware of RAND Corporation and entitled Records, Computers, and the Rights of Citizens.[57] The original FIPs from the Ware Report could be stated as just five simple elements:

- There must be no personal data record-keeping systems whose very existence is secret.
- There must be a way for an individual to find out what personal information is in a record and how it's used.

- There must be a way for an individual to prevent information obtained for one purpose from being used or made available for other purposes without his or her consent.
- There must be a way for an individual to correct or amend a record of identifiable personal information.
- Any organization creating, maintaining, using, or disseminating records of identifiable personal data must ensure the reliability of the data for its intended use and must take reasonable precautions to prevent misuse of the data.[58]

Over the years, the FIPs influenced the development of information privacy laws in the United States and around the world, and over time they were refined to include protections for things like limitations on data collection and use, more explicit protections for data security, including breach notifications, and the availability of remedies when human information is processed wrongfully.[59] It is hard to deny, though, as one eminent privacy historian puts it, that the FIPs have been "the most important single concept in privacy all around the world for more than forty years."[60]

The FIPs have their flaws, just like privacy policies do.[61] But as the foundation of most privacy laws around the world, they take as a given that once human information is known, it must still be regulated, and it must still be protected.[62] A good example of this is Europe's GDPR, which is the strongest embodiment of the FIPs in a privacy law to date. The GDPR broadly covers the processing of all "personal data," and personal data can be processed only if it is authorized by one of the GDPR's exceptions. Many of these exceptions can be quite broad, such as whether there has been meaningful consent or whether there is a "legitimate basis for processing" notwithstanding consent.[63] But the GDPR is yet another example of how privacy law often begins when information gets collected. Our law as well as our language thus clearly recognize the fact that if we want to tackle the problems of human information in a serious way, we have to talk about how that information is *used*, and not just about whether it is *known*.

4. **A matter of *degree*.**   The fourth and final element of my privacy definition worth highlighting is that *privacy is a matter of degree*. Recall the definition of privacy as the *degree* to which human information is neither known nor used. When we talk about privacy, it's too simplistic to talk about whether information is "private," or for that matter whether it is "public." We can talk instead about things being relatively private or not, because we can

talk about the degree to which human information is private. From this perspective, privacy is a continuum rather than a binary on/off state. This insight reflects the reality that most human information is neither fully private (known only to oneself and not written down anywhere, like our most intimate thoughts) or completely public (a fact that virtually everyone knows, like that John Lennon and Paul McCartney were in The Beatles). Most information about most people lives somewhere between these extremes. When it comes to human information, usually some people know it, but not everyone knows it. And for any given person, different kinds of information are at different points on that continuum. Talking about privacy as a matter of degree allows us to talk about privacy the way we experience it in our daily lives.

To make things more concrete, I'll use myself as an example here, and let's assume for the sake of argument that I am a middle-aged law professor. As such, there are a few things about me that lots of people know. Part of my job involves talking to the media about legal issues within my area of expertise. That means when I talk to reporters about privacy law or constitutional law or presidential impeachment (I worked on the Clinton impeachment trial when I was a young law clerk), I assume that whatever I say could end up in the public domain, whether it is clever or foolish. A few Google searches can reveal other things about me as well. These are things like the fact that I'm married, have two children, was born in England, and spend far too much time thinking about Liverpool Football Club—the kinds of things you'd find on a bio of me on my website, on the dust jacket of this book, or on my public Twitter profile. In an internet-mediated world, it's probably a safe bet that these facts are preserved as public forever. Conversely, when I teach classes at my law school, where we typically don't record classes, I assume that anything I say or reveal about myself will be known to my students, and potentially the law school community as a whole, but no further than that. This would include the odd personal story (including stories about my law school colleagues) or "war stories" from practicing law that I might tell in class to illustrate certain points I want to make for my students or to break up the lecture so that they remain engaged and hopefully learning.

There's also information about myself that I feel comfortable sharing only with my friends (including some fairly embarrassing stories in which I'm the unfortunate protagonist). As you might imagine, there's another, different category of things I share with my family (or my doctor or my lawyer), and yet another category I share only with my wife. I won't give examples of these last few categories because it would defeat the point I'm trying to make here: as is the case for most people, there's a lot of information circulating about me, but very little of it is in wide public circulation. Most of it is known to one or another of the overlapping subsets of the people I know, and when I share information with these people, I can be pretty confident that the information won't spread much further than them.

The reason that I am able (like most people) to confidently share information with a few people with relative confidence it won't come back to hurt me is because of a concept that legal scholars call "obscurity." Woodrow Hartzog helpfully defines obscurity as "the notion that when our activities or information is unlikely to be found, seen, or remembered it is, to some degree, safe."[64] I can share personal or sensitive information or opinions with my small circle of friends with pretty good (but not perfect) confidence that it's not going to go into general circulation. For example, I might talk candidly about politics or my religious beliefs with my family or close friends or discuss personal health issues with my doctor. I can share less personal or less sensitive information or opinions with a wider circle of acquaintances with less confidence that it might become common knowledge, but because the harms of this information circulating aren't as menacing, it's also less of a problem. And this commonsense way of thinking about information about ourselves is how most people, most of the time, live their lives.

Unfortunately, American law does not always reflect this commonsense understanding of how human information circulates. Consider a couple of examples, one old and one new. The older example is the famous privacy law case of Bill Sipple, a former marine who saved President Gerald Ford's life in San Francisco in 1975. When would-be assassin Sara Jane Moore attempted to shoot the president, Sipple struck her arm as she was about to fire, thereby foiling her attempt. In addition to being brave and quick-thinking, Sipple was a gay man who was relatively open about his sexuality in 1970s San Francisco, where he was a prominent member of the gay community and a friend of openly gay politician Harvey Milk. However, while the gay community in San Francisco knew about Sipple's sexual orientation, his conservative Michigan family had no idea. But when national news reports on Sipple's heroism disclosed his sexuality, his parents and siblings back in Detroit learned that he was gay and disowned him. As a result, Sipple was not permitted to attend his mother's funeral a few years later, something that understandably caused him great anguish. Sipple sued the media for the intentional disclosure of private facts about him, but he lost. The court ruled that the disclosure of his sexual orientation was needed to "dispel the false impression that gays were timid, weak and unheroic figures" and to dispel some false reports that President Ford had never thanked him, reflecting homophobic bias.[65] (It was later revealed, ironically enough, that Ford had sent Sipple a private thank-you letter shortly after the event.)[66]

Now consider a newer example: American law's failure to come to grips with the problem of "upskirt photography," the practice of photographing the genitals and breasts of women in public spaces. This is, regrettably, an old practice that has taken on new life in recent years with the use of cell phones and smaller, more portable cameras, as the legal scholar Danielle Citron has documented.[67] Here, too, American law has failed to solve this problem. For example, in one recent Georgia case, Brandon Lee Gary used his cell phone camera to record four videos up the skirt of a woman he followed around a supermarket.[68] Though he was convicted of criminal invasion of privacy, the court of appeals reversed his conviction on the somewhat bewildering ground that the video recording was not made "in a private place and out of public view," as the statute required.[69]

Taking the *Sipple* and upskirt cases together, I'd like to suggest that understanding privacy as a matter of degree not only matches how we ordinarily think about privacy in our everyday lives; it also helps to solve these practical legal problems in a principled way. It's easy to feel sympathy for someone like Bill Sipple, who acted selflessly without hesitation and whose act of heroism resulted in such devastation to his personal life. At the same time, it's also important for us to build our privacy rules in ways that protect a free press, something I've written about in other work.[70] But surely, when we are thinking about privacy, and the legal rules that protect privacy, isn't it reasonable to suggest that when we share something about ourselves in one context, we don't waive our right to privacy in all contexts? This is an idea that many privacy scholars have written about at length. For example, Nissenbaum has argued that when we think about privacy, we need to respect what she calls "context-relative informational norms," the idea that our decision to share information in one context (like the community in which we live) doesn't mean that we should share it in all contexts (whether that's all people in the country in which we live or the community where we grew up, as happened to Sipple).[71] Along these lines, law professor Lior Strahilevitz has suggested that when it comes to privacy, we should be entitled to what he calls "limited privacy"—that information can be "public" with respect to one community (like our neighbors or coworkers or fellow students) but "private" with respect to the rest of the world.[72] Similarly, with respect to the problem of upskirt photography, American law has struggled with the problem of "privacy in public," bedeviled by the idea that people might not need to sacrifice their privacy when they are out of doors in "public" places. But a focus on the *degree* to which human information is private allows us to better focus on the precise issue in the upskirt cases. If privacy is a matter of degree, we can concede that fellow supermarket shoppers can justifiably see our face, our clothes, or even what is sitting inside the wire mesh of our shopping carts. But it does not follow that just because other shoppers can see our clothes or our chocolate, they have any reasonable right to photograph our underwear, or that it is reasonable (for example) for the supermarket to deploy a facial recognition network to prevent shoplifting or to nudge us to buy more cheese. Such a conclusion is simply at odds with the ordinary social norms that govern our social relations. It's also a conclusion that courts can apply in a principled way. For example, in Massachusetts, after a man escaped punishment for upskirt photography on the Boston subway on the ground that the victim was not nude, as the statute seemed to require,[73] the legislature amended its privacy law to clarify that upskirt photography is illegal even if it captures only underwear or partial nudity.[74] This was a fact that may have seemed obvious, but as this case and the Georgia case of Brandon Lee Gary illustrate, sometimes laws reflect older, out-of-date understandings, and sometimes courts interpret pretty good laws in ways that are needlessly rigid and needlessly underprotective of important interests. "Judging," after all, requires good judgment.

The Massachusetts amendment to its upskirt law recognizes our intuitive understanding that privacy is a matter of degree. But laws like that can go only a small way toward solving the problems of human information. Many of the examples I've given so far in this chapter have been physical ones: peeping Toms, government searches of property, and the publication of facts in newspapers that people would rather keep secret. But as anyone who has lived through the emergence of the internet can attest, the flow of digital personal information dwarfs these physical examples. It's in this area that the failure to appreciate that privacy is a matter of degree can cause the greatest problems. Consider the third-party doctrine cases discussed earlier—the claims by law enforcement that information shared with a phone or app provider makes it "public" such that the government doesn't need to get a warrant before it can obtain it. Or consider the problems of location data collection through smartphones. In one 2019 study, the *New York Times* obtained a location data company's file containing "more than 50 billion location pings from the phones of more than 12 million Americans as they moved through several major cities, including Washington, New York, San Francisco and Los Angeles." The file represented "just a small slice of what's collected and sold every day by the location tracking industry—surveillance so omnipresent in our digital lives that it now seems impossible for anyone to avoid."[75] If we reject the idea that privacy is a matter of degree, if sharing with *anyone* is sharing with *everyone*, then location privacy and many other problems caused by the overcollection and underregulation of human information become impossible to understand, much less solve. We need to recognize that privacy is a matter of degree across the board.

* * *

Thinking of *privacy as a matter of degree* thus allows us to understand human information the way it actually exists—in a continuum between strictly private on one end and widely public on the other. It allows us to think and talk about—and thus think and talk about regulating—human information in these intermediate states. It is the final element of the idea that *Privacy is the degree to which human information is neither known nor used.* But mindful of the fact that no one has been able to offer a definition of privacy that works for all seasons, let me offer a modest disclaimer. In this book, I'm not offering my definition as one for all time and all circumstances. Instead, the definition I've suggested is fit for my purposes here: how we should think about the issues of human information flow that are dominating our attention at the same time that they are transforming not just our society but what it means to live as a human in our digital age. If we want to understand why privacy matters, we have to talk about privacy, and to do that, we need at least some shared sense of what we mean by privacy. It is in that spirit that I have offered this definition of privacy I will use in the chapters that follow.

2

A Theory of Privacy as Rules

Targeted Marketing

If you're a pregnant woman living in the United States, Target Corporation probably knows that you're expecting—and has a pretty good idea when you're due. In fact, a coupon for baby clothes may already be on its way. A few years ago, the journalist Charles Duhigg told the now-classic story of how human information powered the remarkable growth of sales in the baby and maternity department at the American retail giant.[1] Duhigg discovered that in 2002 Target figured out how to tell "if a customer is pregnant, even if she didn't want us to know." His *New York Times* article on the topic was titled, appropriately enough, "How Companies Learn Your Secrets."

The Target employee who figured out how to do this was a man called Andrew Pole. Pole is a "data scientist," a trendy term that means he was good at using math and computers to learn things from data sets. Target had a pretty good data set, too. It had been amassing a large database about its customers, a combination of information it had observed from purchases in its own stores and other detailed sources of consumer data bought from data brokers. Pole was able to use his skills to mine that data set to discover some interesting things about the people in it. Target had discovered, for example, that pregnant women are more likely than others to buy unscented lotion and that they tend to start doing so around the beginning of their second trimester. This correlation between pregnancy and changes in behavior was one of about twenty-five that the data analysts were able to identify. They combined these correlations with a dash of algorithmic science to generate a "pregnancy prediction" score—one that allowed them not only to identify which of their female customers was pregnant, but also to guess each woman's due date with surprising precision. This in turn gave Target the ability to send coupons timed to the various stages of a customer's pregnancy to different pregnant consumers at the times judged most likely to make them come into Target and use them.

The Target pregnancy story has become well known in privacy circles, and you may well have heard it before.[2] It's often used to talk about how big data technologies can find surprising insights using seemingly innocuous information, and how "creepy" that can be. I'll have much more to say about the problems with "creepy talk" in the next chapter. But the important lesson of this ot-told story is not actually about the power of human information analytics to find surprising *correlations* like the one between lotion and pregnancy. Instead, the real lesson is about the power those insights confer to *control human behavior*. The reason Target wants to know about pregnancy is because Target wants consumers to buy as much as possible of *everything* they sell at their big box stores—not just diapers and baby clothes, but lawn furniture and underwear, wine and electronics. The problem is that, because we consumers are creatures of habit, our buying preferences are sticky and hard to change, even when we are subjected to lots of advertising.[3] However, there are a few times in our lives when our buying preferences are up for grabs, such as when we start college, get married, divorce, or move to a new city to start a new job. Another of those predictable life events when our purchasing habits change is around the birth of a child, when so many other aspects of our lives are also in flux. Target wanted to get to consumers who were expecting before its competitors could get to them. It wanted to get those consumers to shop at Target and to habituate them as Target shoppers for baby formula and maternity clothes before, weary from diapering and feeding their infant, their buying preferences readjusted to new habits—with Target as one of those habits. Target's own data scientist confessed to Duhigg before his superiors ordered him to stop giving away its secrets to journalists:

> "We knew that if we could identify them in their second trimester, there's a good chance we could capture them for years[.] ... As soon as we get them buying diapers from us, they're going to start buying everything else too. If you're rushing through the store, looking for bottles, and you pass orange juice, you'll grab a carton. Oh, and there's that new DVD I want. Soon, you'll be buying cereal and paper towels from us, and keep coming back."[4]

Consumers generally consider advertising to be a basically innocuous activity that companies engage in; they might find advertising annoying or be skeptical of it, but it's hardly something they consider to be insidious.[5] But

Target's pregnancy marketing was different: consumers who became aware of it responded negatively, with reactions ranging from feeling "queasy" to actual anger. One father, for example, stormed into a Target store with a fistful of baby coupons that had been sent to his teenage daughter, only to abashedly apologize after he learned his daughter actually *was* pregnant due to some "activities in our house that I haven't been completely aware of."[6] Knowing that their customers did not appreciate learning that Target was experimenting on them, the company decided to refine its marketing with another secret experiment. It began mailing different combinations of ads to random samples of Pole's list of pregnant women. As one Target executive explained:

> [W]e started mixing in all these ads for things we knew pregnant women would never buy, so the baby ads looked random. We'd put an ad for a lawn mower next to diapers. We'd put a coupon for wineglasses next to infant clothes. That way, it looked like all the products were chosen by chance. *And we found out that as long as a pregnant woman thinks she hasn't been spied on, she'll use the coupons.* She just assumes that everyone else on her block got the same mailer for diapers and cribs. As long as we don't spook her, it works.[7]

Put simply, then, Target wanted to get customers to start shopping at Target when data science suggested they were pregnant, and thus (according to behavioral science) vulnerable to forming a durable habit of more regularly shopping at Target. So they used large amounts of human information to figure out which of their customers were pregnant and marketed baby-related coupons to them at times in their pregnancy that were precisely tailored to be most effective. When those customers freaked out at Target's ability to learn their secrets, it ran another experiment on groups of customers. These additional experiments revealed to the company that if it bundled its payload of targeted coupons with soothingly irrelevant ones, the customers were tricked into thinking that the baby-related coupons were merely happy coincidences. The customers wouldn't know they were being "spied on," so they would use the coupons and likely form the habit of becoming Target customers over the long term. Target's cocktail of behavioral science and data science fueled by the human information of their customers thus became even more effective at getting the consumers to do what Target wanted them to do.

Four Elements of Privacy as Rules

The previous chapter gave us, I hope, a shared understanding of privacy so that we know what we are talking about. In this chapter, I want to go a step further and start to explain the importance of protecting privacy in our information society. Definitions get us only so far. Our working definition of privacy is helpful; more important, it is key to understanding the varied ways that we might want to protect human information. After all, it's more important to have the benefits of privacy than to perfectly define those benefits. To put this another way, if I had to choose, I'd rather have privacy laws that are effective than ones that are conceptually beautiful. No doubt a lot of this has to do with the fact that I am a lawyer and not a philosopher and that this is a book about law rather than about philosophy. Applied subjects are generally less beautiful (though more useful) than pure ones, which is one of the differences between the applied science of engineering and the pure science of physics. Law is an applied subject, too—a kind of applied philosophy— and while it is less beautiful than philosophy, it's more immediately useful in our world. Turning back to privacy, we've already seen how a philosophically beautiful definition of privacy has proven elusive, if not impossible. At the same time, technologies powered by human information march on, caring not a whit for philosophical niceties. Given these stakes, we can't wait until scholars reach a perfect consensus about what privacy means to begin protecting privacy meaningfully. There has to be a better way.

I'd like to suggest one: I believe that a better way of thinking about privacy is to focus less on the *essential nature* of human information and more on the *ways that we regulate* the flows of that information, as well as the consequences of those rules. When we think of privacy, then, we should think primarily about the *rules* that govern the degree to which human information is known or used with an eye to the values we want to achieve by protecting privacy. And we should always be sensitive to the practical consequences of those rules and whether the actual human beings who are subject to them have the practical ability to flourish. When it comes to privacy, we should take people as they actually are rather than as economic or philosophic theories want them to be.[8]

This chapter suggests how and why we should think about privacy as a system of rules. Privacy rules are, logically enough, rules that regulate (such as by constraining, prohibiting, discouraging, or even encouraging or permitting) the extent to which human information is known or used. Thus, privacy rules might prohibit *collection* of information in the first place (like a ban on wiretapping phone calls). Or they might regulate the *use* of information (like a rule allowing use of a certain kind of data for improving service but not to serve advertisements) or its *disclosure* (like a rule preventing doctors from disclosing medical data except under defined circumstances). Privacy rules can also regulate the context in which human information is collected (like a requirement to have a privacy policy before processing human information) or retained (like requirements to keep or destroy documents after a specified period of time).

Recall that in the previous chapter I offered a definition of privacy ("the degree to which human information is neither known nor used"), and I explained four parts of that definition. My theory of privacy as rules also has four features that are worth a little elaboration. The four elements each build on one another, so as I did before, I'll lay them out now, and then go through them one at a time. Here are the four elements:

1. "Privacy" is fundamentally about *power.*
2. Struggles over "privacy" are in reality struggles over the *rules* that constrain the power that *human information* confers.
3. "Privacy" rules of some sort are *inevitable.*
4. So "privacy" should be thought of in instrumental terms to promote *human values.*

In terms of these four elements, the story of Target's pregnancy predictions is one that, as we'll see, illustrates why it's helpful to think about privacy in terms of our *inevitable* need for *human information rules* that restrain *power* to promote *human values.*

Privacy and Power

Information is power, and information about other people can bring power over those other people. This is the first observation I hope we can agree on: that *privacy is fundamentally about power.* It's such an important observation that if you take only one thing from this book, I hope it is that privacy matters because information is power. We've seen evidence of this fact already. In chapter 1, I argued that it is important to understand privacy in terms of *human information* because human information technologies are being used to predict, influence, and increasingly control human behavior. I showed how antiseptic terms like "data" to describe these technologies are used to distance us from what's really at stake in discussions over privacy—how power is being exercised over human beings in various ways. Power is central to understanding what is being done with human information in our societies, and it is the essential reason privacy matters.

As we saw in the introduction, the evangelists of big data and other human information technologies (whether corporate, scientific, or governmental) are fond of suggesting that "data is the new oil."[9] This is a conscious choice of words to frame the debates over our human information policy in ways that benefit the companies, scientists, and governments who would collect it. It was popularized by a cover story in the *Economist* magazine in 2017 titled "The World's Most Valuable Resource Is No Longer Oil, but Data."[10] Data is the new oil, the analogy goes, because the industrial age's cars, trucks, planes, ships, and power plants were fueled by oil, but the electronic engines of the information age will be fueled by human data. *Wired* magazine made a similar claim a couple of years later:

> On the internet, the personal data users give away for free is transformed into a precious commodity. The puppy photos people upload train machines to be smarter. The questions they ask Google uncover humanity's deepest prejudices. And their location histories tell investors which stores attract the most shoppers. Even seemingly benign activities, like staying in and watching a movie, generate mountains of information, treasure to be scooped up later by businesses of all kinds. Personal data is often compared to oil—it powers today's most profitable corporations, just like fossil fuels energized those of the past.[11]

Data as fuel suggests human data as a power source, providing the necessary raw material for the technologies that are making the future.

Putting aside the self-interested, self-justifying framing of data as "the new oil" for a moment, it cannot be denied that human data is being used to fuel a range of information-age technologies. It also cannot be denied that many of these technologies are useful, at least when they are deployed ethically. These technologies range from "personalized" search results and other "filter bubbles" such as Facebook's News Feed to traffic-sensitive GPS navigation algorithms and technologies labeled as "machine learning," "artificial intelligence," or just "AI."[12] From this perspective, human information is being used to power the technologies of the information age the same way that oil and petroleum power the trucks, trains, factories, and shipping of the industrial age. Just as gasoline powers your car, the argument goes, human data powers many of the technologies you rely upon each day to live your life. If data is the new oil, then data is literally a power source.

But of course, framing the issues in this way is a conscious move by those powerful entities that would exploit human data. The "new oil" lens both describes their activities as unobjectionable and even "natural" and minimizes any negative consequences that result from those highly profitable activities. Technology companies have described their processes of data collection as somewhere between a natural, benign activity and the recycling of an unclaimed resource—the "data exhaust"—that would otherwise go to waste.[13] We have seen this move before. The European colonists of North America and the proponents of American westward expansion christened the American West "virgin land" to justify their appropriation of a different resource—land—occupied by the indigenous Americans who were already there.[14]

The Target example that opened this chapter clearly shows the power of human information in the "new oil" sense. Target used aggregated personal data to work out the kinds of behavior changes associated with pregnant women; it used specific data about individual women shopping in its stores to assign them pregnancy prediction scores; and then it used yet more personal data to determine what kinds of advertising would be effective to influence their behaviors in the ways Target wanted. But the Target example also shows the exercise of that power in a more revealing way than the simple mantra "data is the new oil" normally suggests. To be sure, human information is powering algorithms, but it is doing so in the service of established social, economic, and political power, often in connection with applied behavioral science or other forms of social, economic, or political control. Target wanted pregnancy predictions because it knew that pregnant consumers are particularly susceptible to targeted behavioral modification. And when those consumers freaked out when the first version of Target's advertising gave them an inkling of what the company was doing, Target intentionally concealed the targeted coupons for baby formula by bundling them with other coupons that would not give its game away. Data plus behavioral economics plus feedback from more data plus a bit of deception gave Target power—in this case, the power to nudge consumers at a time of vulnerability to acquire the sticky habit of becoming Target customers. It wasn't quite drug dealers giving the first hit away for free, but it was certainly an equally deceptive and habit-forming practice. Whatever we think about the ethics of this kind of manipulation, however, it is undeniably powerful, and powerful in a very different way from the power generated by burning oil.

The Target example thus illustrates not just how human data powers the information revolution but how the technologies of that revolution allow companies, governments, and other entities to exercise power over people—often the very same people whose data is being used to run the technology in the first place. It's a phenomenon that my coauthor Jonathan King and I have elsewhere called the *power paradox of big data*.[15] Privacy is about power because information is power, and information gives you the power to control other people. This is a fact that even the *Economist* recognized. Shortly after claiming that data was the new oil, it conceded that "there is cause for concern. Internet companies' control of data gives them enormous power."[16]

The recognition that information is power is hardly a new one. Sir Francis Bacon famously observed in 1597 that "ipsa scientia potestas est," which translates to English as "knowledge itself is power." The facts that information gives power and that the "privacy" conflicts over human information are struggles over social power should thus not surprise us. An early information privacy article by Daniel Solove titled "Privacy and Power" argued that the best way to understand the state of privacy in the year 2000 was not with George Orwell's famous metaphor of Big Brother but rather by reference to Franz Kafka's *The Trial*, "a world where people feel powerless and vulnerable, without any meaningful form of participation in the collection and use of their information."[17] In a later, expanded version of the argument, Solove noted that collections of personal data were significantly expanding the power of businesses and governments, leading to "unease, vulnerability, and powerlessness—a deepening sense that one is at the mercy of others, or, perhaps even more alarming, at the mercy of a bureaucratic process that is arbitrary, irresponsible, opaque, and indifferent to people's dignity and welfare."[18] More recently, Julie Cohen has explained how digital platforms operating within what she calls "informational capitalism" treat human beings as the raw material for the extraction of data as through a process of surveillance under which the subjects become conditioned as willing providers of the data. This can take the form of competing for artificial prizes like being "mayor" of the local coffee shop in gamified environments like FourSquare, or the work of constant grooming of social media profiles in pursuit of likes and followers on Instagram, Facebook, and Twitter.[19] The Canadian legal theorist Lisa Austin has been even more blunt, arguing that a lack of privacy can be used by governments and businesses to enhance their power to influence and manipulate citizens and customers, whether by changing behavior or by manufacturing "consent" to dense sets of terms and conditions or privacy policies. Austin argues that if we look at the privacy issues raised by human information technologies in terms of power, we can see the real benefit of meaningful privacy protections: they empower human beings individually and in groups to secure their ability to live their lives in the ways that they want to and in ways that are authentically "free."[20] And the philosopher Carissa Véliz argues that the surveillance economy "creates and enhances undesirable power asymmetries."[21]

In our digital, networked age, privacy struggles—human information struggles—remain struggles about social power. Thus far, we have looked at the consumer context with the example of Target. The Target example is a relatively old one, at least by the standards of recent technological change. The events recounted by Duhigg took place between 2002 and 2010, yet the story remains instructive. It is a safe assumption that in the decade since Target perfected its surveillance-based pregnancy marketing (and its maternity and baby business increased by billions of dollars), its techniques have become more sophisticated rather than less. Critically, though, Target is by no means unique or even an outlier in this respect. Many corporations today use similar combinations of data and behavioral science to influence consumers and to try to gain an edge against their competitors—and their techniques have become vastly more sophisticated and widespread than Pole's pioneering work at Target. As the communications scholar Joseph Turow has documented at length, bricks-and-mortar merchants have fought a surveillance arms race over the past two decades, competing with internet companies to turn their stores into zones of ever more finely grained customer surveillance. Using smartphone apps and GPS technology to track their customers, merchants at the cutting edge of consumer surveillance use the data they collect to more efficiently track, market, nudge, and control their shoppers into becoming loyal, habituated customers, often without their knowing they are being manipulated.[22] Turow argues that these activities serve as a "hidden curriculum," habituating customers not just to constant tracking and profiling but to understanding commercial surveillance itself as a "natural" and thus unobjectionable feature of modern living. Turow explains how this trend in "commercial intelligence," in line with Target's earlier techniques, is often hidden, discriminatory, manipulative, and an abandonment of the traditional egalitarian ideals of the American market-place.[23] Turow's ongoing work continues to track new ways in which companies compete through ever more sophisticated surveillance technologies, even ones that may seem at first blush to come from the realm of science fiction, such as the new technologies of "voice intelligence"—using artificial intelligence tools to draw demographic, emotional, and psychological insights from voice prints to further enhance the power of data-driven personalized marketing.[24] In these and other ways, merchants seek ever more intrusive and effective means of surveillance-based marketing as they chase a profit in competition with each other. Target's technology-assisted manipulation is thus memorable, but merely the tip of the iceberg—an iceberg of surveillance in pursuit of the power human information confers.

This insight should not be all that surprising. For many years, companies have tried to exploit the known cognitive biases and vulnerabilities of consumers to market and sell products more effectively. In 1957, the American journalist Vance Packard exposed the use of such psychological techniques in his best-selling book *The Hidden Persuaders*.[25] Packard was particularly concerned about a technique called "depth manipulation," a kind of exploitation of the unconscious mind of the shopper such as the one Chrysler attempted in designing a car that would appeal to married men's alleged subconscious desires to have a mistress.[26] Packard was not the only writer to worry about subliminal advertising; unease about psychological testing and manipulation by companies and governments was rife in the 1950s and 1960s,[27] and Alan Westin's landmark *Privacy and Freedom* (1967) devoted three chapters to the topic, including one he called "Tampering with the Unconscious."[28] While the techniques decried by Packard, Westin, and others were later shown to have had only limited effects on purchasers, marketers remained committed to influencing consumer behavior. Under the relentless financial pressures of the market, they were even willing to turn to practices some would consider deceptive and unethical to do so.[29]

Behavioral economics proved to be the effective tool of influence that the marketers sought. Living at the intersection between economics and psychology, this emerging science marries economics' focus on human behavior with psychological insights about the way the human mind operates in practice. Traditional economics assumes that humans are motivated by self-interest in a rational way. This is the famous "rational actor model," which rests on the classic assumptions of "avarice" (self-interest) and "ingenuity" (rational cleverness). As a model of human behavior, economics explains a lot, though it is often at odds with most people's experience of humanity, which is often altruistic and sometimes neither clever nor rational. Recognizing that human beings often act in ways that are at odds with the rational actor model, behavioral economics seeks a more nuanced understanding of how human beings decide what to do.

Behavioral economics as a field of study originated with pioneering work done by the Israeli psychologists Daniel Kahneman and Amos Tversky starting in the late 1960s. Their work, which won Kahneman a Nobel Prize, has influenced many others, including the American economist Richard Thaler (himself a Nobel laureate for his own contributions to the field).[30] As Thaler puts it well, behavioral economics "is still economics, but it is economics done with strong injections of good psychology and other social sciences."[31] It rejects the assumption of traditional economics, that people always act in a rationally self-interested way; Thaler describes the artificial people in the traditional model as "econs" rather than "humans." Behavioral science instead approaches humans as they actually make decisions and on the basis of experimental evidence rather than the assumptions of the rational actor model.

The injections of experimental psychology into economics are critical, as they have led to the discovery of several dozen ways in which humans behave very differently in reality from the ways the rational actor model would predict. Thus, humans, unlike econs, are bad at estimating probability, due to a host of fallacies and faulty "heuristics," the mental shortcuts and rules of thumb we use to estimate things we can't easily measure. Humans sometimes irrationally reason with emotion rather than facts ("affective reasoning") and make different decisions based upon whether options are described as costs or benefits ("framing effects"). They also irrationally tend to value their current state of affairs over objectively better but different situations ("status quo bias"); they overestimate the likelihood of positive versus negative outcomes ("optimism bias"); and they find that it hurts more to lose something they already own than the thing is rationally worth ("the endowment effect"). These features of the way we humans make decisions that depart from the rational actor model persist systematically across differences in intelligence, wealth, and other factors.[32] They are not defects so much as they are consequences of the way the human brain has evolved to function.[33] As a computer scientist might put it, these aspects of human cognition are "features" rather than "bugs." And critically, they can be demonstrated and replicated repeatedly across populations. We humans thus "systematically behave in non-rational ways."[34] We are, as the behavioral scientist Dan Ariely puts it well, "predict-ably irrational."[35]

The discipline of behavioral economics became popularized by *Nudge* (2008), the best-selling book by Thaler and legal scholar Cass Sunstein that laid out the basic findings of behavioral economics. Resting on the insight that human decisions can be influenced by the ways the structure of decisions affect our cognitive biases, *Nudge*'s basic argument is that we can structure those decisions to improve (as the book's subtitle suggests) our decisions about "health, wealth, and happiness."[36] Thaler and Sunstein helpfully coined the term "choice architecture" to indicate that the conditions under which we make choices affect those choices and that those conditions are subject to manipulation by others. And they call those people who can affect the conditions under which we choose "choice architects."[37] For example, some of Thaler's work had suggested that the best way to get employees to start saving for their retirement was to automatically enroll them in retirement savings plans when they start a new job, rather than giving them one more optional form to fill out their first day.[38] (In this example, the new employer was the choice architect.) The employees would not be required to save by their employers because they would still have a choice, but their choice was now to opt out of saving rather than opting in. This change was based upon an intuition (which turned out to be correct) that because defaults are sticky and humans are creatures of habit, switching the default to automatic enrollment rather than requiring employees to take the action of enrolling themselves would lead to more retirement savings (and better-off employees) in the long run. It worked, and employees saved substantially more, even though they were free to "choose" not to.[39]

Recognizing the power that choice architecture gives to governments, employers, marketers, or anyone else with the ability to structure the terms under which choices are made, Thaler and Sunstein optimistically hoped that choice architects would adhere to a principle they called "libertarian paternalism." This is the idea of structuring choices to encourage human well-being, welfare, and happiness on average, while maintaining the ability of choosers to opt out of choices they did not believe advanced their individual preferences over the alternatives.[40] Yet, as Thaler conceded in a later interview, their advice that nudges should be (1) clear and nonmisleading, (2) easy to opt out of, and (3) likely to improve the welfare of those being nudged was merely an optimistic hope.[41] Nudges (like all forms of applied behavioral economics) confer power, and they are tools that can be used for good, for evil, or to advance the goals of whoever wields the tool. As Thaler confessed, "[W]henever I'm asked to autograph a copy of *Nudge* . . . I sign it, 'nudge for good.' Unfortunately, that is meant as a plea, not an expectation."[42] Nudges confer power for all choice architects, whether they care about the welfare of the choosers or not.

Given the insights behavioral science and choice architecture provide about how human beings make decisions and how those decisions can be influenced, they were unsurprisingly seized upon eagerly by marketers. This eagerness was particularly true for those willing to relax the assumption of "libertarian paternalism" so that they could nudge consumer choices in directions that maximized corporate profitability over consumer welfare. These developments were predicted, documented, and studied by legal scholars. Writing in 1999, Jon Hanson and Douglas Kysar explored the concept of what they called "market manipulation," the exploitation of "cognitive biases to influence people's perceptions, and, in turn, behavior."[43] In a companion paper, the authors documented numerous examples of market manipulation of consumers using the tools of behavioral economics to exploit known biases. One of these examples was the manipulation of consumer perceptions of risk, which characterized much cigarette advertising. Another was the manipulation of consumer perceptions of the costs of products, such as by ending price terms in the number "9." When we see a price of, say, \$199,* our mental heuristics can perceive it as being closer to \$100 than \$200.[44] Crucially, Hanson and Kysar argued, market pressures on businesses mean that the exploitation of known consumer biases using the new science of behavioral economics is inevitable, at least while such exploitation is legal. "Once one accepts that individuals systematically behave in nonrational ways," they explained prophetically, "it follows from an economic perspective that others will exploit those tendencies for gain."[45]

Hanson and Kysar's important work was published just as the rise of the commercial web was turning the internet into the greatest surveillance tool in human history. They described the power of applied behavioral science before it is supercharged with data. But as the Target example illustrates, market manipulation can be made far more personal, and thus more effective, when

---

* Hanson and Kysar's evidence was actually even more interesting than this simplification suggests. They discussed the practice of American gas stations charging not just \$1.99 per gallon but "\$1.99⁹"— with the nine-tenths-of-a-cent upcharge appearing as a superscript after the 99-cent element. Consumers were paying just one tenth of a cent less than \$2.00 per gallon, but their automatic cognitive systems misleadingly registered the price as much less.

combined with data analytics and large amounts of consumer data about consumers in general and the particular consumers that companies seek to influence. Recognizing this fact, Ryan Calo has explored the phenomenon of what he calls "digital market manipulation" by firms, the use of behavioral economics in the data-rich digital environment to influence consumers in a personalized and highly effective way.[46] Calo bluntly describes this phenomenon as "nudging for profit,"[47] arguing that "society is only beginning to understand how vast asymmetries of information coupled with the unilateral power to design the legal and visual terms of the transaction could alter the consumer landscape."[48] He warns that the intimate connection between human information and the mature technologies of consumer manipulation represents a radical shift in the terms of consumer transactions that cannot be ignored by regulators—or by the manipulated consumers themselves.[49] Cohen takes this argument a step further, explaining that digital platforms can use their power over design to enlist consumers themselves as participants in their own manipulation, whether through behavioral nudges, "gamification," or other forms of subtle but effective coercion.[50]

A classic example of this shift was the Facebook game FarmVille. Launching in June 2009, Zynga's social game put its players in control of a small virtual farm. At its peak FarmVille boasted 85 million players, briefly dominating and threatening to overwhelm Facebook itself. Zynga worked hard to make the game engaging for players (again, we could use the word "addictive") with a series of design choices that took advantage of choice architecture and behavioral economics. Zynga created feedback and activity loops that made it hard for players to escape. As one journalist describes it succinctly, "If you didn't check in every day, your crops would wither and die; some players would set alarms so they wouldn't forget. If you needed help, you could spend real money or send requests to your Facebook friends—a source of annoyance for nonplayers who were besieged with notifications and updates in their news feeds."[51] FarmVille ultimately was a passing fad, filtered by Facebook as nonplayers became annoyed by the spam their friends were posting to the platform, and ultimately abandoned by players who came to realize that they were not the farmers but rather the crop itself—it was their own time, attention, and money being farmed by Zynga. Yet FarmVille was a pioneer in the use of embedding cognitive tricks in design to create a deliberately engaging ("addictive") product. Other designers were watching and taking notes, and FarmVille's cognitive tricks—a subset of what are known as "dark patterns"—spread throughout the internet. If you've ever played a game on your phone because of a timer or a notification, if you've ever felt a need to help a friend also playing a game, or if you've ever worried about uploading new content or otherwise "curating" your image on a digital platform, you've experienced the broader legacy of FarmVille. Indeed, as the *New York Times* reported on the occasion of the game finally shutting down on New Year's Eve 2020, "FarmVille once took over Facebook. Now everything is FarmVille."[52]

The power of personal information is one of the hallmarks of our age. It is also a major theme of this book, and we will see its effects in every chapter that follows. For now, it is enough to note that the power effects of privacy extend far beyond marketing to (and manipulation of) just consumers and have spread throughout society. Consider our roles not just as consumers, but as workers. Here, too, is a realm of surveillance in the service of control. The twenty-first-century workplace has become one of increased monitoring and surveillance, as employers seek to exercise ever greater control over their workers.[53] As my Washington University colleague Pauline Kim has documented, employers are increasingly using surveillance tools like GPS tracking devices, RFID (radio-frequency identification) badges, and monitoring algorithms and software to monitor workers under the mantra of productivity.[54] A *Wall Street Journal* report in 2020 even detailed a variety of technologies deployed by corporations to track employee happiness and "delve into the emotional health of their workers," from survey apps to email and Slack channel monitoring.[55] The fruits of these forms of surveillance are increasingly dumped into algorithms to score, separate, reward, and punish individual workers—yet another exercise of power conferred by the use of human information.[56] And in April 2020, as the Covid-19 epidemic began to ravage the world, it came to light that the American grocery chain Whole Foods, owned by Amazon, was using a data-fueled heat map tool to rank which of its stores were most likely to unionize.[57] The map displayed individual risk scores for each of the 510 Whole Foods stores in the United States,

> calculated from more than two dozen metrics, including employee "loyalty," turnover, and racial diversity; "tipline" calls to human resources; proximity to a union office; and violations recorded by the Occupational Safety and Health Administration. The map also tracked local economic and demographic factors such as the unemployment rate in a store's location and the percentage of families in the area living below the poverty line.[58]

Whole Foods' data-fueled anti-union work is not unique; there is good evidence that between 2014 and 2017, American companies spent more than $100 million on fees for anti-union consulting services.[59] Beyond union-busting and employee monitoring, both the technology and the economic incentives are available for companies to use personal data in these or even more insidious ways.

Beyond the economy, political campaigns are increasingly using these techniques to drive voter turnout of their supporters, nudge the undecided in their favor, and suppress the inclination of voters from the other party to turn out and vote.[60] We saw in chapter 1 how the examples of the Facebook emotional contagion study and the Cambridge Analytica scandal show how data can be exploited to influence our emotions and our votes. It is for these reasons and more that governments and companies eagerly seek human information—so that they can control, manipulate, nudge, or otherwise influence human beings more effectively through data.

We'll see these issues again in later chapters, but let's sum up before we move on. Information is power. Not merely power as a raw material, like coal for steam engines, diesel for trucks, and gas for most cars, as the self-interested frame of "data is the new oil" would have us believe. More important, human information confers power over the very humans from whom it is collected by powerful entities. It gives those entities that amass and exploit human information economic, social, and political power, in ways that are magnified by preexisting power asymmetries. And this effect is even greater when mixed with behavioral science or other forms of social control. It may even be the real reason you shop where you shop.

Privacy as Rules

Because privacy is really about power, I'd now like to make a second claim, which is *that our struggles over privacy are in reality struggles about rules*—the rules that will govern the collection and use of the human information the confers power in our information society. As we've seen, human information confers power, and sometimes that power is distributed or exercised in ways that can be unequal, disproportionate, manipulative, or contrary to values we care about. Human societies have long used rules to restrict the ways in which government power is exercised; Anglo-American law traces this tradition back to at least the Magna Carta, the 1215 document extracted from King John by his rebellious barons that is one of the foundations of the rule of law. In the United States, this principle was reaffirmed by the U.S. Constitution of 1787 and Bill of Rights of 1789.[61] But the use of law to regulate the exercise of power is hardly limited to government actors; the law is filled with regulations and restrictions on private power. Consider, for example, the rules that apply in the workplace, from workplace safety rules and the minimum wage to federal civil rights law, which prohibits employers from discriminating on account of (among other things) race, sex, or disability.[62] In the landlord-tenant context, there is the implied warranty of habitability, a term inserted by law into every lease that holds landlords to a promise the property is fit for human habitation. There's the contractual doctrine of unconscionability, which makes certain kinds of contracts unenforceable. This can be procedural, invalidating contracts where there is a gross imbalance in bargaining power or hidden terms, or it can be substantive, such as terms requiring consumers to waive legal rights that are so unfair or unreasonable that judicial enforcement would be inappropriate.[63] There's also a whole host of rules for consumer protection, such as those forbidding unfair and deceptive trade practices, impure food, and dangerous products.[64] Countless legal rules thus constrain power exercised by governments, companies, or other powerful entities.

Recognizing that human information confers both power and the potential for mischief, privacy rules governing the collection, use, and disclosure of personal information have been a feature of Anglo-American law for a very long time.[65] Some of these rules are ones that we typically think of as "privacy rules." Thus, tort law governs invasions of privacy such as peeping (or listening) Toms,[66] the unauthorized use of personal photographs for advertising,[67] and the disclosure of sexually explicit images without consent.[68] The Fourth Amendment requires that the government obtain a warrant before it intrudes on a "reasonable expectation of privacy" and is itself backed up by a complex web of federal and state laws regulating eavesdropping and wiretapping by both government and private parties.[69] In addition to the Privacy Act and the Fair Credit Reporting Act, federal laws regulate the collection and use of financial information, medical and genetic information, and video privacy, among others.[70] States, led by California, have also added privacy protections, such as California's constitutional right of privacy (applicable to both private and government actors), reader privacy laws, data breach notification statutes, the spate of laws in the early 2010s prohibiting employers from asking for the social media account passwords of their employees, and the California Consumer Privacy Act that took effect in 2020.[71] Even the First Amendment, thought by some to be the enemy of privacy, is a kind of information rule that mandates the circumstances in which other laws cannot restrict certain free flows of information, such as the publication of true and newsworthy facts by journalists or truthful and nonmisleading advertisements for lawful products.[72] As I explored in my previous book, the First Amendment also protects a variety of kinds of privacy directly, such as the ability to read freely in one's home and rights of anonymous expression and association, among others.[73]

Then there's the GDPR. Europe has had a set of comprehensive laws regulating the "processing" of virtually all personal information since the 1990s, and this regime was further strengthened by the GDPR, which took effect in May 2018. The GDPR regulates the processing of all personal information about Europeans, even when that processing happens outside Europe. As a result (and indeed, entirely on purpose), the GDPR has had an extraterritorial effect on the ways companies treat human information in the United States, changing business practices, inspiring the California Consumer Privacy Act (and other state privacy laws), and driving at long last a meaningful privacy reform conversation in Washington.[74]

Why, then, you might wonder, are people so worried about the Death of Privacy if there is so much privacy law? The problem is that, at least in the United States, we have a combination of a small number of good rules, a much larger number of bad rules, and lots of outdated and incomplete rules. There are *good privacy rules* in the United States—rules that allow important social activities while also protecting human beings from surveillance, manipulation, or other bad consequences that result from their privacy being violated. For example, the Fourth Amendment's protection against "unreasonable searches and seizures" allows police to get a warrant to obtain evidence if they can demonstrate probable cause to a judge. It has been interpreted flexibly to protect not just the "persons, houses, papers, and effects" mentioned in the text of the Constitution, but also telephones, smartphones, cloud storage, and location data.[75] But it has not always been interpreted in such a flexible, reasonable way. For example, in *Olmstead v. U.S.* (1927) the Supreme Court ruled that, because telephone calls were merely electrons traveling on wires owned by the phone company, police wiretapping did not fall within the meaning of "persons, houses, papers, and effects," and thus the Constitution placed no bar on police wiretapping.[76] It took the Supreme Court forty years to correct this mistake, and in the interim state and federal government agents engaged in widespread surveillance, not just of suspected criminals but of dissidents, outsiders, and other marginalized groups. (We'll see in chapter 5 how this led to a shameful episode in which the FBI tried to blackmail Martin Luther King Jr. into killing himself.) Today, thankfully, there are much stricter rules governing surveillance by the police, the FBI, and (thanks to Edward Snowden) the National Security Agency (NSA), though even these rules are not perfect.[77]

In contrast to such good but imperfect rules, there are also some really *bad privacy rules*. In fact, the basic system governing internet privacy in the United States follows not just a bad rule but a terrible one. We saw in chapter 1 how the Ware Report established the FIPs, the set of Fair Information Practices that have formed the basis for privacy law around the world. The United States almost immediately applied the FIPs to federal government data in the Privacy Act of 1974, announcing in the law that Congress expressly found that "the right to privacy is a personal and fundamental right."[78] Unfortunately, while Congress had originally intended to extend the FIPs to private databases, last-minute lobbying by private industry led to amendments restricting broad privacy protection to government-held data only.[79] The law as passed was also hamstrung by a "routine use exemption," under which routine uses (even those that were privacy-infringing) were exempted from coverage.[80] As Paul Schwartz explains, "[F]ederal agencies have cited this exemption to justify virtually any disclosure of information without the individual's permission."[81] Apparently, legislators thought, doing a bad thing in a bureaucratized way makes it okay—an idea that resonates with C. S. Lewis's reimagining of Hell as a bureaucracy in his novel *The Screwtape Letters*.[82] Time and time again, a combination of legislative indifference to privacy, lobbying, bad drafting, and bad luck have derailed privacy protections for consumers. In the late 1990s, with the rise of the commercial Web raising serious privacy concerns, the bursting of the internet stock bubble combined with the 9/11 attacks to shelve privacy reform.[83] Then, in the late 2010s, after rampant data breaches, Snowden's revelations of NSA spying, and the Cambridge Analytica scandal, privacy reform was once again on the agenda, only for a combination of the Trump impeachments, the 2020 election, and the Covid-19 pandemic to once more sideline privacy reform.

In the absence of comprehensive privacy rules to protect consumers, the American approach to privacy has been "sectoral." Under this system, some types of information, like health, financial, and movie rental data, are covered by individual laws, but no general privacy law fills the holes and provides a baseline of protection like the GDPR does in Europe.[84] The closest thing to a baseline that exists is the Federal Trade Commission Act of 1914, Section 5 of which has, since 1938, outlawed "unfair or deceptive acts or practices" in commerce.[85] While the FTC has done impressive and creative work with this century-old law designed to deal with the problems of the industrial rather than the information age, the general rule of American privacy has been one called "notice and choice."[86] Since the dawn of the internet, as long as tech companies give us "notice and choice" of their data practices, they are judged to be in compliance with the law. This is the case even though both "notice" and "choice" are empty shells. In practice, the "notice" consumers get is little more than vague terms hidden in the bewildering fine print of privacy policies. Moreover, virtually no one reads these privacy policies—a fact documented by a vast academic literature.[87] One *New York Times* study expressed this point memorably: "We read 150 privacy policies. They were an incomprehensible disaster. . . . Like most privacy policies, they're verbose and full of legal jargon—and opaquely establish companies' justifications for collecting and selling your data. The data market has become the engine of the internet, and these privacy policies we agree to but don't fully understand help fuel it."[88] Dense, unreadable privacy policies and other legal documents, including voluminous ones like Apple's infamously lengthy Terms of Service, do not provide notice in any meaningful way to any ordinary consumer of what they are agreeing to. Yet the law allows us to click "I have read the terms and I agree" even when everyone knows that the company is nudging or even forcing us through choice architecture to lie about notice in order to use its service.

The "choice" half of "notice and choice" is an equally dangerous fiction, particularly when the "choice" we are being presented with is essentially the "choice" of whether or not to participate in the digital world.[89] Woodrow Hartzog and I have argued that choice can be empowering for a small number of important decisions where we can vividly understand the risks and benefits of what we are agreeing to—buying a home, a car, or a computer, deciding where to go to college, or deciding whom to marry.[90] Such choices are both practically sound and morally valid when the choice is knowing and voluntary. But consent can be knowing and voluntary only when we are asked to choose *infrequently*, when the potential harms that result from the consent are *vivid* and easy to imagine, and when we have the right *incentives* to consent consciously and seriously.[91] When we overleverage choice, as we have done in the digital environment, choice suffers from a series of systemic pathologies that render it both practically and morally ineffective. First, there is *unwitting consent*, which takes the "knowing" out of "knowing and voluntary." This can happen, for example, when we don't understand either the legal agreement, the technology being agreed to, or the practical consequences and risks of agreeing. Second, there's *coerced consent*, which takes the "voluntary" out of "knowing and voluntary," for example where we are confronted with choosing between consent and something we cannot realistically give up, like our job or our ability to use the internet. Third, there's *incapacitated consent*, in which voluntariness is not available as a matter of law, such as with children or other people who are categorically incapable of legally consenting.[92] Nowhere are these pathologies more evident than under the notice-and-choice regime that has governed much of Americans' digital privacy.

In the absence of meaningful consumer protections, American privacy law's terrible "notice and choice" rule has forced consumers into what Solove has called "Privacy Self-Management": giving people "a set of rights to enable them to make decisions about how to manage their data," including rights of notice, choice, access, offering a form of control under which they can "decide for themselves how to weigh the costs and benefits of the collection, use, or disclosure of their information."[93] Privacy self-management is an ideology that dumps the workload of privacy protection onto individual consumers, who will usually be harried, busy, and confused. It improperly treats humans as econs. It elevates the brutal Roman maxim *caveat emptor*—buyer beware—over a better alternative that actually empowers and protects consumers from misleading choices or a menu of bad ones. It pretends to be agnostic about the substance of the privacy rules, while everyone knows that the power to set defaults over harried and confused consumers is the real power to decide the substance of these rules—literally—by default. It leads to vast numbers of popular articles with titles like "How to Stop Your Smart Home Spying on You" or "All the Ways Facebook Tracks You—and How to Limit It."[94] One thoughtful recent book recognizes that privacy is about power but ultimately concludes with suggestions about how to "take back control of your data" such as using search engines other than Google, tweaking privacy settings, using strong passwords, buying newspapers, and other individual strategies of privacy self-management.[95] Well-meaning works like these contain dozens of helpful tips that we could spend all of our days following (one article for each of the many digital services we use, each with their own "privacy dashboard") and yet still fail to effectively protect our privacy.

Privacy Self-Management sets the defaults of human information collection in favor of powerful companies, and then causes consumers to feel guilty and morally culpable for their loss of privacy by failing to win a game that is intentionally rigged against them. After all, consumers feel, "I consented to that app, so it's my fault if my data is now 'out there' and beyond my control." This is a common sensation when bad design causes human beings to go with the default choices—we blame ourselves because the design that is nudging us in that direction is often invisible or seemingly apolitical.[96] And we blame ourselves even though we know from the social sciences that all design is political and all designed objects have politics, regardless of whether they are tangible or digital.[97] Notice and choice is thus an elaborate trap, and we are all caught in it. *Caveat emptor.*

It gets worse. Even good rules can be co-opted in practice, and institutions can be highly resourceful in watering down or even subverting rules intended to constrain them. In many ways, this is one of the classic stories of law, but it has special application to privacy. There is a large and highly skilled privacy profession, consisting of lawyers, engineers, designers, and many other professionals who work in "privacy on the ground." Many, if not most, of these professionals work conscientiously to promote privacy in their organizations, whether they work in tech or retail, coding or HR, regulatory affairs or a product team.[98] They sincerely mean well—a fact I can attest to from my personal experience of knowing dozens of not hundreds of them, training many students to go into the field, and from having been a privacy lawyer myself in the early 2000s. But detailed sociological fieldwork by Ari Waldman has revealed the ways in which corporate structures and cultures, organizational design, and professional incentives are often deployed by companies to thwart both the intentions of privacy professionals on the ground as well as the spirit of the legal rules and privacy values those professionals attempt to advance.[99]

To routinize surveillance, executives in the information industry use the weapons of coercive bureaucracies to control privacy discourse, law, and design. This works in two ways: it inculcates anti-privacy norms and practices from above and amplifies anti-privacy norms and practices from within. Tech companies inculcate corporate-friendly definitions of privacy. They undermine privacy law by recasting the laws' requirements to suit their interests. And they constrain what designers can do, making it difficult for privacy to make inroads in design. As this happens, corporate-friendly discourses and practices become normalized as ordinary and common sense among information industry employees. This creates a system of power that is perpetuated by armies of workers who may earnestly think they're doing some good, but remain blind to the ways their work serves surveillant ends.[100]

Again, I can attest to the truth of these findings from my own professional experiences.[†] Prominent privacy whistleblowers tell even more striking stories of workplace privacy practices that drove them to go public with their allegations of wrongdoing. Christopher Wylie, the Cambridge Analytica whistleblower, recounts a story of corporate institutionalized indifference to privacy (as well as indifference to the integrity of democracy itself) as the company weaponized Facebook data it had harvested through trickery to influence voters in support of the 2016 Brexit referendum and the Trump presidential campaign.[101] And Edward Snowden has explained at length how he witnessed other intelligence community personnel who spoke up internally about surveillance abuses face professional marginalization, harassment, and even legal consequences—convincing him that the only way to address those abuses was to go to the press with documentary evidence.[102] Cohen goes even further, explaining how powerful institutions are able to shape not just their own organizations but the basic structure of our political and legal language to capture rules and subordinate them to their own purposes through the ideology of neoliberalism. This can happen, for example, by reinterpreting human information as their own valuable property rights or advancing dubious interpretations of the First Amendment like "data is speech" to insulate their information processing from democratically generated state and federal laws that would rein them in.[103] These intertwined phenomena help to explain why there are so few effective American privacy rules at present, and why efforts to improve them have faced serious challenges in the political process, in the courts, and in practice.

Then there are the *outdated privacy rules*. When I teach privacy law to my graduate students, they are frequently amazed by how much of the American law of privacy (including data security) is a creature of the 1980s. Our law governing email privacy—the Electronic Communications Privacy

---

[†] I do want to make clear that I am not equating the great law firm I worked at with Cambridge Analytica or the NSA. But it is undeniable that lawyers working for clients in privacy compliance as I did experience the seemingly unyielding obligation of trying to make the rules work for the client as painlessly as possible rather than as faithful to the spirit of the law as possible.

Act (ECPA)—was passed in 1986, long before most people (including members of Congress) had even sent an email.[104] Our law governing computer hacking—the Computer Fraud and Abuse Act (CFAA)—was passed in 1984. It was initiated by a terrified President Reagan, deeply disturbed after seeing the movie *WarGames*, in which a teenage hacker (played by Matthew Broderick) almost starts a global thermonuclear war after hacking into the NORAD defense mainframe.[105] (I promise, I am not making this up.)[106] And our law protecting movie-watching privacy, the Video Privacy Protection Act (VPPA), was passed in 1988 after a reporter for the alternative *Washington City Paper* obtained a list of all the movies Supreme Court nominee Robert Bork had rented from his local video store, hoping to discover pornographic titles. (He didn't.)[107]

Perhaps unsurprisingly, most of these laws from the days of the VCR have aged badly in the days of the smartphone. While ECPA was farsighted, its dial-up model of electronic communications failed to anticipate cloud email, and its antiquated predictions of what email would turn out to be have led to absurd (and unconstitutional) results, like email more than six months old being protected at a much lower level than recent email.[108] The *WarGames*-inspired CFAA has been interpreted much more broadly, with some courts and prosecutors suggesting that any violation of a website's terms of service could potentially bring down the full weight of federal felony charges. This interpretation had tragic results in the case of Aaron Swartz, a young coder whose attempts to free publicly funded research hidden behind paywalls led to a sad tale of overprosecution and, ultimately, his death by suicide.[109] Ironically, it is only the VPPA, which literally regulated VCRs, that has aged well. The VPPA applies to businesses that rent, sell, or deliver "prerecorded video cassette tapes or similar audio visual materials." Applying this definition, courts have found that the "delivery" of streaming video by companies like Netflix and Hulu is a "similar" enough "audio visual material" to a VHS tape from Blockbuster to keep the VPPA protecting our privacy well into the twenty-first century.[110] While a stream is physically quite different from a videotape, the social practice of watching a movie on our sofa hasn't changed all that much, apart from our TV screens becoming larger and thinner. But because the law regulates the social practice of movie-watching at home rather than the technology of the VCR, it continues to function.

Finally, there are many *incomplete privacy rules*, gaps in the rules governing human information in the United States, places where there should be a rule but there isn't one. We saw in chapter 1 the trend in Fourth Amendment law called the "third-party doctrine." This suggests that information shared with another person lacks a "reasonable expectation of privacy" and thus can be collected by the government without a warrant. This rule made some sense in the context of a prison inmate who confessed a crime to a police informant wearing a wire,[111] but it makes no sense in the context of our networked information society, in which *all* of our email is stored in the cloud (and thus "shared" with Gmail, for instance) and *all* of our location data is uploaded to our phone companies to make GPS mapping work. Indeed, in a series of cases, lower courts agreed with the government's claim that sharing location data with a phone company to make a mobile phone work somehow waived our expectations of privacy in our location—at least until the Supreme Court corrected the absurdity of that position in the *Carpenter* case.[112] As it stands, the third-party doctrine is by no means dead. The legacy of *Carpenter* will be to require courts to undertake a delicate balance between the remnants of the third-party doctrine and a notion of Fourth Amendment protection that is sensitive to the ways in which digital services and devices are essential to our modern way of life and, consequently, our civil liberties. (We will pick this theme up again in chapter 5.)

Another example of incomplete privacy rules is HIPAA, the Health Insurance Portability and Accountability Act, which governs Americans' health information. The fact that most people think the "P" in HIPAA stands for "privacy" when it really stands for "portability" betrays the Act's origins. HIPAA was a health insurance portability bill, one that let Americans "take" their health insurance with them to a new job. It also promoted the development of electronic health records. At the last minute, Congress realized that health insurance and electronic medical records contain a vast amount of sensitive human information, which ultimately led to the HIPAA Privacy Rule and the HIPAA Security Rule.[113] Within the context it came from— health data held by doctors, hospitals, and insurance companies—HIPAA has done and continues to do a pretty good job. It allows these "covered entities" to use health data relatively freely to treat patients, run hospitals, and process payments effectively, and it strictly limits other uses of the data. The problem is that today, unlike in 1996, there are large amounts of health data that aren't held by covered entities—and thus aren't covered by HIPAA. The heart rate and workout data collected by your smartwatch, the results of direct-to-consumer genetic tests like those provided by Ancestry and 23andMe, health-related searches on Google or WebMD, data tracked by dieting apps—all of this is sensitive health data. But almost all of it falls outside HIPAA because it doesn't involve a "covered entity."[114] It's yet another example of the many holes—some of them huge—that run throughout American privacy law.

To be clear, the larger point here is not that American privacy law has many holes and bad rules, but rather that if we are interested in thinking about the ways in which privacy is protected today, we cannot do so without thinking about *privacy rules*. We have already seen that privacy is fundamentally about power; the good news is that we already have a set of tools for dealing with power: legal rules. As we've seen, some of our rules governing government power, like the Magna Carta, the U.S. Constitution, and other public law rules, are of very long standing.[115] There are lots of legal rules that regulate private power too. In fact, a major part of the story of U.S. law in the twentieth century was about the constraint of private power, from workplace safety and the law of labor unions to antidiscrimination law, consumer protection law, and the minimum wage. These rules take advantage of the efficiencies of private economic ordering while attempting to minimize some of its more unpleasant consequences: industrial accidents, pollution, discrimination, and gross inequalities of wealth. And, as we have seen, there are many such rules regulating privacy—setting a human information policy—even though that set of rules has its flaws, gaps, and outmoded elements.

Legal rules are not the only forms of constraint. Privacy law pioneer Joel Reidenberg argued in 1996 that when it comes to regulating technology, we need to focus on what he called *lex informatica*, the idea that the design of computer systems is a source of rules that constrain the users of those systems.[116] We see a contemporary example of this when companies offer us "privacy choices": we can choose only the ones that they offer and build into their systems. As a result, if we are offered the "choice" between accepting software cookies or not using their website, we are constrained by the site's design, giving us only those options and no others. Reidenberg's powerful insight was popularized by Lawrence Lessig, who in turn suggested that when it comes to rules, we should think about the "four modalities" of regulation. Lessig explained that behavior can be constrained not just by *legal rules* but also by *values* embodied in computer code, social norms, and market incentives.[117] Whether we call it *lex informatica* or code, the power that design confers has only increased as the digital environment has become more ingrained into our lives. Thus, Seda Gurses and Joris van Hoboken have shown how the software development kits that platforms allow designers to use to build products are themselves designed in ways that make the protection of privacy in practice very difficult, even where privacy protections are mandated by legal rules. Hartzog has explained more generally the ways in which design is everywhere, is political, and affects our choices through the exercise of power, and how an attention to design should be an important part of our public policy.[118] In crafting privacy rules for our information society, and as we respond to the increased power of design in the digital environment, we should certainly be mindful of each of Lessig's factors. Yet legal rules will continue to remain critically important, not only because they can regulate directly but also because they can direct systems to be designed in certain ways, they can change social norms through law's expressive role, and they can alter market incentives by making certain kinds of activities more costly and by prohibiting others outright. They can also, as Hartzog explains, be sensitive to design in ways that can diminish the power of design over both human users of technology and the law itself. Lessig may have been right that "code is law," but law remains law, too.

There is nothing magical about our information society, nor does it have a fixed, inevitable, evolutionary state. Instead, like every society in human history, it is up for grabs, and its final evolution will be the product of millions of choices about technological design, human preferences, and regulations of both technology and the ways that technology can (and cannot) be used. There is no final, inevitable "information society" we are being led toward by forces external to human beings and human institutions. We face the future, as we always have, facing choices. The future will be determined by how as well as by whom those choices are made. But in making those choices, we will need to commit ourselves to rules. Rules matter, and the decisions we make about which rules will govern human information will come to define what privacy means for future generations.

The Inevitability of Privacy Rules

Thinking about privacy in terms of rules leads us to a third feature of privacy, which is that *privacy rules are inevitable*. Consider again Target's use of data analytics to try to figure out which of its customers are pregnant. Putting to one side whether Target is engaged in an unfair trade practice by spying on its vulnerable customers in that way, let's assume that this practice is currently legal.

The government has a range of regulatory options here. It could continue to allow this kind of practice; it could prohibit the practice on the grounds that it is exploitative; or it could allow the practice but require Target to disclose what it has done in any marketing to the customer. ("Dear Madam, we have been watching your purchases and we have determined, with a 97.43% likelihood, that you are with child. Felicitations. A new federal law requires us to tell you exactly how we know that. You see, from monitoring your purchases, we know you've been buying unscented lotion as well as multivitamins containing folic acid, along with. . . .") Whichever of these options the law takes, we will inevitably have a privacy rule—a rule governing the degree to which human information is known or used.‡ Target can use the data in that way, it can't use the data in that way, or it can use the data but only if it does so in a particular way (and maybe isn't allowed to sell the data to a data broker). Whichever way, we have a privacy rule. And from this perspective we can see how privacy rules are inevitable—even doing nothing is a choice. There is no escaping the question. There are no neutral baselines. And all choices have architecture.

An information society like ours must inevitably have rules for when information can flow and when it must not. This is the case because an information society that doesn't create any new information rules will still have rules. In this case, the rules will just be the permissive ones, like the gaps in HIPAA that effectively permit the processing of sensitive health data by health websites, smartwatches, and other companies that aren't "covered entities." That's a privacy rule, because it allows information to flow, albeit in a way that makes little sense. Or consider the First Amendment, which (correctly, in my view) generally permits a newspaper to publish embarrassing facts about politicians if the information was (a) lawfully obtained and (b) is a legitimate matter of public concern.[119] That's a privacy rule, too—a rule regulating the degree to which human information can be known or used.

We saw in chapter 1 that the secrecy paradigm—the notion that human information ceases to be "private" when it is shared—is a dangerous fallacy

---

‡ You'll note that I've defined privacy as "the degree to which human information is neither known nor used," while my definition of privacy rules ("rules governing the degree to which human information is known or used") removes the negatives of "neither" and "nor." This adjustment of the definitions is not intended as a sneaky moving of the goalposts, but is offered just to make my language clearer. It doesn't change the meaning. For example, if my emails and diary are private, "neither known nor used" by anyone else, and constitutional law requires the police to get a warrant before they read what I have written, I am protected by a privacy rule—a rule governing "the degree to which human information is . . . known or used."

because we need to be able to regulate the uses as well as the collection of information. In the government context, for example, "secrets" and "top secrets" can be known by many people. But even these secrets are protected by a wide variety of legal, technological, and operational tools, including criminal and contract law, encryption and other security tools, and the whole trade of spycraft. The same is true of corporations around the world that utilize confidentiality regimes, nondisclosure agreements, and trade secret protection to protect "secret" information. Our verbal intuitions point up a second observation—one we've seen before—which is that information has always existed in intermediate states between wholly public and wholly private. Many still think of privacy as a binary option of "public" or "private," when our everyday experiences remind us that virtually all information that matters exists in intermediate states between these two extremes.[120] As Hartzog points out, it makes just as little sense to define "privacy" or "private information" in terms of secrets known only to one person as it does to define "public" or "public information" as something that every single person knows.[121] In reality, virtually all information is and has been in intermediate states between these two extreme poles. Faced with such a reality, we should recognize that our law should operate primarily in the vast middle, on information in its intermediate states.

Realizing this important fact, our law has regulated information in intermediate states for a very long time. As King and I have argued, even in the big data context we must recognize that shared private information can remain "confidential."[122] Much of the confusion about privacy law over the past few decades has come from the simplistic idea that privacy is a binary, on-or-off state and that once information is shared and consent given, it can no longer be protected. Binary notions of privacy are particularly dangerous and can erode trust in our era of "big data" and "metadata," in which private information is necessarily shared to some extent in order to be useful. The law has always protected private information in intermediate states, whether through confidentiality rules like the duties lawyers and doctors owe to clients and patients, evidentiary rules like the ones protecting marital communications, or statutory rules like the federal laws protecting health, financial, communications, and intellectual privacy.[123] Neither shared private data (nor metadata) should forfeit their ability to be protected merely because they are held in intermediate states. Understanding that shared private information can remain confidential helps us see more clearly how to align our expectations of privacy with the rapidly growing secondary uses of big data.[124]

And, as critically relevant here, privacy rules are inevitable when we are talking about human information in intermediate states. This is the case even when the rules allow information to flow freely and even when we agree that this is the right way to treat that information, whether we're talking about making public the tax returns (or secret payments to porn star mistresses) of our presidents or the use of sensitive health data to fight a pandemic that threatens the foundations of our society.[125]

Once we realize that we have been using "privacy" to talk about information in intermediate states and that our law has long regulated information of that sort, it's a lot easier to see how privacy rules are really a subset of information rules. "Privacy," in this broader sense, becomes much more than just keeping secrets; it enters the realm of information governance. We live in an information society, and privacy rules are the rules that govern the information in and out of networks and data sets in that society. Understanding privacy rules as information rules radically changes the questions we might ask about regulation of personal information in the big data context. If we think about privacy merely as secrets, the collection of data and its incorporation into a data set would seem to moot any privacy concerns. Information that is collected and shared even to a moderate degree would seem to be "public" or at least "nonprivate," and therefore beyond any regulation. Such a conclusion would likely meet with the approval of many who wield the powerful tools of big data analytics, but it would leave us with an essentially lawless, anarchic, and unsustainable information society. An information society with no restraints on information flow might seem like a techno-libertarian's paradise, but in reality it would be awful. Such a society would have no protection against hackers, malicious code, data breaches, revenge porn, child pornography, cybercrime, or any of our other information age maladies. It would be a libertarian paradise the way the Dark Ages were—a paradise only for the powerful, with no solace for the weak.

By contrast, when we ask the privacy question more constructively as "What rules should govern the collection of personal information?," the answer changes entirely. The answer becomes not about the metaphysics of "privateness" or "publicness" but rather about what kinds of data uses and which kinds of information regulation support the kind of society we might want to live in and which ones do not. When we do this, we see that the collection and sharing of information need not be the end of the regulatory inquiry but rather the beginning of it. Unlike much information contained in databases and read by computers, privacy is not binary. Privacy is about degrees of knowing and using, and as such it requires an ethical rather than a mathematical approach to the management of information flows.[126] It's not about the value of the code or the values in the code; it's about the code of human values that inform the entire enterprise. At bottom, then, privacy (and the decisions we make about it) is ultimately a series of human questions that must be informed by human values. But if the decision to protect or regulate the collection, use, or transfer of personal information is dependent on human values other than the private-ness or public-ness of a data field, we still need to figure out exactly what those values should be. (Much more on that in a bit).

Taken together, when we see (1) that *privacy is about power*, (2) that *privacy is best understood in terms of rules*, and (3) that *privacy rules of some sort are inevitable*, we can better understand what's really going on with the debate about the Death of Privacy that opened this book. Anxiety about the death of privacy is really anxiety about the ways in which human information is being collected and used to influence people in a time of change and anxiety about the increasingly insufficient rules in place to regulate or place limits on that power. It's anxiety that our secrets are being exposed to potentially harm us, and anxiety that we are largely at the mercy of the powerful entities that are amassing and using our human information to make decisions about us: whether we'll get into college, get a particular job, or be approved for a mortgage. There's also anxiety about information uses we are unaware of—to borrow Rumsfeld's Razor, both the "known unknowns" and "unknown unknowns" of information use. This is the real reason the revelations about Target's use of human information and behavioral economics resonated so widely.

"Privacy," then, is best thought of not as some measurable and vanishing thing but as an ongoing conversation about social power—specifically about the social power conferred by human information. This is a conversation that has been going on for a very long time and shows no signs of abating as the uses of human information—and the stakes—continue to increase. In her history of privacy in modern America, Sarah Igo documents a variety of privacy struggles over the past century or so, in which some Americans sought to know more about other people, and how the subjects of that scrutiny resisted those attempts to make them known. Igo convincingly argues that these episodes were invariably fights over social status and power in which privacy was the indispensable "mediator of modern social life."[127] As she puts it well,

"Americans never all conceived of privacy in same way, of course. . . . What remained remarkably consistent, however, was their recourse to privacy as a way of arguing about their society and its pressures on the person."[128] Thus, in 1890 when Justices Earl Warren and Louis Brandeis resisted the new "Yellow Press" prying into the private business of Boston's elites, when in the 1930s African Americans sought social security numbers as a mark of citizenship but unmarried working women resisted them out of fear of age discrimination by employers, and when 1960s research subjects subjected to personality tests objected to their being scrutinized by social scientists, each of these claims on being known or unknown couched in privacy were in reality struggles over social standing.[129] And the familiar fault lines of our society—race, class, wealth, gender, religion, and sexuality—were all too often the conduits of those struggles and all too often dictated their winners and losers. The human information at issue was a source of power, whether that power was used to expose, control, uplift, or harm members of American society. The social power that human information confers is why governments are keen to conduct censuses, register young people for potential conscription, and conduct surveillance of criminals or social undesirables, however defined. It is also why "undesirables" resist being seen, such as when the NAACP successfully used the First Amendment to prevent the state of Alabama from making its membership lists public during the tense years of the struggle for civil rights in the 1960s.[130] Writing for a unanimous Court, Justice John Marshall Harlan explained that "[i]mmunity from state scrutiny of [the NAACP's] membership lists is here so related to the right of [its] members to pursue their lawful private interests privately and to associate freely with others in doing so as to come within the protection of the Fourteenth Amendment."[131] Undeniably, both Alabama's attempt to force the NAACP to divulge its membership lists (and chill its activism) and the NAACP's claims to group privacy in pursuit of its political activities were claims to control the use of human information because of that information's social power. Privacy talk in America, then, has long been a conversation about social power, specifically the forms of power that the control and exploitation of human information confers. Privacy talk is inevitable. So too are privacy rules of one sort or another, whether they are empowering, oppressive, incoherent, or some combination of all three.

Privacy Rules Are Instrumental

Many people believe privacy to be a good thing in itself. Many, for example, believe that having places we can go—a forest, a library, a bedroom—without being observed is good without needing any further justification. Being alone and unobserved can be seen as (as a philosopher would put it) an *intrinsic good*. Intrinsic goods are things that are good in and of themselves, in a way that is separate from any other consequences they produce. They are fundamentally good things, and they are ends in themselves.[132] So let's think a little bit about whether a state of privacy is an intrinsic good. There's pretty good anthropological evidence that humans, like many animals, benefit from having private spaces and relationships, and that this benefit is an intrinsic good.[133] European Human Rights Law, as we've seen, also treats privacy this way. The European Union's Charter of Fundamental Rights and Freedoms recognizes fundamental rights to "private and family life, home and communications" (Article 7) and "the protection of personal data concerning [individuals]" (Article 8). Such fundamental rights are important for their own sake; they are the fundaments—the foundations—of a free society. Full stop. Usually, when I ask my European friends why they think privacy matters, the reaction I get is puzzlement. "Why does it matter?" they say. "What a strange question. *Privacy just does matter.* It's a fundamental right."

I have to confess that I am sympathetic to this view, and not just because it is held by many wise people whose judgment I trust. There's a lot of merit in the idea that privacy is an intrinsic good. I suspect there's a good chance that if you chose to read this book about why privacy matters, you might also agree. In my experience, the students who enroll in my privacy law courses not only tend to be inclined to favor pro-privacy arguments, but they also tend to be more likely to believe in privacy as an intrinsic good. In my experience as well, because privacy is about power, people whose identity or circumstances depart from American society's (socially constructed) default baseline of white, male, straight, rich, native-born Christians tend to be, on average, more receptive to the privacy-as-an-intrinsic-good argument. I suspect that it is an appreciation of how marginalization affects power and how privacy is about power that leads to this tendency. Consequently, there is an important, rich, and expanding literature on the privacy experiences and challenges of marginalized groups.[134]

Unfortunately, as I have also experienced when speaking with others (and having The Privacy Conversation with them), not everyone shares these inclinations. This is particularly true of many (but not all) law enforcement officers and many (but not all) technologists. There remain many people unconvinced that privacy matters, or who are not convinced that privacy is important enough to fight for in the face of other values that conflict with it—values like policing, counterterrorism, public health, innovation, or convenience. A lot of very thoughtful people are inclined to think that privacy just isn't worth the cost of physical safety or our technological marvels, and they don't really care whether or not privacy is intrinsic.

To make the case that privacy matters to those who are unconvinced or skeptical, it's helpful to offer another way to think about privacy. If someone doesn't believe that privacy is fundamental, pounding the table about its fundamentality is not going to be an effective way of changing their mind. Instead, I've found it's necessary to go deeper than just privacy, to explain that privacy can matter not for its own sake but because it gets us other things that we can all agree are important. This is what a philosopher would call an *instrumental* argument. From this perspective, privacy matters not as an end in itself but because privacy lets us pursue other values that we can agree are important (even fundamental). Since privacy rules will inevitably be necessary for any of the many possible information societies we might build, we need to be thoughtful about what those rules are and what values they will serve. Getting this argument right is particularly significant because international conversations about privacy rules frequently break down with the assertion (commonly made by Europeans) that privacy is a fundamental right that needs no further explanation. To many Americans used to thinking about personal information in economic terms, that argument is bewildering. But at the same time, even if all we care about is economics, some international understanding about what privacy is and why it matters is essential to the economic future of Western democracies. Personal data is already a multibillion-dollar trade across the Atlantic Ocean alone, and that trade is being threatened by the massive legal uncertainty surrounding what privacy is and why it matters. Being clearer about "what privacy is" is thus tremendously important however we might want to look at it.

If we want to talk about privacy with those who are unconvinced about its value, intrinsic or otherwise, I believe it's essential to talk and think about *privacy as being instrumental*. There is nothing inherently good or bad about information flowing or not, but as we've seen, information flows and privacy rules have consequences. Because we must inevitably craft privacy rules of one sort or another, we will need to figure out what values we want to advance and what ends we want to achieve when we regulate the collection, flow, use, storage, and life cycle of human information. Because human information is everywhere, privacy discussions will frequently involve difficult trade-offs between privacy or other values. Should we require companies to get affirmative consent from consumers before they serve them ads based upon detailed profiles of their internet reading habits? (Currently, the answer in U.S. law is no, in order to promote "innovation.")[135] Should the government have to get a search warrant before it obtains the location data of a suspected drug dealer from the dealer's mobile phone provider? (Currently, the answer in U.S. law is yes, even though the consequence is that guilty people might be set free on a technicality.)[136] There is no shortage of values that can be placed in conflict with the protection of human information. Undeniably, in some cases those values will prove to be more important. Often, these conflicts will raise hard questions, and ones for which it can be hard to reach a good answer. But our confusion about what privacy is and why privacy matters is not just leading to confusion about the Death of Privacy; it is getting in the way of working out the conflicts between privacy and other values in ways that are clear, intellectually honest, effective, and in the public interest.

Specifying the values that privacy rules can serve is essential if we want to resolve those conflicts in a socially beneficial way. Part 2 of this book identifies three such instrumental values—identity, freedom, and protection—that I believe good privacy rules can and should advance. In chapters 4, 5, and 6, I will say much more about each of them, about why we should care about them, and about how sensible privacy rules can promote and protect them. I'll show how privacy rules should be thought of as instrumental rules that are a useful means to those three ends. But for now, it's enough for us to understand that, if there is disagreement or confusion about privacy, it helps to talk about the values that privacy protection gets us. That approach, I have come to believe firmly, is the best way to talk about why privacy matters.

3

What Privacy Isn't

Four Privacy Myths

The previous two chapters offered a definition of what I mean by "privacy" in this book—a provisional definition of privacy and an emphasis on the importance of thinking about privacy in terms of rules advancing values in practice rather than seeking a perfect philosophical understanding of privacy for all seasons. In doing this, I've tried to offer an account of *what privacy is*. We've also seen how privacy can have many different meanings to different people. We've encountered some of these in passing: the idea that privacy is just about keeping secrets, the related idea that privacy is lost once those secrets are shared with another, and the idea that privacy is best protected by giving people the right to control how their human information is collected and used.

This chapter is about *what privacy isn't*. It changes direction a bit from what's come before in order to clarify what I mean by "privacy." This is all part of the process of defining something. Definitions of course tell us what something *is*, but they are also importantly limiting. Definitions tell us what something *is not* as well. If X and Y are separate, defining something as X is defining it as "not Y." If we say that the sky is blue, we're also saying that it is not red. Alternatively, when the English philosopher Simon Jenkins says that he is a committed fan of Liverpool F.C.,[1] he must also be saying that he is also not a committed fan of rival Premier League clubs Everton or Manchester United.[2] (If you're a baseball fan, it works the same way with the Cubs and Cardinals or the Red Sox and Yankees.) To say you are committed to one is to say that you aren't committed to the other. Legal and philosophical definitions work similarly, particularly when we use definitions to narrow the meaning of a term. For example, if we define the First Amendment as protecting only political speech, as the legal scholar Robert Bork suggested we do in the early 1970s, we have defined it in a way that excludes both pornography and nonpolitical art from its protections.[3] You don't have to agree with Bork's narrow view of free speech in order to appreciate the limiting effect of his definition. Conversely, if we (as I happen to think we should) mean to extend free speech protections to facially nonpolitical artistic expression (whether Nabokov's *Lolita* or Mondrian's abstract paintings), then we need a definition that is broader than a strict limitation to political speech. Yet even if we do that and define the protection of free expression in this broader way, we are still marking out its limits and saying what it does not cover (i.e., child pornography, insider trading, false advertising, rioting in the U.S. Capitol, etc.).[4]

Defining privacy works the same way. Chapter 1's provisional definition of privacy as *the degree to which human information is neither known nor used* is an intentionally broad definition, but it's not a limitless one. In a time of rapid technological and social change, it's helpful to think about privacy in relatively broad terms, particularly given the importance of human information to those changes. This is why most of the leading scholarly definitions of privacy are relatively open-ended, like Daniel Solove's sixteen different conceptions of privacy, Helen Nissenbaum's argument that privacy is about managing the appropriate flow of information with respect for social context, or Beate Rössler's broad focus on privacy as the necessary condition to live an autonomous life.[5] There's a necessary trade-off here between a definition that is broad enough to do the work we want it to do and one that is specific enough to be useful in specific cases. But while it's important to think about privacy in broad terms, we shouldn't think about it in a way that is so broad as to be meaningless. Marking out privacy's meaning and saying *what privacy is* allows us to clarify *what privacy isn't*, whether those things are clarified as misconceptions by its definition or just outside its definition entirely. For example, my own definition excludes other ways we could talk about privacy, such as its being a right to control our personal information or the ability to conceal disreputable information about ourselves.[6] Being specific about what privacy is thus lets us be specific about what it is not, and it lets us clear up misconceptions and myths about privacy. As we've seen, privacy is an idea that can mean many things to many people, and there are lots of misconceptions about it. These misconceptions plague academic, policy, and popular discussions about our human information policy, and they are often repeated by the media, by companies, by the government, and by academics. These misconceptions are not only widespread; several of them are seductive, persistent, and dangerous, meaning that they can be used to obscure or mislead from the critically important issues that are at stake.

This chapter tries to cut through some of the myths about privacy in our digital society. The way we talk about privacy is often infected by dangerous misconceptions about what privacy is or about how our digital society actually works. These privacy myths are not only widespread, but, as we'll see, they are often advanced by some of the people and organizations that have the most to gain from the destruction—or at least the wounding—of the belief that human information should be protected and regulated. Four of these myths are particularly dangerous, and once again I'll list them now so that we can proceed through them in order. They are:

1. Privacy is about hiding dark secrets, and those with nothing to hide have nothing to fear.
2. Privacy is about creepy things that other people do with your data.
3. Privacy means being able to control how your data is used.
4. Privacy is dying.

As I'll explain in the pages that follow, these are all myths. Privacy Isn't About Hiding Dark Secrets; Privacy Isn't About Creepiness; Privacy Isn't Primarily About Control; and Privacy Isn't Dying.

Privacy Isn't About Hiding Dark Secrets

"If you have nothing to hide, you have nothing to fear." It's one of the most frequently heard—and powerful—rejoinders to any argument for privacy, particularly privacy against the government.[7] It's common, it's clear, and it's concise. It's the idea that privacy is no more than the ability to hide unpleasant truths about ourselves from the public, and that if we have no unpleasant truths to hide, we don't need privacy.

The "nothing to hide" argument also has a long pedigree. It's been used by novelists like Richard James and Upton Sinclair. It's been attributed to Joseph Goebbels, the Nazi minister of public enlightenment and propaganda, yet it's been used to justify numerous state surveillance programs in democracies like the United Kingdom and the United States.[8] Influential scholars have also advanced the "nothing to hide" argument. In one widely cited 1970s article, for example, Richard Posner claimed that "everyone should be allowed to protect himself from disadvantageous transactions by ferreting out concealed facts about individuals which are material to the representations (implicit or explicit) that those individuals make concerning their moral qualities."[9] Put in plain English, he's saying that in the market for personal reputation, privacy is a kind of fraud that keeps relevant information away from those who might need it. And people not engaged in fraud don't need privacy.

Unfortunately, while it makes a good sound bite, the "nothing to hide" argument doesn't stand up to close examination. "Nothing to hide" is a fallacy—and a dangerous one at that. There are several problems with it, but I'll focus on three of them here. The first problem with the "nothing to hide" argument is that *it's wrong on its own terms*. This is the case because everyone has something to hide, or at least everyone has facts about themselves that they don't want shared, disclosed, or broadcast indiscriminately. Put another way, everyone needs privacy at one time or another, and this need for privacy is legitimate. Privacy—the rules governing the extent to which our information is known or used—is necessary for all of us. It's necessary for every member of society to separate themselves from others, and it's necessary for society to function. At its most basic, privacy is needed to protect our naked bodies and our intimate bodily activities from the gaze of others. We all wear clothes, and for virtually all of us, we wear them for privacy (as well as for warmth). More pointedly, few if any of us would be comfortable having videos of our activities in the bathroom or bedroom made public, even when we do the typical things one would expect in those rooms. In a judicial opinion written fifteen years after he made the economic case for the "nothing to hide" argument, Judge Posner explained that privacy for such activities is not just a common social norm but one that receives the protection of the law:

> Even people who have nothing rationally to be ashamed of can be mortified by the publication of intimate details of their life. Most people in no wise deformed or disfigured would nevertheless be deeply upset if nude photographs of themselves were published in a newspaper or a book. They feel the same way about photographs of their sexual activities, however "normal," or about a narrative of those activities, or about having their medical records publicized. Although it is well known that every human being defecates, no adult human being in our society wants a newspaper to show a picture of him defecating. The desire for privacy illustrated by these examples is a mysterious but deep fact about human personality. It deserves and in our society receives legal protection.[10]

Posner's admission reveals not only that privacy protections are broader than the disclosure of embarrassing facts, but that they rest upon deep and long-standing cultural norms.

These cultural norms reflect the fact that disclosure of information—images, videos, or descriptions—about our intimate bodily activities can be psychologically and professionally devastating. Americans began a national conversation about bullying and nonconsensual pornography in 2010 after Rutgers University freshman Tyler Clementi killed himself by jumping off the George Washington Bridge because his roommate had used a webcam to record Clementi engaging in private and consensual sexual activities in their dorm room.[11] As the 2010s progressed and connected smartphones with high-resolution cameras became ubiquitous, we began to appreciate the international problem of nonconsensual pornography, sometimes known colloquially as "revenge porn."[12] This phenomenon involves one sexual partner sharing sexually graphic images or video of the other without their consent.[13] Typically (though by no means exclusively) the perpetrator of nonconsensual pornography is male, while the victim is a female former lover.[14] As legal scholar Danielle Citron has described at length, nonconsensual pornography can be devastating.[15] Her scholarship details the many significant harms of nonconsensual pornography, ranging from psychological and emotional harm to diminished professional and personal opportunities.[16]

As a result of advocacy by scholars like Citron, as well as by activists and reform groups around the world, many jurisdictions have passed laws making nonconsensual pornography a crime. According to the Cyber Civil Rights Initiative, a nonprofit group committed to supporting the victims of nonconsensual pornography, there are laws addressing revenge pornography in forty-eight U.S. states, the District of Columbia, and Guam.[17] Legal protections outside the United States can be even stronger. Britain, for example, criminalized the sharing of private sexual images and videos without consent in 2015 and has vigorously enforced the law since then, with 464 prosecutions in 2017–18 alone.[18]

Beyond information about our sexual and bodily activities, another category of human information that many would want to keep private is information about our intellectual activities. This is particularly the case for information about our tastes or activities in politics, religion, reading, movie viewing, and web browsing. Reading and thinking are essential activities in any free society and lie at the foundation of the activities protected in the United States by the First Amendment. In my previous book, *Intellectual*

WHAT PRIVACY ISN'T   75

Privacy, I argued that protection for these intellectual activities is essential if we want to continue to protect the ways we make sense of the world, develop new ideas, and figure out how we want to express them; in other words, meaningful protection of intellectual privacy is essential if we want ourselves and our society to be free and self-governing.[19] Intellectual privacy is particularly important at the present moment in human history, when the acts of reading, thinking, and private communications are increasingly being mediated by computers. When we wonder about someone or something, we frequently use search engines to learn. When we read, we increasingly do so with our phones, laptops, or e-readers. And when we hesitantly test out our new beliefs with those we trust, we often do so over the phone, text, or email. These new technologies undoubtedly advance our abilities to think, to explore new ideas, and to learn, but they have been designed to create records of these intellectual activities—records that can often be easily shared or exposed.

I'll have more to say about intellectual privacy in the next two chapters, but what's important to understand right now is that the unwanted disclosure of many kinds of information about ourselves can have deeply harmful consequences to our identity, to our livelihood, to our political freedom, and to our psychological integrity. More fundamentally, we can see that even on its own terms, the "nothing to hide" claim is wrong. Because we all have something to hide, when privacy protections are absent and our lives are made transparent, we all have something to fear.

The second problem with the "nothing to hide" claim is that *it fundamentally misunderstands why privacy matters.* The most obvious of these misunderstandings is that "nothing to hide" arguments reduce privacy to little more than the claim to keep dark secrets from the public gaze. As we've seen, privacy is about so much more than the very limited "secrecy paradigm." I've argued that, at bottom, privacy matters because *privacy is about power*—the social power that human information provides. Information about our intimate lives certainly provides a vivid example of this power in action. When talking about photos and videos of our naked bodies, sexual fantasies and preferences, illicit affairs, and health conditions, it's easy to see how any and all of them can confer power. "Do what I say or I will tell the world your darkest secret" can be a powerful motivator. It's also blackmail, which has been a crime since Roman times.[20] Blackmail is the crime of making threatening demands without justification and includes coercing someone to behave in a certain way by threatening to disclose their secrets.[21]

What's interesting about the crime of blackmail is that it's criminal even though both asking someone for money and disclosing secrets usually aren't illegal on their own. I can reveal your secret, or I can ask you for money, but if I put them together, I've committed a felony. While we legal scholars have long puzzled over this "blackmail paradox,"[22] for our purposes, it's enough to note that the law's intuitive and long-standing protection against blackmail shows that the ability to disclose secrets confers the kind of inappropriate power that the law needs to safeguard against.

Blackmail is exciting, but it also distracts us from more subtle and important ways that information confers power. The kinds of dark secrets involved in blackmail are ones that draw our attention, particularly if they involve sexual, ethical, or financial impropriety, or if they involve celebrities or politicians. But juicy secrets such as these can distract us from more discreet uses of information to control other people. The secrecy paradigm suggests that privacy interests cease once information is collected, but we've already seen how effectively information can be used to influence people after it is collected. As the Target example illustrated, data science provides powerful tools to influence and manipulate people's behavior. Such tools are far more common and subtle than the blunt instrument of blackmail, particularly when people have no idea they are being influenced. Thankfully, few people are the victims of felonious blackmail or extortion. On the other hand, a vastly larger number of us have been influenced in our shopping, our behavior, and perhaps even our voting by data-driven persuasion. If you have access to the internet, it's almost certain that you have been subjected to such methods in one form or another. The "nothing to hide" argument's suggestion that virtuous, ordinary, boring, or law-abiding people don't need to care about their privacy completely ignores the real reason that companies and governments are eagerly scooping up human information. Human information allows control of human behavior by those who have the know-how to exploit it.[23] And all of us can be nudged, influenced, manipulated, and exploited, regardless of how few dark secrets we might have.

A third and final way that the "nothing to hide" argument misunderstands why privacy matters is that *it focuses narrowly on privacy as an individual matter rather than as a social value.* It's common to describe things we value as rights, particularly if we want the law to protect them, and Americans have been talking about the "right to privacy" ever since Warren and Brandeis's famous *Harvard Law Review* article from 1890. But as we've seen, definitions matter, and calling something an individual right can distract us from appreciating it as something broader that matters not just to individuals but to the broader fabric of our society as a whole. The "nothing to hide" argument offers the worst of both worlds: it doesn't recognize privacy as a right, yet it treats privacy as an individual preference rather than something of broad value to society in general. Framing privacy in this way makes it seem both weak and suspicious from the start. From the "nothing to hide" perspective, all that matters is whether an individual is misbehaving. If you choose not to misbehave, if you act in socially acceptable ways, there is no problem. It's only outliers—people with something to hide—who are in danger. As long as you keep your front lawn (and the rest of your life) tidy, it would seem that you have nothing to worry about.

We've already seen a number of problems with this position, but the individualization of privacy is perhaps the biggest one. Let's assume, for the sake of argument, that you are boring, or at least that your preferences are average. The way you like to live your life and the things you want to do are squarely within the mainstream. You are radical only in the extent of your commitment to the norm. Why should you care about privacy? You have nothing to hide because no one would find your life remarkable, so why should you care about someone else's weird lifestyle or secrets? As an initial matter, and as we've already seen, our experiences of privacy are rarely individual. With the possible exception of our thoughts, very little of our information is known solely to us, lurking in the deep recesses of our minds. Instead, much human information gets shared in relationships, particularly trusted ones in which we share intimate secrets with friends and lovers, health information with doctors and therapists (even ones we've met just a moment before), financial information with accountants, and a vast amount of personal and professional information with our lawyers. The law has long recognized information relationships of this sort, from the absolute confidentiality of the church confessional to a whole host of evidentiary privileges and duties of confidentiality, along with the law of blackmail we've already examined.[24] As sociologist Christena Nippert-Eng has explained, we are not so much strict "Islands of Privacy" as we are social creatures who are constantly sharing information about ourselves and others to build trust, seeking intimacy through selective sharing, occasionally gossiping, and always managing our privacy with others as we maintain our personal, social, and professional relationships.[25]

Even if we ourselves continue to insist that we have no need to explore, surely the other people in our life—our parents, partners, and children, our friends, colleagues, and other relationships of loose social ties—need the space to play with beliefs and identities, lest our radical normalcy creep throughout our immediate society, assimilating everyone we know into a stifling conformity. Beyond personal and professional relationships, each of us also has a broader interest in letting other people in general have privacy. While humans are naturally curious creatures who at times delight in gossip and innuendo, we also have an instrumental interest in letting other people have the privacy to live their lives as they see fit. Undeniably, this value is a cultural one; as law professor Robert Post has argued, privacy rules are a form of civility rules enforced by law.[26] If we have tenants, it's rude to hide a listening and recording device in their bedroom. If someone sends us nude pictures of themselves, it's rude to share them with others or post them on the internet. But privacy law ensures that these things are illegal as well, thereby shoring up the social norms of civility protected by the law.[27] Beyond civility, social privacy serves another, critical function by protecting the freedom of others to experiment with new lifestyles and ideas. Building on Post's work, Solove agrees that privacy's value is social. "Society involves a great deal of friction," he argues, "and we are constantly clashing with one another. Part of what makes a society a good place in which to live is the extent to which it allows people freedom from the intrusiveness of others. A society without privacy protection would be oppressive. When protecting individual rights, we as a society decide to hold back in order to receive the benefits of creating free zones for individuals to flourish."[28]

In the next two chapters, I'll say much more about the critical importance of these free zones and gaps, spaces and refuges from the gaze of others, and how they let us figure out who we are (chapter 4) and what we believe (chapter 5). They let us play—alone as well as with others—with our identity and are an essential shield to the development of political beliefs.[29] They foster our dynamic personal and political selves, as well as the social processes of self-government.[30] In this way, privacy is essential to the kinds of robust, healthy, self-governing, free societies that represent the best hope against tyranny and oppression.[31] As Edward Snowden puts it succinctly, "Arguing that you don't care about the right to privacy because you have nothing to hide is no different than saying you don't care about free speech because you have nothing to say."[32] We are all better off in a society with broad protections for privacy—a perspective that the artificial narrowness of the "nothing to hide" argument cannot envision. The "nothing to hide" argument might be tenacious, but it's a myth, and one that dangerously misdirects us away from what privacy is and why privacy matters. It's just not worthy of serious consideration.

Privacy Isn't About Creepiness

Imagine, for a moment, your reaction to a new practice or technology that collects or uses human information. Maybe it's the city of Baltimore, which installed surveillance microphones on city buses and has authorized spy planes to fly over the city taking high-resolution video of everything on the ground on a dubious crime-prevention rationale.[33] Maybe it's your voice-activated smart television, listening to your conversations and enabled with "automatic content recognition" to automatically monitor and collect everything you watch.[34] Or maybe it's a networked sex toy that records your usage of it.[35] What's your natural reaction to these practices? If you're like most people, you might think "Wow. That's pretty creepy!"

Creepiness may be the most common reaction people experience when they learn of a new privacy threat or invasive information practice. Most discussions of privacy and new technologies run into accusations of creepiness at some point. In privacy, it's everywhere you look. Consider, for example, surveillance-based advertising, Facebook's experiments to control the emotions of its users, NSA surveillance, black-box data recorders in cars, eavesdropping "smart" Barbie dolls, the Internet of Things, drones, Google scanning your Gmail or accessing vast amounts of healthcare data, the use of predictive analytics by employers, Zoom's attention-tracking feature, and police use of the DNA databases and audio captured from smart speakers to investigate crimes. Each of these practices have been labeled "creepy" at one time or another.[36] Target's data-based pregnancy detector discussed in chapter 2 spawned a cottage industry all on its own of journalists lining up to call it "creepy."[37]

These journalists were not alone. Politicians and technologists also frequently equate privacy risks in terms of their creepiness, even when they are trying to do good. Consider, for example, the issue of consumer tracking to serve surveillance-based ads. In a major U.S. Senate report laying the foundations for a sincere attempt at privacy reform, committed privacy reformer Senator Maria Cantwell noted that "[a]s consumers browse the web, interact with social media, or use other online services, they probably see advertisements for items they've previously searched for online (even on another device), purchased in a store, or saw on a nearby billboard. For some consumers, it can feel creepy, invasive, or alarming."[38] Or consider Apple CEO Tim Cook, who remarked, when discussing the same issue, "To me it's creepy when I look at something and all of a sudden it's chasing me all the way across the web.... I don't like that."[39]

The language of creepiness runs through academic books and articles on privacy as well. In advice to technology companies about how to make sure their customers aren't "creeped out" by their business practices, Omer Tene and Jules Polonetsky suggest that there are "several categories of corporate behavior that customers and commentators have begun to label 'creepy' for lack of a better word," activities that don't violate any established law but give their customers the creeps.[40] Tene and Polonetsky advise companies to avoid deploying new technologies (or redeploying old technologies) in ways that seem creepy. Such limits are necessary, they advise, because "social values are far more nuanced and fickle tha[n] any existing (and most likely future) laws and regulations. In order to avoid creep, companies should resist the temptation to act with chutzpah, even though brazen and audacious behavior constitutes a hallmark of Silicon Valley entrepreneurship culture. The challenge is for companies to set the right tone when seeking intimate relationships with consumers."[41] Consider, in this vein, the way Google tweaked its Gmail interface to mollify the creepy reaction. Early versions of Gmail produced small ads triggered when certain keywords were typed into an email. Silicon Valley historian Margaret O'Mara explains, "[A]fter outcry and further refinement, the more obvious signs of surveillance disappeared." The surveillance still happened—indeed, it continued to increase—but the company seems to have decided that secret surveillance that consumers didn't notice was better for its business than the more obvious signals that made its users feel creepy rather than blissfully ignorant.[42]

Even leading theories of privacy can contain overtones of creepiness. Nissenbaum's highly influential theory of privacy as "contextual integrity," for example, relies in substantial part on the creepiness reaction. Under Nissenbaum's nuanced and thoughtful theory, she explains how context matters a great deal when we discuss data practices, because not all data practices are problematic.[43] The challenge for the law, she suggests, is in respecting people's expectations to ensure "appropriate flow" of information. The trigger for considering whether a legal intervention might be appropriate under this approach is to ask whether there has been a violation of a "context-relevant informational norm" when information is shared.[44] These norms, which are "finely calibrated systems of social norms, or rules, govern the flow of personal information in distinct social contexts (e.g., education, health care, and politics)."[45] Individuals experience privacy violations, she argues, when those social norms about information are violated in inappropriate ways.[46] But notice what is at the core of Nissenbaum's claim: a perception by a person that their social norm-based expectations are being violated. Nissenbaum argues further that we should consider privacy issues in the first instance when people react to new information practices by expressing "alarm."[47] In other words, although she does not use the term, something like creepiness in a particular context is the trigger for a potential privacy violation. When we are "creeped out" by a collection or use of data that is context-inappropriate, Nissenbaum's theory would have us ask whether the law should intervene. In this way, the theory of contextual integrity is a theory of creepy. Nissenbaum's theory offers much more than creepiness, but the fact that even a nuanced and influential theory of privacy relies on something very close to the creepiness reaction further illustrates that when it comes to privacy, creepiness is everywhere.

Given how common creepiness has become as a way of thinking about privacy, it should be no surprise that creepiness has entered privacy law. Consider, for example, the Fourth Amendment's famous "reasonable expectation of privacy" test. This idea has influenced privacy law around the world, and it has also entered popular understandings of what privacy is and why privacy matters. Under the test, developed from Justice John Marshall Harlan's concurrence in the case of *Katz v. United States* (1967), the Fourth Amendment applies when a person manifests (1) a subjective expectation of privacy that (2) society is prepared to recognize as objectively reasonable.[48] Thus a police officer who secretly listens in on a telephone call without a warrant has violated the reasonable expectation of privacy of the people on the call because (1) people typically (subjectively) assume that their phone conversations are private, and (2) the Supreme Court ruled in *Katz* and subsequent cases that expectations of privacy against warrantless wiretapping are objectively reasonable expectations under the Fourth Amendment.[49] But by resting the constitutional doctrine on what people expect, and triggering the inquiry on when those expectations are violated, the "reasonable expectation of privacy test," like the theory of contextual integrity, is at bottom a theory of creepiness.

When it comes to privacy, the dominance of creepy talk shouldn't be too surprising. Creepiness is our first impulse when we encounter changing norms or technologies that leave us exposed or vulnerable. It's a visceral sensation of shock, discomfort, and revulsion, a trigger that tells us when privacy might be threatened. If we feel that a practice is creepy, this intuition suggests, maybe we should think about regulating it. But using creepiness as our test for privacy problems creates a problem of its own. If something isn't creepy, the insight suggests, then it probably isn't something we should worry about. And it seems to follow from this that if people aren't aware of a data practice, it's fine.

Despite the dominance of creepiness as a way of thinking about privacy, it's a trap, and we must resist it. Like the very best traps, creepiness is a seductive one, luring us in so gracefully that we don't realize we've been ensnared. Creepiness distracts us from the real issues at stake in privacy, and it has three principal defects.

First, creepiness is overinclusive. As a test for threats to privacy, creepiness proves too much. Lots of new technologies that might at first appear viscerally creepy will turn out to be unproblematic. Some will even turn out to be beneficial. Philosopher Evan Selinger reminds us that early steam train passengers were not merely creeped out by the new iron horses; they were physically terrified. Early passengers fainted and complained of serious maladies like spinal damage, urinary tract blockage, and eye infections, all from traveling at speeds that by today's standards wouldn't even count as speeding in a school zone.[50] New technologies—even useful ones—frequently inspire visceral terror and unease. In the early days of the internet, many consumers refused to buy products online from digital shops, fearing security lapses from electronic technologies they didn't understand.[51] Facebook's News Feed feature creeped out many users when it was first introduced because users were not accustomed to having all their information aggregated in one place for easy consumption.[52] Now the feature is considered fundamental both to the company's success and to the social awareness of many users of its network.[53]

Second, creepiness is underinclusive. New information practices that we don't understand fully, or highly invasive practices of which we are unaware, may never seem creepy, but they can still menace values we care about. Take, for example, surveillance of which we are unaware, like the mass tracking of phone calls by the NSA prior to the Snowden revelations or the use of secret algorithms to score our lives.[54] Such practices may unconstitutionally subject us to criminal or civil punishment (from jail time to designation on "no-fly" or "watch" lists), or they may overcharge us or deny us access to insurance or to economic opportunities (in the case of scoring by credit brokers or university admissions algorithms). Such practices may be illegal, inaccurate, or both, but if they operate behind layers of secrecy, we may never learn about them. And things we are unaware of are unlikely to trigger the creepiness reaction. The fact that creepiness is underinclusive is a real problem, because many of the most threatening and harmful information practices are invisible to ordinary people, such as the use of opaque black-box algorithms to sort (and then act on) citizens and consumers based on their race, gender, politics, vulnerability, or gullibility. This includes many of the most pernicious uses of data-based technologies, including those of digital redlining, fake news, and voter manipulation. If creepiness is our main test for privacy issues, its underinclusiveness represents a massive hole in its ability to do good work for us. As we've already seen, hidden exercises of information power (think Target surveillance, Gmail ad serving, NSA spying, or something entirely unknown to us) can be just as dangerous as overt ones, if not more so.

Third, creepiness is both socially contingent and highly malleable. Creepiness rests on psychological reactions to social practices—reactions that are socially constructed, that can change over time, and that can be manipulated. A pervasive threat to privacy or our civil liberties can be made less creepy as we become conditioned to it. Think, here, about metal detectors at airports or at the entrances of professional sports events and public schools. Such a threat may remain equally serious but become normalized as we fit it into our understanding of the world in which we have to operate, alongside other problems like police corruption, sexism, or drunk drivers. The internet advertising industry, which relies on detailed surveillance of individual web-surfing to target ads, has fallen into this category.[55] It's easy to forget that the internet of the late 1990s was an anarchic, largely untrackable domain of the weird and the private. (Undeniably, it also included a lot of pictures of naked people.) By contrast, the corporate, commercial, mobile app–driven internet of the early 2020s represents probably the most highly surveilled environment in the history of humanity.[56] (Equally undeniably, it too includes a lot of higher-resolution photos and streaming videos of naked people.)[57]

Another good example of creepiness's malleability is the erosion of location privacy expectations on dating apps. In 2012, the Girls Around Me app scraped publicly accessible Facebook and Foursquare check-ins and displayed them on a map around the user's location for dating, meetup, or hookup purposes. It was roundly condemned as "creepy." One widely circulated article in the *Atlantic*, for example, condemned both the app and its vision of privacy—the idea that information shared with a social network somehow became "public" and was fair game for any use that the company or its partners might dream up down the road. (Notice the echoes of the secrecy paradigm here as well.) Castigating this vision of privacy, the well-read *Atlantic* journalist argued that app developers should instead adopt Nissenbaum's contextual integrity framework to dial down the creepy factor.[58] But most app developers don't read Nissenbaum, and they kept pushing and pushing at the social norms of information use that the "notice and choice" regime enables. As a result, by the end of the decade location-based dating apps had become so normalized as to no longer trigger the creepy reaction. For example, one guide to dating apps in *The Guardian*— the privacy-conscious newspaper that broke the Snowden revelations—ran through the location-based features in the leading services. Its review hardly batted an eye about the privacy issues these apps raised. This was the case for Tinder's "geographically defined options" and the "convenience" of Happn, "designed for you to meet someone in your vicinity, ideally someone you have just brushed past on the street or made awkward eye contact with on the train."[59]

How did the experience of privacy in the internet's constructed environment change? Many believe that companies like Facebook had a lot to do with the shift in norms and expectations surrounding privacy, transforming practices that had recently been thought of as "creepy" into ones that blended seamlessly into the "nature"* of the internet. Facebook founder Mark Zuckerberg, as we'll see in more detail later, once bluntly stated that his company decided that since college kids had started to share information about themselves on the internet in blogs, privacy would no longer be a social norm—so he (in his words) "just went for it."[60] But as the legal theorist Lisa Austin has explained, this process was much more complicated—and strategic—than Zuckerberg's breezy assertion that Facebook was just sailing the winds of a changing social norm (and making vast amounts of money almost by accident). Facebook, like other companies, consistently and constantly nudged at those social norms and expectations with the wide variety of tools at its disposal. How was Facebook able to do this? One factor was that, unlike most prior internet companies, Facebook connected people who

---

* Remember that the internet has no "nature" that isn't built by humans. Everything is constructed, and design is everywhere.

actually knew each other using their real names and pictures. This let it piggyback on the greater willingness of people to share their lives and photos with people they actually knew (and who, presumably, already knew many of these things about them). In addition, the social norms developed on Facebook were (at least in the minds of its customers) limited to Facebook activities rather than general norms of "sharing" with the world at large. The trick was using in-person social norms as bait for a much broader privacy heist.

Finally, as Austin puts it, "both the architectural and business choices that Facebook makes exert a strong influence on the formation of these [privacy] expectations and Facebook's choices occur within the context of a business model premised on broad information and use."[61] Using all of the tools of behavioral economics, choice architecture, and data-powered persuasion it could muster, Facebook was able to craft the social network's environment to encourage sharing, nudging by design to advance its own interests. It could engage in vast numbers of experiments using a technique called "iterative A/B testing," in which it could run its standard interface on a control group for half of its test subjects (group A), while it tried out an experimental new interface on the other half of the set (group B).[62] Whichever interface design produced more sharing or whatever other activity Facebook was trying to encourage could be installed as the new default, and then iteratively A/B–tested against other versions of the interface to produce ever more sharing through marginal gains. And with millions upon millions of unwitting test subjects to experiment upon, Facebook could continue to refine its design over many years with scientific precision. With the single-minded persistence of a toddler who wants a cookie (albeit a toddler who never sleeps and has billions of dollars of resources), Facebook could keep pushing at the social and legal norms surrounding privacy, pushing for more information and changing its terms of service to allow it to access ever more personal information.[63] A/B testing can certainly be a legitimate tool for industrial and academic research, but it is a very powerful one that is barely constrained by law, particularly in the private sector. And its use is widespread. Facebook is not the only tech company or social network to use A/B testing to leverage "the surprising power of online experiments," such as whether a particular color or design causes more people to click on an advertising banner.[64] Indeed, one study estimates that "[t]oday, Microsoft and several other leading companies—including Amazon, Booking.com, Facebook, and Google—each conduct more than 10,000 online controlled experiments annually, with many tests engaging millions of users. Start-ups and companies without digital roots, such as Walmart, Hertz, and Singapore Airlines, also run them regularly, though on a smaller scale."[65]

The manipulation of once creepy practices to normalize them under a kind of digital Stockholm Syndrome hardly removes the problem, even if we become accustomed or resigned to it. In the context of privacy, consider the ever expanding reach of data collection, always pushing up against (and seeking to desensitize and then roll back) the creepiness reaction. Google shares culpability with Facebook in this respect. Technology critic Shoshanna Zuboff has shown how Google took unclaimed data about the people using its "free" services and used it to profile, predict, and ultimately influence them through the business model she calls "surveillance capitalism." At the same time as it was building this model, Zuboff argues, Google used a process she terms "psychic numbing" to reduce the creepiness reaction as it changed social norms surrounding human information. In this process, Google's "free" services are best seen as neither free nor a typical transaction. Rather, Zuboff argues, they are "hooks" that lure people into Google's data ecosystem "in which our personal experiences are scraped and packaged" for the goals of Google and its real customers, advertisers.[66] Google thus becomes a "Faustian bargain," because, once entangled, we cannot tear ourselves away without leaving modern, networked life as we know it behind. She explains further:

> Our dependency is at the heart of the commercial surveillance project, in which our felt needs for effective life vie against the inclination to resist its bold incursions. This conflict produces a psychic numbing that inures us to the realities of being tracked, parsed, mined, and modified. It disposes us to rationalize the situation in resigned cynicism, creating excuses that operate like defense mechanisms ("I have nothing to hide") or find other ways to stick our heads in the sand, choosing ignorance out of frustration and helplessness. In this way, surveillance capitalism imposes a fundamentally illegitimate choice that twenty-first-century individuals should not have to make, and its normalization leaves us singing in our chains.[67]

As Google's Eric Schmidt put it all too honestly in 2010, "Google policy is to get right up to the creepy line and not cross it."[68] "Don't be creepy" reminds us of Tene and Polonetsky's advice to companies about not entering into creepy territory. As a corporate philosophy, however, it sounds a lot closer to "Move the goalposts, but don't get caught" than Google's original mission statement, "Don't be evil."

While creepiness may be a natural psychological response to novelty, in the context of privacy law it is ultimately a trap. Even under Nissenbaum's contextual integrity theory, a finding of creepiness ("the violation of a context-relative informational norm") nudges us into thinking that privacy issues are merely subjective matters of psychology and preference. Under this view, different people have different reactions to privacy practices, so we should let them choose what they want. In theory, this sounds reasonable, even empowering. But in the United States at least, we've already seen where this leads in practice: the time-consuming, bewildering, and ineffective model of "notice and choice" and privacy self-management, with its lengthy boilerplate privacy policies and limited, nudgy choices structured by choice architecture and behavioral science. It's why Nissenbaum's thoughtful and nuanced theory was eagerly embraced, watered down, and co-opted by companies. (This is, incidentally, another great example of Ari Waldman's insight, discussed earlier, about how companies rewrite privacy language in self-serving ways.) Under this watered-down view of contextual integrity, if privacy depends on subjective preferences and varies depending upon context, we should just give people a choice about what they want. From this view, consent looks like the only answer to the problem. But as we've seen, under U.S. law, consent is a pathologically ineffective way to protect privacy. In the digital world, consent is frequently unwitting, incapacitated, or coerced.[69] That's the trap: creepiness is not only a poor proxy for identifying privacy problems, but it also manufactures and then justifies empty forms of manufactured consent.

The creepy trap tricks us into thinking that privacy is about psychology, subjective preferences, and consumer empowerment, when privacy is really about money, power, and the ways in which human information rules are used to manipulate consumers and citizens alike. This is why, as I argued in chapter 2, it's essential to understand that privacy is fundamentally about power and how it should be operationalized around rules other than the false friends of notice and choice. Let's return once again to the Target pregnancy case. Recall that the real reason Target was trying to predict which of its female customers were pregnant had nothing to do with creepiness—it had to do with power. Target was trying to determine pregnancy because the birth of a child is one of those critical times when consumer behavior can be manipulated. Expectant parents buy a lot of things, including a lot of new things for the first time from new retailers—and then they have a baby, and they are highly unlikely to start buying from new retailers, at first because they are too overwhelmed and exhausted even to shower regularly, and then because they have become habituated to buying their diapers (for example) from Target. Target even went out of its way to appear noncreepy. When pregnant customers freaked out after Target started sending them coupons for baby formula, Target began to intentionally hide what it was doing by sending the baby coupons (its data-driven payload) alongside other coupons for things that were deliberately chosen to seem irrelevant to the pregnant woman. Human information was used to identify a target (so to speak); it was used to time the relevant coupons; and it was used to select irrelevant ones, all with the intentional goal of manipulating pregnant women into becoming habituated Target shoppers. Through this kind of data-informed sleight of hand, Target was able to minimize the creepiness reaction of its customers so that those mollified customers could be subjected to Target's real purpose: an unwitting control of them using the power of their data analytics.

These sorts of activities are widespread today in industry. Consider the widely shared belief that Facebook "creepily" listens to our conversations through smartphone and smart speaker microphones, then uses those conversations to target ads to us on News Feed. This is a belief that lots of people hold and is certainly not a crazy thing for them to suspect or believe. "Smart home" devices create all sorts of privacy and security vulnerabilities. And we already saw in chapter 2 that capturing the "voice intelligence" of shoppers and subjecting it to AI analysis is the new frontier in surveillance-based marketing.[70] What's more, Facebook has done a lot of things with human information that are ethically dubious, so many people reasonably believed the story of conversation-based ad targeting to be true. In fact, enough people had experienced the phenomenon of seeing an ad on Facebook and then thinking "I was just talking about that with my friend" that reporters started digging into the story. As it turned out, this particular accusation about Facebook's misdeeds is false. Facebook denied that it was listening to our conversations through our iPhones or Alexa speakers, both to journalists and before Congress under oath, and there is every reason to believe it is telling the truth here.[71] If it had been listening in to one—or millions—of private conversations, this would violate the Electronic Communications Privacy Act of 1986. This federal law makes bugging a private room a federal felony and would expose Facebook to being sued for $10,000 for each and every one of potentially millions of violations—enough liability to bankrupt even a tech giant.[72]

But that's not the *really* interesting part of the story. The real reason Facebook wasn't listening in to our conversations was that it didn't need to. Like Target, Facebook uses data science and its vast stores of our human information to pursue highly sophisticated surveillance of us, and it uses this to predict what we might be interested in. These techniques can be highly effective, which is why people suspected they might be listening in. Journalist and Facebook historian Steven Levy puts it well: "[T]he truth is that Facebook didn't need to spy on people's audio. It already had all the [human] data it needed to help advertisers hit the mark not just on the kinds of audiences it wanted to reach, but on the exact individuals who would be in that audience."[73] In other words, Facebook was just doing what Target—and many other companies—have been doing: using data science to track, predict, and influence. The only difference was that Facebook was doing the business of surveillance capitalism so well that these coincidences kept happening. They kept triggering the creepy reaction—but because the creepy reaction is so unreliable, it was for the wrong reason.

When it comes to privacy—particularly when it comes to data-based surveillance and manipulation of consumers—creepiness is a trap. What's really important is not whether the creepy reaction is being triggered. Instead, what really matters is *power*—the substance of what's going on whether we as consumers understand it or not, whether we as consumers notice it or not, or whether we as consumers are freaked out by it or not. Thinking of privacy in terms of creepiness is not only a bad way of gauging whether there's a real privacy issue; it also confuses us about what's really at stake, and it further enables the exercise of power by those who control our data. Given these limitations, when we talk about privacy, we must do much better than talking in terms of creepiness. Creepiness can sometimes be the start of a conversation about privacy, but it cannot be more than that. We need to think more concretely than merely whether something is creepy if we want to build the kind of information society that protects values more meaningful than preventing visceral senses of unease.

Privacy Isn't Primarily About Control

If consumers and citizens are bewildered by the ways in which their human information is collected and used, one logical solution to the problem might be to put them back in control. Like creepiness, this argument is seemingly everywhere in privacy debates. We see it in the "choice" element of "notice and choice" as the aspiration of empowerment through privacy self-management.[74] We see it in the multiplying number of "privacy dashboards" and other kinds of interfaces that companies have provided (often in good faith) to help their customers manage their privacy settings and preferences. When Zuckerberg was called before Congress to testify about Facebook's information practices during the Cambridge Analytica scandal, he argued over and over again that when it comes to privacy, Facebook's goal, first and foremost, is to put its "users" in "control."[75] Facebook is by no means alone in this endeavor, as control has become a staple of the ways technology companies describe their privacy commitments. However we characterize it, the idea of Privacy as Control that runs through privacy debates is an ideal that it seems almost everyone shares.

Privacy as Control runs deep in our legal and cultural understandings of privacy.[76] Warren and Brandeis's seminal article, "The Right to Privacy," offered a theory of Privacy as Control when it argued that "[t]he common law secures to each individual the right of determining, ordinarily, to what extent his thoughts, sentiments, and emotions shall be communicated to others."[77] In the late 1960s, Alan Westin's germinal book, *Privacy and Freedom*, argued that the best way to think about privacy was as the claim of "individuals, groups, or institutions to determine for themselves when, how, and to what extent information about them is communicated to others."[78] Writing in the essentially predigital world of the late 1960s, Westin saw privacy as our ability to share and withhold information from our fellows, an ability, as the book's title suggests, that was essential to preserving freedom.[79] Westin's work has been highly influential; indeed, the basic approach of the Fair Information Practices is all about empowering people to make good, informed decisions about their data.[80] The right to consent to new uses of our data and the right to access our data and correct it if it is wrong are examples of this approach, which has been common in U.S. privacy laws from the federal Privacy Act of 1974 to the California Consumer Privacy Act of 2020.[81] Privacy as Control also runs through European data protection law and particularly through the GDPR, which enshrines strong norms of informed consent, access, correction, data portability, and other control-minded principles. Indeed, the official commentary on the GDPR even declares one of its key purposes to be that "[n]atural persons should have control of their own personal data."[82] Another key part of the GDPR framework is that the organization that is in charge of processing personal data is known as the "controller."[83] American regulators have shared this view. As we have seen, for many years the Federal Trade Commission has called for a "notice and choice" regime to protect consumer privacy, even though the limitations of this approach became apparent over time. Nevertheless, as recently as early 2020, FTC Commissioner Christine Wilson continued to enthusiastically assert that in spite of the "privacy missteps by notable platforms," a comprehensive federal privacy law should "[empower] individuals to make informed choices."[84]

Technology companies also lionize Privacy as Control. Google promises, "[Y]ou have choices regarding the information we collect and how it's used" and offers a wide variety of "privacy controls," touting, "We also built a place for you to review and control information saved in your Google Account."[85] Facebook continues to emphasize control as a solution to privacy in the aftermath of the Cambridge Analytica scandal. In an online manifesto titled "A Privacy-Focused Vision for Social Networking," Zuckerberg mused, "As I think about the future of the internet, I believe a privacy-focused communications platform will become even more important than today's open platforms," and he offered a few key principles that this new, allegedly privacy-protective Facebook would adhere to, the first of which was "Private interactions. People should have simple, intimate places where they have clear *control* over who can communicate with them and confidence that no one else can access what they share."[86] As a follow-up, ads for the Facebook app touted the slogan "You see it. You control it" and boasted of "a new level of transparency and control."[87] Even older companies trumpet the importance of putting their customers in control of data choices. Charter Spectrum (the cable company that delivers internet service to my house) has argued sincerely that any future U.S. privacy law should embody five key principles—the first and most important of which is "control," the idea that "consumers should be empowered to have meaningful choice for each use of their data."[88] And Barclay's Bank trumpets the importance of "putting consumers in control of their data and enabling innovation."[89]

What could possibly be wrong with putting consumers in control of how their data is collected and used? Privacy as Control allows diverse consumers to make choices that reflect their diverse preferences. It resonates with American notions of autonomy and individuality and European notions of human dignity and the fundamental right of data protection. Moreover, it is supported by consumers, regulators, and industry on both sides of the Atlantic. Surely, the problems with privacy just stem from our not getting control right, right?

Unfortunately, it's not that simple. What can be stated simply, though, is that Privacy as Control has been a spectacular failure at protecting human privacy for the past thirty years, particularly in the United States. Privacy as Control is an illusion, though like the best illusions it is a highly appealing one. There are four main problems with using control to solve problems of privacy, but they are big ones: (1) control is overwhelming; (2) control is an illusion; (3) control completes the creepy trap; and (4) control is insufficient.

The first problem is that *control is overwhelming*. It's here that Privacy as Control in theory becomes privacy self-management in practice. More control means more options, and while that can be great in theory (after all, who doesn't want more choices?), the sheer number of choices we can be given can be overwhelming. Consider passwords, for instance. It's all well and good to have a password for a service, and in the early days of the internet, when we had only a few passwords to memorize (our ISP, an email account, and maybe a shopping site or early social network or two), it was fine. It was even fine when password requirements mandated uniqueness and became a little more demanding in terms of length and complexity. But when you have a lot of accounts, each requiring unique complex passwords, on multiple devices, things quickly escalate beyond the ability of our mind to keep them in our head. And then we are asked to add numbers and special characters. And then asked to change our passwords regularly. Little wonder, then, that many people keep all of their passwords written down on a piece of paper or sticky notes on their desk or reuse the same password over and over just so that they can get anything done.[†]

Privacy self-management makes the complexity of passwords look simple by comparison. At least for any given site password, "all" we need to remember for passwords is an account name, a unique password, and ideally

---

† You might be wondering at this point, "What about password managers that keep track of all of our passwords for us?" Password managers have their virtues, but only if you trust the manager's own security enough to keep all of your eggs in their single basket. More important for this example, password managers just store unique identifiers; they don't manage privacy preferences, and despite the dreams of futurists for "privacy butlers" to manage our preferences for us, such technologies have remained in the realm of science fiction, partly because the many other defects of Privacy as Control.

that we should change it once in a while. Privacy choices, by contrast, can be overwhelming. Mobile apps can ask users for more than two hundred permissions, and even the average app asks for about five.[90] How many apps do you have on your phone and your computer? Woodrow Hartzog states the problem well when he explains, "The problem with thinking of privacy as control is that if we are given our wish for more privacy, it means we are given so much control that we choke on it."[91] We therefore get presented with a "dizzying array of switches, delete buttons, and privacy settings," all very sparkly and shiny but ultimately just that.[92] This is particularly the case with services that envision control and transparency as virtues that we can't have enough of. When a company's response to a privacy scandal is "more control," this simply means more bewildering choices rather than fewer, which worsens the problem rather than making it better. As scholars across disciplines have documented extensively, our consent has been manufactured, so we just click "Agree."[93] But talking about "putting people in control" makes a good sound bite for executives, and it distracts us from the real problems of power and manipulation.

All of this assumes, moreover, that we even know what we are agreeing to. In lip service to this idea, every digital service and website has its own privacy policy—the "notice" portion of "notice and choice"—but usually here, too, the notice we need to exercise control is irredeemably deficient. Privacy policies range from airy language that is long on promises but short on detail to dense, turgid prose that can be deciphered only with the help of a law degree and a heavy jolt of caffeine. On the airy side, there's Google's readable but vague platitudes—the verbal equivalent, nutritionally speaking, of a marshmallow:

> We collect information to provide better services to all our users—from figuring out basic stuff like which language you speak, to more complex things like which ads you'll find most useful, the people who matter most to you online, or which YouTube videos you might like. The information Google collects, and how that information is used, depends on how you use our services and how you manage your privacy controls.[94]

Or there's Amazon's impenetrable turgidity, the prunes of the privacy world:

> Amazon Services may include third-party advertising and links to other websites and apps. Third-party advertising partners may collect

information about you when you interact with their content, advertising, and services. For more information about third-party advertising at Amazon, including interest-based ads, please read our Interest-Based Ads policy. To adjust your advertising preferences, please go to the Advertising Preferences page.[95]

Long or short, privacy policies are vague and they are legion. We encounter far too many of them each day for us to stay on top of any of them, much less all of them. As Amazon's policy puts it in a rare moment of absurdist clarity, "Our business changes constantly, and our Privacy Notice will change also. You should check our websites frequently to see recent changes."[96]

In any event, the volume of privacy policies is far too great. One famous 2009 study estimated that if we were to quickly read the privacy policies of every website we encounter in a typical year, it would take seventy-six full working days of nothing but reading just to get through them all.[97] A 2016 study by the Norwegian Consumer Council found that the privacy policies of the thirty-three most common apps on a typical smartphone measured over 250,000 words—longer than the New Testament, twice the length of this book—and would take more than twenty-four hours to read out loud (something the quirky folks at the NCC actually did online).[98] The investigators concluded, "The current state of terms and conditions for digital services is bordering on the absurd. Their scope, length and complexity mean it is virtually impossible to make good and informed decisions."[99] Control over personal information might be attractive in the abstract, but in practice it's an overwhelming obligation. Hartzog is entirely right—we are choking on it.

The second problem with Privacy as Control is that, *when it comes to privacy, control is an illusion.* It's easy to forget, particularly given the way the internet has integrated itself into our lives over the past twenty-five years, but the internet is not natural. It is a human construction built by humans comprised of human decisions serving human purposes. Early tech evangelists imagined the internet's revolutionary potential to empower humans, and while we certainly could have built an internet along those lines, that's not the one we got. What we got instead was one in which the interfaces governing privacy have been built by human engineers answering to human bosses working for companies with purposes other than revolutionary human empowerment (Silicon Valley's advertising claims to the contrary notwithstanding). All of the rhetoric surrounding putting "users" in control belies the fact that engineers design their technologies to produce particular results.

These design choices limit the range of options available to the humans using the technology—Joel Reidenberg's *lex informatica* at work. Companies decide the types of boxes we get to check and the switches we get to flip. They also decide which set of choices goes in the basic privacy dashboard, which set goes in the "advanced settings," and, even more important, which choices "users" don't get to make at all. Facebook, for example, lets "users" manage location settings and turn off facial recognition in photos (with default options originally being set to "share" with the company before an outcry changed the default), but other options are buried deeper in the interface. Notably and intentionally, the "choice" to "control" Facebook's collection of vast swaths of other human information about its customers is never given.[100] Critically, by designing the technology and setting the defaults, Facebook's engineers not only know which options the average user is likely to select, but they can use the nudging effects of choice architecture to produce the outcomes they want and that serve their business interests. As we saw earlier, design can shape outcomes, and large tech companies with millions (or billions) of "users" can conduct large-scale scientific experiments on those human subjects, using A/B testing to figure out which blend of options, choices, decision structure, wording, and even color schemes produces the outcomes the companies want.[101] Deploying the insights of behavioral economics, companies create manipulative interfaces that exploit our built-in tendencies to prefer large shiny colorful buttons and ignore small dull gray ones. ("Delete my account" is always the small gray one, not the large shiny one.) They may also shame us into feeling bad about withholding data or declining options. And we've already seen how companies often make the ability to exercise control possible but costly through forced work, subtle misdirection, and incentive tethering—called "dark patterns."[102] Sometimes platforms design online services to nudge people into oversharing through FarmVille-style gamification, such as keeping a streak going or nudging people to share old posts or congratulate others on Facebook. Or they use other dark patterns to discourage their customers from exercising their privacy controls.[103] Companies know how impulsive sharing can be and therefore set up an entire system to make it as easy as possible.

Third, *the control illusion completes the creepy trap.* Recall our discussion of creepiness. We saw in that section how Facebook shifted social norms on privacy through its own control of the choice architecture and its ever-expanding attempts to collect the personal data of its customers, and it did so with the insistence and persistence of a robotic toddler that doesn't

sleep. Better yet, Facebook was able to mask these activities with the rhetoric of putting its "users in control."[104] When the public or regulators pushed
back, as they did from time to time, Facebook could apologize and wait a
little while. When the heat died down, Facebook could just keep trying
again, month after month and year after year, using the techniques of data-
enhanced choice architecture. ("Can I have a cookie now?" "How about
now?" "Your friends would give me a cookie." "Your dad gave me a cookie
last week." "How about I take a cookie unless you object?") On the legal side
of things, the American "notice and choice" regime enabled these efforts,
giving Facebook's data grab and norm erosion a fictional but legally sufficient
patina of "consent."[105] In this way, what had once been creepy was gradually,
continually, and scientifically worn down into appearing "just the way the internet works," allowing Zuckerberg to claim that Facebook was merely riding
the wave of a changing social norm instead of consciously shaping it with all
of the considerable tools at its disposal. Indeed, in a 2019 statement on privacy control, Facebook's Chief Privacy Officer Erin Egan suggested, "Many
apps and websites are free because they're supported by online advertising.
And to reach people who are more likely to care about what they are selling,
businesses often share data about people's interactions on their websites with
ad platforms and other services. This is how much of the internet works."[106]

It is here that communications scholar Alice Marwick's idea of "privacy
work" is particularly illuminating. Marwick argues that we all engage in "privacy work," uncompensated labor that we must engage in or else be considered at fault. Using a feminist lens that focuses on power imbalances, she
argues that we consumers are all disempowered when it comes to privacy
work. She draws an analogy to "safety work," the kinds of work that women
must perform to determine, for example, whether it is safe to walk home
alone from a party. Just as women who don't engage in safety work are often
blamed for harms they incur as a result, Marwick argues that all of us must
engage in privacy work or be blamed for the consequences. Running through
all of this analysis is the insight that consumers are disempowered by the
structural power imbalances between individuals and entities that process
their information.

And thus the creepy trap is completed. Creepiness is a subjective experience, suggesting that we have divergent privacy preferences. The key to managing divergent preferences is to give people control so they can get what
they want. But when norms and architecture are shaped by powerful engineers wielding the power of data science and behavioral science, the design of

interfaces with limited choices allows control of behavior and the illusion of transparency through vast numbers of overwhelming privacy policies. If you don't do the privacy work, it's your fault, even when the deck is structurally stacked against you. Critically, because creepiness extends only to privacy practices we perceive, companies are largely free to do what they want with that vast iceberg of dark data existing below the waterline of our comprehension. A more recent report by the Norwegian Consumer Council titled (appropriately enough) "Out of Control" documents how a shadowy group of companies most people have no awareness of are tracking vast amounts of human information every time people use their phones, notwithstanding the "putting users in control" rhetoric of tech companies.[107] These are the "adtech" companies—advertising companies processing human information that is below our creepiness threshold with the purpose of selling targeted, surveillance-based ads to manipulate us into buying things. In other words, their private purpose is control, but it's control of us. In these ways, we can see clearly how "putting users in control through notice and choice" is really code for controlling "users" through the overwhelming and manipulative scheme of privacy self-management and then blaming them for failing to do the requisite privacy work.[‡] The illusion of Privacy as Control masks the reality of control through the illusion of privacy. What is really being controlled is us.

Fourth, and finally, *privacy as control is insufficient*. Tech executives and some regulators talk as if the solution to every privacy problem is more control, more dashboards, clearer privacy policies, and more dumping of more privacy work onto already harried and bewildered human minds. These people don't want to engage in privacy work; they just want to email their babysitter to say they are running late or show their friends the loaf of sourdough bread they just baked.[108] We've already seen how fetishizing control does nothing when there is information collection we can't perceive or don't understand. And privacy, as we've seen, is a social value; our privacy depends not just on what choices we make ourselves but on the choices of everyone else in society. In this respect, privacy is like other social goods, like public health or the environment. In dealing with the Covid-19 pandemic,

---

[‡] The late great Joel Reidenberg, a founding figure in information privacy law, anticipated this development a quarter of a century ago at the dawn of the commercial internet. See Joel R. Reidenberg, *Setting Standards for Fair Information Practice in the U.S. Private Sector*, 80 Iowa L. Rev. 497, 499–500 (1995) ("[I]nstead of minimizing the manipulation of citizens and their thinking through unfettered flows of information, the private sector has established a 'smoke screen' that in effect enables subtle, yet significant, manipulation of citizens through hidden control of personal information.").

we counted on other people's decisions to wear masks, follow social distancing guidelines, and get vaccines to help us get through the public and private health crisis. We couldn't do it on our own, and other people's bad or limited choices made the public health situation worse than it needed to be. Treating privacy as a purely individual value that can be given or bartered away (whether through "control" or sale) converts it into an asset that can be chipped away on an individual basis, distracting us from (and ignoring) the social benefits privacy provides.

An example from the environment might help to bring this point into focus. As most people are aware, single-use plastic bottles are undeniably a massive environmental problem. Made from crude oil like other forms of "disposable" plastic, these bottles harm wildlife and plants, and they contain microplastic particles with unknown effects on human health.§ The National Geographic Society has termed the plastic pollution crisis "one of the most pressing environmental issues."[109] However, in 2017 the Trump administration decided to resume selling plastic bottles in America's national parks, including the Grand Canyon, whose stunning natural beauty does not come with an abundance of convenient recycling locations. The decision to make this change, produced after lobbying by the plastics industry, was couched in the familiar terms of consumer choice and control. "It should be up to our visitors to decide how best to keep themselves and their families hydrated during a visit to a national park, particularly during hot summer visitation periods," announced the new acting director of the National Park Service.[110] Notice once again how, control notwithstanding, structuring design and defaults produces predictable outcomes. In this case, the predictable outcome was more bottles sold—and more bottles discarded—in national parks. But notice also how, even if I would like to visit a Grand Canyon unspoiled by millions of pieces of plastic waste, and even if I follow the Wilderness Code scrupulously and leave no trace of my water consumption behind, I cannot, because the "choices" of other people have affected the environment I would like to visit. Privacy works the same way. Even if we engage in superhuman efforts at privacy control, managing our dashboards with the diligence of an air traffic controller, reading our privacy policies and checking back regularly to see if Amazon has made changes, the inevitable actions of other

§ Consumer Reports found in 2020 that the average American ingests a credit-card-size weight of microplastics every week. See Kevin Loria, *How to Eat Less Plastic: Each of Us Might Ingest Up to a Credit Card's Worth of Plastic Weekly Through Food and Water. Here, How to Minimize Exposure,* CONSUMER REPORTS, Apr. 30, 2020.

WHAT PRIVACY ISN'T 99

people have changed the privacy environment. Ordinary consumers (the ones who care about their privacy but are human beings rather than fictional and somewhat obsessed superbeings) will have succumbed to Zuboff's "psychic numbing," worn down to the point of resignation and acceptance by the manufacturing of their consent.[111]

Sometimes there is little or nothing we can do to prevent others from disclosing information about us. This can happen when companies set up pricing systems that rely on information disclosure, like "safe driver" discounts for car insurance contingent on your agreeing to have a black-box data controller in your car, especially if such boxes were to become standard in passenger cars.[112] Or when your child's school decides to use a "learning management system" or other software that has privacy practices only the school can agree to. Or when a company voluntarily discloses data it collected about you to the government. Or when someone discloses their genetic data to a company, which, since blood relatives have very high genetic similarities, means they have also shared sensitive information about their close family members.

This last example is how the notorious murderer and rapist known as the Golden State Killer was caught in 2018, using data from GEDMatch, a basic Florida website that allowed people to upload their genetic profiles to help with genealogical searches and filling in blank spots in family trees.[113] Police took old genetic material from crime scenes and uploaded the sequenced genome to GEDMatch. That produced a pool of potential relatives of the killer, which the police used to identify Joseph James DeAngelo, a seventy-two-year-old man living in Citrus Heights, California. (They also confirmed his identity using DNA of his on a tissue they found in his trash, but that's a different privacy issue.)[114] And while it might be hard to muster too much sympathy for the privacy travails of a serial killer, the Golden State Killer example nicely illustrates how such privacy unraveling could also be used to reveal paternity, disposition to genetically linked diseases like breast cancer, and many other facts about us that (unlike being a serial killer) are no fault of our own. Perhaps even more important, the phenomenon of unraveling happens entirely outside the realm of consent, a gap in consent that is just further evidence that Privacy as Control cannot bear the tremendous weight that has been placed on it.

The limitations of Privacy as Control are thus numerous. Simple to state and noble in theory, it nevertheless operates in practice as a smokescreen under which companies control humans rather than humans controlling their data. The problem isn't that control and choice are always bad—it would be hard to imagine a good life or a free society in which people weren't given real choices and control over their modes of living. But as practiced in the twenty-first-century digital world, by elevating a fiction of control and ignoring choice architecture, design, defaults, and power, Privacy as Control operates as a form of disempowerment rather than the liberating force it is claimed to be. We should certainly focus on giving digital consumers a manageable set of what Austin calls *meaningful choices* rather than the vast number of tightly controlled and ultimately controlling limited choices most consumers face.[115] But in order to do that, we need to think differently about privacy and control. We need to shift our view from looking just at the individual and focus instead on our public norms, our built digital infrastructure, and the ways "control" operates in practice rather than in theory. As Austin helpfully reminds us in another of her articles, "privacy is about power, not control.[116]

Privacy Isn't Dying

At this point in my argument, you might be feeling fairly pessimistic about the future of privacy. I hope you agree that privacy is best understood as the rules governing the extent to which human information is known or used, that privacy is about power, and that protecting it is important. But I've just painted a picture in which we all have something to hide; our intuitive emotional responses of creepiness are not only unreliable but malleable; and the bedrock principle of privacy as being in control of our own data is a dangerous illusion. It can be easy to give up hope and enter into the fatalism that privacy is dying. Even if you accept that privacy rules of some sort are inevitable, the story I have painted so far of the strategic erosion of privacy norms by surveillance capitalism could lead you to despair.

In some respects, this brings us back to where we started. The idea that *Privacy Is Dying* is a weaker but more insidious version of the Privacy Is Dead argument we saw in the introduction. Even if privacy isn't dead, goes this argument, it is dying, slowly whittled away as our society moves toward increasingly digital ways of living. A society fueled by data has no place for privacy, we hear, and we should let it fade into the past like horse-drawn carriages and VHS cassettes. Besides, the argument goes, people in general (and especially young people) don't care about privacy anymore; they might say they care about privacy, but what about the "privacy paradox" under which people talk about the importance of privacy but then act like they don't care about privacy? Perhaps unsurprisingly, a good example of the Privacy Is Dying argument was offered by a young Mark Zuckerberg in 2010, responding to an interview question about the future of privacy on Facebook and the internet in general:

> When I got started in my dorm room at Harvard, the question a lot of people asked was "why would I want to put any information on the Internet at all? Why would I want to have a website?" And then in the last 5 or 6 years, blogging has taken off in a huge way and all these different services that have people sharing all this information. People have really gotten comfortable not only sharing more information and different kinds, but more openly and with more people. That social norm is just something that has evolved over time.
>
> We view it as our role in the system to constantly be innovating and be updating what our system is to reflect what the current social norms are. A lot of companies would be trapped by the conventions and their legacies of what they've built, doing a privacy change—doing a privacy change for 350 million users is not the kind of thing that a lot of companies would do. But we viewed that as a really important thing, to always keep a beginner's mind and what would we do if we were starting the company now and we decided that these would be the social norms now and we just went for it.[117]

There are many problems with Zuckerberg's statement. It is naïve, tone-deaf, self-interested, and arrogant. It failed to recognize what people really wanted, perhaps confusing "what people wanted" with "what made more money for Facebook." (Maybe that's an easy mistake to make when that money is at the scale of billions of dollars.) Zuckerberg's statement also suggested that internet privacy norms just "evolved over time" rather than being influenced by the values embedded in the design of the technologies we use every day, including the technologies Facebook itself designed and marketed.[118] (We've already seen this claim; recall how the creepy trap allows online social norms to be manipulated by the companies that design the internet's built environment.) But at the core of Zuckerberg's claim is the idea that Privacy Is Dying: people, he claims, had started to share more information about themselves on the internet; he took this to mean that they had decided that privacy was dying, and so Facebook "just went for it."

Beyond Zuckerberg's nonsense, though, there is something to the Privacy Is Dying myth, or else it wouldn't be so persistent. Like a lot of myths, the Privacy Is Dying myth has a grain of truth at its core. If privacy concerns the degree to which human information is known or used, as I argue, then more human information is being known or used in the digital present than the analog past. Digital technologies are designed to collect and use human information, and they are good at that task. The amount of human information collected and used is increasing. But does that mean that Privacy Is Dying?

Put simply, no. Just because more information is being collected, it does not mean that Privacy Is Dying. In fact, the Privacy Is Dying claim is erroneous and deeply flawed. Let me explain why. The claim takes an undeniable fact (more human information is being collected), but then adds two more elements. The first of these is an additional empirical claim that people don't care about privacy, and second is the moral claim that it's okay not to worry about privacy because sharing human information is, on balance, a good thing. This argument is a bit is like responding to seeing a house on fire by saying that the homeowners have insurance, may have wanted to move, and that fires have upsides like being pretty and generating warmth on a cold night. However, the pervasiveness of the Privacy Is Dying claim warrants a closer look.

The first set of claims in the Privacy Is Dying argument are empirical: (1) more human information is being collected and (2) people don't care about privacy. The first of these empirical claims is true, but the second is false. People do care about privacy. That is why we talk about privacy so much all the time, and why you are already deep into the theory section of this book. Much has been said about people's attitudes toward privacy over the past few decades—so much attention that volume alone suggests people do care. When we look at the evidence, in fact, it's undeniable that people care about their privacy, and they often care very deeply.

Looking at the evidence closely, Zuboff explains that "in forty-six of the most prominent forty-eight surveys administered between 2008 and 2017, substantial majorities support measures for enhanced privacy."[119] Polls by the Pew Research Center, which does extensive nonpartisan work on public attitudes toward technology, have also found that Americans are increasingly concerned about online data collection, believe the risks of collection outweigh the benefits, and support withholding certain kinds of personal information from online search engines.[120] Other studies reach similar conclusions.[121] Of course, it's always important to take survey evidence with a grain of salt. This is particularly the case in privacy, given the creepy trap's minimization of the threat posed by data collection and the control illusion's suggestion that nothing is wrong and that we cannot blame others for our failure to manage privacy preferences. But the claim that people don't care about privacy is simply and undeniably false.

Moreover, the very institutions that have the most to gain from the acceptance of the Privacy Is Dying myth often go to great lengths to protect their own privacy. The NSA, for example, keeps its surveillance activities hidden behind overlapping shields of operational, technical, and legal secrecy. It took Edward Snowden's illegal whistleblowing to reveal the NSA's secret court orders from the secretive FISA Court. These orders allowed the NSA access in bulk to the phone records of millions upon millions of Americans, without any evidence that international terrorists were involved.[122] Law enforcement agencies have access to "sneak and peek" search warrants that allow them to read emails stored on the cloud, often never giving notice to the people being spied on, and they are secretive about their use of drones and "stingrays," devices that pretend to be cell phone towers that access digital information.[123] Technology companies closely guard their privacy with aggressive assertions of intellectual property rules, trade secrecy law, and the near-ubiquitous use of NDAs, nondisclosure agreements that prohibit employees, visitors, and even journalists from revealing discreditable things about a company. For example, Amazon's aggressive use of NDAs and related tools to protect its methods has prohibited temporary, $12-an-hour warehouse employees from working for competitors for eighteen months, and prohibited cities bidding to be hosts for its second headquarters from discussing any negotiations, tax credits, or related information.[124] Amazon is hardly the only company to employ these strategies.[125] The tech company Grayshift, for example, was able to hide from the public the existence of Hide UI, a software that helps law enforcement agencies unlock suspects' iPhones, for nearly a year in part because Grayshift forced law enforcement agencies to sign NDAs when they purchased the software.[126] More generally, public-private data-sharing partnerships are as ubiquitous as they are secretive thanks to iron-clad memoranda of understanding.[127]

A common variant of the Privacy Is Dying argument is that while old people may care about privacy, young people don't. Young people are (in this view) "digital natives" who have grown up with social media and other networked tools, their lives shared, tweeted, Instagrammed, and Tik Tok–ed**

** One of the challenges about writing about technology in general, and young people and technology in particular, is that the fad apps and trends of the moment change quickly. By the time you constantly.[128] Because young people don't care about privacy, before too long no one living will care about privacy. One colorful journalistic account of young people's privacy preferences expressed this sentiment aptly:

> Kids today. They have no sense of shame. They have no sense of privacy. They are show-offs, fame whores, pornographic little loons who post their diaries, their phone numbers, their stupid poetry—for God's sake, their dirty photos—online. They have virtual friends instead of real ones. They talk in illiterate instant messages. They are interested only in attention— and yet they have zero attention span, flitting like hummingbirds from one virtual stage to another.[129]

Or, as the CEO of Disney put it more succinctly in 2009, when it comes to privacy, "kids don't care . . . they can't figure out what I'm talking about."[130]

It turns out that young people do care about privacy, just differently and on their own terms. Young people have plenty of privacy concerns, and in many respects they are far more sophisticated about privacy—particularly digital privacy—than their elders. Their privacy behaviors reflect the importance of practical privacy management in their lives, a function of the different perspectives they have as young people trying to figure out who they are, as well as their relative inability to connect with their peers without technological assistance. As sociologist danah boyd explains in her book *It's Complicated*, the lives of middle- and upper-class American youth are often programmed to the minute. Most teens enjoy less in-person, unstructured time than prior generations. Teens can either use technology to talk to "their people" or face social isolation. To pursue the former, they guard their privacy with verbal codes and sophisticated strategies of obfuscation, much like trained intelligence officers. For many young people, high-alert surveillance threats are not the NSA or Google, but more immediate figures such as parents, siblings, teachers, coaches, and college admissions officers.[131] Close friends are welcomed in (with code words and little-known accounts) while grown-ups are left out.[132] Young people embrace online platforms as a way to meet like-minded young people, to experiment with identity, and to create safe social spaces. There is also the moonshot chance of "going viral" or becoming a micro-celebrity.[133] Although teens may share intimate personal

---

read this, you may never have heard of these examples, as trends move on. But this is yet another way that young people in general remain constant, by always changing. As the French say, *plus ça change, plus c'est la même chose*—the more things change, the more they stay the same.

information, their behavior shows a deep concern for privacy. Indeed, in their engagement in the processes of "boundary management" with multiple publics, boyd and Marwick suggest that, compared with older people, young people are both more concerned with privacy and have a more sophisticated understanding of the nuances of information flows in digital social environments.[134]

Other studies reach similar conclusions. One Berkeley study of young people's attitudes toward privacy found that they care as deeply about privacy as older people, and that they might even be more vigilant and more likely to engage in privacy-protective behaviors (such as supplying false information) than their elders.[135] Young people are also more likely than older people to engage in sophisticated tweaking of their social media privacy settings. Dutch privacy theorist Mireille Hildebrandt notes that, even given the limits of the control offered by social media companies, "young Facebook users have developed intricate and dynamic privacy strategies, by changing their privacy settings in relation to the targeted audience of their postings."[136] Other platforms call for other strategies by ingenious teenagers, such as the creation of "finstagrams," fake Instagram accounts they don't tell their parents about, in which they engage in expression and identity play that they don't want their parents to see.[137] Anyone who has lived with—or been—a teenager will know that teens are very good at sharing things they want to talk about, yet capable of sullen reserve and not talking about things they don't. Their behavior on social media—showing selective "curated" highlights of their lives but not the whole picture—is fully consistent with this time-honored tradition.

Why, then, if young people care deeply about privacy, have popular accounts suggested otherwise? Young people might share information about themselves that shocks their elders,[138] but young people doing risky things to shock old people has been a defining characteristic of youth culture for millennia. Risky privacy behavior—where young people do not engage in careful boundary management such as code words or hidden accounts— is thus no different from unprotected sex, drug use, or reckless driving. Another explanation is that teens are limited by the use of "free" surveillance capitalist social networks that are designed to collect more information than less and to be public by default. In this respect boyd and Marwick explain that social dynamics in the physical world are typically "private-by-default, public-through-effort."[139] It is difficult to get to know people in the physical environment, and personal information requires effort to obtain.

But in a digital environment in which social networking companies have financial incentives to nudge users toward disclosure and oversharing (in order to amass more data and sell more and better ads), the model is public-by-default, private-through-effort. Facing such radically different default settings, and given a more limited range of choices to opt out, it should thus be no surprise that young people appear less privacy-conscious. Like their elders, teens have a limited range of privacy choices, but they have much less autonomy and fewer financial and other resources to select more private options. So they make the best of the limited options available to them. And of course young people change, growing up to be older people who take fewer risks, with more autonomy and resources and different perspectives and goals. All safe middle-aged drivers were riskier young drivers once.

What, then, of the "privacy paradox," the idea that people of all ages often complain about their privacy going away, and then they act in ways that undermine that privacy? First, we've already seen how the combination of behavioral and data science, design, and defaults can be used to nudge users of computer systems on average toward the outcomes the designers want them to reach. If this is sharing more information, the designer's toolkit is certainly sufficient to nudge it, particularly if the service being used is useful enough, essential enough, or the consumer has invested enough effort in the service to cause them not to leave for a competitor. As with the Death of Privacy, a closer look at public attitudes toward privacy shows that the reality is far more complicated than the simple mantra that people no longer care about privacy. A more accurate interpretation of the available evidence suggests that people do in fact care about privacy, but they are bewildered by the difficulty of protecting their personal information in a time of rapid technological change and limited options. Indeed, the myth that People Don't Care About Privacy suggests a kind of reverse privacy paradox: if people really don't care about privacy, why do they talk about it so much? After all, if we didn't really care about privacy, it wouldn't be regular front-page news, books on privacy wouldn't sell, and it would not be a major topic of public debate.

So much for the empirical claim that Privacy Is Dying. But there's a second claim in the Privacy Is Dying argument, which is that, empirics aside, privacy isn't worth caring about. This is what a philosopher would call a normative claim—a claim not about what *is* the case but what *should be* the case. This book largely makes what is, on the whole, a normative argument: why and how we *should* think about privacy. The normative piece of the Privacy Is Dying argument relies on the opposite argument, that privacy going away is a good thing. We've seen people make this argument before. At the beginning of the introduction, we heard technologist and Googler Vint Cerf suggest that privacy might be a historical anomaly, an intermediate state between the relative intimacy of the village and the mass surveillance of the digital future.[140] And in this chapter, we've heard the NSA argue that those with nothing to hide have nothing to fear, a young Zuckerberg decide for us all that privacy just isn't a social norm anymore, and Posner assert that privacy's ability to keep secrets is a fraud on the market for human reputation.

Many others have dismissed privacy as a normative value. Former Facebook advertising executive Antonio García Martínez suggests that most privacy concerns around the revealing of dark secrets boil down to narcissism, since technology companies care only about your Netflix habits or what you look at when you go to Best Buy—the better to serve targeted ads.[141] Nick Denton, the founder of the celebrity gossip site Gawker, unwittingly echoed Posner in boasting, "If there's a gap between your private behavior and your public status, that's what makes the story for us. To my mind, the only real modern sin is hypocrisy."[142]

I'll be brief here, since most of this book is the explanation of privacy as a normative value. The short version is that these arguments completely misunderstand the importance of privacy as the rules governing the degree to which human information is collected or used—or more simply, the rules governing the social power that human information confers. Many of the people who have made flippant remarks about privacy being unimportant have later come to retract—or at least regret—those statements. To his credit, once he got past thinking about privacy in terms of dark secrets, García Martínez conceded that Facebook's ability to target particular messages to particular consumers would allow it to influence an election. He recalled that, separately and apart from the effect of Cambridge Analytica on the 2016 election, during the 2012 election, "[t]he fact that Facebook could easily throw the election by selectively showing a Get Out the Vote reminder in certain counties of a swing state, for example, was a running joke."[143] Denton's Gawker was driven out of business by privacy law. It was sued into bankruptcy by former professional wrestler Hulk Hogan after it posted a seven-minute video of Hogan having sex with his friend's wife.[144] (It later came to light that Hogan's lawsuit had been funded by billionaire Peter Thiel, who was apparently annoyed that Gawker had disclosed the previously nonpublic fact that Thiel was gay. Privacy is everywhere.)[145] And as for Zuckerberg, after the Cambridge Analytica scandal broke in 2018, he was hauled before

Congress for humiliating hearings (he even had to wear a suit),[146] and he subsequently posted a manifesto called "A Privacy-Focused Vision for Social Networking" in which he assured Facebook's users that "the future is private."[147] Zuckerberg explained, "There are a number of reasons for this. Many people prefer the intimacy of communicating one-on-one or with just a few friends. People are more cautious of having a permanent record of what they've shared. And we all expect to be able to do things like payments privately and securely."[148] So much for "going for it."

More fundamentally, of course, the debate about whether people do or do not care about privacy obscures a much more important point, one we've also seen before. In the English-speaking world at least, we have been using the word "privacy" to capture our anxiety about many of the changes that the digital revolution has enabled. In chapter 2, we saw Sarah Igo's historical explanation that for most of modern U.S. history, struggles around the social power conferred by human information has been expressed as anxiety around privacy. Privacy, as we've seen, is power, which means that privacy talk is power talk and privacy anxiety is power anxiety. Fears that privacy might be dying are often expressions of that anxiety. Assertions that Privacy Is Dying are often no more than self-interested framings of the issue by people and entities who have much to gain from diminished privacy expectations. When we think about privacy more broadly, it becomes clear that people (including young people) definitely care about this problem. They care deeply about it because it is one of the defining questions of our age. Privacy—and privacy talk and privacy anxiety—aren't going away any time soon.

* * *

Privacy, therefore, is about so much more than hiding dark secrets. It's less about our reactions to creepy new human information practices and much more about the reasons those practices occur: to influence and control us. Similarly, privacy is best understood in a broader way than our ability to control our information like an orchestra conductor, as fine-grained control is impossible and helps to complete the creepy trap. Privacy isn't dying, either, but claims of its decline mask the real issue, which is that the content of privacy rules—the rules that govern our human information—are very much up for grabs. Those rules need to be strengthened to safeguard human values. Now that we are equipped with a more sophisticated understanding of privacy and have put aside its most common myths, we can turn to those values.

PART 2
THREE PRIVACY VALUES

I've argued up to this point that privacy is best understood as being about the *power* that human information conveys. I've also argued that the rules governing our privacy should be *instrumental*, that they should advance other human values we care about. We humans are private creatures, but we are social creatures, too. Privacy is best understood not so much as an end in itself but as something that can get us other things that are essential to good lives and good societies. Part 2 offers three such human values that I think privacy rules can and should advance: *identity, freedom,* and *protection.* As we refine and build our privacy law for the challenges of the mid-twenty-first century, these are three values that should be held out at the forefront, animating our law and policy choices toward good privacy rules.

Part 2 is thus organized around the three privacy values of identity, freedom, and protection. I want to make clear that these are just the three that I think are most important. We might have other values that we think should be embodied in our system of human information rules. It's hard to have a good society without equality, for example, and we certainly don't want our digital systems and algorithms to entrench or exacerbate inequality. Similarly, we'll want to make sure that governments and companies can't hide behind spurious claims of institutional privacy to shield injustice or autocracy. These are important conversations to have, but for our present purposes I think these three privacy values are enough to start the conversation. If we're arguing about what precise privacy values best promote a good and fair society going forward, this book will already have been a great success.

It's also important to note that when we treat privacy as instrumental, the way we talk about privacy changes. We stop talking about creepiness, about whether we're Luddites or about whether our friend's privacy preferences are idiosyncratic. Instead, we start asking ourselves what rules about human information best promote values we care about, what the power consequences of those rules might be, and how we should use those rules to advance the values on the ground. From this perspective, privacy becomes more neutral. This is important because privacy rules can promote bad things, too. Feminist scholars have long documented the ways that certain kinds of family privacy have been used to shield domestic abuse.[1] The long struggle for open, accountable government has shown how governments that operate in secrecy can produce corruption, oppression, and injustice. As Louis Brandeis, one of the fathers of modern privacy theory, put it, sometimes "sunlight is the best disinfectant, electric light the best policeman."[2] And sometimes companies have a legitimate point that poorly crafted privacy rules can get in the way of economic activity without protecting anything particularly important. When privacy rules can promote bad things as well as good things, and when privacy is fundamentally about power, we can't get hung up on creepiness or the myth of control. Instead we have to ask what values are animating the inevitable set of rules we need to regulate the flows of human information.

Part 2 offers three of the most important values that should drive any reasonable set of privacy rules. These three privacy values aren't the only ones that matter, but I do think that these three are particularly important and that their protection through privacy rules is particularly necessary. Taken together, they represent a vision of a good and just society and of the ways that privacy rules can and should advance that society and safeguard many of the roles that each of us plays in society. Let's look at them one at a time.

4

Identity

"Authenticity"

Many technology companies are obsessed with "authenticity," but perhaps none so much as Facebook. From its very beginnings, the social network has insisted upon a "Real Name Policy" under which its human customers are required to use their real names rather than pseudonyms. In the early days of the company, a young Mark Zuckerberg told a journalist that Facebook's real-name requirement emerged from his own "strength of conviction" that the future of the internet demanded people to present just their one "authentic" self. "Having two identities for yourself," Zuckerberg argued with no sense of context or irony, was a clear example "of a lack of integrity."[1] Facebook's commitment to "authenticity" has continued to the present. Today the company organizes its "sharing" policies around four "Community Standards," the first and presumably most important of which remains "Authenticity." As the company website explains, "[W]e want to make sure the content people are seeing on Facebook is authentic. We believe that authenticity creates a better environment for sharing, and that's why we don't want people using Facebook to misrepresent who they are or what they're doing."[2] Facebook executives may sincerely believe this, or they may not. What is undisputable, however is that Facebook's Real Name Policy is very good for business. The ability to conduct surveillance on people under their real names makes it much easier to associate and aggregate other information about them. It also allows better microtargeting of advertising, whether commercial or political, which gives the company a significant competitive advantage. As one scholar explains, "Not only is Facebook's user base huge—in June 2019, the company had 244 million monthly active users in the U.S. and Canada alone—but its micro-targeting tools are finely-tailored to individuals' identities and interests."[3] The Real Name Policy is thus undeniably good for Facebook, enhancing both its power and its profitability.

Unfortunately, mandatory real name policies are not nearly as good for many ordinary people, and Facebook's own policy has been the subject of several lines of high-profile criticism. Not all people have names that fit Facebook's normalized, Eurocentric model on which its coding and correlation algorithms are based. The author Salman Rushdie got into a high-profile spat with Facebook after it suspended his account for not matching the name Ahmed Rushdie that appeared on his passport. Rushdie was able to jump on Twitter and shame Facebook into an apology, but real name policies pose even greater risks for ordinary people, particularly those who are members of marginalized groups and who are not world-famous authors.[4] Thus, Native and indigenous Americans with surnames like Creeping Bear have had their accounts suspended because Facebook believed them to be fake, leading to burdensome processes of "verification."[5] Members of the trans and drag communities who did not want to be forced into a single, binary-gendered identity or who wanted pseudonymity to explore their gender identities were forced into limiting and sometimes dangerous choices.[6] As with the Bill Sipple case we saw in chapter 1, pseudonymity is not a mere convenience or affectation for many gay and trans people, for whom revealing their identity could lead to loss of employment, family and social ostracism, and even the threat of violence.[7] Along similar lines, democratic activists in Russia, China, Vietnam, and other countries have been persecuted for their social media posts, a form of oppression enabled by real name policies that reject robust pseudonyms.[8]

The Facebook real name policy scandal is important as a struggle over the ability of people to determine for themselves what names they used on the service, and about whether they or the company got to have the final say. Legal scholar Sarah Haan explains that while psychologists and philosophers use the term "authenticity" in a variety of ways, all of these ways have one thing in common: they produce benefits for the individual self. This is the case whether we understand "authenticity" to mean being true to ourselves after introspection, consistently following our emotional or moral commitments through action, or our being present and engaged in the moment.[9] On the other hand, "authenticity" as used by social media companies often means the exact opposite. First, "authenticity" is judged by the company rather than the individual (think presumptively "fake" Native American names or Salman versus Ahmed Rushdie). Second, this definition of "authenticity" primarily benefits the company by enabling better ad targeting to known humans. Third, insofar as humans are benefited, it is "the community" over the individual, under the theory that linking expression tied to a "real name" is thought to promote truthfulness and accountability.[10] As

Facebook's definition explains, from their perspective "authenticity creates a better environment for sharing."[11]

"Authenticity" can mean more than accurate identification and linkage to a real human being. As Haan suggests, the real significance of authenticity is even deeper because it goes to our ability to develop and express our identities. Being able to say who I am—what my name is—is a basic prerequisite for being human, one that has long been appreciated in Western culture. Victor Hugo's novel *Les Misérables* tells the story of Jean Valjean, a former convict who reforms himself into a paragon of human virtue known as Monsieur Madeleine. Valjean/Madeleine is pursued by a dutiful police officer who can see only the convict and not the good man that Valjean/Madeleine has become. In the Broadway musical adaptation of the book, the officer frequently refers to Valjean/Madeleine as simply "24601," his prisoner number, denying him the ability to determine his identity for himself. We human beings are more than our identifying numbers, at least if we believe that we are defined by more than just algorithms and databases, and we deserve the right to determine for ourselves not just what we are called, but who we are and what we believe.

How Privacy Nurtures Identities

This brings us back to privacy. At the most basic level, privacy matters because it enables us to determine and express our identities, by ourselves and with others, but ultimately—and essentially—on our own terms. Privacy offers a shield from observation by companies, governments, or "the community" within which our identities can develop. In other words, privacy gives us the breathing space we need to figure out who we are and what we believe as humans. My previous book, *Intellectual Privacy*, showed how this process works for purposes of developing our political and intellectual identities. I argued that at the core of political freedom is intellectual freedom—the right and the ability to think and determine what we believe for ourselves.[12] I explained how our long-standing commitments to intellectual and political freedom require the protective, nurturing shield of "intellectual privacy"—a zone of protection that guards our ability to make up our mind freely. More formally, intellectual privacy is the protection from surveillance or interference when we are engaged in the activities of thinking, reading, and communicating with confidants.[13]

In order to generate new ideas, or to decide whether we agree with existing ideas, we need access to knowledge, to learn, and to think.[14] When we do that with the aid of search engines, that means our intellectual wonderings and wanderings should be able to occur in a way that is private—or at least confidentially protected by the search engine from disclosures to others. When we read other people's ideas, particularly with the aid of electronic readers, web pages, and bookstores, we should similarly be able to demand privacy and confidentiality from the merchants and services that provide us access to words. Librarians have long protected the intellectual freedom of their patrons through privacy and confidentiality norms, and we should demand the same from organizations that provide the same service electronically. Similarly, as we develop new ideas and reach out to others to share our half-baked hypotheses before they are ready for sharing with the public, we need to be able to rely on confidential communications. The fight for communications privacy in letters, telegrams, and telephone calls was a long and hard one, and we must ensure that those hard-won protections are extended to emails, texts, and video chats. We also need private spaces—real and metaphorical—in which to do that work. Virginia Woolf's well-known aphorism about the importance of having a "room of one's own" (complete with lock and key)* to enable our ability to think and to write expresses this point well.[15] And to the extent we write from the heart, those spaces also serve as areas in which we can figure out who we are. Private spaces enable us to develop our identities, whether in our teenage bedroom, the family dinner table, the library, or the confessional. Of course, our identities are not created solely by ourselves, alone in our room. Most often, we learn from other people, we are influenced by other people, and we test out our new beliefs with our close confidants. Our identities may be individual, but the processes by which we develop them are undeniably social, and intellectual and other forms of privacy are needed throughout the processes of identity and belief formation, development, and revision.

Our political identities are critically important and have received special protection in the law for centuries. I'll have more to say about our political identities—and their relationship to surveillance—in the next chapter. But for now, I want to talk about human identities more broadly. Our human

---

* Woolf, of course, was particularly concerned about the difficulty of female writers of fiction in a literary environment dominated by men. Her point about vulnerability and the enabling shield of privacy is one that I think has much broader applicability than the important but specific context in which she was writing.

identities are broader than our political selves, even when we define "political" broadly to include religious, intellectual, and other related aspects of
the self as a member of a free and self-governing society. (The second-wave
feminists were of course correct that "the personal is political," but the kinds
of identity I am talking about in this chapter are our identities as a whole,
even those parts of our identity that may be at some remove from everyday
politics.) Privacy shields the whole self, enabling us to develop our whole
personalities and identities, in ways that may be far removed from politics
and society at large. The classic work in this area is by sociologist Erving
Goffman. Using the theater as a metaphor, Goffman explained how identity involves performance: it is often constructed as a kind of character or
characters we play for other people, depending on the circumstances. At the
same time, since this kind of identity play is tiring, there is a need for "backstage" areas in which we can relax and take off the mask and be more relaxed
with our fellows, so to speak.[16] Goffman also uses the theater metaphor to
suggest that we wear different masks and take on different identities for different audiences as typical features of social life.[17] Privacy makes all of this
possible, both in the creation of backstage areas and in the ability to perform
multiples roles, maintaining variations and even inconsistencies in our identities in different social contexts.

   More recently, Julie Cohen has shown how privacy is essential for the processes of identity formation.[18] Privacy, Cohen argues, provides practical
breathing room as we manage the boundaries of our identities in a socially
situated way.[19] Under this view, privacy gives us the space to develop our
identities across all dimensions, on our own terms. Two features of Cohen's
privacy theory are particularly relevant to identity. First, Cohen *rejects the
liberal ideal of the autonomous self* that is common in both liberal political
theory and in much of the talk about privacy. Under the classic liberal view,
we each have an immutable, essential self at the core of our identities that is
separate from social and cultural influences. From this perspective, privacy
rules should operate as carefully calibrated individual rights derived from a
precise definition of privacy. We have seen already in chapter 1 how efforts
to derive a fixed essential definition of privacy for all purposes have been
mired in failure. But Cohen goes further, arguing that the quest for the essential meaning of privacy is misguided. Our identities, our senses of self,
are complicated and gloriously, *humanly* messy. She puts it well: "The self has
no autonomous, precultural core, nor could it, because we are born and remain situated within social and cultural contexts. And privacy is not a fixed

condition, nor could it be, because the individual's relationship to social and cultural contexts is dynamic."[20] I share this view of human nature. We human beings are complicated, we are constantly in flux, and our identities are affected by our environment and by our interactions with others. I am a product of my environment: my childhood in England, my teenage years in Boston, my young adulthood in the D.C. area, and my adulthood and parenthood in St. Louis. I have been shaped by the things I have done, the things I have read, the people I have met and with whom I have lived, and the time in which I have been living. I play different roles: husband, father, son, brother, friend, teacher, student, colleague, professor, lawyer, client, patient, guest, host, and many, many more. I will continue to change throughout my life. Yet it is still possible to say that I am "me" and I am separate from "you."

Rather than trying to pin privacy down to its essential core to protect our (mythical) essential selves, Cohen suggests that privacy rules should protect the ways our identities develop, a process derived not from quasi-scientific assumptions about the Nature of Humans but rather from what we've learned from the social, cognitive, and behavioral sciences about how human identities actually develop. We saw in chapter 2 how these sciences have taught us a lot about how humans make decisions (and how those decisions can be influenced and manipulated). The behavioral sciences have also revealed the ways in which humans, starting in childhood, begin to differentiate themselves from others and develop a sense of their own identities.[21] A real virtue of Cohen's approach to identity is that it is rooted in the behavioral sciences; in this respect, her approach represents a good match for many of the threats to privacy we've seen in this book. Thus, as we develop new privacy rules to protect our emergent, messy, and evolving identities from manipulation by companies deploying behavioral science techniques in the pursuit of profit, a defense of identity play also rooted in the behavioral sciences is helpful. This idea of identity play grounded in the social sciences is thus a well-matched response to privacy threats also grounded in the social sciences. It speaks the same language as the problem it is trying to address, rather than speaking in abstract, quasi-philosophical terms that protect against different risks than the ones that are present.

Cohen does not reject the idea that we have a self, or even liberalism in its entirety; on the contrary, she argues that there is just good evidence that the self is evolving, subjective, and shaped by social forces, and any account of human autonomy must include these facts.[22] This self is neither rigidly determined by the mythic, autonomous core, nor is it rigidly determined by social forces; the self exists somewhere in between these two poles. In other words, there is indeed a Me, but it is complicated, influenced, and shaped by all of the Yous out there. Yet even though You and other Yous influence Me, I can still resist, sometimes with success. We are shaped by our time, our experiences, and our fellow humans, but we are not rigidly defined by them. It is possible to separate ourselves somewhat and be different, unique, individual. This is what it means to be Me, to have what Cohen calls a "post-liberal" identity.[23] Liberalism, from this perspective, remains an ideal even though the evidence shows it may be impossible to fully attain it. As she explains, "The liberal self is an aspiration—an idealized model of identity formation that can be approached only incompletely, if at all. This does not mean that all of its attributes are equally attractive and worth pursuing."[24]

A second key feature of Cohen's theory of identity is that it is defined by what she memorably calls "the play of everyday practice." Our identity doesn't develop by philosophical reasoning but rather through the "ordinary, everyday behaviors" of humans living in their social and cultural environments.[25] We are born, we meet our family and community, and over time we "encounter and experiment with others, engaging in a diverse and ad hoc mix of practices that defies neat theoretical simplification."[26] This identity experimentation goes on throughout our lives as we encounter other people. It is also playful; as we encounter constraints in our lives, we push back against them in creative ways. Subcultures are particularly adept at these practices— think of how hippies, punks, alternative rockers, and hipsters have, generation against generation, dressed and defined themselves in relation both to the dominant culture and the subcultures that have come before.

As this book was being drafted, something of a generational civil war broke out in American popular culture. The Millennials started it. First they went after the Baby Boomers, and the slur "O.K., Boomer" was used to try to silence old people some Millennials believed had been in charge for too long, refusing to deal with climate change, economic inequality, and racial injustice.[27] Then the younger Generation Z went after the Millennials, criticizing them for side-parting their hair and wearing skinny jeans, rather than having center parts and baggy jeans.[28] My own generation, Gen X, stood off to the side in a disaffected way and said "Whatever."[29] Of course, it's possible that much of this feuding was caused by bored young people tired of social distancing during the Covid-19 pandemic, but I think it serves a useful illustration about identities and groups. We are often members of groups that define ourselves in terms of what we are not. Groups engage in identity play in order to define who they are and who they are not (notice definitions once again at work in multiple directions, defining and restricting). As individuals, we can do the same thing—belong to groups, define ourselves in opposition to groups, or be part of a group and also separate from it. As Cohen would put it, our identities emerge and shift through these kinds of play. Play of this sort can be conscious and tactical, but identity play can also be unexpected, coincidental, eccentric, and weird. Privacy enables play of this kind by providing the space in which to simultaneously belong to a culture or group and to critique it. It gives us the opportunity to develop critical faculties and critical perspectives, and it fosters individualism along political and personal dimensions, along with all points in between. Internet memes and political dissent can be part of this, as can other forms of identity signaling, like how (or whether) you part your hair, how tight your jeans are, or whether you own jeans at all.

Again, I'll use myself as an example of this phenomenon. As someone who lived as a child in Manchester during the rise of punk, I don't part my hair and I'm quite fond of skinny jeans (having the scrawny legs of a stereotypical academic probably has something to do with this). You might be surprised to learn that, as an English immigrant living in St. Louis, I'm not much of a fan of the English Royal Family. On the other hand, I do rather like tea. At the onset of the Covid-19 pandemic in March 2020, I was gripped by an irrational but culturally conditioned fear that as supply chains constricted I might not be able to access the tea with which I start each morning.† I bought a catering pack of four hundred bags online that was the size of a sofa cushion and showed it to my students over Zoom when it arrived. They thought it eccentric and humanizing; I found it comforting to lean into something that was culturally familiar as the world descended into chaos.

I didn't need to share this somewhat embarrassing example, either with my students or the readers of this book, but I think it illustrates how identity development can be playful, even in dark times, and how it can operate to define ourselves both in accordance with and in opposition to existing cultural structures. (I like tea but not the Royal Family.) But this kind of identity play depends critically on privacy and on our ability to choose when and where and how (if at all) to disclose parts of our identity to some or all of the people we know. I have deliberately used an innocuous example here, but we could imagine many other examples that are not innocuous.

---

† Taylor's of Harrogate Yorkshire Tea. With milk, naturally.

Imagine a young person confiding in a friend that they are gay, nonbinary, or trans, or that they are having a crisis (or moment) of religious faith, or any one of a hundred other examples. The power of the insight here is that identity depends on privacy for matters that can be important, playful, or, critically, both.

Let's sum up where we are. I've argued that privacy creates a space between ourselves and other people that allows the development of our identities. Good privacy rules help us to develop these identities. Simply put, privacy matters because without meaningful privacy protection, we can't figure out who we are. When we are watched, when we're subjected to surveillance, and when our actions are automatically linked to our permanent records, it's much harder for us to figure out our authentic self across the spectrum of the political and the personal. That authentic self doesn't spring up full-blown when we are born. Throughout our life, we are influenced by where we live, who we meet, and what we read. Our identities are varied and complex, transcend the personal and the political, and are both serious and playful. Like Cohen, I believe that the liberal ideal is just that—an ideal—and that it is important to take the protection and development of identity as we actually find it rather than as we might like it to be. At the same time, recognizing that we are influenced by social and cultural forces does not mean that we are destined to be irresistibly determined by those forces; this is what it means to be a Me that is also part of the broader culture and of subcultures within that culture. We're complicated, and that's okay. More than that, our complexity is essential to the kinds of eccentric, unique individuals we say we want to have in a free society. Freedom must mean more than just the freedom to be like everybody else.

The theory of privacy as protecting identity I offer here is not just abstract. At a practical level it also helps explain why particular information practices involving human identities are problematic. Now that we are armed with a more nuanced understanding of the ways our human identities develop, and of the ways in which privacy is intertwined with the development of healthy, socially minded, but unique personal and civic identities, we can better see how threats like real name policies menace not just our privacy but the fragile and contingent identities that privacy protects and nurtures. But theories are only as good as the assumptions on which they rest and on the ways in which they illustrate particular problems that are worth solving. In order to make my theory of privacy-as-identity concrete, I'll offer a few ways in which current privacy practices are deficient in giving our identities the breathing space they need to develop organically. I call them *forcing, filtering,* and *exposure.*

Forcing

Identity forcing happens when our social or cultural environment defines us, forcing our identities into boxes we might not choose or may not even have drawn in the first place. Adolescence is a time of identity exploration, but the social tyranny of adolescent school peers is an example of forcing. At the American high school I attended, for example, you could be clever or popular, but it was hard to be both (and it was particularly hard to be neither). Salman Rushdie makes a similar observation about his attendance at Rugby School in England in the 1960s, in which there were three cardinal sins, any two of which could be excused: being intelligent, being foreign, and being bad at sports.[30] The stifling cultures of these institutions (themselves a function of the interplay of the history, teachers, and students affecting each other) had the consequence of forcing the students in them into roles—a phenomenon no doubt familiar to most of us who have attended a school or participated in any other hierarchical human institution. While there was certainly room for identity play, the forcing effect of institutions can make play emotionally, psychologically, or socially costly.

Facebook's mandate that the identities of its users be tied to a public, "real" name is another example of forcing. We saw earlier that Facebook prizes authenticity as one of its four core values. (The other three are privacy, safety, and dignity.) Facebook defines "privacy" as follows: "We are committed to protecting personal privacy and information. Privacy gives people *the freedom to be themselves,* and *to choose how and when to share* on Facebook and to connect more easily."[31] To the extent that this definition emphasizes choice and "choos[ing] how and when to share," we've already seen in chapter 3 how pursuing Privacy as Control is a dangerous and disempowering fallacy that subjects us to being controlled and manipulated. But let's look at the other key piece of the definition, "giv[ing] people the freedom to be themselves." Facebook thus adopts the liberal ideal of the fixed self, under which our identities are both unitary and unchanging. Under this view, there is only one authentic Me, and it is fixed; I am forever the one and unchanging Me, and I am not You. Zuckerberg himself said as much in that infamous early interview, arguing, "You have one identity. The days of you having a different image for your work friends or co-workers and for the other people you know are probably coming to an end pretty quickly," going on to claim that having multiple identities "is an example of a lack of integrity."[32]

This is, of course, nonsense, like so many of Zuckerberg's tone-deaf pronouncements about How Things Are. Facebook's design embraces the liberal ideal of a single, unchanging, core, "true" self, the same ideal that behavioral science has shown to be a myth. Our identities are changeable, and it's important to be able to experiment with them. As technology scholars Oliver Haimson and Anna Lauren Hoffmann have explained, "Experimentation with representing one's identity online can also allow people to embody potential future selves, which can be indispensable to developing one's identity broadly."[33] Yet Facebook's design seeks to force its users into a unitary model of unchanging identity. In a similar way, its binary classification of all other users as either "friends" or "not friends" forces choices that are at odds with the ways human beings actually experience circles of intimacy, or intimacy with other people for some things but not others. Friendship—actual human friendship—is messy, in part because friendships involve two or more messy identities coming together. Design choices of the sort Facebook makes about unitary identities or binary friends might be easier for the company to code, and they might make "monetization" of their customers' data more lucrative, but they do not respect the complexity of human identities and friendships, and they represent an attempt to *force* our complicated, gloriously messy selves into a stifling framework that benefits the company rather than its customers.

Our identities aren't just messy; they are also fluid. They change over time and they vary depending upon whom we are with. Members of marginalized ethnic and national groups, immigrants, racial minorities, sexual minorities, and women, among others, are all familiar with the practice of code-switching, whereby we act, speak, perform, and dress differently for different audiences.[34] In fact, everyone code-switches, even if we don't realize it. As an immigrant who has lived in the United States since adolescence, I am sometimes a different person with my American friends than I am with my foreign or fellow immigrant friends. This is not "inauthentic"; it is instead the expression of different aspects of my self, both of which are Me. Privacy matters to the development of our identities not just by allowing us to figure out who we are, alone or in communication with confidants. It also allows us to hold multiple identities without their coming crashing together, giving the lie to Zuckerberg's stingy and self-serving notion of unitary identity as authenticity. As Walt Whitman put it well in his epic poem *Song of Myself*, "I contain multitudes."[35] We are all of us different people at different times each day as we play different roles in society, and we are different people at different times in our lives as we evolve, mature, regress, explore, and play with our identities.[36] We've already seen how, at various times in the same day, virtually every adult can be a friend, a worker, a supervisor, a citizen, a mentor, a student, a musician, a customer, a lover, a child, and a parent. Each of these roles demands different behavior and different aspects of our selves, aspects that need not be consistent. We behave, for example, in different ways with loved ones than with those we encounter in commercial or professional settings. Even among our loved ones, we behave very differently (and often show very different sides of ourselves) to our children, our parents, and our sexual partners. But this is not dishonest, nor is it inconsistent. At the very least, it's no more inconsistent than is the complicated nature of having a self. It is human.

Forcing human beings into compatibility with digital or corporate systems, shaving off our rough or "inauthentic" edges, has undeniable human costs. Like all cultural forces, computer systems shape us, even though a basic principle of computer science is that human beings should direct technology, rather than things being the other way around. This was a basic claim of the early computer scientist J. C. R. Licklider, who argued in 1960 that even though a symbiotic relationship with technology was in our future, we should make sure that it was humans and not computers who were setting the rules.[37] This claim is echoed by contemporary technologist Jaron Lanier's argument that human beings should not be "gadgets," meaning that computers should play an empowering role for ordinary people rather than forcing them and their identities into machine-readable formats that maximize corporate profitability—what he calls "multiple choice identities."[38] The costs of identity-forcing are significant for everyone, but they are even greater for people with nonnormative identities or politics. Haimson and Hoffmann, for example, detail some of the ways in which people with trans identities are systematically excluded and harmed by real name policies.[39] Real name policies, of course, are not the only ways that identities can be forced, and as the legal scholar Scott Skinner-Thompson reminds us, identity coercion of this sort implicates not just privacy but rights of equality and free expression.[40]

We must resist the calls to render ourselves to a single, unitary, boring self, the better to render ourselves amenable to the market in general or to

Facebook's interface in particular. After all, we contain multitudes. If we do have a false, inauthentic self, I would argue that it is the homogenized, flattened, forced self that is the false one. This is the forced self that may be desirable to interfaces, advertisers, and self-appointed arbiters of our middle school social standing, but it is worrying if we care about individuality, eccentricity, and the development of unique, critical individuals and citizens. If we do care about these things (and I believe that we must), privacy is an essential protection, enabling us to develop and express our identities in these varied ways.

Filtering

If our identities are shaped by what we read and whom we talk to, what happens to those identities when all we see is one perspective? This question has particular urgency in the polarized political climate of the early 2020s, but it is a problem that legal scholars have been worrying—and warning— about for decades. Technologists in the heady early days of the internet looked forward hopefully to a day when we would begin each morning with "The Daily Me," Nicholas Negroponte's optimistic characterization of a personalized newspaper that gave each of us all of the content we were interested in and nothing else.[41] Cass Sunstein, however, viewed such predictions of a "personalized" internet not with hope but with dismay. In a series of books over almost twenty years, Sunstein has argued that "The Daily Me" represents a serious threat to our civic lives because what we might *want as consumers* of content and what we might *need as citizens* are often two different things. Sunstein suggests that informational monocultures that present us only with things we want (or that the algorithm predicts we want) reflect only our interests and biases. They include little additional information we might learn from or that might disrupt our preconceptions or beliefs.[42] What is more, there is significant social science evidence that algorithmic "filter bubbles" of what we see and read can push our views to extremes.[43] Likes on Twitter, Facebook, and Instagram and defriending of people with different views can deepen echo chambers, making it more likely that users see posts consistent with their views and none whose views are contrary to theirs. In turn, when groups with similar views get together, their members hear "more and louder echoes of their own voices."[44] These echo chambers are a feature of the way digital services are designed. Programmers designing and writing algorithms have choices about what outcomes the algorithms can favor, and most often these algorithms are optimized to produce maximum *engagement* with the service. This makes obvious business sense under the business models of many "free" internet companies since more engagement equals more customer attention, and more attention means more paying ads and more revenue.[45]

My point here is not to add to the chorus of criticism of filter bubbles, echo chambers, and political polarization, but rather to make a more subtle point about identity in an age of media "personalization." Even a glance at the deeply polarized political and media landscape of the early 2020s offers a striking example of the impoverished civic world that filtering may have helped to create. If we are committed to the development of unique, eccentric individual identities on our own terms, and if we are affected by what we read and whom we talk to, then there is a great irony to "personalization" and filter-produced polarization and echo chambers. By filtering what we see according to what makes us click more, "personalization" ironically makes us more like everyone around us.

Solving the problems of democracy in a digital age—designing a better political and media system that produces civic engagement, a sense of the common good, deliberative decisions, and a respect for civil liberties—is beyond the scope of this book. "The internet," if it's possible to speak of the internet as a single, intentional thing, is not the problem. Digital platforms can boost political accountability as well as help citizens learn information and absorb a wide variety of political opinions, and they can also brew polarization and easily spread fake information.[46] As we've seen, tools are tools; they have politics and they can be used for a variety of purposes. But the theory of privacy as nurturing identity formation that I have offered here suggests one modest solution to the problems we face. Because much filtering, targeting, polarization, and manipulation requires access to identifiable humans (whether under their real names or not), privacy rules that sever the targeting laser beam could improve things. Privacy can thus create a space between our identities and the patterns and information that others would impose on us.[47] It could provide meaningful opportunities for pause and for working things out on our own terms instead. It could sever the trend of surveillance capitalism feared by Zuboff, in which personal data is first used to improve services in a general way, then used to predict human behavior to serve better ads, and finally used to manipulate human behavior according to the wishes of the platform or its partners, as happened in the Cambridge Analytica scandal.[48] At a minimum, it seems undeniable that filtering and polarization, with all of their consequential effects on our identities, are in part a function of a lack of important privacy protections around our own ability to develop our own identities and our political beliefs on our own terms. Intellectual privacy rules that give us the space to figure out what we actually think and who we are rather than bombarding us with what serves the algorithm would be an important first step in reorienting the balance toward Licklider's dream, so that we humans are back in charge calling the shots for the machines.

Exposure

A third way in which current privacy practices are deficient in giving our identities the breathing space they need to develop organically is through the practice of *exposure*. We in the West are fond of telling ourselves that individuality is the bedrock of freedom. Yet digital tools and platforms that create the risk of our oversharing sensitive ideas, beliefs, or aspects of our identities drive those identities toward mainstream homogeneity and away from the eccentric individuality that we say (and our institutions presuppose) we value. Simply put, digital tools *expose* us to others in ways that are normalizing, stultifying, and chilling to the personal and social ways we develop our senses of self. And exposure can be devastating to identity. Alan Westin expressed this idea well:

> Each person is aware of the gap between what he wants to be and what he actually is, between what the world sees of him and what he knows to be his much more complex reality. In addition, there are aspects of himself that the individual does not fully understand but is slowly exploring and shaping as he develops. Every individual lives behind a mask in this manner; indeed the first etymological meaning of the word "person" was "mask," indicating both the conscious and expressive presentation of the self to a social audience. If the mask is torn off and the individual's real self bared to a world in which everyone else still wears his mask and believes in masked performances, the individual can be seared by the hot light of selective, forced exposure.[49]

Westin was writing in the 1960s, long before personal computing and social networking created even wider risks of exposure. And we don't need to agree with his implication that we have a single "real self" in order to recognize his insight that unwanted exposure can be damaging to the development of our identities. The searing heat of exposure can cause us to draw back and stay in the safety of mainstream identity performance, even when we would rather play and explore under the protective shield of privacy.

There are two parts to my argument about the effects of exposure on identity development—a normative part and an empirical part. The normative argument for identity and exposure is easy to state, and you've heard it already. At this point, either you agree with me that what I've been calling "eccentric individuality" as a shorthand is desirable, or you do not. Hopefully you agree with me that an attractive vision of freedom is one in which we are able to work out for ourselves and with those close to us what we like, who we love, what we think is beautiful or cool, and what we think human flourishing looks like. This is not the freedom to be just like everyone else but rather a more radical notion that good lives and good societies are ones in which there is individuality, diversity, eccentricity, weirdness, and dissent.[50] This is an argument for authenticity the way psychologists describe it, not the way Facebook does.

Privacy is the key to making this system work. Behind closed doors (or high garden fences or virtual private networks) we can be who we want to be with those we want to be with, free from the gaze (disapproving or otherwise) of our neighbors. And those same structural privacy rules protect our neighbors from our own gaze. The philosopher Timothy Macklem puts it well when he argues, "The isolating shield of privacy enables people to develop and exchange ideas, or to foster and share activities, that the presence or even awareness of other people might stifle. For better and for worse, then, privacy is sponsor and guardian to the creative and subversive."[51] This is my normative claim in a nutshell.

But there's also an empirical element to my argument. Let's say that you agree with my normative claim—"Bring on the freaks and weirdos," you say—but you wonder whether privacy makes much of a difference at all. Even if we accept that our identities are fluid and that we are influenced by other people, is there any evidence that when other people watch us, we behave or develop differently? This is the empirical claim—the demand for evidence that surveillance, *being watched*, inclines us to the boring, the bland, and the mainstream in matters of identity and politics. It turns out that there is excellent evidence that the empirical claim is true: surveillance normalizes us. It makes us act in ways that are socially acceptable. To put it colloquially, when other people are watching us, it's middle school all over again. A whole book could be written assembling the evidence in its entirety,[52] but I will highlight some of the evidence from the humanities and the social sciences illustrating the stifling effects of surveillance on our expression, our behavior, and our identity development.

Our culture has long reflected the intuition that when we are watched, we act and behave differently, internalizing the norms of what is socially acceptable into our identities. Of course, since our identities are products of our environment, it would follow rather straightforwardly that environments of persistent surveillance would have shaping effects of their own. This is an idea that has been explored by numerous works of literature and philosophy. Many of them owe an outsized debt to Jeremy Bentham's idea of the Panopticon, an ingenious but horrifying prison designed around a central surveillance tower from which a warden can see into all of the cells. In the Panopticon, prisoners have to conform their activities to those desired by the prison staff because they never know when they are being watched. As Bentham describes this system, "To be incessantly under the eyes of an Inspector is to lose in fact the power of doing ill, and almost the very wish."[53] The most famous cultural exploration of the conforming effects of surveillance is of course George Orwell's harrowing depiction in *Nineteen Eighty-Four* of the totalitarian state personified by Big Brother—an image that has been echoed in countless other books and films.[54] Orwell's fictional state sought to prohibit not just verbal dissent from the state but even the thinking of such ideas, an act punished as "thoughtcrime" and deterred by constant state surveillance.[55] Some scholars have documented how the modern surveillance environment differs in important ways from both the classic Panopticon and a fully realized Big Brother.[56] I'll have much more to say about this in the next chapter, but for now it's enough to note that Orwell's insight about the effects of surveillance on thought and behavior continues to resonate—the fear of being watched causes people to act and think differently from the way they might otherwise.

Our cultural intuitions about the effects of surveillance are supported by a second body of evidence from the empirical work of scholars in the interdisciplinary field of surveillance studies. Consider one such study, by psychologists at the University of Newcastle in Northern England. Knowing that their colleagues drank a lot of tea and coffee—perhaps to stave off the bleak ennui of the local climate—the researchers looked to the honesty system by which they paid for the communal milk they drank with their coffee and tea. In the departmental kitchen there was a sign asking colleagues to contribute the agreed amount: 10p for each use of the milk. The experiment involved the background to that sign, which changed every week. On odd-numbered weeks, the background was a pair of human eyes staring at the reader, while on even-numbered weeks, the background was soothing images of flowers. The researchers then measured the amount of tea, coffee, and milk that was consumed, and the amount of money placed in the honesty box. They wanted to see if changing the background to eyes affected the amount of money that was put in the honesty box. That was it. But the results were striking. On the odd-numbered weeks, when the sign displayed the staring eyes, members of the Psychology Department contributed almost three times as much money to the honesty box per liter of milk consumed than on the even-numbered weeks with flowers on the sign. The sensation of being watched by eyes—even fake ones—seems to have triggered behavior in the professors conforming to the established social norm of chipping in for their fair share of the milk.[57] Other studies have produced similar findings that being watched brings behavior into conformity with social norms. Consider the problem of employee theft, of employees stealing from their employers to the tune of hundreds of billions of dollars a year.[58] A study of the problem by one of my Washington University colleagues found that employees at casual dining restaurants such as Applebee's stole significantly less often from the company when they were informed a theft-monitoring system had been installed on the cash registers.[59]

From this perspective, surveillance might sound like a pretty good thing if it causes us to pay our fair share at the workplace tea and coffee station and to steal fewer pens. This, after all, is the classic law enforcement defense of surveillance, with echoes of the "nothing to hide" argument tipped in for good measure. But the tea and cash register studies show only part of the picture. In the aftermath of the Snowden revelations, several studies demonstrated that the new awareness of NSA surveillance had a chilling effect on people's behavior online, including on what information they searched for and what articles they read.[60] One MIT study demonstrated that after Snowden, Google searches for terms like "dirty bomb" and "organized crime" declined, as did noncriminal but sensitive searches like "abortion" and "liposuction."[61] A study by Jonathon Penney showed a similar effect from the Snowden revelations on people's willingness to read about controversial topics on Wikipedia.[62] The message of these and other studies in other areas is clear: surveillance doesn't necessarily drive our behavior in a positive direction, but it does drive it in a *socially conforming direction*. Surveillance doesn't deter us from crime as much as it shapes us into acting in ways that are mainstream.[63]

Remember those dissidents, eccentrics, freaks, and weirdos? We saw in chapter 3 that privacy is a social value, and how it is a good thing to live in a society where people are free to be different and to think for themselves. By letting other people mind their own business, privacy can make society more cohesive. But privacy doesn't just make society more cohesive; it also makes society better by providing an incubator for new ideas about how to live. Privacy acts as a shield for people like this, people who may well be among the most vulnerable in our society. If history is any guide, there are likely dissidents and weirdos out there today whose beliefs might seem dangerous or bizarre, beliefs that may one day become just as cherished as we cherish our other once dangerous, now mainstream articles of political and social faith. Privacy is the incubator for these ideas and ways of living, exemplified by Woolf's demand for a "room of one's own," in which women could defy conventions that would keep them subordinate and where they could learn, write, and create art. The empirical work on the normalizing effects of surveillance helps us to see why. If surveillance just made us follow the law, then it would not be so dangerous, at least as long as we could be sure that the law was always just. But even when our laws are just, surveillance is still a problem because it has a normalizing effect on what we do, what we say, and what we read. If we want to freely figure out who we are, if we want to experiment with new ways of living, if we want to live in a diverse and truly free society, the normalizing glare of surveillance makes that difficult because it exposes the gaps and spaces of unmonitored freedom in which the fragile processes of identity experimentation can take place.

We will return to surveillance and explore other benefits privacy gives us against it in the next chapter, but the point I want to make here is that even if we are completely happy with an identity and a lifestyle that happen to coincide with average or "normal" habits, we should still want to live in a society that allows dissenters and free thinkers, difference and eccentricity to thrive. Such a society is not only intrinsically richer, but as we'll see, it instrumentally affords its eccentrics the space to generate new ideas that can improve society in the future. And insofar as privacy rules offer credible protection from surveillance that exposes our activities to others, this is another meaningful way in which privacy supports our abilities to develop our identities.

* * *

To sum up, privacy matters if we are interested in developing a diversity of interests, opinions, and identities as a society. It also matters if we are concerned that social norms may be stifling or oppressive, or that filter bubbles and echo chambers might divide and polarize us. And it matters if we agree with Cohen that a critical perspective and distance on our social norms is important. That is, privacy matters if we wish to encourage human flourishing through the development of identities that value difference, individuality, and eccentricity rather than in stifling those characteristics in favor of bland conformity. These processes can be threatened in a variety of ways, such as by forcing, filtering, and exposure. But privacy supplies spaces in which the personal and social processes of identity development and experimentation can flourish. In this way, by shielding and supporting our efforts to develop actually authentic, messy, and changeable identities, privacy matters because it enables us to be human.

5

Freedom

The "Truth Bomb"

Edward Snowden disclosed many things about the scope of U.S. government surveillance in the summer of 2013, but one revelation that went under the radar was the National Security Agency's pornography surveillance program. Almost six months after Snowden first revealed the magnitude of NSA spying in June 2013, Glenn Greenwald and two colleagues broke the porn story: "The National Security Agency has been gathering records of online sexual activity and evidence of visits to pornographic websites as part of a proposed plan to harm the reputations of those whom the agency believes are radicalizing others through incendiary speeches."[1] The NSA wanted to identify and surveil "radicalizers"—people who were not terrorists but merely radical critics of U.S. policy. The plan was to surveil them to find their vulnerabilities, then expose those vulnerabilities to discredit them publicly. As the leaked (and now declassified) NSA document put it, an earlier "assessment report on radicalization indicated that the radicalizers appear to be particularly vulnerable in the area of authority when their public and private behaviors are not consistent. . . . Some of these vulnerabilities, if exposed, would likely call into question a radicalizer's devotion to the jihadist cause, leading to the degradation or loss of his authority." These vulnerabilities included "viewing sexually explicit material online or using sexually explicit persuasive language when communicating with inexperienced young girls."[2] When pressed on the program, an intelligence community spokesman argued that the U.S. government "uses all of the lawful tools at our disposal to impede the efforts of valid terrorist targets who seek to harm the nation and radicalize others to violence."[3] Former NSA general counsel Stewart Baker, an outspoken supporter of mass surveillance, put it even more bluntly: "If people are engaged in trying to recruit folks to kill Americans and we can discredit them, we ought to[.] On the whole, it's fairer and maybe more humane" than bombing a target, he said, describing the tactic as "dropping the truth on them."[4]

Talk of a "truth bomb" is a great sound bite for cable news, but it's worth considering exactly who was being surveilled here. The NSA program did not involve the porn-viewing habits of members of Al-Qaeda, and while it's worth noting that pornography found on Osama Bin Laden's computer was also used to discredit him after his death, that case is quite different from the one that Snowden revealed to Greenwald. According to the NSA's own documents, its porn surveillance program dealt only with "radicalizers," people whose views the NSA didn't think were good for U.S. interests, but "very few of [whom] were associated with terrorism."[5] Some of these "radicalizers" were "respected academics"; some were religious leaders or celebrities. At least one was described as a "U.S. person," which means either a U.S. citizen or resident, someone entitled to the full protections of U.S. law. If a government were to drop an actual bomb on such a person, it would be murder, a fact which puts the "truth bomb" claim in perspective. It also raises troubling questions about the government's ability and willingness to black-mail its critics for nothing more than sincerely speaking on core matters of political speech protected by the First Amendment.

* * *

In the previous chapter, we saw how meaningful privacy protections are necessary for the development of our identities and how surveillance stifles the development of authentic identities and produces social conformity in its subjects. Privacy shields the development not just of our personal iden-tities but of our political ones as well.[6] Privacy can also nurture the devel-opment of political ideas and expression, and is thus an essential source of political power for citizens against the state. Simply put, privacy permits us to act as self-governing citizens, and it is hard to envision a functioning de-mocracy without privacy. Not all human societies have placed a premium on privacy; in particular, totalitarian societies have largely failed to respect any line between the state and the subject. Alan Westin explained in 1967 that "the modern totalitarian state relies on secrecy for the regime, but high surveillance and disclosure for all other groups. With their demand for a complete commitment of loyalty to the regime, the literature of both fas-cism and communism traditionally attacks the idea of privacy as 'immoral,' 'antisocial,' and 'part of the cult of individualism.'"[7] These ideas have been reflected in our literature and culture as well, most famously in the society of Oceania portrayed by George Orwell in his novel Nineteen Eighty-Four, whose defining metaphor of Big Brother (as we saw in chapter 4) continues to frame (and occasionally distort) discussions of surveillance and privacy nearly seventy-five years later.[8]

We have numerous cultural warnings and laws protecting us from unregulated government surveillance, from the Fourth Amendment and Laura Poitras's excellent Snowden documentary, *CitizenFour,* to the Foreign Intelligence Surveillance Act and movies like *Minority Report* and *The Lives of Others.* These warnings are commonplace, but they are rarely very specific. Other than the vague threat of an Orwellian dystopia, as a society we don't really know why surveillance is bad and why we should be wary of it. We've been able to live with this state of affairs because for most democracies, the threat of constant surveillance has been relegated to the realms of science fiction and failed totalitarian states. But these warnings are no longer science fiction. The digital technologies that have revolutionized our daily lives have also created minutely detailed records of those lives. In an age of terror, our government has shown a keen willingness to acquire this data and use it for unknown purposes, a fact that Snowden's revelations only served to further illustrate.

In the digital age, privacy against the state remains an essential part of political freedom. The extraordinary public attention prompted by Snowden's revelations in 2013 about the scale and scope of U.S. government surveillance produced a fierce and durable debate that continues to run years later. Yet we remain confused about the dangers of surveillance. We have made some progress against the specter of unregulated government surveillance, most notably with the passage of the 2015 USA Freedom Act, but we still lack a clear understanding of why surveillance can be harmful and how it can threaten political freedom.

This chapter explains how privacy matters to political freedom. We'll start with the Big Brother metaphor we typically use to talk about surveillance. I'll argue that while it can be helpful and powerful, it can also be incomplete and misleading. Instead, I'll offer a more nuanced way of thinking about surveillance, and I'll show how contemporary surveillance is both more complex and sometimes more beneficial than our basic intuition might suggest. Drawing on the work of scholars of surveillance studies, I'll explain how any understanding of the dangers of surveillance requires us to grapple with surveillance by private parties as well as surveillance by the state. Yet a more sophisticated understanding of surveillance reveals a problem: we need an explanation for when and why surveillance is dangerous and when it is not.

Next, I'll do just that, by offering a couple of reasons why surveillance can be dangerous. First, surveillance threatens the intellectual privacy we need to think, read, and communicate with others so we can make up our minds about political and social issues. Just as surveillance can drive our identities to the mainstream, being watched when we think, read, and communicate can cause us not to experiment with new, controversial, or deviant ideas.[9] Second, surveillance changes the power dynamic between the watcher and the watched. The power that surveillance gives to watchers creates risks of blackmail and discrediting, discrimination, and coercive persuasion.

Before getting into the details, it's worth noting that surveillance's threat to democracy is more than just a theoretical academic or philosophical problem—it is of critical and practical importance for both humans and companies. For example, in spite of the enormous attention given to surveillance by the NSA and other government entities since 2013, U.S. courts hearing challenges to government surveillance programs too frequently fail to understand the harms of surveillance and too frequently fail to allow legitimate claims to go forward. If you want to sue in federal court in the United States, you have to show "standing" to sue, including that you have suffered a legal injury that would be made better by your lawsuit. Many American judges believe that standing requirements should be strict, which in practice has kept out many kinds of privacy and environmental law claims.[10] For example, Section 702 of the Foreign Intelligence Surveillance Act was passed in 2008 to give U.S. intelligence agencies greater power to collect electronic communications where the target was not known to be an American. It was challenged the day it went into effect by a group of plaintiffs, including human rights activists from Amnesty International, journalists, and lawyers communicating with clients held in Guantanamo Bay—all of whom knew that their clients almost certainly would be placed under government surveillance by the new powers. They argued that Section 702 violated the First and Fourth Amendments because their own professional communications with those clients were going to be captured as well. The Supreme Court was unsympathetic, dismissing the case as lacking standing since the plaintiffs hadn't argued that the government was "imminently" targeting their communications, and that their lawsuit was merely "speculative."[11] After the Snowden revelations, Wikipedia's parent company joined the plaintiffs in a second lawsuit, adding empirical evidence that unlawful capture of Americans' use of Wikipedia was occurring under Section 702 to a mathematical certainty. But almost fifteen years later, the challenge to Section 702 remains mired in

the federal courts on standing grounds. The result of all these legal technical-
ities is that the constitutionality (or not) of Section 702's wide-ranging surveillance powers has never been conclusively determined.[12] Rights that can't
be heard in court are not very useful, to say the least.

Beyond constitutional rights, the failure of U.S. courts to come to
grips with surveillance has significant economic consequences. Literally
thousands of American companies with customers, employees, or other operations in Europe depend on the ability to bring data about Europeans back
to the United States in order for their businesses to function. United Airlines
as well as companies like St. Louis–based Enterprise Rent-A-Car bring
travel data from all over the world to the United States to process airline
and car rental transactions. These and thousands of other companies with
European employees bring data back to corporate headquarters to run their
human resources departments (and hire and pay those overseas employees).
Technology companies in particular also need access to European data,
whether it is for Google to fulfill search queries or send GPS navigation
directions to smartphones; for social networks like Twitter, Instagram,
and Pinterest to send their customers the posts of their friends and others
whom they follow; or for any one of a thousand other uses of human information. Shortly after the Snowden revelations, an Austrian privacy activist, Maximilian Schrems, asked the Irish Data Protection Commission
to investigate whether the NSA's mass surveillance of Facebook violated his
European privacy and data protection rights. The case went all the way to
the European Court of Justice, which ruled in Schrems's favor in 2015. In
so doing, it struck down the Safe Harbor Agreement, the main legal mechanism allowing the transatlantic data trade under European Law.[13] The economic chaos the ruling produced led to a stronger version of Safe Harbor
called the Privacy Shield. But Schrems challenged that as well, along with
the EU's model contractual clauses for data transfers, the other main mechanism by which American companies can lawfully import European data. In
the summer of 2020, the European Court of Justice struck down the Privacy
Shield and cast doubt on the legality of the model contracts. Its reasoning?
That American surveillance practices are broad, that the law gives insufficient remedies to Europeans claiming that their rights had been violated, and
that a major part of the problem was U.S. law's stingy approach to standing
doctrine.[14]

The transatlantic data trade is certainly important, but my argument here
and elsewhere in this book is about more than just economics. The value of

privacy is far greater than the mere economic value that companies can coax out of "monetized" human information, particularly when privacy will help to determine whether Western democracy continues in its historic form or morphs into something that is less free. It is to these much more important issues that we now turn.

Understanding Surveillance

When we think of surveillance in the English-speaking world, the conversation almost inevitably turns to *Nineteen Eighty-Four*. Orwell wrote what would be his final novel in 1948, in the aftermath of a Second World War that had left the totalitarian surveillance society of Nazi Germany in ruins but Joseph Stalin's totalitarian surveillance society of the USSR ascendant. Orwell's book depicts the fictional surveillance society of Oceania, one of three totalitarian superstates that have carved up the world among themselves. Oceania includes Airstrip One, a near-future version of Britain, where the book is set, which is dominated by a ruler known as Big Brother. Big Brother is everywhere in Oceania, rewriting history and the English language to achieve his goal of the total control of society, even down to people's thoughts and beliefs. A primary tool of the totalitarian state is the complete elimination of privacy. The streets are filled with posters featuring a gigantic face whose eyes "follow you about when you move" and which are captioned "BIG BROTHER IS WATCHING YOU."[15] Another of Big Brother's tools of control are "telescreens," two-way video communicators installed in every home. The telescreen is both television, propaganda device, and monitoring device for Big Brother. As Orwell describes them:

> There was of course no way of knowing whether you were being watched at any given moment. How often, or on what system, the Thought Police plugged in on any individual wire was guesswork. It was even conceivable that they watched everybody all the time. . . . You had to live—did live, from habit that became instinct—in the assumption that every sound you made was overheard, and, except in darkness, every movement scrutinized.[16]

With echoes of the Panopticon we saw in the previous chapter, telescreen surveillance enabled totalitarian control. Like actual dissidents in unfree societies, those who spoke or believed undesirable things were seized by the police and "disappeared," every record of them removed as if they had never existed.[17]

Orwell's depiction of Big Brother has dominated cultural and political discussions of surveillance and totalitarianism since his book was published in 1949, even among people who have never read it.[18] This should be no surprise; the Big Brother metaphor is vivid, terrifying, and accurately brings together the ways in which uncontrolled surveillance can be used to destroy individual political freedom and even a sense of self. The Big Brother metaphor was informed by Orwell's own experiences in the Spanish Civil War fighting the fascist forces of General Franco. As someone for whom telling the truth was a moral and political imperative, Orwell was repulsed by the way some allied communist forces adopted convenient political fictions on orders from Moscow.[19] The importance of truth and the dangers of lies in pursuit of politics were major themes that ran though Orwell's body of work, reflected in both his Spanish Civil War memoir, *Homage to Catalonia,* and his classic essay "Politics and the English Language."[20] Orwell's insight about the dangers of lies continues to be relevant in an age of misinformation, "fake news," and the rise of elected demagogues who lie incessantly and who have what we could accurately call an Orwellian relationship with the truth.

But with respect to surveillance in the digital world, the Big Brother metaphor fails to fully capture the nature of the problem. Daniel Solove made this observation in the early days of the Web, arguing that commercial data collection was happening not in pursuit of totalitarian domination backed up by fear and violence but for more effective marketing of goods and services. Solove argued that instead of Big Brother, we should use Franz Kafka's depiction of a bewildering bureaucracy in his novel *The Trial* to better capture the essence of the problem as one of powerlessness and confusion.[21] We can certainly quibble with Solove about the best literary metaphor with which to understand modern surveillance.[22] (I'd nominate, for example, Aldous Huxley's *Brave New World* and its "soft" dystopic vision of a deeply unequal society numbed into apathy by sex, drugs, consumerism, and other endless distractions.)[23] But the point remains that while we still have much to learn from Orwell nearly seventy-five years after his death, the Big Brother metaphor neither fully captures nor accurately diagnoses all of the problems of surveillance we face today.

How, then, should we think about surveillance? Scholars working around the world have produced a thick descriptive literature examining the nature, causes, and implications of our age of surveillance.[24] Working under the umbrella term "surveillance studies," these scholars span both the social sciences and the humanities, with sociologists making many of the most significant contributions.[25] Like privacy, surveillance is a complex subject, and like privacy, it is neither always good nor always bad. But a better understanding of what surveillance is and how it works can help us to understand how to protect privacy when it matters. Reviewing the vast surveillance studies literature, sociologist David Lyon explains that surveillance is primarily about *power*, but it is also about *personhood*.[26] (Recall how in chapter 4 we saw social networks exert power to shape the identities of their human customers.) Lyon also offers a helpful definition of surveillance as "the focused, systematic and routine attention to personal details for purposes of influence, management, protection or direction."[27] Four aspects of this definition are noteworthy, as they expand our understanding of what surveillance is and what its purposes are. First, surveillance is focused on learning information about *individuals*. Second, surveillance is *systematic*, which is to say that it is intentional rather than random or arbitrary. Third, surveillance is *routine*, part of the ordinary administrative apparatus that characterizes modern societies.[28] Fourth, surveillance can have a wide variety of *purposes*—sometimes totalitarian domination, more often subtler forms of influence or control, and sometimes oversight or protection.[29] The NSA and FBI monitor suspected terrorists, marketers profile consumers, employers oversee their employees, and parents install baby monitors to keep the new addition to the family safe. As the sociologist Gary Marx puts it well, surveillance "is neither good nor bad, but context and comportment make it so."[30]

To Lyon's four features of surveillance, I'd like to add a fifth, which is that surveillance *transcends the public-private divide*. The Big Brother metaphor focuses on a totalitarian society in which the primary threats to political freedom and identity come from the state: government-owned telescreens and propaganda and a knock on the door in the middle of the night from the secret police. In our world, surveillance is performed by the government, by the private sector, and by a thriving combination of the two. The sociologist Zygmunt Bauman has noted this "liquid" feature of surveillance, as it flows throughout our society in ways that can be hard to measure or regulate.[31] Thus, we have government surveillance like the NSA's "Stellar Wind" program, ordered by President George W. Bush less than a month after 9/11 to collect telephone and internet data en masse: who called whom when and for how long, and what everyone read on the internet and when, for an *entire* democratic society.[32] We also have private-sector surveillance, like when internet advertising companies compile detailed lists of all of the websites you visit in order to figure out how to deliver the ads that you are most likely to click on. And then there is hybrid surveillance, like when data brokers buy or just take data in government databases to assemble consumer profiles, or when facial recognition companies like Clearview AI scrape millions of photos from the internet, combine them with government photo ID databases or Facebook profiles (both of which associate photos with real names), and then sell facial recognition products to the government. In August 2020, the U.S. Immigration and Customs Enforcement Agency, an agency well known for its terrible human rights record,[33] signed a contract with Clearview for the company to provide "mission support" in Dallas.[34] The fact that surveillance transcends the public-private divide in ways like this is a real problem under U.S. law because constitutional protections like the Fourth Amendment typically apply only against government surveillance. Private actors can undermine civil liberties free from constitutional constraint, so government agencies are relatively free to enlist private actors to do things for them they would otherwise be constitutionally forbidden from doing.

The NSA pornography surveillance program nicely illustrates all five of the elements of surveillance I've highlighted. It was focused on learning information about *individuals*—the pornography preferences of "radicalizers" that the U.S. government was hoping to neutralize. It was *systematic* and intentional because it was part of a broader plan of information warfare against people considered to be ideological enemies of U.S. interests. It was *routine*, part of what the government spy agency saw its mission to be. It also had a *purpose*: neutralizing the expression of these critics, either by exposing their vulnerabilities to discredit them or by threatening to do so to keep them compliant with the NSA's interests. Finally, although we still don't know all of the details, the surveillance likely *transcended the public-private divide* under another program revealed by Snowden, the NSA's so-called PRISM program, which permitted access to data held by Microsoft, Google, Yahoo!, Facebook, YouTube, and Apple.[35] Like so many other privacy issues we've examined, the program was also undoubtedly about the exertion of *power*, in this case the power to manipulate those seen as enemies and inconvenient critics, as well as *personhood*, dealing as it did with the targets' sexual preferences and behaviors.

Another important example of surveillance is the Cambridge Analytica scandal. We've seen it several times in passing, but looking at its details is appropriate here. Cambridge Analytica was a British company that used Facebook's interface to offer an innocuous-sounding "personality test" to people on Facebook, encouraging those who had taken the test to share their results (and the "fun" test) with their friends. Unbeknownst to the people taking the test, the fine print of their "consent" to take the test also gave Cambridge Analytica access to their entire Facebook profile, including everything they could observe of their Facebook friends' accounts. The company copied everything it could see with these permissions—vast amounts of personal data from across the Facebook platform. It then used the data to assemble the detailed psychographic profiles it used to target ads to potential voters ahead of the two key votes of 2016: the British Brexit referendum on continued membership in the European Union and the U.S. presidential election contested by Hillary Clinton and Donald Trump. (Both the Trump campaign and Leave.EU, a pro-Brexit group were paying clients for the company). Although hard proof is difficult to establish given the variables involved and given other forms of foreign interference in these consequential votes, it is likely that Cambridge Analytica had some effect on these outcomes, nudging them toward British withdrawal from the EU and toward the election of Trump to the presidency.

The Cambridge Analytica scandal also nicely illustrates the five features of modern surveillance. Like the NSA's porn surveillance program, Cambridge Analytica intentionally targeted *individuals* (potential voters) for *systematic* observation and profiling as part of the company's *routine* business that it offered as a service. Here the *purpose* was clear: to influence democratic votes in directions that served the company's clients. And the surveillance *transcended the public-private divide* in innumerable ways, by the combination of voter rolls and Facebook data, by private companies seeking to influence public elections, and by private campaigns attempting to use surveillance to influence the nature of the state itself (in Britain) or the winner of a presidential election (in the United States). Insofar as it involved the creation of psychographic profiles to influence the outcome of votes, Cambridge Analytica's surveillance was also undeniably about both *personhood* and *power*—the kind of power conferred by the use of human information we've seen again and again.

Of course, in modern democratic societies, surveillance of all kinds is on the rise. There are numerous examples of this, including location tracking from smartphones and smart cars, facial recognition technology (whether used by Clearview or by smartphone makers to unlock devices), or AI and "big data" algorithms fueled by human information from a variety of sources and used for an ever greater variety of purposes.[36] Surveillance is used for contact tracing of infectious diseases, by parents using "Find My Friends" functionality to track their teenage drivers, and by athletes curious about how far they ran or cycled and how many calories they ingested or burned.[37] Here too it is helpful to think about Bauman and Lyon's idea of "liquid surveillance"—the spread of surveillance beyond government spying to a sometimes private surveillance in which surveillance subjects increasingly consent and participate.[38] But here, too, consent can become an illusion. We cannot consent to secret surveillance, nor can we consent to structural surveillance like ubiquitous CCTV cameras installed by businesses or on public transport. Then there is the problem of the "unraveling" of privacy described by legal scholar Scott Peppet, which occurs when other people opt in to surveillance, leaving the vulnerable exposed and isolated. We saw one example of this in the case of genetics databases the Golden State Killer in chapter 4. Another example is Progressive Insurance's "MyRate" program, in which drivers can receive reduced insurance rates in exchange for the installation of a surveillance device that monitors driving speed, time, and habits.[39] Drivers who don't participate in this surveillance program not only pay more for their insurance, but their "privacy may unravel as those who refuse to disclose are assumed to be withholding negative information and therefore stigmatized and penalized." In circumstances like these, there is no way to avoid the unraveling of privacy.[40]

Now that we have a better understanding about what surveillance is and how it manifests in our world in all of its complexity, we face a problem. If we are ambivalent about surveillance; if we see that it can be sometimes useful, sometimes menacing, and often both; if we see surveillance as necessary to our daily lives and societies yet potentially corrosive to democracy, how do we separate the good from the bad? The complexity, liquidity, and ubiquity of surveillance means that we need to be critical of it, but realizing its complexity does not mean we must be resigned to accepting all surveillance in all forms. But we need a better understanding of the dangers of surveillance. In the remainder of this chapter, I will try to do just that, and also show how privacy rules can protect us against two different kinds of dangers that unconstrained surveillance poses: surveillance can menace our intellectual privacy and thus our ability to govern ourselves, and it changes the power relationship between the watcher and the watched, creating the opportunity for blackmail, manipulation, and discrimination. Good privacy rules can protect us from each of these dangers.

Intellectual Privacy and Political Freedom

The clearest harm of surveillance is that it can menace our intellectual privacy. We saw this in chapter 4 in the context of privacy protecting identity, but in a democracy there is also a special relationship between intellectual privacy and political freedom. We've already seen how, when we are watched, we act differently, and that the effect of surveillance on our behavior extends to what we read, what we think, and who we become. Chapter 4 explained how surveillance and other privacy threats can warp the processes by which we develop our identities. In this chapter, I want to say more about the link between privacy and the formation of our political beliefs as citizens of democratic self-governing societies.

Intellectual privacy theory suggests that new ideas often develop best away from the intense scrutiny of public exposure, that people should be able to make up their minds at times and places of their own choosing, and that a meaningful guarantee of privacy—protection from surveillance and interference—is necessary to promote this kind of intellectual freedom. It rests on the idea that free minds are the foundation of a free society, and that surveillance of the activities of belief formation and idea generation can affect those activities profoundly and for the worse.[41] I want to be clear at the outset that intellectual privacy theory protects "intellectual" activities, broadly defined—the processes of thinking and making sense of the world with our minds. Intellectual privacy has its limits. It is only a subset of all things that we might call "privacy," but it is a very important subset. Intellectual privacy is also not just for intellectuals; it is for everyone with an intellect, which is to say that it is an essential kind of privacy for us all. The foundation of Anglo-American civil liberties is our commitment to free and unfettered thought and belief—that free citizens should be able to make up their own minds about ideas big and small, political and trivial. This requires at a minimum protecting the ability to think and read as well as the social practice of private conversations with confidants. It may also require some protection of broader social rights, whether we call them rights of association or rights of assembly, since our beliefs as well as our identities are socially constructed.[42] Protection of these rights and social practices allows us the space to develop intellectual diversity, eccentric individuality, and the sense of both belonging to a group and being separate from it that we explored in chapter 4. It reflects the conviction that in a free society, big ideas like truth, value, and culture should be generated organically from the bottom up rather than dictatorially from the top down.

Just as intellectual privacy protections can safeguard the development of our identities, similar protections are necessary if we want to refine our political beliefs or develop new (and potentially unpopular) ideas. As we saw in the context of privacy and identity, surveillance and interference chill activities and beliefs that are dissident, eccentric, or unpopular, driving them toward the boring, the bland, and the mainstream. Government surveillance can also threaten our political freedom by chilling our ability to think, read, or communicate politically unpopular ideas or associate with people who hold those ideas. This matters because many of our most cherished beliefs— the equality of all people regardless of race, gender, or sexual identity; the separation of church and state; political and religious dissent; and democratic self-government itself—were once deeply controversial ideas that people were willing to die for (and many them did die for these ideas). As we face the complex problems of the mid-twenty-first century, we are deluding ourselves if we think that all of the answers to our problems can be found in current beliefs or in dusty political or religious texts from the past. New ideas will be needed, and likely they will be controversial to many. But it was once highly controversial to say that women should be entitled to the vote, or that the institution of slavery was an affront to the most fundamental human rights. If we are interested in the development of new ideas, we must protect the social processes by which those ideas originate and are nurtured and developed. A meaningful measure of intellectual privacy offers the breathing space for the development of these new and potentially transformative political and personal ideas.[43] Surveillance, as we saw in chapter 4, tends to drive our behavior and reading habits toward social conformity, whittling away our capacity to engage with the eccentric and the weird, the heretical and the deviant.

In addition to its role in nurturing the creation of new political ideas, intellectual privacy is essential to the development of informed, engaged, active democratic citizens. In this respect, intellectual privacy theory is like free speech, which Justice Louis Brandeis famously described as "both an end and a means."[44] Brandeis believed that free speech is important because it allows citizens to make better democratic decisions, because it protects political opinions, because it lets speakers rather than governments check dangerous ideas, and because all of these activities themselves produce better individual democratic citizens. As we saw in chapter 4, our personal identities are shaped by our social and cultural environments, but they are also not inescapably defined and determined by them. Our political identities are the same. Privacy protects the space between the individual and society, a space that lets us both observe our world and critique it at the same time. Thus, we can be proud of our national identity and at the same time insist that our nation may have failed in its moral commitments to equality or to justice. It allows us an external perspective on our culture to observe, to learn, and to demand change. If we were rigidly determined by our society, we would lack the critical perspective from which to dissent and demand better.

Privacy, as Julie Cohen reminds us, is essential if this distance is to be maintained. And she warns us that networked surveillance and manipulation threaten to eliminate this distance, as the new technologies of "pervasively distributed surveillance" nudge "citizen-consumers" toward search results and personalized "content" prioritized to generate advertising revenue without concern for unprofitable democratic deliberation.[45] Brandeis also warned that gossip in newspapers threatens to drive out the important matters of public interest that citizens need to know if they are to govern themselves effectively.[46] But our new media, "personalized" by surveillance, is so much more engaging and insidious than either the Gilded Age gossip columns that worried Brandeis or the specters of totalitarianism that haunted Orwell. Cohen explains that the new technologies of surveillance do not have as their purpose or effect the "'normalized soul training' of the Orwellian nightmare. They beckon with seductive appeal."[47] Bernard Harcourt similarly points out that, unlike the drab, colorless, Orwellian world, the new technologies of surveillance are colorful, fun, and addictive, seeking to enlist us in our own surveillance and our own exposure.[48]

Without privacy—without a space between our political selves and the always-on notification pings of surveillance-based media—we may never have the time or capacity to think critically about the direction in which our world is heading. What we do read is likely to be shaped by what advertisers desire rather than what advances thoughtful, rational, and ethical democratic decision-making. Paradoxically, we may be nudged and herded into increasingly polarized but profitable "filter bubbles" while being deprived of the social and intellectual habits of mind to look at the big picture and think for ourselves. For all of the liberational promise of early internet evangelists, we have been left instead with a digital politics of increasingly hardening division and distrust, driven by lucrative advertising algorithms and seemingly producing more misinformation and conspiracy theories than the thoughtful, deliberative culture that democratic self-government requires.[49] Without intellectual privacy, then, we risk a world in which new political ideas are hard to come by, and in which we and our fellow citizens are less able to come to terms with what we believe. Without intellectual privacy, meaningful democratic self-government itself is at risk.

Surveillance and Power

The mechanics of intellectual privacy discussed so far depend upon knowing, or at least fearing, that someone might be watching us. Recall that we change our behavior when we know we are being watched. But what if we have no idea? If we have a sense of privacy, even one that turns out to be an illusion, we might not change our behavior. Could an illusion of intellectual privacy be just as good as the real thing? Truly secret and unexpected surveillance, from this perspective, might appear not to violate our intellectual privacy at all. If we have no inkling that we are being watched, if we really do not care that we are being watched, or if we fear no consequences of being watched, it could be argued that our intellectual freedom is unaffected. It can thus be argued that if the NSA wiretapping program had never been leaked, it would have posed no threat to intellectual privacy—that it was Snowden, and not the NSA, who was really at fault.

There are two problems with this justification for secret surveillance. First, no program of widespread surveillance is likely to remain secret forever. At some point, such a program will inevitably come to light. It can be leaked, which is what happened with the NSA program and previous surveillance abuses by the U.S. government stretching back across the twentieth century. Alternatively, secret surveillance programs can come to light when they are declassified, or when people are prosecuted (or assassinated) based upon their findings. In these cases, the injury suffered by those thus punished can serve as an example to the rest of us, and the mechanisms of intellectual privacy would come into effect at that point.

There is a more fundamental problem with surveillance that happens even where government or corporate surveillance is never disclosed. Once again, this lesson comes from the scholarship of surveillance studies. Recall that in

Lyon's definition of surveillance it has a purpose, even while the purposes of contemporary surveillance rarely include totalitarian domination.[50] All the same, most forms of surveillance seek some form of subtler influence or control over others. And even when we are unaware of surveillance, it can be problematic, because surveillance is another form of power that gives the watcher power over the watched. Surveillance brings us right back to the insight in chapter 2 that human information confers human power. Ultimately, *power is why surveillance happens*: all forms of surveillance seek some kind of influence or control over other people, whether in overt or in subtle ways. Even when surveillance is not Orwellian, it is usually about influencing or being able to respond to someone else's behavior. And while surveillance can sometimes have benign goals (like traffic safety or parents using baby monitors or GPS trackers to keep tabs on their teenage drivers), it is invariably tied to a particular purpose. Critically, the gathering of information affects the power dynamic between the watcher and the watched, giving the watcher greater power to influence or direct the subject of surveillance. Here as elsewhere the power of personal information lies at the heart of why surveillance happens and how its products are used. The power effects of surveillance illustrate three additional dangers of surveillance beyond its threat to intellectual privacy: *blackmailing and discrediting, discrimination,* and *persuasion.*

1. **Blackmailing and discrediting.** The crudest and most direct use of surreptitiously collected information is to *blackmail or discredit* opponents by threatening to reveal or actually revealing embarrassing secrets. U.S. political history over the past hundred years furnishes numerous examples of this phenomenon, but none more compelling than the treatment of Martin Luther King Jr., who was blackmailed by the FBI, which threatened to expose his extramarital affair if he didn't commit suicide. King received the following chilling letter:

King, look into your heart. You know you are a complete fraud and a great liability to all of us Negroes. White people in this country have enough frauds of their own but I am sure they don't have one at this time anywhere near your equal. You are no clergyman and you know it. I repeat you are a colossal fraud and an evil, vicious one at that. You could not believe in God.... Clearly you don't believe in any personal moral principles.... King, there is only one thing left for you to do. You know what it is. You have just 34 days in which to do it (this exact number has been selected for a specific reason, it has definite practical significance). You are done. There is but one way out for you. You better take it before your filthy, abnormal fraudulent self is bared to the nation.[51]

The FBI's letter is so outrageous that it's worth pausing on it for a moment to appreciate what happened. The U.S. government's primary law enforcement agency subjected the most significant American political dissident in the modern era to surveillance because they thought he might be a Soviet agent trying to destabilize America's racially segregated social order. The official government investigation into the Dr. King wiretaps concluded in 1976, "The FBI . . . acknowledged 16 occasions on which microphones were hidden in Dr. King's hotel and motel rooms in an 'attempt' to obtain information about the 'private activities of King and his advisers' for use to 'completely discredit' them."[52]

The FBI's surveillance revealed that King was no communist agent. He was certainly trying to destabilize America's racially segregated social order, but his motivations were his deeply held political and religious convictions about the basic equality of human beings, and because (as he put it so memorably) he had a dream for a better future for the country of his birth. Yet while the FBI's surveillance revealed that King wasn't a communist, it did reveal that he was having an extramarital affair, something which (to borrow the language of the NSA's porn surveillance program) was a "vulnerability." The FBI's letter, accompanied by surveillance photos of King with his mistress, was an attempt to "neutralize" him as a threat to what the FBI saw as America's national interest: Kill yourself, or we will unleash our "truth bomb" on your family and on your political movement.

The FBI has certainly reformed its practices since its attempt to "neutralize" King. Some of these reforms have been a result of professionalization within the agency,[53] while others have resulted from federal privacy law, which has prohibited warrantless wiretapping since 1968.[54] But risks—and abuses—are inevitable, even by otherwise well-meaning agents who zealously pursue their targets and are "just doing their jobs." This is a particular worry at a time in American politics when nonpartisan law enforcement agencies have in the recent past been placed under significant pressure to show loyalty above all else to the president, a phenomenon documented in great detail by Andrew McCabe, a career FBI agent who served as acting FBI director during and witness to such pressure during the Trump administration.[55]

Beyond the ethical pressures on law enforcement, the risks of surveillance abuses are even greater in our digital world, in which more sensitive information is created and stored in digital formats and our security services have access to far more sophisticated tools than the ones used by J. Edgar Hoover's FBI to investigate King. Imagine a dissident like Dr. King living in today's information age. A government (or political opponent) that wanted him silenced might be able to obtain access not just to his telephone conversations but also to his reading habits and emails. This critic could be blackmailed outright; he could be discredited by disclosure of the information as an example to others; or he could be shamed or "canceled" on social media. Perhaps he has not been having an affair but has some other secret. Maybe he is gay, or has a medical condition, or visits embarrassing websites, or sent intemperate tweets as a teenager, or has cheated on his taxes. All of us have secrets we would prefer not be made public. Consider the case of Representative Katie Hill, one of many young female Members of Congress who were elected in 2018 in reaction to the first two years of the Trump administration. Hill was pressured to resign after details of her affair with a campaign staffer were published by conservative media, along with nude photos of her.[56] Outside the realm of government, digital blackmail has become big business, such as in the common web-cam scam of "sextortion," in which criminals pose as attractive women soliciting naked pictures that then become the basis for financial blackmail.[57]

There is no evidence that the disclosures of Hill's secrets were produced by government surveillance. Many such disclosures are purely private, part of the digital age phenomenon of nonconsensual pornography, or "revenge porn." Sometime after her resignation, Hill disclosed her belief that her public shaming and political downfall resulted from "a toxic mix of 'revenge porn', partisan politics and the media's insatiable appetite for clicks."[58] The important point here, though, is that surveillance allows those secrets more opportunities to come out, and it gives power to the watchers that can be used nefariously, whether those watchers are former lovers or foreign spies. The risk of the improper use of surveillance records also persists over time. Most of the former communist states in Eastern Europe have passed laws strictly regulating access to the surveillance files of the communist secret police. The primary purpose of such laws is to prevent the blackmail of political candidates who may have been surveilled under the former regime.[59] The experience of these laws reveals, moreover, that the risk of such blackmail (or discrediting via a "truth bomb") is one that the law cannot completely prevent after the fact. Professor Maria Los explains that "[s]ecret surveillance files are routinely turned into a weapon in political struggles, seriously undermining democratic processes and freedoms."[60]

The Arab Spring revolutions also revealed some of the dangers of electronic blackmail. Many observers argued at the time that the political turmoil in Tunisia, Libya, and Syria showed the liberating potential of digital technologies.[61] But the crisis also illustrates the potential of modern surveillance technologies, which were deployed by authoritarian governments across the Middle East. The Libyan government of Moammar Gadhafi, for example, attempted to capture internet and phone communications with the assistance of Western technology companies for later review. One journalist remarked about the availability of such " 'massive intercept' technology" to governments around the world, "Today you can run an approximation of 1984 out of a couple of rooms filled with server racks."[62] Using these technologies, the Libyan government obtained information about dissidents that it was able to use to blackmail them into silence. And while the Gadhafi regime did not hesitate to use violence against its critics, it found blackmail and harassment to be even easier tools.[63] The fact that the Gadhafi regime ultimately collapsed does not diminish surveillance's blackmail threat. Oppressive governments around the world continue to be able to use social media monitoring and surveillance technologies to profile, track, and round up dissidents.[64] This should be no surprise, because the truly powerful big data technologies running on human information are usually held not by dissidents but by governments, corporations, and other powerful institutions.[65] The struggles over personal information that we have lumped under the rubric of "privacy" are the struggles that are defining the allocation of political, economic, and social power in our new technological age.[66]

Even in democratic societies, the blackmail threat of surveillance is real. Surveillance (especially secret surveillance) often detects crimes or embarrassing activity beyond or unrelated to its original purposes. The surveillance of Dr. King, for instance, produced evidence of his marital infidelity, while the NSA surveillance produced pornography use and other behaviors that were inconsistent with the targets' public images. To be fair, sometimes surveillance produces helpful information. In another infamous case, national security surveillance of a terrorist suspect in St. Louis produced chilling evidence of the suspect's murder of his own daughter for dating the wrong boy.[67] Whether these discoveries are important, incidental, or irrelevant, all of them give greater power to the watcher. Unscrupulous government officials could engage in blackmail, whether motivated by policy, political, or pecuniary considerations. Even faithful government agents who discover illegal activity would now possess the weapon of selective prosecution, which could be used to influence the subject, and would be able to wield the separate threat of mere disclosure of legal but embarrassing activity.

Looking forward, it does not take much paranoia to imagine a spy agency in a democracy interfering in an election by blackmail (through the threat of disclosure) or even disclosure itself. We have already seen evidence of disclosure used as a political weapon, most likely by foreign powers. For example, both the Clinton campaign in the U.S. presidential election of 2016 and the Macron campaign in the French presidential election of 2017 were plagued by hacks, leaks, and misinformation against these candidates thought to be disfavored by Russia.[68]

The step beyond blackmail is of course discrediting, whether we talk in terms of "neutralization" or "truth bombs." Sensitive information can be released to discredit, as with Representative Hill. The public use of information to discredit or "neutralize" political enemies by intelligence agencies is something we might call the "Praetorian Guard problem." Familiar to students of Roman history, the Praetorian Guard were the military unit that performed bodyguard and intelligence services for the Roman emperors. Unfortunately, during the political chaos that characterized the Roman Empire, the Praetorians occasionally took it upon themselves to murder or depose emperors they didn't like and arrange for emperors they did like to take power.[69] Thus, in 41 CE, the Guard famously assassinated Emperor Caligula and installed his successor, Claudius, on the throne.[70]

Now, it's important for me to be clear here. I am not suggesting that the NSA or MI6 might be planning a coup. But the Praetorian Guard problem raises the perennial question "Who watches the watchers?" In a democracy, giving intelligence agencies free rein to discredit or "neutralize" radicals by exposing their sexual or other secrets gives them a great power. And the use of such powers need not be confined to radicals. There is evidence that U.S. intelligence services have spied on politicians and staffers. In 2014, CIA Director John Brennan apologized to the leaders of the Senate Intelligence Committee after it came to light that CIA personnel had broken through a firewall to spy on Senate staffers who were investigating the CIA's torture practices, including a keyword search of emails.[71] And although the CIA did not confirm it, sitting senators raised concerns that the U.S. intelligence community may have been spying on Congress more generally.[72] Such concerns appear to be bipartisan in the United States. While Democrats were prima-rily the ones concerned by allegations of intelligence community spying on Congress, Republicans were outraged by surveillance conducted on the cam-paign of presidential candidate Trump to investigate (once again) links to Russian influence.[73] Given these precedents, the Praetorian Guard problem does raise the risk of, say, a spymaster using a politician's secrets to influence a vote on a bill regulating or funding intelligence agencies. It also raises the risk that intelligence agencies might attempt to affect the outcome of an elec-tion in their own country. (We will see in the next section that this is exactly what happened in South Korea in 2017, though not through blackmail.)

Recognizing that certain private matters (e.g., nude photos and sexual preferences) are no one's business would be a good place to start, but when it comes to blackmail and discrediting, privacy protections can help, such as limits on information collection, retention, and disclosure and requiring good data security. Blackmail will perhaps inevitably be a problem in poli-tics, but when sensitive human information is harder to come by, it follows that it will become harder to "neutralize" inconvenient critics. When we think about the linkages between the power to blackmail and democratic self-government, we must keep in mind the last of the five features of sur-veillance that I highlighted earlier: that surveillance transcends the public-private divide. When we talk about surveillance, we constantly find instances of privately gathered information being used by government, government-gathered information being used by private actors, and even more compli-cated ways in which human information can pass between companies and governments. Any approach to the problem of blackmail will need to grapple with the complexity of government and private actors, but it remains unde-niable that the power effects of surveillance that enable blackmail are likely to become only greater as new digital tools for processing human information are developed and deployed.

2. Persuasion. Blackmail, for all its power, is a crude tool. Surveillance gives the watcher another, more subtle power: the power to *persuade*. The online ad industry operates on the premise that fine-tuned surveillance of internet users will give them the ability to serve the perfect ad to the per-fect consumer at the perfect time—surveillance-based digital persuasion through algorithm. We've already seen many examples of this practice, such as Facebook's infamous "emotional contagion" study and the more recent allegations of the emotional manipulation of teenagers. (This is also, as we saw in chapters 2 and 3, the real lesson of Target's surveillance of its pregnant customers—not that it is creepy, but that women about to have their first baby are unusually susceptible to persuasion and unlikely to switch to a competitor for several years thereafter.) Governments also use the power of surveillance to control behavior. One of the justifications for massive CCTV networks in modern urban areas, for example, is that they allow police greater ability to watch and influence what happens on city streets.[74] Certainly, the presence of cameras or police can persuade citizens to obey the law, but it can have other effects as well. In Britain, where the science of surveillance-based control is at its most advanced, CCTV has been used in connection with court-ordered injunctions, sometimes known as Anti-Social Behavior Orders, or ASBOs, to move groups of teens out of the commercial cores of cities. This is yet another way that surveillance transcends the public-private divide—using surveillance and the coercive power of the state to ensure that commerce continues efficiently.[75] Government use of persuasive surveillance is still in its relative infancy, but since the technologies of surveillance and big data analytics are available to the state as well as to private companies, we can imagine the government becoming increasingly able to engage in Target-style persuasion in the future.

Perhaps the most worrying trend in surveillance-enhanced persuasion by the government has happened in the context of elections. American political campaigns have long fought each other with any tools that were at hand, as a young James Madison found to his chagrin, losing his first political campaign to an opponent who cheerfully distributed free liquor to win votes among local planters. (The next time, Madison made sure that his campaign was well stocked in the drinks department, and he won.)[76] Modern political campaigns have undergone a similarly transformative arms race, though the weapon of choice is no longer drinks but data. Shortly after President Obama won his second term in office, I participated in a conference on big data at which the Obama campaign's chief data scientist explained their use of data in a keynote address. He boasted that their use of the human information obtained from publicly available electoral registrations had been central to the use of data science to get out the vote for Obama. The audience at that conference skewed both pro-Democratic and pro–data use, and I can remember murmurs of agreement at the cleverness of the campaign. I can also recall my friend and co-author Jonathan King turning to me at that moment with horror in his eyes and whispering something to the effect of "If this really works, democracy in practice will just boil down to an arms race between which campaign hires the best data scientists."[77]

Over the next five years, Jonathan's horrified prediction came to pass, and I suspect that quite a few of those conference attendees changed their minds about whether the influx of data science into political campaigns was such a good thing after all. A *New York Times* examination of the data industry explained that "Silicon Valley ha[s] come to transform politics itself" and that the American political establishment has come to rely heavily on

> companies like Google and Facebook—not because of whom they supported but because of what they did. The surveillance capitalists didn't just sell more deodorant; they had built one of the most powerful tools ever invented for winning elections. Roughly the same suite of technologies helped elect Obama, a pragmatic liberal who promised racial progress and a benevolent globalism, and Trump, a strident nationalist who adeptly employs social media to stoke racial panic and has set out to demolish the American-led world order.[78]

Recent U.S. presidential elections have thus been marked by the aggressive application of big data analytics to the voter rolls in ways that raise big questions about the integrity of democracy itself. As we've seen, both Democrats and Republicans have availed themselves of these technologies. Obama's team of data scientists and software engineers combined dozens of pieces of information on each registered voter in the United States to develop patterns to help them with fundraising and get-out-the-vote activity.[79] Trump's team used Cambridge Analytica's scraped Facebook profiles to create detailed psychographic profiles to aid in the targeting of radicalizing political ads.[80] Regardless of one's politics, these developments make clear that digital surveillance technologies have reached the point when they threaten self-government itself. Going forward, data science techniques like these will offer a powerful boost to campaign fundraising activities, but they raise the risk of "personalizing" a candidate to make them appear like us and shape our voting decisions in ways that we do not yet understand.[81]

Data-driven personalized political persuasion is already being deployed against voters. One of the ways campaigns use data to persuade is through "microtargeting," essentially little more than an updated version of Target's data-based pregnancy detector. It's something that Roger McManee, an early Facebook investor turned critic, suggests "transforms the public square of politics into the psychological mugging of every voter."[82] Let's take a closer look at how the Obama campaign used data science. Microtargeting can be used for a variety of purposes by campaigns, but all of them boil down to trying to change the behavior of voters through personalized messaging based upon what the campaign knows about the voter. This should be no surprise to us as this point, as we have seen again and again how privacy is about power, and surveillance is about control.

In a nutshell, here's how microtargeting works. Let's say you are running a political campaign and have used the campaign's data to identify a voter you believe supports your candidate. Maybe they've told you as much on your website or over the phone, but this isn't really necessary, as it's often surprisingly easy for campaigns to figure out a voter's basic political inclination. (Any of us can do this at a basic level by consulting the public voter rolls that show party affiliation, but there are more granular and accurate ways to do this using personal data analysis or AI.) We've already seen how this information can enable the campaign to ask the voter for money or remind them right before election day to vote, something that is merely a more transparent version of Target sending pregnant women those precisely timed coupons for baby formula.

But microtargeting can be used for other messages for other voters. Let's say that you've identified a voter you think does not support your candidate. We'll call this voter "Chris." You know Chris is likely to vote for your opponent, and this is a problem for you since you want to win the election by getting more votes for your candidate than the opposing candidate gets. Microtargeting allows two different options to influence Chris. The first option is *persuasion*. If you know enough about Chris (let's say you know Chris is really concerned about the environment, or that they really dislike environmental activists), you can use technology to deliver precisely targeted ads to them (a series of ads pointing out how your candidate is stronger on environmental protection, or how they, too, are critical of environmental activists). This is the best option, because if you can persuade Chris to vote for your candidate, your candidate gets one more vote and your opponent gets one less—a two-vote swing in your favor. But let's say that Chris is a die-hard member of the other party, and you know from microtargeting and AI modeling that people like Chris are almost never going to cross the aisle and vote for the party they see as the "bad guys." That's where a second strategy comes in, which is *suppression*. Suppression is less about changing Chris's mind and much more about making Chris so displeased about the candidate they would typically support that they just stay home and don't vote on election day. You can do this using microtargeting, by sending negative messages to Chris about the other candidate. (Perhaps it's about the candidate's poor record on the environment, or alternatively by pictures of the candidate hanging out with those environmental activists alternate Chris hates so much, or really by any other negative fact or image that the AI predicts is likely to disgust Chris with the whole project.) This strategy can be used to make Chris stay home and not vote for anyone. If you succeed in suppressing Chris in this way, the strategy still denies one vote to your opponent than they otherwise would have received and represents a one-vote swing in your favor. Not quite as good as the persuasion strategy, but still a net victory.

But that's not the whole story of how microtargeting works. What's truly remarkable here is that the strategy for persuading Chris doesn't work on just a single Chris. Because it operates at what the technology companies call "scale," this strategy of automatic microtargeting can be used on *all* Chrises, which is to say, microtargeting at scale can be used on all voters. It might not work every time, but if it works even some of the time, it can be used to tip a close election, at least if one side uses better microtargeting than the other. This is what McManee means when he calls microtargeting the "psychological mugging of every voter." It's also what the Trump campaign of 2016 did when it labeled 3.5 million African American voters for "Deterrence" and served them targeted Facebook ads in an effort to get them to stay home on election day 2016—an election in which African American turnout declined for the first time in twenty years.[83]

We have an ideal of politics and public debate being about persuasion toward issues and the character of the candidates. Even though we know that politics are often much dirtier than that in practice, it's a useful ideal to strive toward, even if we will ultimately fall short of it. We might concede that our elections have their problems (too much money in politics, concerns that voters might not treat female or racial minority candidates equally, too much focus on sound bites or looks or family name rather than ability) yet still believe that they are fundamentally democratic. But a system deploying data science and behavioral science to microtarget voters at scale represents a new and ominous threat to democratic self-government. It might be bad enough that money seems to edge out values and ability in many elections, but a system of unregulated microtargeting means that elections might be determined by data science rather than democratic practices, under which swing voters are subjected to the same processes by which "consent" to data practices are manufactured by companies. And this problem might be made even worse by the reality that many democratic elections in the West of late have been decided by razor-thin margins—and in U.S. presidential elections determined by the Electoral College, frequently by candidates who have failed to achieve more votes than their opponent, much less a majority of total votes cast. Maybe elections shouldn't be a competition about who can better use tech powered by human information to persuade voters, because if that's all they are, then we really don't have a democracy anymore.

Human information allows electoral manipulation in other ways as well. The use of social media platforms to manipulate voters through misinformation has been well documented, with scandals like Cambridge Analytica and attempts by foreign states to influence democratic elections with misinformation delivered through targeted ads. But concerns about electoral manipulation using the fruits of surveillance also raise the Praetorian Guard problem in a way that should worry anyone concerned about the integrity of democratic elections. Intelligence services using the tools of human-information-powered persuasion represent a real threat to democratic self-government, and this is true for domestic as well as foreign agencies. Such fears are neither outlandish nor to be dismissed as paranoid science fiction. In 2017, for example, the South Korean National Intelligence Service admitted it had conducted a secret campaign in its own country to ensure that its preferred candidate, the conservative Park Geun-hye, won (which she narrowly did), as well as earlier campaigns that sought to influence parliamentary elections.[84] The NIS deployed approximately thirty teams with expertise in psychological warfare that were (as its own report disclosed) "charged with spreading pro-government opinions and suppressing anti-government views, branding them as attempts by pro–North Korean forces to disrupt state affairs."[85]

Taking a step back for a moment, it should be no surprise that surveillance threatens democracy by enhancing the powers of persuasion. The use of surveillance to persuade people follows logically from the reasons surveillance happens in the first place. Consider once more the five features of surveillance derived from surveillance studies. Information collected about (1) *individuals* in a (2) *systematic* and (3) *routine* way is literally the business model of tech companies and political campaigns. Critically, human-data-powered political persuasion has a clear (4) *purpose* of control in fundraising as well as voter encouragement and vote suppression. Equally important, the symbiosis of political campaigns and technology companies in the most public context of elections amply illustrates yet another way that modern surveillance practices (5) *transcend the public-private divide*.

Yet all is not lost. As with the problem of blackmail, privacy protections can help. Privacy rules limiting the extent to which human information can be known or used can disrupt some of the more sinister applications of the data-political complex. Better restrictions on the ability of Facebook partners like Cambridge Analytica to siphon off vast amounts of sensitive data could have prevented the creation of the psychographic profiles that caused such problems. Regulations on fine-grained collection and targeting of human information can limit the effect of microtargeted political advertisements that prey on the vulnerabilities of voters, or that intentionally dump misinformation into the sphere of public debate. The precise formula for reform here is beyond the goal of this book, which is of course to make the case for why and when privacy matters. We can—and should—debate the appropriate level of regulations on microtargeting given the dangers of regulation of political activity. What we don't need to debate, however, is the undeniable fact that avoidable incursions on privacy have upended our political system, enabling both good- and bad-faith interventions on voters that are powered by human information. If we care about self-government and elections, if we care about the autonomy of political decisions made by citizens in digital democracies, and if we care about the integrity of our democracy itself, then we need to care about privacy.

3. Discrimination. Finally, surveillance brings the power to *discriminate*. As we've seen, many kinds of surveillance are routinely used to sort people into categories. Some of these forms of sorting are obviously harmful. Consider, for example, the use of census records by the U.S., Canadian, and German governments during the Second World War to identify citizens to relocate to the Japanese internment camps in North America and the concentration camps in Europe.[86] Others forms of sorting may seem innocuous or even benign. As we've seen more than once, the vast preference engines that power the "free" internet are used to profile people for marketing purposes. Companies like Google and Facebook amass vast detailed profiles of our web-surfing habits, our interests, and our buying habits.[87] Data brokers like Acxiom and LexisNexis create even more detailed consumer profiles by combining various kinds of data and then selling it to a wide variety of sources, including direct marketers, background-check companies, and companies consumers may already have a relationship with, such as car dealerships or Target.[88] Commercial data of this kind can be used to offer discounts or selective promotions to more or less desirable customers. From one perspective, the use of the fruits of data surveillance in this way might look like ordinary or even "innovative" marketing. But consider the power that data-driven marketing gives companies in relation to their customers. The power of sorting can bleed imperceptibly into the power of discrimination. A coupon for a frequent shopper might seem innocuous, but consider the power to offer shorter airport security lines (and less onerous procedures) to rich frequent fliers, or to discriminate against customers or citizens on the basis of wealth, politics, religion, geography, gender, sexuality, race, or ethnicity.

The sorting power of surveillance has been studied extensively by surveillance scholars. In the 1990s, sociologist Oscar Gandy described the "panoptic sort": the use of consumer databases to profile consumers, sort them into categories, and then discriminate among the categories, allocating opportunities on the basis of the classification.[89] As we saw in the previous section, these techniques of microtargeting also allow the delivery of messages with fine precision, messages that can encourage racism and division. Shoshana Zuboff notes that the "radical indifference" many tech platforms have toward the "content" on their sites permits the spread of false and abusive messages with scientific precision.[90] Journalist Julia Angwin and her colleagues at ProPublica found, for instance, that Facebook enabled targeted ads to people who expressed an interest in subjects like "Jew Hater," "How to burn Jews," and "History of why Jews ruin the world."[91] Another team of journalists found that Google allowed hateful or racist ads to be targeted to people who entered search terms as "Jewish parasite" and "Black people ruin everything."[92] While the platforms removed these specific capabilities in response to the bad press, they did not remove the capability of specific microtargeting, because it is a core feature of what Zuboff calls their "surveillance capitalism" business model. Indeed, other work by the ProPublica team had already demonstrated that microtargeted ads could be blocked from being seen by racial minorities.[93]

Governments, too, are increasingly using tools like these that enable invidious sorting. Lyon and other scholars building on Gandy's pioneering work have shown some of the ways software is increasingly used to sort citizens and consumers by governments seeking profiles of criminal risk and by companies seeking profiles of commercial opportunity.[94] The power to treat people differently is without doubt a dangerous one, as our many legal rules prohibiting discrimination in the areas of fair credit, civil rights, and constitutional law recognize. Surveillance however, particularly when fueled by big data, puts pressure on those laws and threatens to upend the basic power balance on which our consumer protection and constitutional laws operate. Danielle Citron argues that algorithmic decision-making based on data raises issues of what she calls "technological due process."[95] The sorting power of surveillance only raises the stakes of these issues. After all, what sociologists call "sorting," has many other names in the law, "profiling" and "discrimination" being just two of them.

One of the defenses that companies sometimes make to charges that their platforms allow racist targeting is that those categories were generated either by their customers or by the algorithms themselves. In other words, companies argue that it was AI algorithms finding racist patterns in the data that permitted the racist microtargeting rather than the companies' own human employees. But this is precisely the point: algorithms being trained on data reflect biases already present in the data. Even if such tools were "neutral" in the sense that they were not encouraging racist outcomes, the data itself can reflect inequality, racism, and many other human problems. And if that is the case (which it indisputably is), it can be no defense for these companies to maintain that their products are neutral. When it comes to algorithms, because they are creations of human beings who rely on data about the world, they cannot be neutral. If the algorithms run on bad or unrepresentative data, their outputs are bad or unrepresentative, as in the old programmer's cliché "garbage in, garbage out." If they are trained on data inputs reflecting racism, inequality, or bias, their decisional outputs will reflect that bias. One representative study, for instance, examined hiring algorithms that had been trained to predict employability based upon past hiring patterns by the company. However, when the algorithms were given identical résumés with different names, they chose the résumés that had White-sounding names over the ones with Black-sounding names.[96] But even where the data is of high quality and does not reflect racism or inequality, algorithms are still not neutral. "Algorithms are, in part, our opinions embedded in code," explain data scientists Gideon Mann and Cathy O'Neil. "They reflect human biases and prejudices that lead to machine learning mistakes and misinterpretations. This bias shows up in numerous aspects of our lives, including algorithms used for electronic discovery, teacher evaluations, car insurance, credit score rankings, and university admissions."[97]

O'Neil goes further in her excellent book *Weapons of Math Destruction*, arguing that algorithmic tools are inevitably biased for an additional reason, which is because they must contain a definition of success.[98] Often, this definition of success is "volume." Headline-generation algorithms are optimized for the number (or "volume") of clicks they generate, which leaves us awash in actual headlines like "Top 11 Fake Clickbait Headlines: You Won't Believe Number 4!" and (my favorite) "Are You Smart Enough to Avoid Clickbait? Take This Quiz to Find Out."[99] Social media platforms are often similarly optimized for "engagement": the more you are engage with and use a platform, meaning the more time you spend and more things you do there, the more ads you see and the more money the platform makes. It's hard to make a nuanced point in a single tweet or comment; it's much easier to insult than to inform; and it seems likely that anger drives engagement more than nuance or human connection do. These platforms may have a business interest in your thinking that they are "the new public square."[100] However, they are not, as Cass Sunstein has pointed out helpfully, optimized for democratic deliberation and creating an informed public with access to a shared set of reliable, truthful facts.[101] The human bias that inevitably infects algorithms, the data they run on, and the outputs they produce has been repeatedly documented by scholars across the disciplines of sociology, information science, data science, and law over the past two decades. This is not to say that algorithms are always bad—in fact, when responsibly designed and used, they can sometimes help to mitigate human bias, though in practice this usage seems rare compared to its alternatives.[102]

In the surveillance of our physical bodies, privacy and equality remain deeply intertwined. Even in a digital world, invasions of privacy—and exercises of the power human information confers—will continue to be unequally experienced along the familiar fault lines of inequality that characterize our society. As Sarah Igo has shown powerfully, the right to privacy—the right not to be known by the powerful—is a fundamental right of citizens, broadly defined, in any free society. It should thus be no surprise that privacy claims in U.S. history have often operated as claims against discrimination or unequal treatment. Citizens (in the past as well as now) making a privacy claim have often been making broader claims about modern citizenship. Igo explains further: "To invoke [privacy's] shelter was to make a claim about the latitude for action and anonymity a decent, democratic society ought to afford its members. Responses to that claim evoked the fault lines of civic membership. Which citizens, after all, could be entrusted with privacy, and therefore be liberated from official scrutiny?"[103] Surveillance that pierces anonymity imposes that kind of scrutiny, and does so in ways that often replicate and expose the divisions in our society over time. Many vulnerable and marginalized groups have been targeted by surveillance, and their identification has led to their being treated in ways that are separate and unequal. In fact, the amount of privacy people have been granted in practice correlates closely with their legal, cultural, and social status in the larger society. Igo gives numerous examples of this phenomenon from the past century of U.S. history. These include the supervision and surveillance of women's sexual and reproductive lives (from Gilded Age requirements that affluent young women be chaperoned to "protect their virtue" to abortion record-keeping requirements), the thoroughgoing surveillance of the lives of the poor by the welfare system, the policing of (and raids on) gay public spaces like bars and parks, and the fewer privacies granted children and adolescents in both homes and schools, particularly in the current age of app-enhanced helicopter parenting and "Find My Friends." In particular, though, departures from the norm of heterosexual white male citizen privacy have been greatest for ethnic and racial minorities and for immigrants.[104]

Facing digital surveillance targeted by human information today, marginalized groups frequently lack a meaningful ability to claim the right of privacy, whether in the case of overpolicing of African American youth,[105] the widespread government surveillance of Muslim Americans after 9/11,[106] widespread monitoring of recipients of government welfare or other benefits,[107] or contemporary militarized policing of American Latino communities as part of the Trump administration's (for lack of a better word) racist immigration policies.[108] It should thus be no surprise that a key purpose of the U.S. government's use of Clearview AI's facial recognition technology is to identify undocumented immigrants for seizure and deportation, often accompanied by violence or the proverbial hammering on the door in the middle of the night.[109] Indeed, the defining image of contemporary immigration policing in America in the late 2010s—Latin American children placed in cages—is in many respects the perfect metaphor for why privacy matters. To look at a photograph of a caged child is to see *power*, with metal bars restricting movement. It is to see an invasion of *privacy*, in which the spaces between those bars allow constant surveillance and eliminate any practical ability of those imprisoned to claim privacy or dignity. And it is, above all, a story of *human* vulnerability and helplessness.

Privacy protections can disrupt the power that human information grants to those who would sort and discriminate. When data-driven technologies are used to sort us, we should be as wary of them as we are when a human being is doing it. To put this another way, we should look critically at algorithms that sort us and examine their goals, the quality of their data, and any disparate impact of their results. Moreover, those who would discriminate based upon data cannot discriminate if they cannot collect or purchase the data in the first place, and we should certainly consider rules that limit using certain categories of sensitive data. Government agencies can also be restricted from acquiring sensitive data about race or sexuality (for instance) through the power of law, or from using AI to find proxies for those facts elsewhere in the data set. And our laws protecting us from discrimination on the basis of race, gender, and sexual orientation may well need to be updated to deal with the problems of algorithmic discrimination. To the extent that existing civil rights laws focus on intentional discrimination by human beings, it may be necessary to come up with additional tests for discrimination by AI that may lack a discriminatory "intent" in the way we are accustomed to thinking about human decisions. Regardless of how we confront these problems, however, the increased power that human information technologies give to those who would sort are undeniable, and any response to discrimination in the digital age must deal seriously with the increasingly discriminatory potential that surveillance provides.

* * *

Surveillance, as we've seen, is complicated. It's traditionally thought of as a government activity, but it's also widely practiced by the private sector, with at best a blurry and permeable barrier separating the two. It's an inextricable part of every modern political state, a highly profitable business, and a perpetually lurking threat to democratic self-government. These threats can take many forms, from inhibiting dissenting thought and voices to blackmail, microtargeted persuasion, and discrimination. It can boost democratic participation and legitimacy when used to get out the vote, or it can make us less free through targeted voter suppression and manipulation. Privacy disrupts these practices, whether of sorting, discrimination, or other forms of oppression. Where surveillance allows microtargeted manipulation, for example, privacy protects the processes of democratic freedom, whether we think of them in terms of autonomy or a broader sense of human empowerment that transcends some of the limitations of traditional liberal theory.

By contrast, rules protecting citizens (and noncitizens) against surveillance can safeguard political freedom and political equality. At the most basic level, data that is never collected cannot menace intellectual privacy, nor can it be used to blackmail, persuade, or sort people for discriminatory treatment. Surveillance may flow like liquid between the public and private spheres, but law can certainly restrict the government's ability to purchase or otherwise access private data, as well as its ability to make sensitive information available to the public. American law already restricts these activities in some areas. Indeed, these rules have constitutional foundations in the Fourth Amendment's warrant requirement and in the constitutional right of information privacy recognized in *Whalen v. Roe* (1977), which envisions constitutional limits on the government's ability to disclose sensitive data about its citizens, such as their medical records.[110] Changes in technology, changes in corporate business practices, and the increasingly liquid nature of surveillance have enabled many of the new forms of surveillance discussed in this chapter, and the arms race between surveillance and law continues, as it must, if we are to continue to protect democracy from the power effects of human information technologies.

The right to claim privacy is thus the right to be a citizen entrusted with the power to keep secrets from the government, the right to exercise the freedom so lauded in orthodox American political theory and popular discourse. It is a claim to equal citizenship, with all the responsibility that comes with such a claim, and an essential and fundamental right in any meaningful account of what it means to be free. In order to achieve this promise in practice, privacy protections must be extended as a shield against inequality of treatment. Privacy enables democracy, and it can be used to secure democracy in the digital age by limiting access to and regulating the use of new technologies of suppression and oppression powered by human information. We saw in chapter 4 how privacy rules that allow identity development help us to develop as *humans*. To this list we can now add that privacy rules can serve the function of allowing us to exist as free and self-governing *citizens*.

6

Protection

The Matchstick Men

When I was a little boy growing up in the North of England, my parents hung a framed Lowry print in our dining room. Laurence Stephen Lowry was an amateur painter from Manchester, and like many artists, he painted what he knew. What Lowry knew were the urban industrial landscapes of Northern England, and today he is regarded as the iconic painter of the British Industrial Revolution. Two things about Lowry's style were distinctive. First, there were the "Lowry Men," the teeming masses of stick-figure humans going about their daily business in town, working in factories, or maybe going to circuses or football matches. Second, in the background were the brooding gray skies of Northern England, punctuated by burning chimneys and industrial smokestacks.

Lowry's paintings reflected the reality that Northern England was the first place in the world to industrialize, creating both large urban populations and unprecedented pollution. Industrialization brought urban jobs in factories and unprecedented economic opportunity—especially for the new titans of industry whose ownership of factories, shipyards, and mills allowed them to amass great fortunes like those of today's tech billionaires. It also brought a cornucopia of new products: industrial textiles for cheap clothing and bedding, mass-produced tools and toys of all kinds, and, as technology advanced, great machines like the car and the aeroplane. Lowry's matchstick men and women—including my great-grandparents and their friends—enjoyed many of these new marvels.*

* The disruption of the industrial age also caused many to flirt with seductive but dangerous political ideologies—nationalism, fascism, and communism—and with demagogues and dictators whose rise was smoothed by the new technologies of mass communications. No account of industrialization would be complete without considering the many wars (including the two world wars and the Cold War) that followed. These wars were of course made deadlier by other marvels of the industrial age such as machine guns, tanks, poison gas, aircraft, and bombs made first of TNT and then of uranium and plutonium. My great-grandparents and my grandparents suffered from these marvels as well, in the British Army in both world wars and as civilians during the World War II Blitz. For example, my great-grandfather Lance Corp. George Nain served in the First World War with the

Industrialization brought unprecedented problems as well. Artisans lost their livelihoods, "disrupted" (in today's parlance) by mass-produced goods that were often inferior but always vastly cheaper to buy. The Luddites were among the artisans who were "disrupted" by industrialization. They were artisan weavers whose livelihoods and communities were destroyed by the new textile mills in early nineteenth-century Britain, and they organized to break the mills. They were not particularly concerned about technology; their real concerns were the ways the new technologies were being deployed to eliminate traditional professions and ways of life, creating vast swaths of hungry poor people at the same time as they created fabulous industrial fortunes for a lucky few. The Luddites were demonized by the new industrial press, and as a result the term "Luddite" is used today to refer to someone who is unskilled in or opposed to new technologies. But it's worth remembering that technologies produce political consequences—winners and losers—and the original Luddites were people whose long-standing ways of artisanal life in their communities were suddenly and brutally wiped out by the cold logic of the market and the ruthless business practices of the new wealthy industrialists.[1]

The factories that produced these textiles and goods produced other things as well: unsafe working conditions, child labor, and discrimination in the industrial workplace. They also produced pollution, the billowing clouds of coal smoke filling the skies of Lowry's urban masterpieces. Pollution in Northern Britain became so bad that it produced the iconic case study on natural selection. The peppered moth, as its name suggests, was originally a small white moth with little black specks. Its coloring provided effective camouflage against the tree bark and rocky surfaces of its native habitat in the English wilderness. But as soot and other pollution from industrial factories blackened the British landscape, darker versions of the moth gained

King's Regiment (Liverpool) and was killed by a German sniper in August 1917. This meant that his wife, Catherine, became a widow in her twenties and her seven-year-old daughter, Bet (my future grandmother), grew up without her father like so many little children of her generation. On the other side of the family, my grandfather Capt. George Richards served in North Africa with the Royal Electrical and Mechanical Engineers and spent the war in a series of Italian and German prisoner of war camps. He was an engineer skilled with the new industrial technologies. Consequently, his technical knowledge made him too valuable to release back to the British Army even as the Germans retreated through Africa and Italy in 1944 and 1945. George's third son, Peter (my own father), was born about ten months after George was released and repatriated in mid-1945, making my dad a true Baby Boomer. The risks of demagogues and the horrors of industrial warfare are beyond the scope of a chapter on consumer protection, but no treatment of the challenges of the industrial age would be complete without at least mentioning them. We may reasonably fear similar horrors from the information revolution if we ignore the lessons of the past—all the more reason to bring these wonderful and worrying technologies under control through law.

a survival advantage. In a relatively short period of time, natural selection worked on the moth population, selecting against the white moths such that the population shifted to darker variants. Recently, scientists at the University of Liverpool identified the genetic mutation underlying this transformation and pinpointed its origin to 1819. (With the success of environmental protection laws in Britain in recent decades, the moth population is apparently becoming more pale again in the absence of the sooty selective pressure.)[2]

The new industrial products created other problems. In the pre-industrial world of artisans and farmers, the men and women who worked in that economy knew how to make and fix, to knit and hammer, to build and mend. There were fewer goods to buy, but by and large they knew how to use, assess, and fix them. If they didn't know how to do that, they likely knew someone in their village who did. But the Industrial Revolution changed that, and for all of the efforts of the Luddites, the pastoral way of life was gone for many. Seeking work, they, their children, and their grandchildren, moved to the cities to toil in factories and offices. Some of them moved to the United States or Canada, where the Industrial Revolution was also beginning to happen. These new generations rarely learned the old artisanal skills, but they developed others, whether blue or white collar. These new "consumers" of industrial products had a much harder time assessing the goods and services the industrial economy offered, and very little idea how to fix them. Consider your own set of skills: how would you begin to fix a radio or a washing machine? What about a zipper or a doorbell?

New problems created by industrialization required new solutions, and the law was not always responsive. Old legal rules were repurposed to smooth the path for industrialization, and new doctrines were developed to further entrench the power of the industrialists, often to the detriment of ordinary people. In the United States, this was the *Lochner* era (roughly 1890-1940), in which unelected judges resisted many of the economic policy reforms passed by elected legislatures to deal with the new industrial problems. Consider, for example, progressive reforms for workplace safety or the minimum wage, which ran into an interlocking set of constitutional objections that frustrated consumer protection. Federal laws to protect workers were struck down by conservative judges as exceeding congressional power under the Commerce Clause. The theory was that such laws regulated "manufacturing," a stage of economic activity that occurred before "commerce" and was the responsibility of the states to regulate.[3] But when states passed laws to protect workers, they were struck down in turn as violating the "liberty of contract," an extratextual doctrine implied into the Fourteenth Amendment for precisely this purpose.[4] Other laws were struck down as infringing the validity of contracts under a separate constitutional provision, while attempts to give flexibility to expert and nonpolitical administrative agencies were struck down as impermissible delegations of executive and legislative authority.[5]

The conservative judges in the *Lochner* era had sincere concerns that the new reforms would destabilize the existing constitutional framework between state-level economic rules and national rules. They feared that the power to set the terms of contracts for the price of labor could lead to redistribution of wealth and a slide to communism, and that giving power to unelected experts in administrative agencies would represent a major incursion into democratic accountability for regulations.[6] The constitutional framework they clung to may have accurately represented the economic world of the mid- to late eighteenth century (a time of pewter mugs, yeoman farmers, and human slavery), but it bore little resemblance to the one the Industrial Revolution had wrought (a time of radio, steel mills, and Jim Crow segregation). The judges who were unwilling or unable to see those changes merely created an ever more complicated, artificial, and unjust set of legal doctrines that ultimately collapsed in the late 1930s.

Slowly but surely, legal rules were created to deal with industrialization's excesses. In the United States, the programs of the New Deal and the Great Society were by no means perfect, but they were at least intended on the whole to mitigate the very real problems of the industrial age. Today we have laws regulating road and car safety, safety in the workplace, the fitness of industrial consumer products, the truthfulness of advertising, the purity and labeling of food, and clean air and water.[7] (It's laws like this last group that brought the pre-industrial pale pepper moth back to unpolluted English fields and hedgerows.) These solutions may not have been perfect, but they were good enough to capture the undeniable benefits of industrialization while minimizing or mitigating its equally undeniable harms. To be sure, we are still struggling with many of the problems wrought by industrialization, like climate change, economic inequality, and the increased risk of pandemics wrought by international air travel. But on the whole, we benefit undeniably from this "protective countermovement" that reshaped both the law and legal institutions to grapple with the industrial challenge.[8]

Toward Consumer Protection for the
Information Revolution

We are now, of course, in the midst of a technological and social transformation every bit as significant as the Industrial Revolution. Just like
the Industrial Revolution, our information revolution is creating new
ways to live and new marvels and conveniences. It is creating vast personal fortunes while it reshapes and destroys old professions—just ask Bill
Gates or Elon Musk, or the long-haul truck drivers whose livelihood is
on the verge of being eliminated by autonomous cars. As advances in au-
tomation and robotics continue, other professions are in danger—store
clerks, taxi drivers, typists, and even computer coders and lawyers skilled
in the review of documents. At the same time, the information revolution
is creating new products that today's consumers have no way of understanding. Few consumers today can take apart a computer and identify
its main components, much less fix them, and the percentage of such consumers is dwindling as devices become smaller and more complex and
as they are increasingly put together with permanent glue rather than re-
movable screws. Beyond physical devices, the digital society encourages
consumers to depend ever more upon information products that operate
in a virtual black box. How do the algorithms of Google's search engine,
Apple's Siri, or Amazon's Alexa work?[9] How can we best secure our devices
against hackers or viruses? How does Twitter decide which advertisements
to serve us? And how, if at all, can we use digital technologies without
being tracked? These questions have answers, but due to a combination of
technical complexity, trade secrecy, and other factors, those answers remain beyond the ability of ordinary consumers to even learn, let alone adequately comprehend. Consider again the humble password, once touted
as the solution to information security but now increasingly vulnerable
as consumers have so many accounts and passwords to remember that
many simply write them down on a piece of paper. Consider also privacy
settings, provided by many companies out of a stated desire to "empower"
consumers with "choice," but which offer so many choices that consumers
are rarely able to find them, much less adjust them.[10] Unfortunately, the
consumer problems brought about by the internet and mobile phases of
the information revolution look likely to become even worse as we move
into the age of the "Internet of Things." We face the onslaught of connected
cars and homes filled with devices that lack screens, previously inanimate

and nonnetworked objects that are yet more data collection points and sources of security vulnerabilities in our lives.

The "protective countermovement" of the industrial age recognized both the benefits and the inevitability of industrialization and worked to mitigate the problems of industrialization, shaping both law and society in a positive way. One of the products of this movement, as we have seen, was consumer protection law. Today the digital consumer confronts not just the goods and services of the industrial age but those of the information age as well. Often these products will be merged, further complicating these problems. For example, some industrial-age consumers could change the oil or tune the transmission of their car, fix a broken radio with a soldering iron, or (later) build a homebrew PC from component parts and software discs. Few, if any, information-age consumers can replace the chipset on their car's motherboard handling the antilock braking system or driver-assist AI, or build themselves a smartphone from scratch. Partly this is a function of the way these new systems are designed,[11] but largely it is a function of their vastly increased complexity. Just as our ancestors found themselves unable to use, assess, and repair the products of the industrial age, so are we now even more adrift with respect to the products we find we need to live our lives. As we confront the changed reality of the information age, one thing is clear: the information revolution has created massive conceptual and practical challenges for consumers navigating the digital economy. Perhaps not all of these issues are strictly privacy issues, but virtually all of them involve the collection and exploitation of human information in one way or another by companies. Because privacy rules are information rules, this is in effect a privacy problem, broadly understood. And privacy rules will be necessary for the next stage of consumer protection law.

Just as consumer protection law developed in the twentieth century to manage the excesses and the new risks of the industrial economy, we will need to develop a consumer protection law for the twenty-first century to manage the excesses and the new risks of the information economy. Because of the central importance of human information to the information economy, and because of the power imbalances that it can create, consumer protection law in the twenty-first century will increasingly need to merge with privacy law. In fact, this trend is already occurring. European countries typically have both a consumer protection agency and a newer data protection agency. The consumer protection agencies usually predate the information age, while the data protection agencies date from the 1970s to the 1990s. Unlike European countries, the United States has only the Federal Trade Commission at the national level, an industrial-age consumer protection agency charged with preventing "unfair and deceptive trade practices."[12] The FTC has tried, heroically at times, to solve information-age problems with industrial-age tools, even though it remains underequipped and underfunded.[13] But the FTC's consumer protection work on privacy issues also demonstrates the ways in which these two bodies of law are becoming inextricably intertwined as so many consumer products are also information products.

This is a book about ideas more so than law reform, but it is worth imagining what a new consumer protection law for the digital age might look like, because it helps to illustrate why privacy matters in the consumer context. Such a new regime could disrupt the ways human information is processed by data science and leveraged by behavioral science to exert unreasonable power on consumers. By limiting the ability of businesses to know or use human information in targeted ways, information-age consumer protection law could meaningfully protect humans from economic activity we might consider manipulative or exploitative. A protective countermovement of this sort could be an information-age analog to the consumer protection law of the industrial age. By focusing on the manipulation of human information, it could continue the project of its industrial-age ancestor—protecting vulnerable consumers from corporate power and economic and other harms. This chapter attempts to sketch out the features that I believe a reasonable consumer protection regime for the information revolution should possess, as a way of showing how and why privacy can matter in the consumer protection context of the information age.

Recall how the two previous chapters showed why privacy matters to the development of human identity and the protection of political freedom. I think it is easier for us to imagine in general terms how privacy rules can protect our individual and political identities than it is for us to talk in that way about our economic identity. Partly this is a function of culture and history. Humans have been talking about and expressing their identities at least since the time of the cave painters, whether in the Australian Outback, at Lascaux and Pech Merle in the French Dordogne, or at countless other prehistoric sites throughout the world. We have been developing laws and vocabulary to talk about the problem of government power since at least the ancient Greek philosophers, and in Anglo-American law since at least the Magna Carta of 1215. But our cultural understandings of private power are far less mature. In Anglo-American law we have a rich vocabulary with which to talk about government censorship. Consider, for example, John Milton's admonition in *Areopagitica* (1644) that restraints on publishing were "a dishonour and derogation to the author, to the book, to the privilege and dignity of Learning."[14] Or consider Oliver Wendell Holmes's famous metaphor of the "marketplace of ideas" in *Abrams v. United States* (1919), in which he argued that we should protect the expression of "opinions that we loathe and believe to be fraught with death" because they might turn out to be correct. Holmes explained (in language that is as close as judicial opinions come to poetry):

> [W]hen men have realized that time has upset many fighting faiths, they may come to believe even more than they believe the very foundations of their own conduct that the ultimate good desired is better reached by free trade in ideas—that the best test of truth is the power of the thought to get itself accepted in the competition of the market, and that truth is the only ground upon which their wishes safely can be carried out.[15]

There are literally dozens more examples I could have chosen from American constitutional law because it is filled with rules and expressions restraining government power—so much so that many of them have escaped into the broader culture. But when it comes to equivalent statements about private power, it is a real struggle, in American law at least, to come up with more than a few examples. None of them is half as memorable as Holmes's statement of the "marketplace of ideas" in *Abrams*, or his even more famous quip from a different case that year: "The most stringent protection of free speech would not protect a man in falsely shouting fire in a theatre and causing a panic."[16] What this means in practice is that if we want to talk about private power with the richness with which we can talk about the humanities or political freedom, part of our challenge is that we need a better vocabulary. Lacking the shared cultural power of generally accepted words like "individuality," "separate but equal," or "totalitarianism," when it comes to the problems of private power, we have no choice but to talk with greater specificity.

For this reason, this chapter is structured differently from the two that preceded it. It first offers some thoughts on how we should talk and think about consumer protection and informational power in the digital age. Rather than talking like tech companies about rational "users" making "choices" in an "ecosystem" of "innovation," I will argue it is far better to talk about consumers as they actually are. This is something I call a "situated" consumer, which the second part of the chapter describes in some detail. Third, I will suggest a few specific features that will be essential to an effective information-age regime of consumer protection. Fourth, and finally, I will describe a more general way that privacy rules can protect consumers by enhancing trust in relationships. The goal of this chapter, however, is the same as the others: to illustrate one more of the human values that privacy law can (and I think should) advance—in this case, consumer protection.

How Should We Talk About Consumer Protection?

One of the primary arguments I've made in this book is not merely that the words we use matter, but that they are particularly important to the ways that we talk and think about privacy. Perhaps this is so because privacy can have so many meanings (as we saw in chapter 1), because there are so many misconceptions about it (as we saw in chapter 3), or even because "privacy" is often used as a shorthand for so many of the problems of the information age. But whether these or other explanations are the reason, the words we use to talk about privacy undoubtedly matter a great deal.

When we talk about human information in the context of consumer protection, however, our vocabulary problem becomes particularly acute. On top of both the vagueness of our existing vocabulary for privacy and the limited vocabulary we have for talking about private power, we confront a problem of rapid technological change. At the intersection of these three problems, we enter a realm where words can be used in ways that are both bizarre and self-serving. Let's consider three examples that, working together, aptly describe the way many tech companies talk about consumer privacy: (1) *users* making (2) *choices* in an environment of (3) *innovation*.

1. "Users." It's commonplace in the technology industry for companies to refer to the people who use their products as their "users." Twitter and Instagram, for example, have User Agreements, while software engineers who design interfaces work in UX, short for "user experience."[17] Do you think of yourself as a "user"? To my knowledge, the only other industry in which customers get described this way is the illegal drug trade. The use of the word "user" may have something to do with distancing the company both psychologically and legally from having responsibility to its customers, particularly when those customers receive a "free" service in exchange for the opaque exploitation of their data by the company. Even customers

who pay for a service—like those who entrust their safety to Uber and its fleet of drivers—can get called a variation of "user." Uber calls these people merely "riders,"[18] in part because its app is intended to link up two groups of people—the ones driving and the ones being driven in Uber cars—while the company tries to avoid as much responsibility (and liability) as possible. Thus, Uber calls the people driving its "riders" merely "drivers," and it fights as hard as it can to avoid owing any legal duties to either group, including resisting treating drivers working for Uber as "employees" who can draw benefits.[19] Not every technology company engages in this kind of linguistic doublethink, to be sure, but it is common enough and intentional enough to recognize as a trend.[20] Such tactics are intentional, seeking to deny the kinds of mutual relationships that are familiar from predigital commerce. Yet consumers still expect that the companies exercising power over them owe them moral and legal duties as part of the relationship—why else would you get into a private car driven by someone you've never met? Perhaps it's because companies seek such blind trust without responsibility that much of their rhetoric continues to suggest something like an obligation. One study of data breach notifications, for example, found that over a third of them contained some variation on the line "Here at [tech company], we take your privacy and security seriously."[21]

Some observers have suggested that human "users" aren't really customers at all, but are actually the product itself. From this perspective, "users" are no more than consumer eyeballs served up to advertisers by what law professor Tim Wu calls "the attention merchants."[22] This idea is most often expressed by the somewhat controversial internet adage "If you aren't paying, you might be the product." Technology writer Nicholas Carr took this critique one step further. He argued, at the dawn of the social web, that social media's model of users producing content—Facebook and MySpace profiles, YouTube videos, tweets, blog posts, Amazon and Yelp reviews, and Instagram feeds—was a form of unjust and uncompensated work. As he put it back in 2006:

> Strip away the happy-face emoticons from the social web, and you're left
> with a sad-face truth: By putting the means of production into the hands
> of the masses but withholding from those same masses any ownership over
> the products of their work, the internet provides an incredibly efficient
> mechanism for harvesting the economic value of the free labor provided by
> the very many and concentrating it into the hands of the very few.[23]

Carr gave this phenomenon the evocative name "digital sharecropping."[24]

No matter how we characterize these practices, my point is that many tech companies try very hard not to call the ordinary human beings who are the source of their profits any one of the many words the English language has developed to show gratitude, reciprocity, and the existence of legal duties in commercial relationships—words like "guest," "patient," "customer," and "client."[25] The words we use matter, as they both structure our perceptions of reality and often have legal consequences as well. As a result, beneath the happy sloganeering of "Here at company X, we care about you and your privacy," Google's "Don't Be Evil," and Facebook's "open and connected," technology companies have been highly strategic in their use of language to structure the perception and legal status of their products for their own advantage. We should recognize it, and in so doing reject the attempt of such verbal heists to create new realities.

2. "Choice." Another example of this problem is how we use the word "choice" to describe the experience of consumers in the digital age. We can certainly talk about the enormous range of choices consumers face in the products and services they can purchase. Literally millions of different products are available for delivery from Amazon, for example.[26] But in the privacy context we most frequently use the word to talk about the "choices" consumers have with respect to the ways in which their human information is collected and used. As we saw in chapter 2, when it comes to human information, talk of "choice" is an illusion, as least if we mean the kind of meaningful, knowing, and voluntary "choice" among attractive alternatives that the word has traditionally evoked in both law and common usage. Beneath the veneer of choice rhetoric lies the thick and inescapable reality of control and manipulation of those exposed consumers.[27] This *pathological* form of digital choice, we have also seen, suffers from a series of defects—choices that are unwitting, coerced, involuntary, or some combination of the three.[28] It should go without saying, but a "choice" that doesn't give you a choice is not a choice at all. These pathologies are worsened by the American regime of "privacy self-management" that puts the legal responsibility squarely on "users" of services to make "choices" about their privacy after "notice" from the company in the form of a privacy policy, many of which pull off the impressive linguistic feat of being both vague and dense at the same time, saying a lot without really saying anything at all. On top of all of this is the myth of Privacy as Control that we saw in chapter 3, shifting moral responsibility onto consumers for failing to make the proper choices to control how their

information is collected and used, even when that control is also an illusion in practice.[29]

One of the major themes of this book is of course how issues of privacy and human information largely come down to *power*, particularly the power to control human behavior. Nowhere have these techniques been used as frequently or as successfully as in the case of profiling and controlling consumers. Consider again Target Corporation's use of the pregnancy prediction score to identify and lock in pregnant consumers (profiled in chapter 2). In that case, human information was combined with data science to identify the consumers Target wanted to manipulate. Data science was used to identify the consumers, and then behavioral science was used to market to them in ways that were both highly effective and closely tailored to their known, predictable, cognitive vulnerabilities. As one Target employee explained:

Take a fictional Target shopper named Jenny Ward, who is 23, lives in Atlanta and in March bought cocoa-butter lotion, a purse large enough to double as a diaper bag, zinc and magnesium supplements and a bright blue rug. There's, say, an 87 percent chance that she's pregnant and that her delivery date is sometime in late August. What's more, because of the data attached to her Guest ID number, Target knows how to trigger Jenny's habits. They know that if she receives a coupon via e-mail, it will most likely cue her to buy online. They know that if she receives an ad in the mail on Friday, she frequently uses it on a weekend trip to the store. And they know that if they reward her with a printed receipt that entitles her to a free cup of Starbucks coffee, she'll use it when she comes back again.

In the past, that knowledge had limited value. After all, Jenny purchased only cleaning supplies at Target, and there were only so many psychological buttons the company could push. But now that she is pregnant, everything is up for grabs. In addition to triggering Jenny's habits to buy more cleaning products, they can also start including offers for an array of products, some more obvious than others, that a woman at her stage of pregnancy might need.[30]

These techniques were applied not just to the fictional Jenny Ward, of course. They were applied to "every regular shopper in Target's national database"—tens of thousands of women Target had determined were highly likely to be pregnant, and thus vulnerable to the targeted marketing that could change their habits. Recall also that this strong cocktail of data and behavioral science was given to them in ways that were deliberately hidden, as consumers who were aware of what Target knew and what it was trying to do would become "queasy," reducing the effectiveness of the marketing.[31]

If we think about Jenny Ward in terms of the pathologies of consent from chapter 2, there's an argument that all three of them are present here. First, Jenny's consent to Target's information practices was *unwitting* because she would have no idea of Target's surveillance into her reproductive state, and by extension their ability to change her habits. Jenny also had no way of learning about what Target was doing, apart from possibly vague language buried somewhere on Target's website. Recall also that when "queasy" customers started to freak out about Target's information practice (thereby expressing their firm refusal to consent), Target just changed its coupon practices to camouflage what it was doing and allay any suspicions of creepiness. Her consent (at least to the surveillance) was also clearly *coerced* because it preyed directly and secretly on her cognitive vulnerabilities to manipulate her behavior and form Target-friendly shopping habits. Finally, Jenny's consent was *involuntary* because she was never given a meaningful opportunity to "choose" Target's real offer: "Can we run data analytics on everything you buy from us and everything else we can learn about you from data brokers to send you a coupon we've timed to your moment of maximum vulnerability so we can make you a habitual Target customer once the baby comes? Oh, and congratulations on that, by the way." Instead, her choice was framed as "Would you like to use these coupons, one of which is for baby formula?"

Remember also that this example is not unique to Target; these business practices are well-developed and widespread as data science has been adopted throughout the corporate world, and they have been significantly improved and refined in the decade since they were pioneered by Target. They are also largely legal under current law. It's also worth noting that the Target example took place in the physical environment of human customers visiting physical stores with paper coupons delivered by physical mail. The more a shopping or other commercial environment takes place in the online context, the more the interface and other interactions of the transaction can be designed (by UX designers) to further influence the consumer.[32] Yet this "choice" is precisely what American law approves as legally valid under the pathological "notice and choice" regime governing data practices, and it is one that companies literally swear to as meaningful choice in court and before administrative agencies. The undeniable fact that this "choice" is so far from any notion of gold-standard knowing and voluntary consent seems to be entirely beside the point under current American law.

3. "Innovation." The final piece of the puzzle for the rhetoric of privacy coming from many tech companies is to portray these rationally choosy users as operating in an environment of "innovation." Many companies go a bit further with the environmental analogy and refer to the technology sector itself as an innovation "ecosystem." And at face value, who wouldn't want a range of choices they can use in an ecosystem of innovation? Innovation is one of the buzzwords of the twenty-first century, a shorthand used to describe everything fantastic and shiny, magical and helpful, all "it just works," curved chrome edges, and smiling app icons. It's not just companies that love innovation; regulators talk about it too, as they try to make sure privacy regulations are reasonable and don't damage innovation's "fragile" ecosystem. The Obama White House unveiled its proposal for a Consumer Privacy Bill of Rights in February 2012, subtitled "A Framework for Protecting Privacy and Promoting Innovation in the Global Digital Economy." The accompanying fifty-two-page memorandum contained the word "innovation" seventy-seven times.[33] Perhaps because of the way the endeavor was framed, nothing meaningful resulted from that process. Technology companies essentially refused to compromise on their adherence to the "notice and choice" regime that gives them maximum flexibility and minimum liability, and the administration ultimately refused to press the issue in Congress.[34]

Innovation is a funny concept, and there are four features of the way it's used in privacy conversations that are worth noting. First, *"innovation" is vague.* It doesn't really have a definition, other than perhaps "good things from technology." This vagueness is a virtue for innovation's acolytes. It allows innovation to be whatever (and only whatever) companies might want it to be, even as those needs vary over time. But here's an experiment: take any sentence from a technology company about "innovation," and replace the word "innovation" with "magic" to see if the meaning of the sentence changes at all. In my own experience playing this game many times over the past decade, it almost never changes the meaning.[†] You can also replace the adjective form "innovative" with "magical" and the ugly verb form "innovate" with "make magic." Consider these sentences from President Obama's introduction to his administration's proposed Consumer Privacy Bill of Rights:

[†] In the mid-2010s, you could also play this game with most sentences featuring the phrase "big data analytics."

- In just the last decade, the Internet has enabled a renewal of direct political engagement by citizens around the globe and an explosion of commerce and *innovation* creating jobs of the future. Much of this *innovation* is enabled by novel uses of personal information.
- With this Consumer Privacy Bill of Rights, we offer to the world a dynamic model of how to offer strong privacy protection and enable ongoing *innovation* in new information technologies.[35]

Or consider these sentences from Mark Zuckerberg's 2018 Senate testimony following the Cambridge Analytica scandal:

- The potential for further growth and *innovation* based on collection of data is unlimitedless [*sic*].
- And the third point is—is just around enabling *innovation*. Because some of the abuse cases that—that are very sensitive, like face recognition, for example—and I feel there's a balance that's extremely important to strike here, where you obtain special consent for sensitive features like face recognition, but don't—but we still need to make it so that American companies can *innovate* in those areas, or else we're going to fall behind Chinese competitors and others around the world who have different regimes for—for different new features like that.
- So there's a lot of different choice and a lot of *innovation* and activity going on in this space.[36]

Of course, given the demands on their jobs, it's often quite useful for politicians and CEOs to have pleasant-sounding but empty words to reach for when it suits them. "Innovation" certainly serves this purpose, but the fact remains that "innovation" is so devoid of content as to be meaninglessly and dangerously vague. We should call them on it.

The second problem with the use of "innovation" is not just that it is vague, but that *it is selectively vague*. When technologists and others talk about "innovation," as in the examples from Obama and Zuckerberg, "innovation" is invariably used in a positive way. Technological innovation, from this perspective, is all good things and no bad ones. It is instantaneous email and videoconferencing, GPS navigation in your car, a library in the palm of your hand—all undeniable good things enabled by the information revolution, to be sure. But it is never voter manipulation, targeted advertisements, denial-of-service attacks, doxing, revenge porn, middle schoolers with access to rape videos, weaponized behavioral economics, political polarization, the resurgence of overt white supremacy, demagogues threatening nuclear war over Twitter, racially biased algorithms, or any one of dozens of other ready examples from what journalists have deemed the "techlash." Innovation is held up as what technology companies do—and to be clear, technology companies certainly do some wonderful, even close to magical things—but innovation is always implicitly defined so as to exclude the bad things that come with new technology. Yet criminals can "innovate." The foreign hackers that broke into the Democratic National Committee were innovative in the way they used hacking and the internet to influence a U.S. election. The use of human information for both get-out-the-vote efforts and voter suppression that we saw in chapter 5 is innovative, too. The vast online repositories of hard-core pornography feared by parents of middle-school children are just as innovative as Google's YouTube platform that so many of those same parents encourage their tweens to use. We saw in chapter 2 how design is political and designed objects have politics, whether we are talking about door handles, nail guns, or Pinterest. These objects make some results easier and others harder, and design choices affect everything. The rhetorical construction of "innovation" by the tech sector slices off everything bad and leaves only the gleaming stainless steel of a technological utopia, one that is all Thomas More and no George Orwell. While I hope we can agree that reality, like the politics of design, is complicated, the way that "innovation" is deployed in technology policy debates is shorn of that complexity in a way that directs our attention away from the bad things that technologies can also be used to do. It is deceptive, and intentionally so.

A third problem with the rhetoric of innovation is that it has a *strength of convenience*: when it suits companies, "innovation" can vary from being strong and powerful or weak and feeble. When technologists are in advertising mode, when their CEOs are on stage at a product launch in jeans and a dress shirt, it seems like there is no force on earth more powerful than innovation. Apple famously promoted its App Store in 2009 with the slogan "There's an app for that!," suggesting that whatever problem you might have, an iPhone plus an app from the App Store could solve it. The internet critic Evgeny Morozov has termed this approach "solutionism," the false idea popular in Silicon Valley that every human problem is amenable to a quick-fix technological solution.[37] It is curious, however, that innovation's strength is immediately flipped as soon as regulation is proposed. Tech executives often complain that regulation could deprive us of the magic of innovation, and their favorite metaphor is to say that innovation would be "stifled." Search engine results for this expression receive literally millions of hits, as its usage has exploded in recent years, becoming instantly familiar to many. In fact, as we search with difficulty for a common cultural vocabulary with which to think critically about private power in the information age, fears about regulation "stifling innovation" (perhaps with the older but still common "red tape") are far more common—another legacy of our rich vocabulary for critiquing state power. For all of the strength of "innovation" that its rhetoric offers when it is convenient, innovation seemingly becomes weak—so easily stifled—in the face of the merest restriction.

There is of course an alternative way of framing this problem: the old proverb that "necessity is the mother of invention." From this perspective, if innovation were truly as strong as its proponents claim it to be, innovative companies could easily continue to work their magic notwithstanding the constraints that reasonable regulation might place upon their progress. What would be better than the power of "innovation" harnessed to do magic while also protecting human consumers? But of course, we are considering here not invention per se, but a peculiar and self-serving use of the term "innovation" as a shield from regulation, diminished profitability, or corporate inconvenience. And one of the hallmarks of innovation rhetoric is its protean ability to shift from powerful to powerless—taking with it all of its promised magic—when regulation threatens. To use an expression from Lowry's Britain, when regulation appears, "innovation" takes its ball and goes home.

This brings us to the fourth and final problem with innovation rhetoric, which is that innovation is sometimes *framed as a fundamental right*. This is related to innovation rhetoric's strength of convenience, though somewhat more subtle. We've seen how innovation rhetoric frames business practices as positive but fragile when regulation threatens to curtail current practices, and that this fragility is often expressed in the form of fears of "stifling innovation." What is particularly interesting about this framing is that it is strikingly similar to the rhetorical ways in which civil liberties are described. In the United States, for example, orthodox First Amendment law prevents prior restraints (requiring speakers to get permission to speak in the first place) and requires content-based regulations of protected expression to satisfy a high level of scrutiny.[38] Part of the reason for this high level of scrutiny is that the law is concerned about *chilling effects*—the fear that an overbroad law might deter far more free expression than is appropriate. Thus, for example, under the *Brandenburg* test governing incitement to lawbreaking,

First Amendment law allows the government to punish speakers who intentionally use words to get other people to break the law imminently (i.e., soon)
where those words have a high likelihood of success. But the government has
to prove all three elements of *intent* ("I want you to break the law"), *immi-
nence* ("break it now"), and *likelihood* (that you are likely to break the law), or
the speaker can walk away. This is because of the fear of chilling effects; if the
law allowed the government (as it used to) to punish speech that merely had
some tendency to produce lawbreaking, it could be used (as it used to be) to
suppress speakers who had no intention of causing riots or revolutions but
who were merely irritating critics of government policy.

Innovation rhetoric often takes a similar form. Technologists and others
take umbrage at the idea that a business might have to get permission from
the government to try a new business practice, so they call for "permissionless
innovation,"[39] an idea that has a direct analog to First Amendment prior re-
straint doctrine. Regulations that require permission to deploy potentially
dangerous technologies are thus seen as being like disfavored prior restraints.
Regulations of the content of business practices are also challenged rhetor-
ically as "stifling" innovation, an idea with an equally direct analog to the
chilling effects doctrine. From this perspective, regulations of "technological
freedom" are particularly dangerous because they might sweep too broadly
and suppress uses of technology that were not squarely within the set of
harms that the regulator was trying to address. It also gives tech companies
leeway to "move fast and break things," Facebook's unofficial early motto, a
mantra that was plastered all over the walls of its first campus.[40] This lets tech
companies ask for forgiveness rather than permission, and to move forward
disrupting things we might not want disrupted, laying infrastructure, and
setting norms and inertia in such a way that forgiveness is a moot point because we're stuck with whatever the tech companies give us. Lather, rinse,
and repeat.[41]

My point here is not that regulations don't ever sweep too broadly (they
often do), or that regulation can't sometimes be a terrible idea (it often is).
Instead, it is that innovation rhetoric frequently deploys "innovation" as if
it were a fundamental right, using the same argumentative structure as First
Amendment or other civil liberties claims. (To be clear, "innovation" is not
such a fundamental right.) This is particularly ironic in the privacy context,
where fears of "stifling innovation" are commonly and frequently used to resist any attempts to protect privacy, an *actual fundamental right* protected
not just by European law but by American law as well.[42] Of course, here too

we run into our lack of a common vocabulary to talk about private power, as in contrast to European law, American law has difficulty articulating fundamental rights against private power. This is the most basic consequence of our lack of a good vocabulary for talking about private power: in part because it lacks the words to do so, American law places far fewer constraints on private actors than on government actors, the result being that in American law, private power is far less constrained than government power. Nevertheless, it is instructive that for all of its acceptance of innovation rhetoric, the Obama administration did try to articulate privacy rights through a "consumer bill of rights" in commerce, and even a few American technology companies (notably Microsoft) have taken the position that in a digital world, consumer privacy is a fundamental right.[43] But the appropriation of rights talk and chilling effects by companies pushing strong forms of innovation rhetoric creates the misleading impression that corporations and not individuals are the ones whose fundamental rights are menaced in the privacy context.

It gets worse. Companies aren't just increasingly framing "innovation" as a fundamental right; they are also beginning to make legal claims along those same lines. In recent years, companies have argued that the First Amendment protects, for example, search engine results, the use of algorithms by drug reps to persuade doctors to prescribe particular drugs, and the ability to create computer code unaffected by government regulation.[44] A few scholars have also made arguments to the effect that privacy law is a kind of censorship because it stops companies "talking" about you through the exchange of data or because "data" is somehow "speech" protected by the First Amendment, but by and large courts have resisted accepting these blunt arguments for constitutional immunity for privacy invasions.[45]

In a series of articles over the past fifteen years, I have offered a number of reasons why courts should and do correctly reject these kinds of seductive, self-serving, and incorrect First Amendment arguments.[46] Three of them are particularly relevant here. First, given how much of what companies do involves processing human information for commercial purposes, giving constitutional immunity to these business practices would place a significant chunk of information-age commerce outside the scope of regulation by democratically elected legislatures. In other words, if everything rests on data, and data is "speech," regulation of everything becomes censorship. Second, business practices like behaviorally targeted advertising or data-driven manipulation simply don't raise the kinds of core expressive interests that warrant First Amendment protection. Target's alleging a right to target and manipulate the Jenny Wards of the world is not remotely equivalent to articles in newspapers criticizing the government or protestors marching in the streets for racial justice. Third, and most significant, courts that were to adopt broad economic libertarian readings of the First Amendment to insulate companies from basic information-age regulations would be repeating the mistake of the *Lochner* courts that adopted broad economic libertarian readings of the Fourteenth Amendment to insulate companies from basic industrial-age regulations. The parallels are striking and have been recognized by numerous scholars and commentators. Indeed, Justice Stephen Breyer put this point well in *Sorrell v. IMS Health*, which struck down a restriction on the use of targeted marketing by drug reps under the First Amendment. "At best," he wrote, by striking down the restriction "the Court opens a Pandora's Box of First Amendment challenges to many ordinary regulatory practices that may only incidentally affect a commercial message. At worst, it reawakens *Lochner's* pre–New Deal threat of substituting judicial for democratic decision making where ordinary economic regulation is at issue."[47] To be clear, *Sorrell* struck down the regulation on technical First Amendment grounds, but it rejected the data broker's full-blooded *Lochner* claim that its use of targeted algorithms to sell drugs was essentially protected expression.[48] But the more we accept corporate framing of their "innovative" commercial uses of human information to be like a fundamental right, the more we run the risk that American courts will one day accept these claims as *actual* fundamental rights, judgments that would make meaningful information-age consumer protection by democratically elected legislatures all but impossible.

Let's take a step back and put together the pieces of the dominant corporate rhetoric about consumers in the information revolution. The human beings who use their products are *users* making *choices* in an ecosystem of *innovation*. While this story might sound good in theory, in practice it misdescribes the situation of most consumers. It calls them "users," distancing them from the reciprocal relationships of clients and patients that consumers often expect (and corporate rhetoric often suggests) in what are actually relationships with a power imbalance. It describes them as making "choices," suggesting that those consumers have far more power (and thus more legal and moral responsibility for their actions) than is actually the case. And by placing the choosy users in an ecosystem of "innovation," it suggests that any regulatory interventions would have an equivalent effect on technological development to the censorship or chilling effects on the fundamental right of free expression, making them more likely to get recognized as such by courts. We need a better way of talking about digital consumers, which the next section will offer.

Toward a "Situated Consumer"

As we have seen, the basic assumptions of American privacy law have long treated consumers as if they were more capable than they really are. The law frequently treats consumers as *rational actors* who diligently read *privacy policies* to intelligently inform themselves about the range of options they face, and who then make rational *choices* about which services to use and which options to invoke so they can *control* their privacy. As we have also seen, every piece of this story is a self-serving myth. Consumers are not rational actors, as we have learned from the behavioral sciences. We are sometimes rational, but we are also consistently and predictably irrational and available to be manipulated in ways that companies can (and do) exploit for profit. Human information makes this manipulation even easier. Consumers do not read privacy policies because most of us cannot understand them and because reading the policy of every service we encounter would take up a sizable chunk of our working lives (not to mention the terms of service, warranties, contracts, product recalls, and the many other dense legal documents that the average consumer encounters with every new product or service they encounter). Moreover, it's hard for consumers to understand the law, the technologies, and the risks they face. Legal scholar Paul Ohm explains that even though American law treats people as if they were "superusers . . . most Internet users are unsophisticated, exercising limited power and finding themselves restricted by technological constraints."[49]

The reality of consumer life in the 2020s is very different from the one described by Silicon Valley and Madison Avenue. Real consumers—you, me, and everyone we know—are very different from the idealized "users" that the language of "choice," "control," and "innovation" suggests. Abstract models of rational actors popularized by the Chicago School appear to track the lived experiences of consumers on the ground about as well as the strict liberal model of an autonomous self that we saw in chapter 4 tracks the actual experiences of human identity development. We are not empowered by this approach; instead, as the critical theorist Bernard Harcourt puts it well, we are *exposed*.[50] This exposure, he argues, is encouraged by the flashing lights and dopamine hits of engineered social and corporate interaction and is dulled by "decades of blind faith in the virtues of entrepreneurialism, self-interest, and self-centeredness, and in the illusion of free markets."[51] In this vein, as we develop a consumer protection law for the digital age the way we developed one for the industrial age, we must recognize that individual consumers do not have the financial, cognitive, temporal, and legal resources of corporations or law firms. Instead, consumers are often harried, distracted, short-sighted, cognitively impaired, impoverished, and sometimes even a bit drunk.

In addition to evaluating consumer goods and services, consumers have varying combinations of industrial-age commitments: jobs to go to, children or elderly parents to care for and transport to sports practices and doctors' appointments, taxes and voting to do, travel to plan, groceries to buy, meals to prepare, homes and gardens to maintain, healthcare appointments to navigate, health insurance companies to fight with over reimbursement or prescription approvals, healthy diets and exercise to manage, extended family and friends to keep in touch with, and somehow also to try to get a good night's sleep. (Phew!) And those are just the industrial-age commitments. They don't include the information-age tasks of emails to read and file, news to read, home network security to maintain, photos to back up, social media feeds to update and check, and all those ads to watch before they can watch the videos and other marvels of the "free" internet. Modern life and the incentives placed on human beings living in late capitalist, modern, networked societies have overleveraged the time and energy of most consumers, sometimes up to and beyond the breaking point, and we should not pretend otherwise. This is why so many of us believe that "modern life is so busy." Modern society has externalized (i.e., dumped) work onto us as a condition of participation in that society, such that we have become overwhelmed. No wonder we don't read privacy policies. In her book *Can't Even*, Helen Petersen argues that Millennials have become the burnout generation, paralyzed by endless errands, tasks, to-do lists, "side hustles," and the need to feel constantly busy and constantly market themselves. But it's not just Millennials; it's everyone.[52] Our consumer protection law should recognize the *situation* consumers are actually in and not treat them as if they had limitless resources of time and money, strong bargaining power, and access to sophisticated lawyers. This is what it means to think in terms of a *situated consumer*—taking consumers as they actually are in all of their complexity, rather than as some rhetoric and ideology might like them to be.

As we approach the challenges of consumer protection law for the information age, recall from chapter 2 how the economist Richard Thaler explained that we have learned from behavioral science that humans behave not like econs, the rational actors in economic models and textbooks, but rather like *humans*, like the people we actually know. We know from the experimental evidence that our situated consumers are bad at mental accounting and tend to be creatures of habit. How many automatically renewing subscriptions to services like cable TV, magazines, software, and streaming services do you have, and how many of them offered you a "free" first month? Defaults matter, too, because they are sticky—how often do you re-optimize your retirement account? (You might want to look at that.) Situated consumers are *particularly* bad at assessing future risk, which they tend to discount. This can be a problem when consumers are asked to "rationally" make choices about their human information that can expose them to future data-based risk of harm, and it's particularly a problem when they don't fully understand the legal agreements they are implicitly agreeing to, the technology they are using, or the future risks they are exposing themselves to.

Situated consumers are also really bad at making lots of choices. Hard thought is costly for our brains, depleting its glucose reserves in ways that are analogous to the ways the glucose in our muscles are depleted when we run or ride a bike. As Daniel Kahneman explains, this means that "decision fatigue" is not just a metaphor; it's a phenomenon with a biochemical basis.[53] This is also why, however we frame it, choice, consent, and control can be valid only when they are infrequent.[54] We can make a limited number of big choices well, but we can't possibly make hundreds of little ones, whether all at once or one after the other. Thus, we can rationally choose which candidate to vote for, whom we want to marry, or what car we want to buy,‡ but we cannot rationally and carefully make thousands of decisions about the privacy and security practices of websites, apps, mobile games, social networks, video services, or health insurance selections, in addition to all of the thousands of similar little decisions we are asked to make each day. Michael Pollan's concept of the "omnivore's dilemma"—what to have for dinner each and every day[55]—is particularly hard when it is added on top of all of these decisions. ("Don't you want to receive more relevant ads?" "Do you want to rate this product online for a coupon?" "Slacks or jeans today?" "Would you like a free

---

‡ Though beware the cognitive tricks and choice architecture of unscrupulous car dealers, particularly when it's time to visit the financing department.

month of premium service?" "What combination of ingredients in my house will make a satisfying and healthy meal that everyone I live with will like?") It's even harder when consumers also have to fight *choice architecture*—psychologically nuanced loaded questions that serve the interests of the company rather than those of the customer. (There are so many examples, but consider [a] prechecked default boxes to receive marketing or to auto-renew; [b] "Are you *sure* you want to forgo future valuable offers?" pop-ups; [c] "And which of our yummy chocolate cakes will you be having for dessert, sir?" questions from waiters, etc.) Companies, after all, usually want more sales or engagement, while customers want to save money, preserve time, make good decisions, and not overeat. What is more, the more we deplete our limited reserves of rational choice with trivial decisions from the ceaseless barrage of architected choices, the less glucose (or bandwidth, if you prefer) remains for making choices that matter to us. This creates a real risk that situated consumers become too overwhelmed by the trivial choices dumped on them in their daily commercial roles that they are too tired for rational choice when it really matters—like whether it's a good idea to answer that text while driving or whom they should vote for in their capacity as citizens. We should design our laws not just to preserve spaces for privacy but also to preserve spaces for thoughtful democratic participation.

Corporations know that people aren't econs, and they take advantage of it. When they put their innovation rhetoric to one side, when they design interfaces and incentive programs, target ads and set prices at $19.99 rather than $20, corporations are treating consumers as humans rather than econs. Our law should also treat us as humans rather than econs. It should recognize that consumers aren't perfectly rational actors, that they are limited in time, mental bandwidth, legal training, money, and rationality. They are *situated* in their economic and social context, and consumer protection law should meet situated consumers where they actually are: exposed, tracked, sorted, marketed, and at risk of manipulation. A situated consumer model is one that more accurately reflects the situations consumers actually find themselves in and the way that ordinary people behave. It is certainly more honest than insisting on consumers being econs exercising rational notice and choice in ignorance of the enormous body of scientific evidence to the contrary. Consumers certainly need to bear some responsibility for their choices, but the old doctrine of *Caveat emptor*—"Buyer beware"—should not be the lodestar for consumer protection in the information economy. (Even Roman law had some consumer protection rules, it turns out, designed of course for its own time and for its own consumers.)[56] But if we ignore the situated consumer in a world where companies can deploy those potent cocktails of behavioral science and data science against us, we risk returning to that brutish world of the consumer state of nature.

The situated consumer approach to consumer protection I am suggesting would certainly represent a change in how we think about consumer protection. But it need not be a radical transformation. The situated consumer model as I have described it is not so different from the basic principles of consumer protection law as they developed in response to the problems of the industrial age. It is merely an updated model that reflects changed power dynamics and the more advanced state of the behavioral sciences, both what we know about consumers in practice and how firms can and do use that knowledge to manipulate them. Twentieth-century American consumer protection law first tried to deal with the immediate industrial problems of monopolies and trusts by protecting consumers from unfair competition.[57] The law continued to evolve over the course of the twentieth century, adding consumer protections such as prohibitions on unfair and deceptive trade practices. These came from the federal government, first with the Federal Trade Commission Act of 1914's prohibition on "unfair methods of commerce" (to which "unfair and deceptive trade practices" were added in 1938),[58] and they were followed by a thicket of state regulations of unfair and deceptive practices in the 1960s.[59]

Legal scholar Ryan Calo and ethnographer Alex Rosenblat argue that while consumer protection law certainly has its complexities, two of its features are salient:

> First, the law assumes the marketplace will function improperly and to the detriment of consumers absent government intervention of some sort. Second, determining what acts or practices are permissible requires the regulator or court to look at both the real-world options consumers have in the marketplace and the prospect that consumers will be able to exercise meaningful choices regarding goods and services in practice. Detecting and addressing harmful asymmetries of information and power among firms, and between firms and consumers, is thus at the heart of consumer protection law.[60]

This is an excellent starting point from which to approach the consumer protection problems of the information age. To Calo and Rosenblat's statement of the goals of consumer protection, I would propose two friendly additions. First, looking at people in the real world as situated consumers will require a more searching inquiry and greater protection than American law has given them to date. Digital technologies and behavioral science now offer more opportunities for manipulation, more asymmetries of power, and more opportunities for the marketplace to function improperly. American consumer protection law's inability to move much past "notice and choice" in the quarter of a century that we have been talking about "electronic," "internet," and now "digital" privacy is simply inexcusable. America's failure to produce a comprehensive privacy law for the age of the internet has dragged on for over twenty-five years, spanning the personal computer revolution, Windows 95, the arrival of the Web, the dot-com boom, the bursting of the dot-com bubble, the September 11 attacks, the rise of Google and Facebook, mass adoption of smartphones with location services, the rise of smartphone apps, the Snowden revelations, uncounted data breaches, the Cambridge Analytica scandal, the Covid-19 pandemic, and many other massive issues of privacy and the use and misuse of human information. It has been a failure of policy leadership, a failure of regulation, a failure of courage, and a failure of imagination. These failures has been made all the more apparent by European practice, in which the EU Data Protection Directive of 1995 was in effect for over twenty years before it was replaced by the more robust GDPR in 2018.[61] American law needs to do better to protect situated consumers as they are, in ways that are informed not by the increasingly inaccurate assumptions of the rational actor model but rather by what we know about consumer behavior and decision-making from behavioral science.

The second addition that I would offer to Calo and Rosenblat's formulation is that the future of consumer protection law will be *human information policy*, regardless of whether we think of privacy law moving in a consumer-protective direction or of consumer protection law coming to terms with the power of human information. The two bodies of law are distinct, but there must be substantial overlap if we are to develop the kind of protective countermovement for the information revolution that adequately grapples with the power effects of human information. Critically, consumer privacy law must protect consumers from deception and manipulation with increasingly *substantive* rules, not just fictional notice and the illusion of consent. Let's turn to what that would mean in practice.

Privacy Protections as Consumer Protections

When we look past the empty rhetoric of autonomous users of services receiving notice and making informed choices about how to control their privacy, we can see that consumer privacy law and consumer protection law—particularly in the United States—have a lot of work to do. At least, that's the case if American practice is to catch up with European practice and with the actual needs of consumers rather than the "needs" the rational actor model would assume. Consumer protection will require new privacy rules, but it's not obviously apparent precisely what privacy and consumer protection rules will be needed to protect the situated consumer. If we do nothing, we are likely to have business as usual, in which "free" services are provided in exchange for exploitation, in which privacy settings and data security protection are left to the self-management of overwhelmed and underinformed consumers, and in which situated consumers have no meaningful redress against exploitation and manipulation.[62] As we saw in the Cambridge Analytica scandal, this situation has ramifications beyond consumer protection to include the future of democracy itself. The stakes are high.

As I've mentioned already, this is a book about ideas rather than law reform, but given the stakes I have just laid out, it might be helpful for me to sketch out a few basics of what I think a situated consumer protection law for the information age should look like in the United States. At a minimum, there should be baseline protections for personal data. Unlike the rest of the world, the United States lacks a general data protection law, preferring to regulate privacy through sector-specific laws, oversight by the Federal Trade Commission for "unfair and deceptive" trade practices, and a record of industry self-regulation that is spotty at best and fraudulent at worst. However, even a general data protection law that merely gives consumers notice of data practices and the choice to opt out of services they don't want would be insufficient.[63] Even better notice and choice would still be notice and choice. Consumers rarely read or understand the notices they are given—the dense legal terms or vague advertising copy of many privacy policies and terms of service. Similarly, they usually lack meaningful choice. In response to the Trump administration's rollback of Federal Communications Commission privacy rules in April 2017, Representative Jim Sensenbrenner stated the rationale, "Nobody's got to use the Internet."[64] If not using the internet is a "choice," then this is an apt illustration of just how weak a "notice and choice" regime of privacy protection can be.

Instead of the thin proceduralism of "notice and choice," privacy law must be *substantive*, outlawing particularly harmful, dangerous, unfair, or misleading data practices instead of tiptoeing around these issues by focusing on the falsity of notice and the illusion of choice. Consumer privacy law for the information economy must ultimately become consumer *protection* law. What might that look like in practice? I think that as the law evolves to meet the changed and changing needs of situated consumers in digital environments, four initial strategies—two new and two old—seem most promising. The two old strategies would be to reinvigorate protections against *deception* and *unfairness*, while the two new ones would be to protect against *abusive* practices and consider *regulating services marketed as "free"* when they are really not. Let's look at each of them briefly in turn.

1. Deception. Deception, as we've already seen, is a basic element of consumer protection law. In the United States, the FTC has had authority over deception at least implicitly since its creation in 1914, and it has explicitly been able to prosecute cases of commercial deception since just before the Second World War.[65] The basic idea behind protecting consumers from deceptive business practices, just like the old law of fraud, is that if you lie to consumers, they can be tricked into making bad choices. Thus, false claims made to consumers in advertising, product labeling, and about the usefulness or safety of products, among other things, have long been basic violations of consumer protection law. In the digital context, the FTC has pursued deception claims since the late 1990s, notwithstanding its inability to seek fines in the first instance or to engage in regulatory rule-making on privacy.[66] Its early internet cases were carefully chosen to involve favorable prosecutorial facts like harm to children, and deception rather than unfairness.[67] These were used to elicit settlement agreements that could be enforced for money damages, as most notably with Facebook's $5 billion fine for its Cambridge Analytica–related breach of an earlier deception settlement.[68] As the FTC's activities in cyberspace developed, it encouraged companies to have privacy policies as a commercial norm. This norm was further encouraged by privacy policy requirements in sector-specific laws and by business arguments that self-regulation under a "notice and choice" model (where the "notice" was provided by privacy policies) was a better alternative to federal regulation.[69] Thus, between 1998 and 2001, the use of privacy policies exploded such that by 2001, "virtually all of the most popular commercial websites had privacy notices."[70] While privacy policies have long been an extremely limited tool for letting consumers know what is happening to their human information, they proved much more useful to the FTC in its role as privacy cop when, as frequently happened, the actual behaviors of companies "mov[ing] fast and break[ing] things" were quite different from the promises made in their privacy policies.[71] These "broken promises of privacy" cases thus became the leading edge of FTC privacy enforcement, which became more useful as the legal and economic incentives for companies to have privacy policies increased.[72] But they have been limited to policing the often vague assertions made by companies in their privacy policies and limited by the FTC's budget to bring enforcement actions with no fines for first-time offenders.

We can do better on deception. The FTC approach in the United States has been a carefully engineered and entrepreneurial approach based upon its limited legal and financial resources. (Some might even call it "innovative.") But it is insufficient to deal with the vast complexity of digital commerce in the 2020s. One minimal step might be to require more than just privacy policies—we could require standard-form information practice labeling the way we have nutritional labels on packaged foods and credit term disclosures on credit applications.[73] Such notices must go beyond the passive boilerplate; they must be for terms that matter, and they must be ones that the consumer is aware of, whether under Calo's idea of "visceral notice" or the duty of affirmative honesty that Woodrow Hartzog and I have called for.[74] We could also expand "deception" to cover not just broken promises but broken expectations that consumers might reasonably have about what companies do and should do with their data, expectations that we should measure from the transaction as a whole and not just from what is buried and often unread in the privacy policy.[75] This would be important where situated consumers bring inaccurate assumptions and cognitive biases to transactions, and particularly so when those assumptions and biases are encouraged or exploited by companies through design of interfaces or choice architecture.[76] We could also solve some of the current limits on FTC enforcement by giving it more funding and new tools or by allowing consumers to sue under private rights of action for liquidated damages, the way many other privacy and consumer protection statutes (including some state unfair and deceptive practices statutes) work.

2. Unfairness. The other classic tool of consumer protection law is unfairness. Unlike deception, which asks about whether company statements are true or false, unfairness looks to the substance of the terms and asks whether they are the kinds of business practices that are commercially reasonable in their operation. Unfairness has been more controversial in the United

States than deception, and the FTC's unfairness authority is limited by a test requiring it to prove a firm has engaged in a business practice that "causes or is likely to cause substantial injury to consumers which is not reasonably avoidable by consumers themselves and not outweighed by countervailing benefits to consumers or to competition."[77] In practice, the two additional limitations of consumers not being able to reasonably avoid a practice and injury that is outweighed by a benefit to competition have restrained unfairness authority. Nevertheless, the FTC has used its unfairness authority in its privacy enforcement actions, arguing, for example, that it is an unfair business practice to make retroactive changes to a privacy policy, to collect data under false pretenses or through spyware, to use data in improper ways, and to design software or websites in ways intended to trick consumers.[78]

The FTC has been particularly aggressive in using its unfairness authority in data security and data breach cases, arguing that it is an unfair business practice for companies to fail to develop "reasonable" information security safeguards.[79] Data security law is an important subset of privacy law. Data security obligations placed on those who collect and use a person's information are less about what the company does with the data with respect to the person and more about protecting that data from unlawful access by hackers and other third parties. William McGeveran has argued forcefully that a duty of data security that is "reasonable under the circumstances" is emerging in the United States, driven by a variety of forces. As he puts it:

> [B]oth public law and the private sector have converged on a clear under-
> standing of the duty of data security owed by companies ... when they store
> personal data. Regulated parties are already shaping their data security
> measures in response. Like most businesses, they try to do so with common
> sense: they weigh costs and benefits, assess risk, and invest accordingly.[80]

Of course, the emerging consensus hasn't stopped businesses from pushing back on the emerging duty of data security on the grounds that it is vague and imposes requirements that they cannot understand. Wyndham Hotels raised a claim like this after it had done nothing to respond to a series of breaches of vast amounts of customer credit card numbers and other data facilitated by its own "atrocious" data security practices.[81] Wyndham challenged the FTC's unfairness authority in court and made a series of increasingly hyperbolic arguments that the court on the whole dismissed. To Wyndham's argument that unfairness required proof that it had acted inequitably, the appellate court responded, "A company does not act equitably when it publishes a privacy policy to attract customers who are concerned about data privacy, fails to make good on that promise by investing inadequate resources in cybersecurity, exposes its unsuspecting customers to substantial financial injury, and retains the profits of their business."[82] And the court had even less patience with Wyndham's claim that the FTC's assertion of unfairness authority had no limits, arguably giving it the power to regulate locks on hotel room doors or letting it prosecute supermarkets that were "sloppy about sweeping up banana peels."[83] "The argument is alarmist to say the least," responded the court, noting that "it invites the tart retort that, were Wyndham a supermarket, leaving so many banana peels all over the place that 619,000 customers fall hardly suggests it should be immune from liability under [the FTC Act]."[84] That may be both true (and funny) in the context of Wyndham's "atrocious" security practices, but FTC unfairness authority over the content of data security practices in harder cases remains in dispute.[85]

Just as with deception, when it comes to the consumer protection problems of the information age, we can do better with unfairness. Here, too, we could imagine an FTC with both rule-making power and the ability to bring damages actions in the first instance as being a more effective enforcer across the field of human information practices, and not just in the area of data security and data breach. Rule-making—the power to specify more detailed requirements—would also provide better notice to companies of what is required than merely being "reasonable under the circumstances." It would also take away the ability of companies to argue that they didn't know what the law required them to do in the first place, banana peel retorts notwithstanding. (I'll note in passing the hypocrisy that companies have long thought the vague notice in privacy policies should be enough for consumers to understand what their own risks and liabilities are.) Retaining a general prohibition on "unfairness" will remain important in a time of changing technology so that the FTC can keep up with the times as it has rather well since 1914.

Beyond these issues, the law of commercial unfairness should recognize the pathologies of consent. Even when companies don't lie in their privacy policies, most consumers have no idea what they are agreeing to in digital contracts, have little understanding of the technologies or risks, and are subject to choice architecture that makes them dance to the tune of the designer. As Hartzog and I have suggested elsewhere, our law could thus invalidate consumer contracts that are premised on consent that is unwitting, coerced, involuntary, or some combination of the three.[86] Doing so would cut through the fiction perpetuated by "notice and choice" and privacy self-management that we have consented to all of this and that companies thus owe little to no responsibility—*Caveat emptor*. Potential rules like these show how unfairness could (and arguably should) develop into a law of substantive prohibitions rather than relying on procedural manufacturing of consent through privacy policy notice and "Nobody's got to use the Internet" fictional choices. It would not mean the end of choices about privacy, but it would mean the end of fictions like privacy self-management letting companies dictate the terms of privacy while pretending consumers had both agreed and had a meaningful choice to do so. This includes the fictional "consent" that by using the internet we all "agree" to have everything we read tracked, sorted, assessed, and sold to unknown buyers, all so that this surveillance can deliver us "more relevant ads"—a bully's argument of the worst kind, and one that is clearly unfair.

3. **Abusiveness.**   As we've seen, deception and unfairness are industrial-age tools that have done heroic work for almost a century. But as Justice Brandeis reminded us in 1928, "Time works changes, brings into existence new conditions and purposes. Therefore a principle to be vital must be capable of wider application than the mischief which gave it birth."[87] Deception and unfairness are useful concepts with which to understand and group particular kinds of business practices that are problematic when used against consumers. They are also industrial-age concepts; as we've seen, the FTC has had the power to prosecute unfair and deceptive trade practices since the early twentieth century. A century further on, as we envision a consumer protection law for the information age, we should imagine new concepts to understand and group problematic information-age business practices. One concept that we should seriously consider is the idea of an "abusive trade practice." We've already seen the ways in which insights from the behavioral sciences can be built into the designs of interfaces, websites, choice architecture, and other places of interaction between companies and consumers to nudge consumers into spending more time or money to the benefit of the company. These engineered spaces can be physical as well as digital; the power of design is frequently used by casinos, amusement parks, and supermarkets to build the physical environments in ways that benefit the companies wielding the power of design.[88] And of course, all of these forms of manipulative design are made more powerful when combined with the insights of data science

about how both consumers in general and individual consumers in particular behave. In his book *Privacy's Blueprint: The Battle to Control the Design of New Technologies*, Hartzog argues that these new forms of "abusive design" are especially problematic because they are intended to misrepresent reality and subvert expectations—put bluntly, they target our mental heuristics to get us to do what the companies want rather than to make what would be "rational" choices. Hartzog argues that our "law should be concerned about designs that *interfere* with people's ability to discern whom to trust . . . or that *take unreasonable advantage* of people's *understanding, limited abilities*, or *reliance* on relationships and transaction costs. In other words, privacy law should ask whether a particular design interferes with our understanding of risks or exploits our vulnerabilities in unreasonable ways with respect to our personal information."[89] Protections of this sort already exist in the law. In addition to the older example of restrictions on subliminal advertising we saw in chapter 2, the Dodd-Frank Act passed in the aftermath of the financial meltdown in 2009 gives the Consumer Financial Protection Bureau the ability to prohibit "abusive" trade practices that interfere with a consumer's ability to make rational decisions. Extending these sorts of protections to transactions structured by choice architecture and powered by personal data and intentional cognitive nudges would represent a meaningful and appropriate first step towards information age consumer protection.

4. **Rethinking the "free" internet.**   Let me offer a final, more radical way in which consumer protection rules might safeguard privacy, which is to question the whole notion of the "free" internet itself. This is the argument that one way to protect consumer privacy might be to treat promises of "free" services as inherently deceptive, unfair, or abusive. Consider that for many years, Facebook's website displayed the slogan "It's free and always will be." Although the sign was quietly removed in August 2019, the company continues to maintain that it is free, a promise that covers well over a billion customers.[90] Other tech companies—most notably Google—call their services free, as do many apps and digital games that use advertising and the sale of customer data to (as they would put it) "monetize user data." But "free" in this context is misleading. It also nicely illustrates both the data science and behavioral tricks that warrant a consumer protection law for the information age. This is the case for three distinct reasons.

First, these services may be touted as free to the extent that they don't charge money, but they are certainly not free because there is an economic transaction taking place. A few years ago, I traded a child's bicycle that my daughter had outgrown to my friend Alex in exchange for an adult bicycle that he didn't need after buying a nicer one. Although this transaction took place between friends, it was not free: we each gained a used bike (one for me, and one for Alex's daughter), but we each lost a bike as well. We each purchased a new bike from a bike shop as well: Alex bought his new bike, and I bought a new bike for my daughter. None of these bike transactions was free. By the same token, it is not free when I have to watch a thirty- or sixty-second advertisement before I watch a video on YouTube. I certainly get something (a video I likely will enjoy), but I also lose something (up to a minute of watching an ad that I almost certainly will not). That's a transaction, and it's not free. Companies know full well that these fake-free digital transactions are enormously valuable, particularly in the aggregate. Ten billion transactions worth only one cent each are worth $100 million in total. This is the inescapable economic logic of tech companies offering "free" services "at scale." You might not notice the value of your time wasted watching an ad, but their services do, tracking it, aggregating it, and sending a bill to their advertiser clients. In this way, taking a little bit of value from lots of people who don't notice it, they generate a vast fortune.[§] As the commercial law scholar David Adam Friedman puts it bluntly, truly free offers are gifts, and ad-supported services are not gifts. These are economic transactions with highly profitable companies, and those profits are generated often entirely from these assertedly "free" transactions for work performed by their "users."[91] Calling this "free" sounds a lot like deception.

There's a second way in which "free" services are problematic, which goes to the business model of what Shoshanna Zuboff calls "surveillance capitalism." We saw in chapter 3 how technology companies noticed that every transaction with their human customers generated additional "metadata" about the transaction. This was the case, for example with serving up search results, YouTube videos, Gmail, or ads. Zuboff documents how Google took this unclaimed data generated by people using its "free" services and used

[§] This is, incidentally, strikingly similar to the plot of the movie *Superman III*. In that film, computer programmer Gus Gorman (played by Richard Pryor) learns that his paycheck for $143.80 likely includes a fraction of a cent extra due to taxes, rounding, and other mathematical factors. Gorman then writes a computer program to take all of those fractions of a cent from other people's paychecks (as tech companies would say today, "at scale"), making his next paycheck $85,789.90. Innovative, no? The Tesla not having been invented yet, he drives to work the next day in his new Ferrari. This technique is known as "salami slicing," named for the practice of taking tiny slices off a large salami such that no one notices they are missing. Cf. Kevin Carr, *Getting Rich With Richard Pryor's Banking Scheme From Superman III*, FILM SCHOOL REJECTS, Aug. 14, 2011. To be clear, Gus Gorman is the bad guy.

it to profile, predict, and ultimately influence them as part of the new "surveillance capitalism" business model.[92] Because the metadata could be used to enhance their model for better consumer predictions, it could be used to serve more effective—and more lucrative—advertisements to them. As Zuboff puts it, with "Google in the lead, surveillance capitalism vastly expanded the market dynamic as it learned to expropriate human experience and translate it into coveted behavioral predictions."[93] Companies can talk all they want about the power of "personalized" ads, but we have seen time and time again in this book how personal information confers power over other people, and how that power can be used to control behavior, whether subtly or bluntly. Notice that what's taken here is not just the time spent watching the ad (to which the consumer presumably consented) but also the metadata from the transaction that is then used for the company's purposes, usually to the detriment of the consumer. And remember that when Target delivered "personalized" ads to pregnant women, it deceptively buried its payload of manipulation—the coupon for baby formula—in the coupon page surrounded with innocuous and deliberately irrelevant ads for wine glasses and lawn mowers. From this perspective, "free" surveillance capitalism is both deceptive and unfair.

But there's a third problem with "free" services, which goes to why many companies are so keen to brand their services as "free" in the first place. Companies have long had the intuition that "free" is a powerful signal to consumers, notwithstanding the old saying "There's no such thing as a free lunch." Emerging evidence in the behavioral sciences indicates that something curious happens to our minds when we see those four magical letters F-R-E-E. When we think about something being free, we tend to overvalue its benefits to the extent that it skews our ability to engage in rational cost-benefit analysis.[94] In practice, this means that consumers overwhelmingly (and perhaps irrationally) choose "free" services and apps over those that have a nominal cost, and that "free" services tend to drive out the ones that cost money, even when that cost is nominal or insignificant.[95] Chris Hoofnagle and Jan Whittington, a lawyer and a social scientist, explain how "free" pricing acts as a psychological enticement to consumers to try products without appreciating future costs or risks. In the context of digital services, they argue, particularly where there is the "hidden charge [of the] forfeit of one's personal information" the word "free" can create a biased perception by consumers of the true nature of the transaction.[96] This occurs all too frequently because consumers cannot adequately assess the value of their personal information to themselves or to the company and cannot assess the risks of the transaction.[97] It's yet another of the mental heuristics that behavioral science has uncovered as a way that we depart from the rational actor model, and it's yet another opportunity for consumer manipulation. The intentional use of the word "free" by companies involved in data transactions creates predictably irrational calculations in consumers, imposes costs upon them that they often cannot recognize or assess, and does so in a way that is hidden. This sounds like deception, unfairness, and abusiveness.

Let me be clear at this point: I am not arguing that companies should not be able to give away free samples or have advertiser-supported products. But I am suggesting that it is problematic for tech companies to offer "free" products that exploit cognitive bias, affect a consumer's rational risk calculus, take customer information in a way that is not transparent, and then use that data to make advertising ever more effective (and perhaps further manipulative) for company profit. What is more, these practices are problematic in ways that traditional consumer protection law has failed to properly comprehend and protect against. In part, this is because these practices present new challenges as a consequence of the information revolution. We should not be surprised that our existing law has failed to grapple with these new challenges. But by the same token, we should not assume—as some suggest—that existing law is adequate to the task and must be left alone to avoid "stifling" innovation. The goal of consumer protection law, after all, is to protect consumers from the kinds of exploitation and injury that we cannot reasonably expect them to avoid on their own. "Free" digital services of the sort I have described here would seem to fall squarely within this category.

Banning, of course, isn't the only way to deal with problematic business practices. There are many ways to regulate that fall well short of a complete ban. Hoofnagle and Whittington suggest, for example, that when digital services are offered in return for data we could require companies to be more explicit about the data portion of the transaction, or we could require them to offer a reasonably-priced paid option instead of a data grab.[98] Other options might include banning "free" months of a service with automatic enrollment for a fee. Or we might use behavioral science to protect consumers by flipping the default and requiring a consumer to opt in to continue service after the free month. This would require consumers to take a conscious step to re-enroll, turning the default around to ensure actual consent rather than passive consent. (It's also how free samples work at the food court: if I accept a free bite of fried chicken, I have to take an affirmative step to buy the whole chicken sandwich.) My argument here, as elsewhere in this section, is not so much to call for a particular reform as it is to illustrate the ways in which privacy rules can advance the mission of consumer protection in a digital age—and in particular the ways in which they can counteract the new techniques generated by the power of human information and leveraged by research in the behavioral sciences. It's all about meeting—and protecting—situated consumers where they actually are and the way they actually are.

Building Digital Trust Through Privacy Rules

Cambridge Analytica's efforts to influence elections using Facebook's human data had been known in the privacy community since at least 2015. But when, as noted in chapter 4, the story became a global scandal in early 2018, Facebook founder Mark Zuckerberg was compelled to respond publicly. What he said was fascinating, at least for anyone interested in the ways we think about privacy and the rules governing human information. Zuckerberg conceded not just that the scandal resulted from a "breach of trust" between Facebook and Cambridge Analytica, but that "it was also a breach of trust between Facebook and the people who share their data with us and expect us to protect it."[99] He also explained:

> [T]he feedback that we've gotten from our community and from the world is that privacy and having the data locked down is more important to people than maybe making it easier to bring more data and have different kinds of experiences. And I think if we'd internalized that sooner and had made these changes that we made in 2014 in, say, 2012 or 2010 then I also think we could have avoided a lot of harm.[100]

In so doing, the man who infamously declared in 2010 that "the age of privacy is over" and thus "went for it"[101] confessed not only that he had been grievously wrong but that privacy rules are essential because they build trust.

Trust is beautiful. The willingness to accept vulnerability to the actions of others is the essential ingredient for friendship, commerce, transportation, and virtually every other activity that involves other people. It allows us to build things, and it allows us to grow. Trust is everywhere, even where it is not obvious, and as Zuckerberg belatedly realized in 2018, trust is crucially at the core of the information relationships that have come to characterize our modern, digital lives. We trust that architects and builders have created bridges that will support us when we cross them. We trust that merchants will accept the small, green pieces of paper (or digital code) we've earned in exchange for goods and services. We trust that airplanes will arrive safely and at the correct airport. We trust that professionals in our service will act in our best interests, and we trust that our friends will support us and look out for us. Without trust, our modern systems of government, commerce, and society itself would crumble. Trust is also the essential ingredient for our digital lives. So much of modern networked life is mediated by information relationships, in which professionals, private institutions, and the government hold information about us as part of providing a service. Such relationships are everywhere we look. We see them when we share sensitive (and not so sensitive) personal information with internet service providers, doctors, banks, search engines, credit card companies, and countless other information recipients and intermediaries. We also see these relationships as we get information via full-sized and pocket-sized computers to access apps, social media, and the internet at large. As we have seen, even relationships that used to have no significant informational component—those with grocery stores, airlines, political parties, and the like—are now part of the data game. Merchants use data to predict what shoppers will do. Companies give away products and services "for free" just to get the information that comes with it. Data brokers amass vast troves of data to enable their clients to profile, segment, and influence people as consumers or as voters. The stampede for big data and the construction of the "Internet of Things" are only accelerating these developments. If we want a sustainable digital society, we need strong, trusted information relationships.

Relationships between people and their ISPs, social networks, and hired professionals are properly understood in terms of privacy. But the way we have talked about privacy has a pessimism problem: privacy is often thought of in negative terms, which leads us to mistakenly look for "creepy" new practices, focus excessively on harms from invasions of privacy, and place too much weight on the ability of individuals to opt out of harmful or offensive data practices. In addition, privacy advocates are frequently seen as standing in the way of progress, complaining about the things technology companies are not doing (like protecting human data) rather than the good things they are doing (like cloud storage, email, and "free" GPS apps). From this perspective, privacy claims start to look like an obstacle, a cost, or a barrier in the way of a sparkling digital future.

There is another, better way to think about privacy as we reshape our laws. Privacy rules don't just protect us from harm; they can also be used to create good things, like trust. In a series of academic papers, Hartzog and I have argued that privacy can and should be thought of as enabling trust in our essential *information relationships*.[102] Information relationships are ones in which information is shared with the expectation it will not be abused and in which the rules governing the information sharing create value and deepen those relationships over time. If privacy is increasingly about these information relationships, it is also increasingly about the trust that is necessary for them to thrive, whether those relationships are with other humans, governments, or corporations. This vision of privacy creates value for all parties to an information transaction and enables the kind of sustainable information relationships on which our digital economy must depend. The work that Hartzog and I have done on trust has not been done in isolation; it has been developed with the aid of a growing community of scholars in law, business, and the social sciences who see the potential of privacy rules to enable the trust our emerging digital society needs to thrive.[103]

If we want to build trust in our technologies that run on personal information, four factors will be essential. These factors apply to any institution (whether a company or a government) that wants to develop sustainable trust relationships with the humans whose data it wants to collect, hold, and use. First, trustworthy institutions are *discreet* about the human information they hold. When it comes to human data, we should be able to presume that our data will not be disclosed or sold without our knowledge. Of course, many of our technologies do require some sharing of human information; when that happens, a second trust principle—*honesty*—comes into play. Trustworthy institutions are *honest* about their data practices. Since the 1970s, privacy laws in the United States and around the world have required institutions to give notice about the ways they use human data. In practice, as we've seen, this notice has often been reduced to no more than densely worded legalese tucked away in a privacy policy that few people bother to (or are able to) read. Honesty requires more—it requires an affirmative obligation to correct misunderstandings and ensure that the humans whose data is processed understand what is going on. Third, trustworthy institutions are *protective* of the human information they hold. Unlike discretion, which requires institutions to limit their own ability to promiscuously share data with friendly (and often paying) third parties, being protective requires institutions to safeguard the data against hostile third parties such as hackers or identity thieves. Most telling, this means taking reasonable precautions to secure human data against breaches and to minimize the damage caused by those breaches and by the lapses that will inevitably happen over time. Finally, and perhaps most important, trustworthy institutions are *loyal*. Loyalty means that an institution should take a page from the law of fiduciaries and put our well-being over its own short-term financial gain from our data.[104] Loyal companies will act in our best interests to the extent of our relationship and use data only to the extent it doesn't endanger or negatively affect us. Companies and governments should not use our data to affect our moods[105] (or influence our voting),[106] nor should they try to mold us into the kinds of consumers or voters they (or their advertisers) might desire us to be.[107] Loyalty means empowerment, not manipulation.

These four foundations of trust—discretion, honesty, protection, and loyalty—can certainly be built into the business practices of companies and governments that build or use the technologies of human information. Many companies do indeed try to build trust with their customers. For example, we can view Apple Corporation's battle with the FBI over the San Bernardino shooter's iPhone data as an example of such trust-building practices.[108] But as we are all too aware, many companies or government actors fail to build trust. There may also be market incentives for untrustworthy behavior—if your competitor is cheating with data, and you have to remain profitable, there can certainly be pressures to cheat like them. When that happens, the law can help promote trust by either creating incentives to act in trust-producing ways or (in more serious cases) by punishing practices that threaten or destroy trust.

Notice, though, how a focus on trust can change how we think about privacy in the consumer protection context. When there is trust, you can have choice again. When the law allows consumers to trust that they will not be exploited or harmed, the stakes on individual choices about privacy become lower. So, too, do the stakes on notice, where the need to read the fine print at one's peril are lessened by the company's legally binding promise that "I've got your back." Similarly, when privacy-backed trust enables successful long-term commercial relationships between businesses and consumers, privacy becomes a source of value for companies, because it enables them to keep their trusting customers.

Since the emergence of the World Wide Web in the mid-1990s, technologies powered by human information have promised us much, whether it was Google's "free" but ad-powered search engine, Facebook's and Twitter's "free" but ad-powered social networks, or the new generation of machine-learning technologies, including Netflix's (paid) recommendation engine and (likely very expensive) self-driving cars. Each of these technologies required human information—information about us—to function, and each of them requires a relationship of trust to function successfully for both the company and the customer. As we look into our digital future, trust will be even more important in developing new and seemingly magical technologies. Consider the emerging technology of precision medicine—the promise that scientists and doctors can use our individually sequenced genomes to determine what treatments, what drugs, and what doses are best calculated to improve our health in ways that are specific to each and every one of us. Precision medicine promises much, from personalized wellness programs to cancer-fighting treatments tailored to the unique genomes of individual tumors. But in order for these treatments to work, our doctors must sequence, keep, and safeguard our individual genomes—each person's unique genetic code.[109] Curing cancer has been a dream for a long time, and precision medicine holds the promise of bringing us closer to that goal. But it requires us to trust our doctors, insurance companies, genomic laboratories, and other healthcare corporations with our most sensitive information: the source code locked in our cells that tells our individual bodies how to function. Like most human technologies, genomic science is a tool with good and bad uses. While we hope that these techniques will be used to improve our health, they could also be used to set insurance premiums, determine who gets into which college and gets given which job, and drive the algorithms of dating services. The society of genetic apartheid depicted by the 1997 science fiction movie *Gattaca* no longer looks so remote a possibility. Yet privacy rules that promote trust can help steer the use of these emerging technologies in productive directions, particularly where those rules require those holding our genomes to be discreet, honest, protective, and loyal.

Trust is important for our emerging technologies, but it is equally essential to preserve many of the values and practices we've held dear for generations. As we confront the digitization of our democracy, our faith in the democratic process has been shaken by the manipulation of our politics and our elections by data-driven campaigning, the microtargeting of voters, and the prospect of digital voting machines being hacked by those seeking to undermine the integrity of democracy. Here, too, the four foundations of trust principles can help us identify the risks and propose solutions to safeguard our processes of government. We must ensure that governments and the companies that build our voting machines ensure that the privacy of the voting booth is *discreet*, that they are *honest* about the data risks of digital democracy, that the accurate tabulation of votes is *protected* from malicious outsiders so that we can have faith (so we can trust) that the outcomes are the product of processes that are *loyal* to the intentions of the voters and the long-established principles of our democracy. Where market incentives alone do not create trust, as will often be the case, we should consider imposing these duties through law.

* * *

It's a truism in military history that generals fight each war with the mindset—and the tactics—of the previous one. Thus, in the First World War, the French Army went to war with higher morale, hoping to avenge their defeat in the Franco-Prussian War. The French marched to war in their beloved red trousers (*les pantalons rouges*) alongside martial bands playing jaunty tunes to keep the troops in line. That army was destroyed in the industrialized misery of the Western Front in 1914–18, in trenches and dugouts and at the indescribably horrific Battle of Verdun. For the Second World War, the French generals learned from their mistakes and built the Maginot Line, the greatest military fortification in history, only for the German Blitzkrieg to go around it and over it with tanks and planes. There is a fundamental point here: human beings use strategies they think are likely to work. And what has worked in the past is likely to work again in the future, unless, like the French Army, we confront significant or revolutionary change. Law is similar: it is evolutionary and works from analogy from things in the past. Most of the time this is a highly successful strategy, until we confront a revolution. Thus, the strategies of classical liberalism with which lawyers approached the Industrial Revolution failed. Industrial financiers, workers, and consumers were simply too different from the model that had taken the Jeffersonian yeoman farmer as the basic building block of society. Financiers were just too wealthy, workers were too disempowered, and consumers lacked the knowledge to fix the items in their lives. Industrial-age consumer protection law helped to remedy these problems. It was never perfect, but as a tool it was better suited for the job than the old tools that were found to be ineffective. In this way, the law developed to help the matchstick men and women of the new industrial economy.

Today we confront the information revolution with a set of tools that we built for industrial life but that are proving inadequate for informational life.

The control theory of privacy was developed in a world where there was far less human information being collected and far fewer burdens placed upon consumers. In that bygone world, some version of notice and choice might have been possible. But those days are over, and we should avoid using outdated tools when we need to develop new ones. The information revolution, like the Industrial Revolution before it, represents a challenge to the law's imagination. We need to update our tools, develop new ones, and use legal rules to encourage trustworthy information relationships between companies and consumers. The new consumer protection law for the information age will need to merge with privacy law if we want it to be successful. But if we are successful, privacy rules protecting consumers will enable us to thrive as *situated consumers* in our information society, just as they also enable us to be *humans* and *citizens*.

Conclusion

Why Privacy Matters

There are remarkably few privacy absolutists. In fact, I don't know any. There may be some hermits or recluses out there, but none of the literally hundreds of privacy scholars, lawyers, and advocates I know would call for privacy all of the time. Humans are social creatures, and we long to connect and share with others. The academic discipline of privacy is no exception; it is a thriving community of scholars across disciplines who enjoy gathering to talk about their work on the future (and past) of privacy rules in our societies.* Connection is not merely a good thing for us humans; it's often essential. This is why Facebook's slogan of wanting to make the world "more open and connected" made such a good sound bite on the surface. What is more, the needs of human society often require incursions into the privacy of its members, whether for crime prevention, economic activity, or numerous other justifications. One such justification emerged seemingly out of the blue when I was finishing this book: the Coronavirus pandemic of 2020. When lockdown hit, human data became essential for treatment and tracing, and much of our communications and our life were driven to Zoom and other digital platforms. In our household alone, work, law school, high school, middle school, learning, volunteering, soccer practice, birthday and holiday celebrations, and privacy conferences—among many other things—became mediated by videoconferencing. Many of those meetings began with the notice that by entering the videoconference we were "consenting" to being recorded. At the same time, mandatory mask rules made all of us more anonymous when we left our homes. As I suggested at the beginning of Part 1, privacy is indeed everywhere you look.

Privacy, of course, must inevitably be reconciled with other competing values, often ones that might seem more pressing or urgent. When criminals

---

* That said, it's still funny when someone—usually one of my cousins—says to me, "How was the privacy conference? I bet you can't tell me!"

or terrorists are afoot, when an emergency is all around us, or when a disease is spreading and killing hundreds of thousands, it's easy to get scared and focus on the problems right in front of our eyes rather than on the longer-term interests privacy often protects. That's part of human nature. This problem is worsened because it's been difficult to agree on a definition of privacy that we all share. Is it about our bodies, our ability to control information, our homes, a right to hide discreditable things about ourselves, a "context-relative informational norm,"[1] or something else? Is it a quaint and old-fashioned value that gets in the way of positive things like health, safety, and "innovation"? As one leading privacy scholar put it aptly, "privacy has an image problem," and that image problem means privacy suffers when there are calls to "balance" the negative value of privacy against positive social goods.[2]

This book has had relatively little to say about the values that are often in tension with privacy. This is intentional. It's been my goal in this book to make the continued case for privacy on the occasion of its supposed death. I hope that I have succeeded in persuading you that (as the saying goes) reports of privacy's death have been greatly exaggerated. Privacy is, however, under attack, and I have attempted to explain why privacy matters on its own terms. I've done this because we are so used to thinking of privacy in terms of what we might lose on the other side of the calculus that we have forgotten to some extent what privacy does for us in the first place. If we must reconcile (or, as some would say, "balance") privacy against other values, we first need a better understanding of Why Privacy Matters. We need a better understanding of what it is and what it does for us. Otherwise, the scales will be tipped from the outset in favor of whatever real or concocted need of the moment asks for incursions into and increased knowledge about our lives. The choice architecture of our privacy calculus will already be rigged against it. We saw, for example in chapter 6, how, when a thin notion of privacy as rational choice is unfairly balanced against an overbroad and puffed-up notion of "innovation," consumers lose out. If we are going to reconcile privacy with other things we care about, let's do so with intellectual honesty, with an appropriately nuanced understanding of the many ways privacy is important and the human values it can promote.

That honest and nuanced understanding of privacy is precisely what I have tried to offer in this book. And now that we have seen the argument in all of its detail, it will be helpful to put the pieces back together so that we can appreciate it as a coherent (and hopefully persuasive) whole. To recap: Privacy is the degree to which human information neither is known nor used. Human information confers power over humans. Because privacy is about power, we should think about it in terms of the rules that govern human information, rules that constrain and channel that power. Because human information rules of some sort are inevitable, we should think about privacy in instrumental terms to promote human values. This focus allows us to dispense with some of the myths about privacy, like that it's about hiding dark secrets, that it's about control or creepiness, and that it is dying. Privacy isn't dying, but it is up for grabs. We should craft our human information rules to promote human values like human identity, political freedom, and consumer protection the way we have crafted our rules for free speech around the search for truth, self-government (which is very close to "freedom"), and autonomy (which is related to "identity"). If we do that, then we might have an information revolution that is closer to the promises of the tech industry and lives up to those promises of human connection, empowerment, and flourishing with which the internet broke onto the public stage in the 1990s. That, in a nutshell, is my argument, and it's what I hope that you, the reader, will take with you once you close this book. You may not agree with it, but I hope that you take it seriously and in the good faith with which it is intended.

Beyond summing up, it's customary in conclusions to books of this sort to offer some thoughts about where we should go from here. Privacy is everywhere in our lives, and offering a detailed reform agenda would likely be both disappointing and a distraction from the main point of this book, which is to make the case for privacy in a world that often thinks it is outmoded. Other work of mine has and will continue to explore how to protect privacy when it conflicts with other values, and how to do so concretely and with a level of technical legal detail that is useful in practice. It is in the details that our privacy will be preserved or whittled away, but without some sense of the big picture informing those details we will be unable to protect privacy effectively at all. We must also remember that we can have privacy *as well as* other values we care about, even where there is tension between and among them. For example, in my previous book, I showed how privacy lawsuits against the media are often in dangerous tension with free expression, but that commercial privacy rules and protections from nonconsensual pornography can live happily alongside the First Amendment. More fundamentally, I argued that intellectual privacy, far from being in tension with the values of free speech, is actually an essential if underappreciated bedrock value for anything remotely resembling effective democratic self-governance.[3] In this way, we can have privacy *and* free expression, independent journalism *and* regulation of both big tech and revenge porn.

When it comes to privacy, Helen Nissenbaum reminds us that context matters.[4] What may be an appropriate protection of privacy in one context may be inappropriate in another. Contexts vary across time and from culture to culture, however, which can complicate privacy analysis and turn context into a complicating factor. Context matters when it comes to privacy, but values matter as well, and privacy claims are at their strongest when they advance human values. As we approach the inevitable and inevitably hard decisions on the rules governing human information, we should approach those decisions with an appreciation of the human values that should guide our judgment. We should avoid privacy's myths, and we should strive to ensure that we have a shield of privacy to protect our human identities, our political freedom, and our protection from harm and manipulation as situated consumers. This book used three examples of the human values that privacy can serve, but there are others, including democratic deliberation, tolerance, and equality. Good privacy rules can also build trust in our social, political, and economic institutions, a trust that seems in desperate need of shoring up as I write these words in early 2021.

I will, however, offer one observation for the future, which is that, given the importance of privacy, we should start treating it as what it is: a *fundamental human right* that should be protected against the efforts of governments and private actors, whether those are companies or other individuals. Privacy, as we've seen, is already recognized as a fundamental right in Europe. Article 8 of the European Convention on Human Rights has recognized a fundamental right of privacy since 1950, while, as we've seen, the newer EU Charter of Fundamental Rights and Freedoms protects two kinds of privacy: private life in Article 7 and data protection in Article 8.[5] These rights are of course further protected in the EU's comprehensive General Data Protection Regulation.[6] American law does not protect privacy so robustly, but occasionally it hums the same tune. Congress passed the Privacy Act of 1974 in the aftermath of Watergate and Richard Nixon's White House tapes scandal. That law applied the Fair Information Practices to human information held by the federal government, and it declared in the Act's preamble that "the right to privacy is a personal and fundamental right protected by the Constitution of the United States."[7] But for last-minute lobbying by insurance companies and others, as we've seen, the Privacy Act would have applied to all databases of human information and not just those held by the federal government.[8] If Congress had held firm to its initial intent to protect data privacy across the board, the United States would have had a comprehensive privacy statute twenty years before the EU Directive of 1995 and forty years before the GDPR. As it happened, when the GDPR went into effect in May 2018, the United States lacked a comprehensive privacy statute. In the light of our experience over the past five decades, Congress's failure to extend the right to privacy to private-sector data in 1974 and in succeeding decades appears to have been a grievous error, enabling not just the surveillance-based ad model of the internet but clear and present threats to democracy itself, like the Cambridge Analytica scandal.

Of course, merely declaring privacy to be a fundamental right is just a first step, one that gives privacy the rhetorical heft and social power to do work. We need to preserve privacy against the government by continuing to interpret the Fourth Amendment in ways that offer protection (as Brandeis advised) as time passes and technology changes. We need to shore up the Fourth Amendment with revisions to our wiretapping laws that bring them out of the 1980s and offer both privacy protection and reasonable process for government access in a way that is suited to the 2020s. We need a comprehensive commercial privacy law that includes both more robust agency oversight as well as private rights of action for those whose privacy has been violated. We need to worry about data brokers, facial recognition, AI, and the ways that information can flow between companies and the government. And we need to preserve the ability of states to experiment with new kinds of privacy protections,[9] as California has done with reader and cloud privacy and Illinois has done with biometrics and facial recognition.[10] Because information power operates along existing fault lines and vulnerabilities in our society, we should be particularly sensitive to the privacy needs of marginalized groups and the contexts in which privacy rules operate on the ground.[11] And we should be sure that privacy remains vital on the ground rather than merely an airy right that we talk about and then ignore. Julie Cohen has argued that we often come at privacy questions backward, assuming autonomy rather than worrying about the conditions that make private and privacy-valuing individuals possible, and focusing on choice rather than focusing on the design, operational, and other practical details that make privacy possible and enable its personal and social benefits.[12] This is particularly a problem when privacy rules encounter a compliance culture that shows remarkable ingenuity to redefine privacy language and water down and co-opt regulations intended to make things better.[13] So as we work to protect privacy, let's do it the right way around, making sure it protects the most vulnerable as well as the powerful and is sensitive to how it operates in practice to advance the human values it enables.

As this book has explained, privacy protections have become central to our ability to participate in our digital society as individuals, citizens, and situated consumers. Even though we might think of privacy as being in tension with being part of a society, I've tried to argue that privacy makes being social possible. By allowing us to manage our boundaries and by protecting us from information power, privacy has become as necessary to our ability to participate fully in society as the First Amendment is necessary to our political freedom. Without privacy, we lack respite, our identities are shaped, our votes are nudged, we are exposed as consumers, and we cannot trust the digital world in which we live. Such a future would be a bleak one. We must reject it and work hard to ensure that it never comes to pass. If we are to learn from the mistakes of the past as we approach the future, we should recognize that privacy is fundamental to our digital lives and that a society without meaningful protections for privacy is inadequate. Privacy is a fundamental right, and we should recognize it—and broadly protect it—as such. As a fundamental right, privacy cannot simply be one that we can waive implicitly. Privacy must be built into the structure of our society the way that other protective structures are built in—like the rule of law, independent judiciary, a free press, and free expression in pursuit of democratic self-government and artistic expression.[†] And it cannot be protected just against the state. American law has recognized privacy as a fundamental right against the government since the 1960s, but its inability to articulate and protect privacy against private actors has a lot to do with the mess that we are in. Privacy as an idea is under threat, to be sure. But it is not dead, and we must not give up fighting for it. Meaningful protection of our privacy safeguards all of these values and more. It is indispensable, and we must fight to preserve it along with our other hard-won fundamental rights.

I'll offer one final thought about privacy. We are living in an information society, which means that our ability to have a meaningful say in how our human information is used is *everything*. Information is power, after all, and this is an information society. Within a few short years we will likely

---

[†] As I write this in early 2021, all of these essential institutional structures are under assault in the West from neoliberalism and demagogues, many of them taking advantage of new digital communications technologies and the fundamental right of free expression to disseminate and amplify their messages.

be surrounded by self-driving cars, connected smart homes, ubiquitous tracking of employees, augmented reality, artificial intelligence, and "precision medicine." Other marvels of the information age lie before us. As technological marvels do, they bring the promise of innovative and disruptive good and innovative and disruptive harm. As we confront these disruptions and challenges, human information will only become more important, not less, and privacy rules will continue to increasingly define how we live our lives as humans, citizens, and situated consumers. Information—particularly the ability to exploit information—is power. Human information and the technologies that run on it are becoming the foundation of our society. As more and more human information is collected, and as more and more activities are fueled by the exploitation of that data, the rules we set (or don't set) for our human information will determine what kind of society we live in. Is it one in which people are empowered to develop their identities, to be free from observation and domination by the state, and to fairly participate as consumers in the economy without being manipulated by the data-informed social sciences? Or will it be a society ordered from the top down, in which governments, companies, and other institutions can track and manipulate us for their own purposes, in which our data serves their ends rather than our own? If the past is any guide to the future, the answer will most likely lie somewhere in between these two poles. Yet where that answer lies is important—at least if we care about identity development, political freedom, consumer protection, and building trust in our digital future. Without a doubt, in the evolving information society that we live in, privacy has become the whole ball game. And that's why privacy matters.

Acknowledgments

I've been working on this book directly for about five years, but I've been struggling with the legal and social definitions of privacy ever since Dick Turkington and Anita Allen's *Privacy Law* casebook arrived unexpectedly in the mail in the autumn of 1999, when I was a twenty-five-year-old postdoc at the University of Alabama. Law school casebooks don't usually make for engrossing reading, but I sat in my office with it that afternoon for about two hours, completely transfixed by the organization of so many areas of the law that I loved into a single, more or less coherent whole. That book prompted me to realize that this thing Turkington and Allen called "privacy law" captured so many of my intellectual interests: history, computers, civil liberties, social power, and the fuzzy lines not just between public and private law but also among ourselves, other people, and the state.

As I mentioned in the introduction, I've learned an enormous amount from the hundreds of people I've talked with about privacy over the years. Perhaps none was more important to my decision to write this book than the Uber driver who took me from my hotel in Palo Alto to Stanford Law School for my *Intellectual Privacy* book talk in April 2015 and who assured me unequivocally that "Privacy Is Dead." Fittingly, in a book about privacy, I don't know her name, but of course Uber still does. That fifteen-minute conversation made me realize that I'd been having The Privacy Conversation for a while, and that maybe I should try to write it up for a broader audience. This book is the result.

I am incredibly grateful to have been able to work with amazing current and former colleagues at Washington University, a university with a vibrant interdisciplinary community of generous and brilliant scholars. At the risk of omission, for their repeated support and engagement with the ideas in this book, many thanks to Scott Baker, Patrick Crowley, Dan Epps, Trevor Gardner, John Inazu, Clare Kim, Pauline Kim, Frank Lovett, Greg Magarian, Sunita Prakash, Rachel Sachs, Bill Smart, Andrew Tuch, and Peter Wiedenbeck. My dean, Nancy Staudt, has been both a friend and a supporter of my work since 2003, when she was not yet an administrator but just a member of the appointments committee. She and Lee Epstein persuaded Wendy and me, on the basis of a couple of very good meals and a city tour in the back of Lee's tiny Audi, that St. Louis was the place we should start our life as parents and the place I should start my academic career. We are very glad that they did. I am also grateful to the other deans I've worked with for their support and encouragement: Joel Seligman, Dan Keating (twice), and Kent Syverud. Thanks also to my colleagues at the Cordell Institute for Policy in Medicine & Law at Washington University—particularly Jon Heusel and Patti Hageman—who have been tremendously supportive of this project and who have each improved it and made it easier for me to get it finished in a variety of ways.

This work has been shaped directly and indirectly by the dozens of scholars who are part of the international privacy scholars community, especially the participants at the annual Privacy Law Scholars Conference. One of my greatest professional delights has been the growth of this community over the years into the vibrant, brilliant, diverse, kind, and fun group of scholars that it is today. Again at the risk of omission, many thanks to Anita Allen, Lisa Austin, Jack Balkin, Ken Bamberger, Michael Birnhack, Vince Blasi, Joseph Blocher, Matt Bodie, Frederik Zuiderveen Borgesius, danah boyd, Julie Brill, Ryan Calo, Danielle Citron, Julie Cohen, Jen Daskal, Helen Dixon, Matt Dyson, Sarah Eskens, Chad Flanders, Amy Gajda, Sue Glueck, Seda Gurses, Gautam Hans, Woody Hartzog, Natali Helberger, Mike Hintze, Susan Hintze, Dennis Hirsch, Anna Lauren Hoffman, Chris Hoofnagle, Margaret Hu, Kirsty Hughes, Sarah Igo, Kristina Irion, Meg Jones, Thomas Kadri, Margot Kaminski, Leslie Kendrick, Ian Kerr, Orin Kerr, Jonathan King, Orla Lynskey, Alice Marwick, Hideyuki Matsumi, Bill McGeveran, Mark McKenna, Ed McNicholas, Kirk Nahra, Helen Nissenbaum, Paul Ohm, Jon Penney, Gavin Phillipson, Dave Pozen, Judith Rauhofer, Joel Reidenberg, Austin Sarat, Lauren Scholz, Paul Schwartz, Evan Selinger, Andy Serwin, Scott Skinner-Thompson, Dan Solove, Lior Strahilevitz, Joe Turow, Bart van der Sloot, Nico Van Eijk, Joris van Hoboken, Salome Viljoen, David Vladeck, Ari Waldman, Peter Winn, Chris Wolf, Tal Zarsky, Elana Zeide, Tim Zick, and Michael Zimmer. I am particularly grateful to Ari, Danielle, Julie, Ryan, and Woody, who each read large chunks of the draft and whose good humor helped keep me sane while I was finishing the manuscript during the pandemic lockdown. Our community lost both Joel and Ian while this book was being written. I miss them both and wish I could continue to talk with them about why privacy matters—and about so much else.

Two scholars in particular have had an outsized influence on the ideas in this book. The first of these is my Washington University colleague Pauline Kim. It is remarkable that the first thing Pauline said to me (a question at my Washington University job talk in October 2002) was to ask what I meant by "privacy." I tried and failed to give her a good answer that day—in fact, I think I also mistakenly called her by someone else's name—but somehow I still got the job. Over the nearly two decades since, Pauline has repeatedly asked me politely for a definition of privacy (and I have kept failing to give her a satisfactory one), until she finally told me that she thought I had implicitly developed one, a version of which appears in chapter 2 of this book as my "working definition." More generally, she has been an outstanding mentor, model colleague, and friend to me for a very long time, and I am extraordinarily grateful to her for her generosity and wise counsel over the years.

The second scholar whose work has influenced this book disproportionately is N. Woodrow Hartzog,* currently at Northeastern University. Woody has been my dear friend and coauthor for a decade now, and many of the new ideas in the argument of this book were developed either in conversations with him or in articles we have written together. This is particularly true of the trust idea developed in chapter 6, but it is true in other areas as well. I'm grateful for his friendship, for his partnership on the many things we have worked on together, and of course for his trust.

Both the book as a whole and the individual chapters have benefited from invitations to give lectures and feedback I've received at workshops at a variety of institutions around the world, including the University of Alabama, the University of Amsterdam, the annual meeting of the American Medical Informatics Association in San Francisco, Berkeley Law, Boston University School of Law, Dartmouth College, the Kenan Center for Ethics at Duke University, University of Edinburgh School of Law, the Federal Trade Commission, Florida State College of Law, Fontbonne University, Microsoft Corporation, Northeastern Law School, Notre Dame Law School, Ohio State Law School, Osgoode Hall Law School, the Privacy Law Scholars Conference at Berkeley and George Washington University, the Society of Law Scholars annual meeting at the University of Central Lancashire, Stanford Law School, St. Louis University School of Law, Tel Aviv University School of Law, UCLA

---

* Most people don't know this, but Woody's given first name is actually Neal, though he spells it the wrong way—with an "a" instead of an "i." He and I struggle to come up with things to disagree about, and so this and the relative merits of coffee versus tea are about the best we have come up with.

School of Law, the Washington University Institute for Informatics, the Washington University Political Theory Workshop, Washington University School of Law, and Yale Law School.

Many of the ideas that are advanced in this book were first developed in earlier academic articles. For example, some of the arguments in chapters 2 and 4 were first made in a series of articles I wrote with Jonathan King;[†] some of the arguments in chapter 3 are an updated version of some of the claims in my essay "Four Privacy Myths" and an article with Woody Hartzog that explored "the creepy trap";[‡] some of the arguments in chapters 4 and 5 were first made in my article "The Dangers of Surveillance";[§] and chapter 6 builds on a series of articles on privacy and trust, again with Woody Hartzog.[**] I am tremendously grateful to Jonathan and Woody for allowing me to expand on our joint work in this book.

I am also grateful to my many current and former students at Washington University who have brought their enthusiasm and intellectual gifts to the study of privacy law in my classes, particularly Information Privacy Law and my seminar (currently titled Digital Civil Liberties Seminar). I've had the great pleasure of working with many of these students as research assistants on either this book or some of the articles in which the ideas in it were first developed. For their help on this book, I'd like to thank Zach Barron, Juhi Patel, David Reck, and Casey Waughn. For their help with some of the underlying academic articles that influenced this book, I would like to thank Chini Bose, Matt Cin, and Carolina Foglia.

I am very lucky to have had the same faculty assistant for the past fifteen years. Rachel Mance is smart, resourceful, hard-working, creative, kind, generous, forthright, dependable, and unafraid to say what needs to be said when it needs to be said. So much of my professional success has been with

[†] Neil M. Richards & Jonathan H. King, *Three Paradoxes of Big Data*, 66 STAN. L. REV. ONLINE 41 (2013); Neil M. Richards & Jonathan H. King, *Big Data Ethics*, 49 WAKE FOREST L. REV. 393 (2014); Neil M. Richards & Jonathan H. King, *Big Data and the Future for Privacy*, in HANDBOOK ON DIGITAL TRANSFORMATIONS (F. Xavier Olleros & Majlinda Zhegu eds. 2016).

[‡] Neil Richards, *Four Privacy Myths*, in A WORLD WITHOUT PRIVACY? (Austin Sarat ed. 2015); Neil Richards & Woodrow Hartzog, Taking Trust Seriously in Privacy Law, 19 STAN. TECH. L. REV. 431 (2016).

[§] Neil Richards, *The Dangers of Surveillance*, 126 HARV. L. REV. 1934 (2013).

[**] Richards & Hartzog, *Taking Trust Seriously in Privacy Law*, *supra*; Neil Richards & Woodrow Hartzog, *Trusting Big Data Research*, 66 DEPAUL L. REV. 579, 590 (2017); Neil Richards & Woodrow Hartzog, *Privacy's Trust Gap: A Review*, 126 YALE L. J. 1180 (2017); Neil Richards & Woodrow Hartzog, *The Pathologies of Digital Consent*, 96 WASH. U. L. REV. 1461 (2019); Woodrow Hartzog & Neil Richards, *Privacy's Constitutional Moment and the Limits of Data Protection*, 61 B.C. L. REV. 1687 (2020).

her loyal help, and I am immensely grateful for all of her assistance and for our friendship.

My editor at Oxford University Press, Dave McBride, believed in the project from the beginning and, along with his OUP colleague Holly Mitchell, was once again a fantastic supporter and professional. Editors and academic publishers are tremendously important in the generation, improvement, and dissemination of ideas, and we do not treasure them as much as we should as a society—or as professional academics. Dave and Holly were also very gracious with revised deadlines as this project took longer to complete than I had anticipated, for which I am also very grateful.

I owe a great debt of thanks to my family and friends, some of whom I neglected to thank in my previous book, and one of whose names was misspelled in its first edition. (Sorry about that!) Special thanks to Chris & Keith, Dan & Lesley, Don & Peggy, Gretchen & Steve, Kassie, Kit & Anita, Jonathan & Christina, Matt & Cath, Scott & Victoria, Sue & Roy, Tom & Susan, as well as to my dad, Peter, my siblings, Emma and Adam, and their spouses, Jason & Leah.

Finally, and most of all, I owe enormous thanks to the three people I live with and love the most and who had the great misfortune to be locked in a house with me for months while a pandemic upended our society and I finished this book. My wife, Wendy, is the smartest, kindest, and most loving person I know. She has lived this project in long form over its twenty-year life, from its beginnings to the final proofreading and all points in between. For thirty years our life together has been a Grand Adventure, and I can't wait to see what happens next. I love you.

Our children, Fiona and Declan, are our greatest joy. They are smart, funny, ethical, kind, and resilient teenagers, and they are growing into the most amazing young adults. They have illustrated not just why privacy matters for young people but how young people manage their privacy as part of their lives, even when choices and practical capabilities are limited, whether through bedroom and bathroom doors, finstagrams, verbal codes, text pseudonyms, or other forms of resourcefulness. Young people like Declan and Fiona know that they need privacy and that privacy matters because it is about power, agency, and ultimately personhood. Like other young people, they are our future, but it is to these two young people in particular that this book is lovingly dedicated.

Notes

Introduction

1. Andrew Burt & Dan Geer, *The End of Privacy*, N.Y. TIMES, Oct. 5, 2017, https://www. nytimes.com/2017/10/05/opinion/privacy-rights-security-breaches.html.
2. Polly Sprenger, *Sun on Privacy: Get Over It*, WIRED, Jan. 26, 1999, http://www.wired. com/politics/law/news/1999/01/17538.
3. Jacob Kastrenakes, *Google's Chief Internet Evangelist Says "Privacy May Actually Be an Anomaly,"* THE VERGE, Nov. 20, 2013, https://www.theverge.com/2013/11/20/ 5125922/vint-cerf-google-internet-evangelist-says-privacy-may-be-anomaly.
4. Thomas Friedman, *Four Words Going Bye-Bye*, N.Y. TIMES, May 21, 2014, at A29.
5. Marshall Kirkpatrick, *Facebook's Zuckerberg Says the Age of Privacy Is Over*, READWRITE, Jan. 2, 2010, https://readwrite.com/2010/01/09/facebooks_zuckerberg_ says_the_age_of_privacy_is_ov/. In 2019, Zuckerberg recanted (or at least qualified) this statement in the wake of repeated Facebook privacy scandals, promising to "[build] a privacy-focused messaging and social networking platform." See Mike Isaac, *Facebook's Mark Zuckerberg Says He'll Shift Focus to Users' Privacy*, N.Y. TIMES, Mar. 6, 2019. I explore some of the privacy problems with this qualification in chapters 1 and 2.
6. E.g., Jonathan Vanian, *Why Data Is the New Oil*, FORTUNE, July 11, 2016, http://fortune.com/2016/07/11/data-oil-brainstorm-tech/; Joris Toonders, *Data Is the New Oil of the Digital Economy*, WIRED, July 2014, https://www.wired.com/insights/2014/07/ data-new-oil-digital-economy/. For a thoughtful exploration of the promise (and pitfalls) of this metaphor, see Dennis D. Hirsch, *The Glass House Effect: Big Data, the New Oil, and the Power of Analogy*, 66 MAINE L. REV. 373 (2014).
7. See Neil Richards & Woodrow Hartzog, *Privacy's Trust Gap*, 126 YALE L. J. 1180 (2017).
8. NEIL RICHARDS, INTELLECTUAL PRIVACY: RETHINKING CIVIL LIBERTIES FOR THE DIGITAL AGE (2015); see also Julie E. Cohen, *Examined Lives: Informational Privacy and the Subject as Object*, 52 STAN. L. REV. 1373–1438 (2000).
9. Justin McCurry, *South Korea Spy Agency Admits Trying to Rig 2012 Presidential Election*, THE GUARDIAN, Aug. 4, 2017, https://www.theguardian.com/world/2017/ aug/04/south-koreas-spy-agency-admits-trying-rig-election-national-intelligence-service-2012.

Part 1

1. Christine Utz et al., *(Un)informed Consent: Studying GDPR Consent Notices in the Field*, 2019 ACM SIGSAC Conference on Computer and Communications Security, Sep. 5, 2019, at 1 ("Since the adoption of the General Data Protection Regulation (GDPR) in May 2018 more than 60% of popular websites in Europe display cookie consent notices to their visitors.").

2. Lily Hay Newman, *Think Twice Before Giving Gifts With a Microphone or Camera*, WIRED, Nov. 29, 2019, https://www.wired.com/story/tech-gifts-microphones-cameras-be-careful/.

3. See, e.g., Carole Cadwalladr & Emma Graham-Harrison, *Revealed: 50 Million Facebook Profiles Harvested for Cambridge Analytica in Major Data Breach*, THE GUARDIAN, Mar. 17, 2018, https://www.theguardian.com/news/2018/mar/17/cambridge-analytica-facebook-influence-us-election; Issie Lapowsky, *How Cambridge Analytica Sparked the Great Privacy Awakening*, WIRED, Mar. 17, 2019, https://www.wired.com/story/cambridge-analytica-facebook-privacy-awakening/. The Cambridge Analytica whistleblower recounts his version of the Cambridge Analytica tale in CHRISTOPHER WYLIE, MINDF*CK: CAMBRIDGE ANALYTICA AND THE PLOT TO BREAK AMERICA (2019).

4. E.g., Joe Mandese, *How Palantir Enables ICE to Target Illegal Immigrants*, MEDIAPOST, July 15, 2019, https://www.mediapost.com/publications/article/338139/how-palantir-enables-ice-to-target-illegal-immigra.html (citing Homeland Security documents released through a FOIA request, *Unaccompanied Alien Children Human Smuggling Disruption Initiative: Concept of Operations*, May 5, 2017); Sam Levin, *Tech Firms Make Millions from Trump's Anti-Immigrant Agenda, Report Finds*, THE GUARDIAN, Oct. 23, 2018, https://www.theguardian.com/us-news/2018/oct/23/silicon-valley-tech-firms-making-money-trump-anti-immigrant-agenda-report.

5. See, e.g., Solon Barocas & Andrew D. Selbst, *Big Data's Disparate Impact*, 104 CALIF. L. REV. 671 (2016); Pauline T. Kim, *Data-Driven Discrimination at Work*, 58 WM. & MARY L. REV. 857 (2018); Pauline T. Kim, *Manipulating Opportunity*, 106 VA. L. REV. 867 (2020). For one journalistic account of the use of big data in college admissions, see Willard Dix, *Big Data's Influence on College Admission Is Growing*, FORBES, Dec. 17, 2017, https://www.forbes.com/sites/willarddix/2017/12/27/big-datas-influence-on-college-admission-is-growing/#331cb5195e33.

6. BRUCE SCHNEIER, DATA AND GOLIATH: THE HIDDEN BATTLES TO COLLECT YOUR DATA AND CONTROL YOUR WORLD (2015) ("Google's CEO Eric Schmidt admitted as much in 2010: 'We know where you are. We know where you've been. We can more or less know what you're thinking about.'"); SHOSHANNA ZUBOFF, THE AGE OF SURVEILLANCE CAPITALISM 256 (2019); Ina Fried, *What Google Knows About You*, AXIOS, Mar. 11, 2019.

7. For example, "Targeting options for Facebook advertisers" include location, gender, "ethnic affinity," age, "conservatives and liberals," and "relationship status." Caitlin Dewey, *98 Personal Data Points That Facebook Uses to Target Ads to You*, WASHINGTON POST, Aug. 19, 2016, https://www.washingtonpost.com/news/the-intersect/wp/2016/

08/19/98-personal-data-points-that-facebook-uses-to-target-ads-to-you/.; see also
NEIL RICHARDS, INTELLECTUAL PRIVACY: RETHINKING CIVIL LIBERTIES IN THE
DIGITAL AGE 1–3 (2015).

Chapter 1

1. *Katz v. United States,* 389 U.S. 347 (1967) ("reasonable expectation of privacy"); *Roe v. Wade,* 410 U.S. 113 (1973) (fundamental decisions); *Griswold v. Connecticut,* 381 U.S. 479 (1965) (somewhere in between). See also Neil M. Richards, *The Information Privacy Law Project,* 94 GEO. L. J. 1087 (2006) (discussing these cases).

2. The classic explanation of privacy-as-control is ALAN WESTIN, PRIVACY AND FREEDOM (1967). The idea of privacy-as-control has remained remarkably tenacious since Westin was writing in the 1960s; in his testimony before Congress in the wake of the Cambridge Analytica scandal in 2018, Facebook founder Mark Zuckerberg repeatedly stressed the importance of control to Facebook's privacy/data exploitation model, stating at one point, "Every single time that you share something on Facebook or one of our services, right there is a control in line where you control who you want to share with." Todd Haselton, *Zuckerberg Says You Control Your Facebook Info—but It's Much More Complicated Than He Says,* CNBC.COM, Apr. 11, 2018, https://www.cnbc.com/2018/04/11/zuckerberg-says-you-control-your-facebook-info-but-its-complicated.html. Indeed, in his written testimony, Zuckerberg used the word "control" more than a thousand times. *Written Testimony from Facebook to House Energy and Commerce Committee for Record of April 11, 2018 Hearing,* June 29, 2018, https://docs.house.gov/meetings/IF/IF00/20180411/108090/ HHRG-115-IF00-Wstate-ZuckerbergM-20180411.pdf [https://perma.cc/B7LR-L7XU]. See generally Neil Richards & Woodrow Hartzog, *The Pathologies of Digital Consent,* 96 WASH. U. L. REV. 1461, 1472 (2019).

3. E.g., HELEN NISSENBAUM, PRIVACY IN CONTEXT: TECHNOLOGY, POLICY, AND THE INTEGRITY OF SOCIAL LIFE (2009).

4. E.g., Daniel J. Solove & Danielle Keats Citron, *Risk and Anxiety: A Theory of Data Breach Harms,* 96 TEX. L. REV. 737 (2018).

5. Blackstone famously wrote, "Eaves-droppers, or such as listen under walls or windows, or the eaves of a house, to hearken after discourse, and thereupon to frame slanderous and mischievous tales, are a common nuisance." 4 WILLIAM BLACKSTONE COMMENTARIES 169. For an overview of concerns about eavesdropping in American law in both the physical and electronic contexts, see SARAH E. IGO, THE KNOWN CITIZEN: A HISTORY OF PRIVACY IN MODERN AMERICA 166–70 (2018).

6. E.g., Robert S. Gerstein, *Intimacy and Privacy,* in PHILOSOPHICAL DIMENSIONS OF PRIVACY (Ferdinand D. Schoeman ed. 1984); JULIE INNESS, PRIVACY, INTIMACY AND ISOLATION (1992).

7. Samuel Warren & Louis Brandeis, *The Right to Privacy,* 4 HARV. L. REV. 193 (1890).

8. There are some important differences, not the least because European Union countries, as members of the Council of Europe, actually have a second "Bill of Rights," the European Convention on Human Rights of 1950, which is enforced through the European Court of Human Rights.

9. Chris Jay Hoofnagle et al., *The European Union General Data Protection Regulation: What It Is and What It Means*, 28:1 INFO. & COMM. TECH. L. 65 (2019).

10. See, e.g., *id.*; Woodrow Hartzog & Neil Richards, *Privacy's Constitutional Moment and the Limits of Data Protection*, 61 B.C. L. REV. 1687 (2020); Anupam Chander, Margot Kaminski, & William McGeveran, *Catalyzing Privacy Law*, MINN. L. REV. (forthcoming 2021); Paul M. Schwartz & Karl-Niklaus Peifer, *Transatlantic Data Privacy*, 106 GEO. L. J. 115 (2017); Paul M. Schwartz, *Global Data Privacy the EU Way*, 94 NYU L. REV. 771 (2019).

11. DANIEL J. SOLOVE, UNDERSTANDING PRIVACY (2006).

12. *Id.*, at ix.

13. *Id.*, at 103–6.

14. M. Ryan Calo, *The Boundaries of Privacy Harm*, 86 IND. L. J. 1, 9–12 (2011).

15. This, in fact, is the story that actually emerges from the careful ethnographic work inside tech companies by the lawyer-sociologist Ari Waldman. See ARI EZRA WALDMAN, INSIDE THE INFORMATION INDUSTRY (2021).

16. See, e.g., MILTON FRIEDMAN, FREE TO CHOOSE: A PERSONAL STATEMENT (1980) (identifying three categories of equality: equality before God, equality of opportunity, and equality of outcome).

17. E.g., *id.*; see also Anne Phillips, *Defending Equality of Outcome*, J. OF POLITICAL PHILOSOPHY 1–19 (2004) (arguing that equality of outcome is the appropriate measure of fairness).

18. E.g., *Shelley v. Kraemer*, 334 U.S. 1 (1948).

19. See, e.g., *Grutter v. Bollinger*, 539 U.S. 306 (2003) (holding that a public college may favor "underrepresented minority groups" in its admissions process).

20. See, e.g., ANDREW KULL, THE COLOR-BLIND CONSTITUTION (1992).

21. E.g., *Regents of the University of California v. Bakke*, 438 U.S. 265 (1978); *Gratz v. Bollinger*, 539 U.S. 244; *Grutter*, 539 U.S. 306 (2003).

22. E.g., Kelly M. Bower et al., *The Intersection of Neighborhood Racial Segregation, Poverty, and Urbanicity and Its Impact on Food Store Availability in the United States*, 58 PREVENTATIVE MED. 33 (2014); Christopher Jencks & Meredith Phillips, *The Black-White Test Score Gap: Why It Persists and What Can Be Done*, Brookings Institution Report, Mar. 1, 1998, https://www.brookings.edu/articles/the-black-white-test-score-gap-why-it-persists-and-what-can-be-done/; Karishma Furtado et al., *Falling Through the Cracks: Disparities in Out-of-School Suspension in St. Louis at the Intersection of Race, Disability, and Gender*, Washington University George Warren Brown School of Social Work Report, https://forwardthroughferguson.org/falling-through-the-cracks/.

23. Cf. Bilyana Petkova, *Privacy as Europe's First Amendment*, 25 EUR. L. J. 140 (2019).

24. For an exploration of this point, see Frederick Schauer, *Facts and the First Amendment*, 57 UCLA L. REV. 897, 916–17 (2010).

25. VINCENT BLASI, IDEAS OF THE FIRST AMENDMENT (2006).

26. *Jacobellis v. Ohio*, 378 U.S. 184 (1962) (Stewart, J, concurring) (emphasis added).

27. On the multiple justifications for American First Amendment law, see Neil Richards, *Intellectual Privacy*, 87 TEX. L. REV. 387 (2008) ("No single theory of the First Amendment adequately explains the doctrine, with a host of utilitarian theories offering competing explanations."); Frederick Schauer, *The Boundaries of the First Amendment: A Preliminary Exploration of Constitutional Salience*, 117 HARV. L. REV. 1765, 1785 (2004) ("Prescriptive theories abound, but descriptive or explanatory accounts of the existing coverage of the First Amendment are noticeably unsatisfactory."). On the difficulties of defining obscenity in the time of both print and the internet, see Thomas C. Arthur, *The Problems with Pornography Regulation: Lessons from History*, 68 EMORY L. J. 867 (2019).

28. See CEOS Mission, U.S. Dept. of Justice, Child Exploitation and Obscenity Section, https://www.justice.gov/criminal-ceos/ceos-mission.

29. For example, Anita Allen defines "spatial privacy" as being "disturbed when a person's efforts to seclude or conceal himself are frustrated." ANITA L. ALLEN, UNPOPULAR PRIVACY: WHAT MUST WE HIDE? 4 (2011).

30. See, e.g., *Griswold v. Connecticut*, 381 U.S. 479 (1965); *Roe v. Wade*, 410 U.S. 113 (1973); *Planned Parenthood v. Casey*, 505 U.S. 833 (1992); *Gonzalez v. Carhart*, 550 U.S. 124 (2007).

31. *Planned Parenthood v. Casey*, 505 U.S. 833 (1992).

32. Paul M. Schwartz & Daniel J. Solove, *The PII Problem: Privacy and a New Concept of Personally Identifiable Information*, 86 N.Y.U. L. REV. 1814 (2011).

33. Video Privacy Protection Act, 18 U.S.C. § 2710(a)(3).

34. GDPR Art. 4(1). The full GDPR definition is actually a bit broader than the excerpt I provided in the text. It reads in full: "'[P]ersonal data' means any information relating to an identified or identifiable natural person ('data subject'); an identifiable natural person is one who can be identified, directly or indirectly, in particular by reference to an identifier such as a name, an identification number, location data, an online identifier or to one or more factors specific to the physical, physiological, genetic, mental, economic, cultural or social identity of that natural person."

35. For a detailed examination of this phenomenon, see SHOSHANNA ZUBOFF, THE AGE OF SURVEILLANCE CAPITALISM (2019).

36. E.g., Charles Duhigg, *How Companies Learn Your Secrets*, N.Y. TIMES, Feb. 16, 2012.

37. E.g., ROGER MCNAMEE, ZUCKED: WAKING UP TO THE FACEBOOK CATASTROPHE 63 (2019); SHOSHANNA ZUBOFF, THE AGE OF SURVEILLANCE CAPITALISM 449–51 (2019). See also B. J. FOGG, PERSUASIVE TECHNOLOGY: USING COMPUTERS TO CHANGE WHAT WE THINK AND DO (2003) (textbook on the use and ethics of how technologies can be applied to persuade human minds); NATASHA DOW SCHÜLL, ADDICTION BY DESIGN: MACHINE GAMBLING IN LAS VEGAS (2014) (study of the use of design, technology, and behavioral psychology to make casinos addictive to gamblers).

38. Adam D. Kramer et al., *Experimental Design of Massive-Scale Emotional Contagion Through Social Networks*, 111 PROCEEDINGS OF THE NATIONAL ACADEMY OF SCIENCES, No. 24, 8788–90 (2014).
39. Robert M. Bond et al., *A 61-Million-Person Experiment in Social Influence and Political Mobilization*, 489 NATURE, No. 7415, 295–98 (2012).
40. Matthew Rosenberg, Nicholas Confessore, & Carole Cadwalladr, *How Trump Consultants Exploited the Facebook Data of Millions*, N.Y. TIMES, Mar. 17, 2018, https://www.nytimes.com/2018/03/17/us/politics/cambridge-analytica-trump-campaign.html; Scott Detrow, *What Did Cambridge Analytica Do During the 2016 Election?*, NATIONAL PUBLIC RADIO, Mar. 20, 2018, https://www.npr.org/2018/03/20/595338116/what-did-cambridge-analytica-do-during-the-2016-election.
41. Lori Bezahler, *We Should Be Alarmed by Schools' Creepy Plan to Monitor Students*, THE GUARDIAN, Oct. 18, 2019, https://www.theguardian.com/commentisfree/2019/oct/18/school-shootings-surveillance-police-database-privacy.
42. *Black Mirror*, "Shut Up and Dance," Season 3, Episode 1 (2016).
43. See HARTZOG, PRIVACY'S BLUEPRINT, *supra*.
44. GDPR Art. 4(2) ("processing").
45. DANIEL J. SOLOVE, THE DIGITAL PERSON: TECHNOLOGY AND PRIVACY IN THE DIGITAL AGE 42 (2005).
46. For an overview of the third-party doctrine, including a discussion of its limits and its future, see Neil Richards, *The Third-Party Doctrine and the Future of the Cloud*, 94 WASH. U. L. REV. 1441 (2017).
47. *Hoffa v. United States*, 385 U.S. 293 (1966).
48. *United States v. Miller*, 425 U.S. 435 (1976).
49. *United States v. Warshak*, 631 F.3d 266 (6th Cir. 2010) (email); *Carpenter v. United States*, 138 S.Ct. 2206 (2018) (location data).
50. Google Privacy Policy, available at https://policies.google.com/privacy?hl=en-US.
51. *Id.*
52. There is a vast academic literature documenting the flaws in the privacy policy model. For a small sample, see Allyson W. Haynes, *Online Privacy Policies: Contracting Away Control Over Personal Information?*, 111 PA. ST. L. REV. 587, 588 (2007); Aleecia M. McDonald & Lorrie Faith Cranor, *The Cost of Reading Privacy Policies*, 4 I/S: J. L. POL'Y INFO. SOC'Y 543 (2009); Daniel J. Solove, *Introduction: Privacy Self-Management and the Consent Dilemma*, 126 HARV. L. REV. 1879 (2013); OMRI BEN-SHAHAR & CARL E. SCHNEIDER, THE FAILURE OF MANDATED DISCLOSURE (2014); *250,000 Words of App Terms and Conditions*, NORWEGIAN CONSUMER COUNCIL, May 24, 2016, http://www.forbrukerradet.no/side/250000-words-of-app-terms-and -conditions [http://perma.cc/RK5B-4E5N]; Joel R. Reidenberg et al., *Disagreeable Privacy Policies: Mismatches Between Meaning and Users' Understanding*, 30 BERKELEY TECH. L. J. 39 (2015); Joel R. Reidenberg et al., *Privacy Harms and the Effectiveness of the Notice and Choice Framework*, 11 I/S 485, 487–88 (2015); FINN BRUNTON & HELEN NISSENBAUM, OBFUSCATION: A USER'S GUIDE FOR PRIVACY AND PROTEST 30–31(2015). But see Mike Hintze, *In Defense of the Long Privacy Statement*, 76 MD. L. REV. 1044 (2017) (arguing that dense, long-form privacy policies have some surprising virtues in terms

of corporate privacy hygiene and disclosure to regulators and other sophisticated actors).

53. For a few of many examples, see, e.g., Alex C. Madrigal, *Reading the Privacy Policies You Encounter in a Year Would Take 76 Work Days*, THE ATLANTIC, Mar. 1, 2012, http://www.theatlantic.com/technology/archive/2012/03/reading-the-privacy-policies-youencounter-in-a-year-would-take-76-work-days/253851 [http://perma.cc/2ZJN-BYLA]; JULIA ANGWIN, DRAGNET NATION (2014); Kevin Litman-Navarro, *We Read 150 Privacy Policies: They Were an Incomprehensible Disaster*, N.Y. TIMES, June 12, 2019, https://www.nytimes.com/interactive/2019/06/12/opinion/facebook-google-privacy-policies.html.

54. EXECUTIVE OFFICE OF THE PRESIDENT, BIG DATA: SEIZING OPPORTUNITIES, PRESERVING VALUES 46 (May 2014). Julie Brill, Comm'r, Fed. Trade Comm'n, *Keynote Address at Proskauer on Privacy* 2, Oct. 19, 2010, http://www.ftc.gov/sites/default/files/documents/public_statements/remarkscommissioner-julie-brill/101019proskauerspeech.pdf [http://perma.cc/CQH4-TA8R] ("[T]he Notice and Choice model, as it is often deployed today, places too great a burden on consumers."); Jon Leibowitz, Chairman, Fed. Trade Comm'n, *Introductory Remarks at the FTC Privacy Roundtable* 3, Dec. 7, 2009, http://www.ftc.gov/sites/default/files/documents/public_statements/introductory-remarksftc-privacy-roundtable/091207privacyremarks.pdf[http://perma.cc/XCQ5-PXLW] ("We do feel that the approaches we've tried so far—both the notice and choice regime, and later the harm-based approach—haven't worked quite as well as we would like.").

55. See Neil M. Richards & Daniel J. Solove, *Privacy's Other Path: Recovering the Law of Confidentiality*, 96 GEO. L. J. 123 (2007) (cataloging these bodies of law).

56. NISSENBAUM, PRIVACY IN CONTEXT, supra.

57. U.S. DEPT. OF HEALTH, EDUC. & WELFARE, RECORDS, COMPUTERS AND THE RIGHTS OF CITIZENS: REPORT OF THE SECRETARY'S ADVISORY COMMITTEE ON AUTOMATED PERSONAL DATA SYSTEMS (1973).

58. *Id.*

59. See COLIN J. BENNETT, REGULATING PRIVACY: DATA PROTECTION AND PUBLIC POLICY IN EUROPE AND THE UNITED STATES (1992); Robert Gellman, *Fair Information Practices: A Basic History* (Version 2.19), Oct. 7, 2019, https://papers.ssrn.com/sol3/papers.cfm?abstract_id=2415020; Robert Gellman, *Willis Ware's Lasting Contribution to Privacy: Fair Information Practices*, IEEE SECURITY & PRIVACY (July/Aug. 2014), at 51.

60. Robert Gellman, *Willis Ware's Lasting Contribution to Privacy: Fair Information Practices*, IEEE SECURITY & PRIVACY (July/Aug. 2014), at 51.

61. For an extended critique of the limits of the FIPs as the principal mechanism of human information governance, see Hartzog & Richards, *Privacy's Constitutional Moment, supra.*

62. Woodrow Hartog, *The Inadequate, Invaluable Fair Information Practices*, 76 MD. L. REV. 952 (2017).

63. GDPR Art. 6.

64. WOODROW HARTZOG, PRIVACY'S BLUEPRINT: THE BATTLE TO CONTROL THE DESIGN OF NEW TECHNOLOGIES 15 (2018). In full disclosure, Professor Hartzog knows quite a few embarrassing stories about me, though since he features in a few of them, I am, to some degree, safe. See *id.*

65. *Sipple v. Chronicle Publ'g Co.*, 154 CAL. APP. 3d 1040 (1984).

66. See Dean Morain, *Sorrow Trailed a Veteran Who Saved a President's Life and Then Was Cast in an Unwanted Spotlight*, L.A. TIMES, Feb. 13, 1989, at Part 5, 1. See also DANIEL J. SOLOVE & PAUL M. SCHWARTZ, INFORMATION PRIVACY LAW: CASES AND MATERIALS 126 (5th Ed. 2015).

67. See Danielle Citron, *Sexual Privacy*, 128 YALE L. J. 1870, 1914–15 (2019).

68. *Georgia Appeals Court Says "Upskirting" Is Legal*, CBS NEWS, July 25, 2016, https://www.cbsnews.com/news/georgia-appeals-court-upskirting-is-legal.

69. *Gary v. State*, 790 S.E.2d 150, 154 (Ga. Ct. App. 2016).

70. See RICHARDS, INTELLECTUAL PRIVACY, *supra*, at 41–56.

71. NISSENBAUM, PRIVACY IN CONTEXT, *supra*, at 140–41.

72. Lior Strahilevitz, *A Social Networks Theory of Privacy*, 72 U. CHI. L. REV. 919, 940 (2005). To be sure, Strahilevitz suggests that the *Sipple* case was correctly decided, but only in a way that illustrates the breadth of his "limited-privacy principle." As he puts it, the court in *Sipple* correctly held that "once hundreds of homosexuals in several cities knew of Sipple's sexual orientation, and once Sipple's heroic actions to thwart the attempt on President Ford's life thrust him into the national limelight, then it was inevitable that Sipple's orientation would spread from the social network of homosexuals to the social network of heterosexuals." *Id.* at 976 n.216.

73. *Commonwealth v. Robertson*, 5 N.E.3d 522, 523 (Mass. 2014) (holding that upskirt photography on a Boston subway car was not actionable under an existing law that protected only against photography of people in a nude or partially nude state).

74. *Commonwealth v. Wassillie*, 125 N.E.3d 682 (Mass. 2019) (explaining the revision of Mass. G.L. c. 272, § 105(b) to cover the secret recording of a person's clothed genitals even while in "public").

75. Stuart A. Thompson & Charlie Warzel, *One Nation, Tracked: An Investigation Into the Smartphone Tracking Industry From Times Opinion*, N.Y. TIMES, Dec. 19, 2019, https://www.nytimes.com/interactive/2019/12/19/opinion/location-tracking-cell-phone.html.

Chapter 2

1. CHARLES DUHIGG, THE POWER OF HABIT: WHY WE DO WHAT WE DO IN LIFE AND BUSINESS (2014); Charles Duhigg, *How Companies Learn Your Secrets*, N.Y. TIMES, Feb. 16, 2012, https://www.nytimes.com/2012/02/19/magazine/shopping-habits.html.

2. Neil Richards & Woodrow Hartzog, *Trusting Big Data Research*, 66 DEPAUL L. REV. 579, 582 (2016) ("The Target Pregnancy story is the evergreen anecdote justifying big

data paranoia."). For illustrative examples, see, e.g., Hugh J. Watson, *Addressing the Privacy Issues of Big Data*, 19 BUS. INTELLIGENCE J. 2, 4 (2014); Nada R. Sanders, *How to Use Big Data to Drive Your Supply Chain*, 58 CAL. MGMT. R. 26, 26 (2016); J. Jeffrey Inman & Hristina Nikolova, *Shopper-Facing Retail Technology: A Retailer Adoption Decision Framework Incorporating Shopper Attitudes and Privacy Concerns*, 93 J. OF RETAILING 7, 8 (2017); Samuel Fosso Wamba et al., *Big Data Analytics and Firm Performance: Effects of Dynamic Capabilities*, 70 J. OF BUS. RES. 1, 5 (2017); Zeynep Tufekci, *Engineering the Public: Big Data, Surveillance and Computational Politics*, 19 FIRST MONDAY 7 (July 2014); Joni R. Jackson, *A Perfect Fit: Personalization Versus Privacy*, 18 J. OF ORG. PSYCHOLOGY 33 (2018); Kate Crawford & Jason Schultz, *Big Data and Due Process: Toward Framework to Redress Predictive Privacy Harms*, 55 B.C. L. REV. 93, 94 (2014).

3. Duhigg, *How Companies Learn Your Secrets*, supra.

4. *Id.*

5. E.g., MARK BARTHOLOMEW, ADCREEP: THE CASE AGAINST MODERN MARKETING 23–25 (2017); Dakota Shane, *96 Percent of Consumers Don't Trust Ads: Here's How to Sell Your Product Without Coming Off Sleazy*, INC., May 31, 2019, https://www.inc.com/dakota-shane/96-percent-of-consumers-dont-trust-ads-heres-how-to-sell-your-product-without-coming-off-sleazy.html.

6. Duhigg, *How Companies Learn Your Secrets*, supra.

7. *Id.* (emphasis added).

8. See Julie E. Cohen, *Turning Privacy Inside Out*, 20 THEORETICAL INQUIRIES IN LAW 1 (2019) (arguing that we should be particularly attentive to the conditions and institutional arrangements that are needed to produce privacy, rather than focusing on artificial abstractions like "autonomy" and "choice").

9. E.g., Lim Zenghao, *Data Is the New Oil and Electricity*, ASIAN SCIENTIST, Mar. 11, 2020, https://www.asianscientist.com/2020/03/features/smu-ai-ip-conference-data-new-oil/ [https://perma.cc/6HNB-HXW3]; Adeola Adesina, *Data Is the New Oil*, MEDIUM, Nov. 13, 2018, https://medium.com/@adeolaadesina/data-is-the-new-oil-2947ed8804f6 [https://perma.cc/8LCD-WC6D]; Anders Aslund, *Data Is the New Oil and Facebook Is Standard Oil*, THE HILL, Apr. 18, 2018, https://thehill.com/opinion/finance/383617-data-is-the-new-oil-and-facebook-is-standard-oil [https://perma.cc/867Y-E89L]; Kiran Bhagesphur, *Data Is the New Oil—And That's a Good Thing*, FORBES, Nov. 15, 2019, https://www.forbes.com/sites/forbestechcouncil/2019/11/15/data-is-the-new-oil-and-thats-a-good-thing/#4450124d7304 [https://perma.cc/NF5J-YYCN]; Kirsten Gillibrand, *The U.S. Needs a Data Protection Agency*, MEDIUM, Feb. 12, 2020, https://medium.com/@gillibrandny/the-u-s-needs-a-data-protection-agency-98a054f7b6bf [https://perma.cc/U4SK-Y34P]; Jory Heckman, *Valuable, Messy and Contentious: How Big Data Became "New Oil,"* FED. NEWS NETWORK, Feb. 6, 2019, https://federalnewsnetwork.com/big-data/2019/02/valuable-messy-and-contentious-how-big-data-became-new-oil/ [https://perma.cc/H3NW-QAAP]; Chandrashekar Srinivasan, *"Data Is the New Oil, the New Gold": PM at "Howdy, Modi!" in Houston*, NDTV, Sept. 23, 2019, https://www.ndtv.com/india-news/data-is-the-new-oil-the-new-gold-says-pm-modi-in-houston-2105338 [https://perma.cc/T3ZA-TR6R].

10. *The World's Most Valuable Resource Is No Longer Oil but Data*, THE ECONOMIST, May 6, 2017, at 9.

11. Louise Matsakis, *The WIRED Guide to Your Personal Data (and Who Is Using It)*, WIRED, Feb. 15, 2019, https://www.wired.com/story/wired-guide-personal-data-collection/.

12. SHEILA JASANOFF, THE ETHICS OF INVENTION 35 (2016); Daniel Faggella, *Your Feed Is All You: The Nuanced Art of Personalization at Facebook*, VICE, Aug. 18, 2016, https://www.vice.com/en_us/article/d7ywxa/facebook-newsfeed-personalization-hussein-mehanna [https://perma.cc/HG98-B67W]; Ahmed El Deeb, *So What Is Machine Learning Good for Anyway?*, MEDIUM, Mar. 19, 2017, https://medium.com/rants-on-machine-learning/so-what-is-machine-learning-good-for-anyway-3cb38621383f [https://perma.cc/SN6T-8XFZ]; Francesca Baker, *The Technology That Could End Traffic Jams*, BBC, Dec. 12, 2018, https://www.bbc.com/future/article/20181212-can-artificial-intelligence-end-traffic-jams [https://perma.cc/DK34-E4MC].

13. SHOSHANNA ZUBOFF, THE AGE OF SURVEILLANCE CAPITALISM 63–70 (2019); JULIE E. COHEN, BETWEEN TRUTH AND POWER: THE LEGAL CONSTRUCTIONS OF INFORMATIONAL CAPITALISM 51–52 (2019).

14. For the classic exposition of the self-serving description of the American West as "Virgin Land," see HENRY NASH SMITH, VIRGIN LAND: THE AMERICAN WEST AS SYMBOL AND MYTH (1950).

15. Neil Richards & Jonathan H. King, *Three Paradoxes of Big Data*, 66 STAN. L. REV. ONLINE 41 (2013).

16. *The World's Most Valuable Resource*, THE ECONOMIST, May 6, 2017, at 9.

17. Daniel J. Solove, *Privacy and Power: Computer Databases and Metaphors for Information Privacy*, 53 STAN. L. REV. 1393, 1398 (2001).

18. DANIEL J. SOLOVE, THE DIGITAL PERSON: TECHNOLOGY AND PRIVACY IN THE DIGITAL AGE 148 (2004).

19. COHEN, BETWEEN TRUTH AND POWER, *supra*, at 5, 82–83.

20. Lisa A. Austin, *Why Privacy Is About Power, Not Consent or Harm*, in A WORLD WITHOUT PRIVACY? WHAT LAW CAN AND SHOULD DO (Austin Sarat ed. 2015).

21. CARISSA VÉLIZ, PRIVACY IS POWER: WHY AND HOW YOU SHOULD TAKE BACK CONTROL OF YOUR DATA (2020).

22. JOSEPH TUROW, THE AISLES HAVE EYES: HOW RETAILERS TRACK YOUR SHOPPING, STRIP YOUR PRIVACY, AND DEFINE YOUR POWER (2017).

23. *Id.* at 13–17.

24. JOSEPH TUROW, THE VOICE CATCHERS: HOW MARKETERS LISTEN IN TO EXPLOIT YOUR FEELINGS, YOUR PRIVACY, AND YOUR WALLET (2021).

25. VANCE PACKARD, THE HIDDEN PERSUADERS (1957).

26. *Id.* at 97–98. See also Mark Bartholomew, *Hiding in Plain View: The Past and Present of Manipulative Advertising*, L.A. REV. OF BOOKS, Sept. 24, 2017, https://lareviewofbooks.org/article/hiding-in-plain-view-the-past-and-present-of-manipulative-advertising/.

27. SARAH E. IGO, THE KNOWN CITIZEN: A HISTORY OF PRIVACY IN MODERN AMERICA 183–84 (2018).

28. Alan H. Westin, Privacy and Freedom, 211–97 (1967). Chapter 9, "Truth Through Stress," deals with the polygraph test; chapter 10, "Prove That You're Adjusted," considers the use of personality testing; and chapter 11, "Tampering With the Unconscious," addresses subliminal manipulation.

29. Bartholomew, *Hiding in Plain View, supra.*

30. See generally Daniel Kahneman, Thinking Fast and Slow (2011); Michael Lewis, The Undoing Project (2016). Both Kahneman and Thaler have won Nobel prizes for their work; Kahneman believes firmly that Tversky would have equally shared Kahneman's had he not died prematurely at age fifty-nine in 1996, since the Nobel cannot be awarded posthumously. See Kahneman, Thinking Fast and Slow, *supra,* at 10.

31. Richard H. Thaler, Misbehaving: The Making of Behavioral Economics 261 (2015).

32. Jon D. Hanson & Douglas A. Kysar, *Taking Behavioralism Seriously: The Problem of Market Manipulation,* 74 N.Y.U. L. Rev. 632, 633, 745–49 (1999).

33. Thaler and Judge Richard Posner, the godfather of the modern law and economics rational actor model in the legal academy, apparently clashed over this very point at an infamous workshop at the University of Chicago Law School in the mid-1990s. See Thaler, Misbehaving, *supra,* at 261.

34. Hanson & Kysar, *Taking Behavioralism Seriously: The Problem of Market Manipulation, supra,* at 632, 635.

35. Dan Ariely, Predictably Irrational: The Hidden Forces That Shape Our Decisions (2008).

36. Richard H. Thaler & Cass R. Sunstein, Nudge: Improving Decisions about Health, Wealth, and Happiness (2008).

37. *Id.* at 11–13.

38. Richard H. Thaler, *Psychology and Savings Policies,* 84 Am. Econ. Rev. 186–92 (1994).

39. Thaler & Sunstein, Nudge, *supra,* at 106. Thaler explains the genesis of this idea, along with a variant called "Save More Tomorrow," in which new hires commit to increase their savings over time as part of any future raises in his highly readable intellectual autobiography *Misbehaving.* See Thaler, Misbehaving, supra, at 310–22.

40. Thaler & Sunstein, Nudge, *supra,* at 248–52.

41. Richard H. Thaler, *The Power of Nudges, for Good and Bad,* N.Y. Times, Oct. 31, 2015, https://www.nytimes.com/2015/11/01/upshot/the-power-of-nudges-for-good-and-bad.html.

42. *Id.*

43. Hanson & Kysar, *Taking Behavioralism Seriously: The Problem of Market Manipulation, supra,* at 632, 637.

44. Jon D. Hanson & Douglas A. Kysar, *Taking Behavioralism Seriously: Some Evidence of Market Manipulation,* 112 Harv. L. Rev. 1420 (1999).

45. Hanson & Kysar, *Taking Behavioralism Seriously: The Problem of Market Manipulation, supra,* at 632, 637.

46. Ryan Calo, *Digital Market Manipulation,* 82 Geo. Wash. L. Rev. 995 (2014).

47. *Id.* at 1001.

48. *Id.* at 1006.

49. *Id.* at 1006–7.

50. See COHEN, BETWEEN TRUTH AND POWER, *supra*, at 75–107.

51. Daniel Victor, *FarmVille Once Took Over Facebook: Now Everything Is FarmVille*, N.Y. TIMES, Dec. 31, 2020.

52. *Id.*

53. See, e.g., Don Peck, *They're Watching You at Work*, THE ATLANTIC, Dec. 2013, https://www.theatlantic.com/magazine/archive/2013/12/theyre-watching-you-at-work/354681/.

54. Pauline T. Kim, *Data-Driven Discrimination at Work*, 58 WM. & MARY L. REV. 857 (2018); Pauline T. Kim, *Manipulating Opportunity*, 106 VA. L. REV. 867 (2020).

55. Chip Cutter & Rachel Feintzeig, *Smile! Your Boss Is Tracking Your Happiness*, WALL ST. J., March 7, 2020, file:///C:/Users/nrich/AppData/Local/Microsoft/Windows/INetCache/Content.Outlook/D71YR0W3/Smile!%20Your%20Boss%20Is%20Tracking%20Your%20Happiness.%20-%20WSJ.pdf.

56. Danielle Keats Citron & Frank Pasquale, *The Scored Society: Due Process for Automated Predictions*, 89 WASH. L. REV. 1 (2014).

57. Hayley Peterson, *Amazon-Owned Whole Foods Is Quietly Tracking Its Employees With a Heat Map Tool That Ranks Which Stores Are Most at Risk of Unionizing*, BUSINESSINSIDER.COM, Apr. 20, 2020, https://www.businessinsider.com/whole-foods-tracks-unionization-risk-with-heat-map-2020-1.

58. *Id.*

59. *Id.*

60. Dan Patterson, *How Political Campaigns Use Big Data to Get Out the Vote*, TECHREPUBLIC, Feb. 12, 2018, https://www.techrepublic.com/article/how-political-campaigns-use-big-data-to-get-out-the-vote/ [https://perma.cc/U642-NF78]; Dan Patterson, *How Political Campaigns Use Big Data to Micro-Target Voters*, CBSNEWS, Nov. 6, 2018, https://www.cbsnews.com/news/election-campaigns-big-data-analytics/; Sean Illing, *A Political Scientist Explains How Big Data Is Transforming Politics*, Vox, Mar. 16, 2017, https://www.vox.com/conversations/2017/3/16/14935336/big-data-politics-donald-trump-2016-elections-polarization [https://perma.cc/XFW3-Q8MX] ("'Big data revolutionized the way American politicians win elections. In the process, it broke American politics.' This was the central claim in a recent column by NBC's Chuck Todd and Carrie Dann. The argument is simple enough: Politics 'broke' because the system is paralyzed by polarization, and it's paralyzed by polarization because technology and demographic data have made it easier (and less risky) for campaigns to target their base instead of appealing to a broad swath of voters."); Chuck Todd & Carrie Dann, *How Big Data Broke American Politics*, NBCNEWS, Mar. 14, 2017, https://www.nbcnews.com/politics/elections/how-big-data-broke-american-politics-n732901.

61. See generally LEONARD W. LEVY, ORIGINS OF THE BILL OF RIGHTS 1–43 (1999).

62. See Occupational Safety and Health Act of 1970, 29 U.S.C. §§ 651–78 (providing workplace safety standards); Fair Labor Standards Act, 29 U.S.C. § 206 (setting a

minimum wage); Civil Rights Act of 1964, 42 U.S.C. §§ 2000e–2000e-17 (prohibiting employer discrimination on the basis of race or sex).

63. E.g., *Chalk v. T-Mobile USA, Inc.*, 560 F.3d 1087 (holding substantively unconscionable an arbitration clause waiving class action rights in a consumer internet service agreement).

64. See Federal Trade Commission Act of 1914, 15 U.S.C. § 45(a) (containing Section 5 of the Federal Trade Commission Act, outlawing unfair and deceptive trade practices); Pure Food and Drug Act of 1906, 21 U.S.C. §§ 341–350I-1 (setting standards for food safety including impurities); Consumer Product Safety Act, 15 U.S.C. §§ 2051–89 (giving the Consumer Product Safety Commission the power to regulate dangerous products).

65. See generally Daniel J. Solove & Neil M. Richards, *Privacy's Other Path: Recovering the Law of Confidentiality*, 96 GEO. L. J. 123 (2007).

66. E.g., *Hamberger v. Eastman*, 206 A.2d 239, 241–42 (N.H. 1964) (finding a tortious invasion of privacy where a landlord installed a concealed listening and recording device in the bedroom of his tenants).

67. See generally RESTATEMENT (SECOND) OF TORTS § 652C (1977); state supreme courts have recognized this cause of action for well over a century. E.g., *Pavesich v. New England Life Ins. Co.*, 50 S.E. 68 (Ga. 1905).

68. E.g., *Michaels v. Internet Entm't Grp.*, 5 F. Supp. 2d 823, 840–42 (C.D. Cal. 1998). See generally DANIELLE KEATS CITRON, HATE CRIMES IN CYBERSPACE (2014); Danielle Keats Citron, *Sexual Privacy*, 128 YALE L. J. 1870 (2019).

69. See, e.g., Electronic Communications Privacy Act of 1986, 18 U.S.C. §§ 2510–22 (2012); CAL. PENAL CODE § 632(a) (Deering 2008); *Katz v. United States*, 389 U.S. 347, 357–58 (1967); *United States v. Carpenter*, 442 U. S. 735 (2018).

70. See generally Privacy Act of 1974, 5 U.S.C. § 552a (2012); Fair Credit Reporting Act (FCRA), 15 U.S.C. § 1681 (2012); Gramm-Leach-Bliley Act, 15 U.S.C. §§ 6801–9 (2012); Video Privacy Protection Act of 1988, 18 U.S.C. §§ 2701–12 (2012); Health Insurance Portability and Accountability Act (HIPAA) of 1996, 42 U.S.C. §§ 201–300ii (2012).

71. E.g., CAL. CONST. art. I, § 1; CAL. CIV. CODE § 1798.82 (West 2014) (requiring notification of certain data breaches); Reader Privacy Act, CAL. CIV. CODE § 1798.90 (West 2012); CAL. LABOR CODE § 980 (West 2014) (prohibiting certain employer actions with regard to social media); California Consumer Privacy Act of 2018, CAL. CIV. CODE § 1798.100 *et seq.* (2018) (giving consumers rights over data collected by companies, including the right to know, the right to delete, the right to opt out of sale, and a right against nondiscrimination for exercising CCPA rights).

72. See NEIL RICHARDS, INTELLECTUAL PRIVACY: RETHINKING CIVIL LIBERTIES IN A DIGITAL AGE, chapter 5 (2015).

73. *Id.*

74. For a small sampling of the voluminous sources on the content and influence of the GDPR, see, e.g., Michael Birnhack, *The EU Data Protection Directive: An Engine of a Global Regime*, 24(6) COMPUT. L. & SEC. REP. 508, 508 (2008) (noting the global impact of the EU's predecessor to the GDPR); Anupam Chander, Margot E. Kaminski,

& William McGeveran, *Catalyzing Privacy Law*, Aug. 7, 2019, at 4 (unpublished manuscript), https://papers.ssrn.com/sol3/papers.cfm?abstract_id=3433922); Lillian Edwards, *Data Protection: Enter the General Data Protection Regulation, in* LAW, POLICY AND THE INTERNET 77, 77 (Lilian Edwards ed. 2019) (calling the GDPR the most important development in data privacy law's history); Graham Greenleaf, *The Influence of European Data Privacy Standards Outside Europe: Implications for Globalization of Convention 108*, 2 INT'L DATA PRIVACY L. 68, 75 (2012) (showing the EU's influence on other nations' data privacy laws); Woodrow Hartzog & Neil Richards, *Privacy's Constitutional Moment and the Limits of Data Protection*, 61 B.C. L. REV. 1687 (2020); Chris Jay Hoofnagle, Bart van der Sloot, & Frederik Zuiderveen Borgesius, *The European Union General Data Protection Regulation: What It Is and What It Means*, 28 INFO. & COMM. TECH. L. 65, 67 (2019); Paul M. Schwartz, *Global Data Privacy: The EU Way*, 94 N.Y.U. L. REV. 771, 772–73 (2019) (noting that the new GDPR has caused U.S. corporations to spend billions of dollars on compliance, and that the European framework is making its way into discussions on data privacy throughout the United States); Lee A. Bygrave, *Transatlantic Tensions on Data Privacy* 12 Transworld, Working Paper No. 19, 2013, http://transworld.iai.it/?p=1149) (claiming the "overwhelming bulk of countries that have enacted data privacy laws have followed, to a considerable degree, the EU model"); Ira Rubinstein & Bilyana Petkova, *The International Impact of the General Data Protection Regulation*, Apr. 23, 2018, at 1 (unpublished manuscript), https://papers.ssrn.com/sol3/papers.cfm?abstract_id=3167389 (arguing the GDPR's right to be forgotten, international adequacy standards, and large fines for noncompliant corporations are the most likely provisions to impact nations outside of Europe); see generally LEE A. BYGRAVE, DATA PRIVACY LAW: AN INTERNATIONAL PERSPECTIVE (2014); Paul De Hert & Vagelis Papakonstantinou, *Three Scenarios for International Governance of Data Privacy: Towards an International Data Privacy Organization, Preferably a UN Agency?*, 9 ISJLP 271 (2013). The best general account of the California Consumer Privacy Act's genesis is Nicholas Confessore, *The Unlikely Activists Who Took On Silicon Valley—and Won*, N.Y. TIMES MAG., Aug. 14, 2018, https://www.nytimes.com/2018/08/14/magazine/facebook-google-privacy-data.html. The California Consumer Privacy Act of 2018 is codified at Cal. Civ. Code § 1798.100 *et seq.* (2018).

75. *Katz v. United States*, 389 U.S. 347 (1967); *Riley v. California*, 573 U.S. 373 (2014); *Carpenter v. United States*, 138 S. Ct. 2206 (2018).

76. *Olmstead v. United States*, 277 U.S. 438, 466 (1928).

77. See Electronic Communications Privacy Act of 1986, Pub. L. No. 99-508, 100 Stat. 1848 (1986) (codified as amended in scattered sections of 18 U.S.C.); CAL. PENAL CODE § 1546 (West 2020) (containing CalECPA, California's electronic communications and wiretapping law); MD CODE ANN. CTS. & JUD. PROC. § 10-402 (West 2018) (containing Maryland's electronic communications and wiretapping law); MO REV. STAT. § 542.402.2 (2017) (containing Missouri's electronic communications and wiretapping law); Foreign Intelligence Surveillance Act of 1978, 50 U.S.C. §§ 1801–85; USA Freedom Act, Pub. L. No. 114-23, 129 Stat. 268 (2015) (codified at various sections of 12 U.S.C., 15 U.S.C., 18 U.S.C., and 50 U.S.C.).

78. See Privacy Act of 1974, Pub. L. No. 93-579, § 2(a)(4), 88 Stat. 1896 (1974) (codified as amended at 5 U.S.C. § 552a. NOTE (1974)) (containing the Congressional
Findings and Statement of Purpose).
79. See Privacy Act of 1974, Pub. L. No. 93-579, 88 Stat. 1896 (1974) reprinted in
JOINT COMM. ON GOV'T OPERATIONS, 94TH CONG., LEGISLATIVE HISTORY OF
THE PRIVACY ACT OF 1974, at 185–86, 231 (1976) (containing the Act's legislative
history, including mentions of concentrated lobbying efforts by the direct-mail industry); 5 U.S.C. § 552A (containing the Privacy Act of 1974).
80. 5 U.S.C. § 552(a)(7).
81. Paul M. Schwartz, *Privacy and Participation: Personal Information and Public Sector
Regulation in the United States*, 80 IOWA L. REV. 553, 585 (1995).
82. C. S. LEWIS, THE SCREWTAPE LETTERS (1942).
83. While Congress passed a number of information privacy statutes alongside the rise
of the public and commercial internet in the late 1990s, the September 11 attacks
halted that legislative agenda and switched the primary focus of privacy attention
and reform to government surveillance, in connection with the Snowden revelations, for almost a decade. Daniel J. Solove, *A Brief History of Information Privacy
Law* in PROSKAUER ON PRIVACY, 1-36 through 1-46 (2006) (highlighting the many
sector-specific privacy reforms such as HIPAA and COPPA that took place in the
late 1990s, followed by the loosening of federal privacy protections following 9/11 in
the early twenty-first century).
84. See, e.g., DANIEL J. SOLOVE & PAUL M. SCHWARTZ, CONSUMER PRIVACY AND DATA
PROTECTION 1920 (2015); Neil M. Richards, Andrew B. Serwin, & Tyler Blake,
Understanding American Privacy, in RESEARCH HANDBOOK ON PRIVACY AND DATA
PROTECTION LAW: VALUES, NORMS AND GLOBAL POLITICS, at 6 (Gloria González
Fuster, Rosamunde van Brakel, & Paul De Hert eds. 2018).
85. Federal Trade Commission Act of 1914, Pub. L. No. 63-203 § 5, 38 Stat. 717, at 719
(1914) (codified as amended at 15 U.S.C. § 45(a)).
86. For scholarly treatments of the FTC's use of Section 5 in the privacy context, see
generally CHRIS JAY HOOFNAGLE, FEDERAL TRADE COMMISSION PRIVACY LAW
AND POLICY (2016); Daniel J. Solove & Woodrow Hartzog, *The FTC and the New
Common Law of Privacy*, 114 COLUM. L. REV. 583 (2014).
87. E.g., Neil Richards & Woodrow Hartzog, *The Pathologies of Digital Consent*, 96
WASH. U. L. REV. 1461, 1463 (2019); Neil Richards & Woodrow Hartzog, *Taking
Trust Seriously in Privacy Law*, 19 STAN. TECH. L. REV. 431, 445 (2016); Daniel J.
Solove, *Privacy Self-Management and the Consent Dilemma*, 126 HARV. L. REV.
1880, 1884 (2013); Jon Leibowitz, Chairman, Fed. Trade Comm'n, *Introductory
Remarks at the FTC Privacy Roundtable* 3, Dec. 7, 2009, http://www.ftc.gov/sites/
default/files/documents/public_statements/introductory-remarksftc-privacy-
roundtable/091207privacyremarks.pdf [http://perma.cc/XCQ5-PXLW] ("We do
feel that the approaches we've tried so far—both the notice and choice regime, and
later the harm-based approach—haven't worked quite as well as we would like.");
HELEN NISSENBAUM, PRIVACY IN CONTEXT 105 (2010); Fred H. Cate, *The Failure of*

Fair Information Practice Principles, in CONSUMER PROTECTION IN THE AGE OF THE INFORMATION ECONOMY 314, 314 (Jane K. Winn ed. 2006).

88. Kevin Litman-Navarro, *We Read 150 Privacy Policies: They Were an Incomprehensible Disaster*, N.Y. TIMES, June 12, 2019, https://www.nytimes.com/interactive/2019/06/12/opinion/facebook-google-privacy-policies.html.

89. Neil M. Richards, *Four Privacy Myths*, in A WORLD WITHOUT PRIVACY? WHAT LAW CAN/SHOULD DO 33 (Austin Sarat ed. 2015); Richards & Hartzog, *Taking Trust Seriously, supra*, at 444.

90. Richards & Hartzog, *The Pathologies of Digital Consent, supra*.

91. *Id.* at 1464–65.

92. *Id.* at 1466.

93. Solove, *Privacy Self-Management and the Consent Dilemma, supra*, at 1880.

94. See, e.g., Davey Winder, *How to Stop Your Smart Home Spying on You*, THE OBSERVER, Mar. 8, 2020, https://www.theguardian.com/technology/2020/mar/08/how-to-stop-your-smart-home-spying-on-you-lightbulbs-doorbell-ring-google-assistant-alexa-privacy; David Nield, *All the Ways Facebook Tracks You—and How to Limit It*, WIRED, Jan. 12, 2020, https://www.wired.com/story/ways-facebook-tracks-you-limit-it/?bxid=5bd673cb24c17c1048009686&cndid=30788676&esrc=AUTO_PRINT&source=EDT_WIR_NEWSLETTER_0_DAILY_ZZ&utm_brand=wired&utm_campaign=aud-dev&utm_mailing=WIR_Daily_011320&utm_medium=email&utm_source=nl&utm_term=list1_p4

95. VÉLIZ, PRIVACY IS POWER: WHY AND HOW YOU SHOULD TAKE BACK CONTROL OF YOUR DATA (2020) 175–201. Véliz, a philosopher, does have a chapter in which she calls for more regulation of tech companies along lines proposed by privacy law scholars and advocates, including "stop personalized advertising," "stop the trade in personal data," "impose fiduciary duties," and "improve cybersecurity standards." However, the proposals lack detail and ultimately rest on the control paradigm of privacy—a problematic idea that I take up in detail in chapter 3.

96. DON NORMAN, THE DESIGN OF EVERYDAY THINGS 65–73 (Rev. ed. 2013).

97. WOODROW HARTZOG, PRIVACY'S BLUEPRINT 44–51 (2018); LANGDON WINNER, THE WHALE AND THE REACTOR: A SEARCH FOR LIMITS IN AN AGE OF HIGH TECHNOLOGY (1989).

98. E.g., KENNETH A. BAMBERGER & DEIRDRE K. MULLIGAN, PRIVACY ON THE GROUND: DRIVING CORPORATE BEHAVIOR IN THE UNITED STATES AND EUROPE (2015).

99. ARI EZRA WALDMAN, INDUSTRY UNBOUND: PRIVACY, PRACTICE, AND CORPORATE POWER (2021).

100. *Id.* at 6.

101. CHRISTOPHER WYLIE, MINDF*CK: CAMBRIDGE ANALYTICA AND THE PLOT TO BREAK AMERICA (2019).

102. EDWARD SNOWDEN, PERMANENT RECORD 235–40 (2019).

103. COHEN, BETWEEN TRUTH AND POWER, *supra*, at 8–10.

104. See Electronic Communications Privacy Act of 1986, Pub. L. No. 99-508, 100 STAT. 1848 (1986) (codified as amended in scattered sections of 18 U.S.C.); *Electronic*

Communications Privacy Act (ECPA), Elec. Privacy Info. Ctr., https://www.
epic.org/privacy/ecpa [https://perma.cc/N8KR-9ENH] (last visited May 7, 2020)
("When ECPA was passed in 1986, web-based e-mail, such as Gmail, did not exist.
Instead, e-mail primarily existed in local intranets where clients would download
their messages from the server and the server would, generally, not keep a backup.");
Samuel Gibbs, *How Did Email Grow From Messages Between Academics to a Global
Epidemic?*, The Guardian, Mar. 7, 2016, https://www.theguardian.com/tech-
nology/2016/mar/07/email-ray-tomlinson-history [https://perma.cc/7Q2P-A839]
(providing a timeline for the invention of email, noting the arrival of Microsoft Mail
in 1988 and the first internet-based email service in 1989, both of which came after
ECPA's passage in 1986).

105. Computer Fraud and Abuse Act of 1984, 18 U.S.C. § 1030; Declan McCullagh, *From
"Wargames" to Aaron Swartz: How U.S. Anti-Hacking Law Went Astray*, CNet.com,
Mar. 13, 2013, https://www.cnet.com/news/from-wargames-to-aaron-swartz-how-
u-s-anti-hacking-law-went-astray/.

106. Fred Kaplan, *"WarGames" and Cybersecurity's Debt to a Hollywood Hack*, N.Y.
Times, Feb. 19, 2016, https://www.nytimes.com/2016/02/21/movies/wargames-
and-cybersecuritys-debt-to-a-hollywood-hack.html.

107. Video Privacy Protection Act of 1988, 18 U.S.C. § 2710; Neil Richards,
Intellectual Privacy: Rethinking Civil Liberties in a Digital Age 132
(2015); Michael Dolan, *The Bork Tapes Saga*, The American Porch: An Informal
History of an Informal Place, https://web.archive.org/web/20071009144531/
http://www.theamericanporch.com/bork2.htm.

108. *United States v. Warshak*, 631 F.3d 266 (6th Cir. 2010) (holding the Stored
Communications Act's allowance for obtaining a subpoena for emails older than
180 days unconstitutional, instead requiring a search warrant based on probable
cause); Stored Communications Act, 18 U.S.C. §§ 2701–12 (requiring the government to obtain a search warrant for emails stored for less than 180 days, but allowing
merely a subpoena, known as a 2703(d) order, for emails stored for more than
180 days, the provision that was held to be insufficiently protective as a constitutional matter in *Warshak*).

109. McCullagh, *From "Wargames" to Aaron Swartz, supra*. Swartz's story is best told in the
documentary *The Internet's Own Boy* (2014), which is available on YouTube under a
Creative Commons license, https://www.youtube.com/watch?v=9vz06QO3UkQ.

110. Video Privacy Protection Act, 18 U.S.C. § 2710(a)(4). See also *In re Hulu Privacy
Litigation*, 2012 WL 3282960 (N.D. Cal. 2012) (extending the VPPA to digital movie
streaming services).

111. See *United States v. White*, 401 U.S. 745 (1971).

112. See *United States v. Graham*, 824 F.3d 421, 427 (4th Cir. 2016) (holding that the government does not need a warrant to access historical Cell Site Location Information
("CSLI") because of the third-party doctrine); *United States v. Thompson*, 866 F.3d
1149, 1154 (10th Cir. 2017) (holding the government's obtaining of historical
CSLI did not constitute a search and require a warrant because of the third-party
doctrine); *United States v. Stimler*, 864 F.3d 253 (3d Cir. 2017) (holding that the

third-party doctrine does not apply, but nonetheless noting the "less precise" nature of CSLI compared to GPS in rationalizing the lack of warrant required to obtain the data); *Carpenter v. United States*, 585 U.S. ____, 138 S. Ct. 2206 (2018) (abrogating the above decisions, holding the government must obtain a search warrant when seeking more than seven days of historical CSLI).

113. Health Insurance Portability and Accountability Act of 1996, Public Law 104-191 (104th Cong. 1996); HIPAA Privacy Rule and the HIPAA Security Rule, 45 C.F.R. Parts 160, 162, and 164.

114. See Samual A. Garner & Jiyeon Kim, *The Privacy Risks of Direct-to-Consumer Genetic Testing: A Case Study of 23andme and Ancestry*, 96 Wash. U. L. Rev. 1219, 1225 (2019). See also Charles Ornstein, *Privacy Not Included: Federal Law Lags Behind New Tech*, ProPublica, Nov. 17, 2015, https://www.propublica.org/article/privacy-not-included-federal-law-lags-behind-new-tech [https://perma.cc/P8RA-KPW6] (detailing accounts of access to publicly available results of at-home paternity tests, sexual activity tracked by Fitbit wearables, and genealogy websites); Peter Pits, *The Privacy Delusions of Genetic Testing*, Forbes, Feb. 15, 2017, https://www.forbes.com/sites/realspin/2017/02/15/the-privacy-delusions-of-genetic-testing/#711544871bba [https://perma.cc/XTS7-8ZR2] (noting that the genetic testing industry's "rapid growth" is based on a "dangerous delusion: that genetic data is kept private"); Julie Brill, Comm'r, Fed. Trade Comm'n, *Welcome Remarks at the FTC Spring Privacy Series on Consumer Generated and Controlled Health Data*, May 7, 2014, https://www.ftc.gov/system/files/documents/public_events/195411/2014_05_07_consumer-generated-controlled-health-data-final-transcript.pdf (explaining that "consumer-generated health information is proliferating" and noting that "when health data is stored outside of silos, outside of the HIPAA silo that was created a fairly long time ago now, it seems like eons ago, in terms of the digital age, it will be health data that is not being controlled by doctors or hospitals or insurers").

115. See Brian Z. Tamanaha, On the Rule of Law: History, Politics, Theory 25 (2004).

116. Joel R. Reidenberg, *Lex Informatica: The Formulation of Information Policy Rules Through Technology*, 76 Tex. L. Rev. 553 (1998).

117. Lawrence Lessig, Code and Other Laws of Cyberspace 235 (1999).

118. See Hartzog, Privacy's Blueprint, *supra*, at 21–55.

119. See Richards, Intellectual Privacy, *supra*, at 44–50.

120. *Id.* at 44.

121. Woodrow Hartzog, *The Public Information Fallacy*, 98 B.U. L. Rev. 459, 494–96 (2019).

122. Neil Richards & Jonathan King, *Big Data Ethics*, 49 Wake Forest L. Rev. 393 (2014).

123. Solove & Richards, *Privacy's Other Path*, *supra*.

124. *Id.*

125. E.g., Aaron Blake, *Trump's Bogus "Simple Private Transaction" Defense of the Stormy Daniels Payment*, Wash. Post, Dec. 10, 2018, https://www.washingtonpost.com/

politics/2018/12/10/trump-gops-dishonest-minimizing-stormy-daniels-payment/ [https://perma.cc/2Q86-93AJ]; Alan Feuer, *What We Know About Trump's $130,000 Payment to Stormy Daniels*, N.Y. TIMES, Aug. 27, 2018, https://www.nytimes.com/ 2018/08/27/nyregion/stormy-daniels-trump-payment.html   [https://perma.cc/ C3DN-693E] ("In the landslide of news last week about guilty pleas, immunity deals and criminal convictions, you no doubt heard something astonishing: President Trump's ex-lawyer said in open court that Mr. Trump directed him to pay a pornographic film star quite a bit of money not to tell the world that they had sex."); Marie Huillet, *New Blockchain Solution to Fight COVID-19 Complies With EU Data Privacy Regs*, COINTELEGRAPH, Apr. 17, 2020, https://cointelegraph.com/news/ new-blockchain-solution-to-fight-covid-19-complies-with-eu-data-privacy-regs [https://perma.cc/FME7-WEPM] ("Collecting and analyzing data en masse appears to be key to tackling the public health crisis—and encrypted blockchain systems can potentially help mitigate the worst effects of surveillance on individuals' privacy, particularly when it comes to sensitive health data."); Danielle Citron & Geng Ngarmboonanant, *Be Very Wary of Trump's Health Surveillance Plans*, WASH. POST, Apr. 16, 2020; Kim Lyons, *Senators' Plan for Reining in Contact Tracing Apps Doesn't Make a Lot of Sense*, THE VERGE, May 1, 2020, https://www.theverge.com/2020/5/ 1/21243977/gop-senators-contact-tracing-data-coronavirus-covid-19-privacy [https://perma.cc/Z8QR-BFK9].

126. Richards & King, *Big Data Ethics, supra,* at 409. Cf. NISSENBAUM, PRIVACY IN CONTEXT, *supra.*

127. SARAH E. IGO, THE KNOWN CITIZEN: A HISTORY OF PRIVACY IN MODERN AMERICA 12 (2018).

128. *Id.* at 11.

129. See, e.g., *id.* at 21, 24–25 (the Warren & Brandeis article and "instantaneous photography"); *id.* at 62–63, 72–73 (the creation of Social Security); *id.* at 185–93 (modern research data ethics).

130. *NAACP v. Alabama*, 357 US 449 (1958).

131. *Id.* at 1174.

132. TAMANAHA, LAW AS MEANS TO AN END, *supra,* at 128.

133. Or at least one that confers a survival advantage. Alan Westin, for example, notes that "one basic finding of animal studies is that virtually all animals seek periods of individual seclusion or small-group intimacy." ALAN F. WESTIN, PRIVACY AND FREEDOM 8 (1967); see also *id.* at 8–11 (exploring this point further); Judith DeCew, *Privacy*, STAN. ENCYCLOPEDIA OF PHILOSOPHY, at 3.3, 3.4 (2018), https://plato.stanford.edu/entries/privacy/#PriInt [https://perma.cc/FNN5-E68W] ("Privacy is valuable because it allows one control over information about oneself, which allows one to maintain varying degrees of intimacy.") (citing CHARLES FRIED, AN ANATOMY OF VALUES (1970)); James Rachels, *Why Privacy Is Important*, 4 PHIL. & PUB. AFFAIRS 323, 326 (1975) ("I want now to give an account of the value of privacy based on the idea that there is a close connection between our ability to control who has access to us and to information about us, and our ability to create and maintain different sorts

of social relationships with different people. According to this account, privacy is necessary if we are to maintain the variety of social relationships with other people that we want to have and that is why it is important to us.").

134. For just a few of the leading book-length examples, see, e.g., SCOTT SKINNER-THOMPSON, PRIVACY AT THE MARGINS (2020); VIRGINIA EUBANKS, AUTOMATING INEQUALITY: HOW HIGH-TECH TOOLS PROFILE, POLICE, AND PUNISH THE POOR (2019); KHIARA BRIDGES, THE POVERTY OF PRIVACY RIGHTS (2017); CITRON, HATE CRIMES IN CYBERSPACE, *supra*.

135. FED. TRADE COMM'N, FTC STAFF REPORT: SELF-REGULATORY PRINCIPLES FOR ONLINE BEHAVIORAL ADVERTISING, at 1, Feb. 2009, https://www.ftc. gov/sites/default/files/documents/reports/federal-trade-commission-staff-report-self-regulatory-principles-online-behavioral-advertising/p085400behavadreport.pdf ("[A]ny self-regulatory program in this area should address practices that raise genuine privacy concerns without interfering with practices—or stifling innovation—where privacy concerns are minimal."); FED. TRADE COMM'N, PROTECTING CONSUMER PRIVACY IN AN ERA OF RAPID CHANGE: RECOMMENDATIONS FOR BUSINESSES AND POLICYMAKERS 36, 48, Mar. 2012, https://www.ftc.gov/sites/default/files/documents/reports/federal-trade-commission-report-protecting-consumer-privacy-era-rapid-change-recommendations/120326privacyreport.pdf (discussing that generally affirmative express consent is not required for marketing, but that individuals should be given a "Do Not Track" option by companies as part of the self-regulatory regime). But see Glenn Fleishman, *How the Tragic Death of Do Not Track Ruined the Web for Everyone*, FAST COMPANY, Mar. 17, 2019, https://www.fastcompany.com/90308068/how-the-tragic-death-of-do-not-track-ruined-the-web-for-everyone [https://perma.cc/5J2W-4WBC] ("A decade ago, a simple browser setting promised to make it easy to protect your online privacy. Too bad it never came anywhere near to living up to its promise."); *The "Do Not Track" Setting Does Not Stop You From Being Tracked*, DUCKDUCKGO, Feb. 5, 2019, https://spreadprivacy.com/do-not-track/ [https://perma.cc/S2RT-RBBG].

136. See *United States v. Jones*, 565 U.S. 400, 404 (2012) (affirming the Court of Appeals reversal of a drug dealer's conviction where the government introduced at trial evidence from a GPS monitor attached to the drug dealer's car without obtaining a warrant); *Carpenter v. United States*, 585 U.S. ___, 138 S. Ct. 2206 (2018) (reversing the robbery conviction of a defendant where the government introduced historical CSLI obtained without a warrant at trial). See also *United States v. White*, 62 F. Supp. 3d 614, 619 (E.D. Mich. 2014) (denying a motion to suppress evidence where a warrant for CSLI was obtained but not supported by probable cause for an alleged drug dealer's cell phones because of a good-faith reliance on the probable cause finding by the magistrate) *vacated on other grounds*, 138 S.Ct. 641 (2018).

Chapter 3

1. SIMON JENKINS, WHAT WE THINK ABOUT WHEN WE THINK ABOUT SOCCER 35 (2017).

2. *Id.* at 19–20 ("I should also confess that this book is not written from a neutral perspective. My only religious commitment is to Liverpool Football Club. All my family came from Liverpool, and although there was an Evertonian wing in my mother's family, LFC always predominated. I was raised with a fanatical devotion to LFC and a belief that my team was not just very good, but that its fans were special and its culture unique. . . . I know how irritating this can be to fans of other teams, because LFC supporters always seem so self-righteous and to think that what happened to them happened first/better/more intensely/more profoundly than elsewhere. This is obviously completely delusional and empirically wrong."). I should myself also confess that I share Jenkins's attachment, if that were not already apparent.

3. See Robert Bork, *Neutral Principles and Some First Amendment Problems*, 47 IND. L. J. 28 (1971).

4. E.g., Frederick Schauer, *The Boundaries of the First Amendment: A Preliminary Exploration of Constitutional Salience*, 117 HARV. L. REV. 1765 (2004). Schauer discusses the boundary problem and ultimately concludes that, in practice, the boundaries of First Amendment protection in the cases are best explained by the sociological phenomenon of "constitutional salience" rather than a strict definition that marks what is in and what is out of coverage.

5. DANIEL SOLOVE, UNDERSTANDING PRIVACY 172 (2008); HELEN NISSENBAUM, PRIVACY IN CONTEXT: TECHNOLOGY, POLICY, AND THE INTEGRITY OF SOCIAL LIFE 2, 7 (2009); BEATE RÖSSLER, THE VALUE OF PRIVACY 17 (2005).

6. E.g., ALAN WESTIN, PRIVACY AND FREEDOM (1967) (privacy as control); Richard A. Posner, *The Right of Privacy*, 12 GA. L. REV. 393, 400 (1977) ("[E]veryone should be allowed to protect himself from disadvantageous transactions by ferreting out concealed facts about individuals which are material to the representations (implicit or explicit) that those individuals make concerning their moral qualities.").

7. For an earlier version of my argument here, see Neil Richards, *Four Privacy Myths*, in A WORLD WITHOUT PRIVACY? WHAT LAW CAN AND SHOULD DO (Austin Sarat ed. 2015).

8. Evan Bartlett, *Tory MP Richard Graham Accused of Quoting Joseph Goebbels in Defence of New Surveillance Bill*, THE INDEPENDENT, Nov. 4, 2015, https://www.indy100.com/article/tory-mp-richard-graham-accused-of-quoting-joseph-goebbels-in-defence-of-new-surveillance-bill--bklSCE9nOg.

9. Posner, *The Right of Privacy, supra*, at 400.

10. *Haynes v. Alfred Knopf*, 8 F.3d 1222 (7th Cir. 1993).

11. Ian Parker, *The Story of a Suicide*, THE NEW YORKER, Feb. 6, 2012, http://www.newyorker.com/reporting/2012/02/06/120206fa_fact_parker.

12. See generally DANIELLE KEATS CITRON, HATE CRIMES IN CYBERSPACE (2014), Danielle Keats Citron, *Sexual Privacy*, 128 YALE L. J. 1870 (2019).

13. Danielle Keats Citron & Mary Anne Franks, *Criminalizing Revenge Porn*, 49 WAKE FOREST L. REV. 345, 346 (2014).

14. E.g., Asia A. Eaton et al., *2017 Nationwide Online Study of Nonconsensual Porn Victimization and Perpetration*, CYBER CIVIL RIGHTS INITIATIVE 12, June 2017, https://www.cybercivilrights.org/wp -content/uploads/2017/06/CCRI-2017-Research-Report.pdf (finding women almost two times more likely than men to have been the victims of actual or threatened nonconsensual pornography).

15. CITRON, HATE CRIMES IN CYBERSPACE, *supra*, at 149.

16. Citron, *Sexual Privacy, supra*, at 1875.

17. Cyber Civil Rights Initiative, *48 States + DC + One Territory Now Have Revenge Porn Laws*, https://www.cybercivilrights.org/revenge-porn-laws/.

18. Lin Taylor, *"Revenge Porn" Victims Could Win Anonymity in UK Courts*, REUTERS, June 26, 2019, https://www.reuters.com/article/us-britain-women-crime/revenge-porn-victims-could-win-anonymity-in-uk-courts-idUSKCN1TR2JL.

19. NEIL RICHARDS, INTELLECTUAL PRIVACY: RETHINKING CIVIL LIBERTIES FOR THE DIGITAL AGE (2015).

20. See R. H. Helmholz, *The Roman Law of Blackmail*, 30 J. L. STUD. 33 (2001).

21. "Blackmail," *Black's Law Dictionary* (11th ed. 2019).

22. James Lindgren, *Unraveling the Paradox of Blackmail*, 84 COLUM. L. REV. 670 (1984) ("In blackmail, the heart of the problem is that two separate acts, each of which is a moral and legal right, can combine to make a moral and legal wrong."); James Lindgren, *Blackmail: An Afterword*, 141 PENN. L. REV. 1975, 1976–77 (1993); Leo Katz, *Blackmail and Other Forms of Arm-Twisting*, 141 PENN. L. REV. 1567, 1613–14 (1993); Peter Westen, *Why the Paradox of Blackmail Is So Hard to Resolve*, 9 OHIO ST. CRIM. L. J. 585 (2012).

23. Cf. SHOSHANNA ZUBOFF, THE AGE OF SURVEILLANCE CAPITALISM: THE FIGHT FOR A HUMAN FUTURE AT THE NEW FRONTIER OF POWER 127 (2019) ("With Google in the lead, surveillance capitalism vastly expanded the market dynamic as it learned to expropriate human experience and translate it into coveted behavioral predictions."). Zuboff notes further that these activities are largely beyond democratic control; as she puts it memorably, referring to Google's founders, "Two men at Google who do not enjoy the legitimacy of the vote, democratic oversight, or the demands of shareholder governance exercise control over the organization and presentation of the world's information."

24. Neil M. Richards & Daniel J. Solove, *Privacy's Other Path: Recovering the Law of Confidentiality*, 96 GEO. L. J. 123, 129–30 (2006).

25. CHRISTENA E. NIPPERT-ENG, ISLANDS OF PRIVACY (2010).

26. Robert C. Post, *The Social Foundations of Privacy: Community and Self in the Common Law Tort*, 77 CALIF. L. REV. 957 (1989).

27. *Hamberger v. Eastman*, 206 A.2d 239 (N.H. 1964) (listening device in tenant bedroom is an invasion of privacy); Mass. Gen. Laws Ann. ch. 272, § 105(b) (West 2014) ("upskirt" photography); Va. Code Ann. § 18.2-386.1(A)(ii) (2014) (same); 13 Vt. Stat. Ann. tit. 13 § 2606 (West 2015) (upheld as constitutional by *State v. VanBuren*, 214 A.3d 791 (Vt. 2019)) (criminalizing knowing disclosure of nude photos without

consent); 720 Ill. Comp. Stat. 5/11-23.5 (2012) (criminalizing nonconsensual dissemination of private sexual images); Ga. Code Ann. § 16-11-92 (2019) (criminalizing "intentionally coercing" an adult to distribute any photograph/video or image depicting an individual in nudity/sexual conduct); Cal. Penal Code § 528.5(a) (West 2020) (criminalizing impersonation, including deep-fake sex videos). See also Cyber Civil Rights Initiative, *46 States + DC + One Territory Now Have Revenge Porn Laws*, *supra*; Citron, *Sexual Privacy*, *supra*, at 1929–38; Mary Anne Franks, *Drafting an Effective "Revenge Porn" Law: A Guide for Legislators*, Aug. 17, 2015, (unpublished manuscript), https://ssrn.com/abstract=2468823.

28. DANIEL J. SOLOVE, NOTHING TO HIDE: THE FALSE TRADEOFF BETWEEN PRIVACY AND SECURITY 50 (2011). An earlier version of Solove's argument appears as Daniel J. Solove, *"I've Got Nothing to Hide" and Other Misunderstandings of Privacy*, 44 SAN DIEGO L. REV. 745 (2007).

29. See RICHARDS, INTELLECTUAL PRIVACY, supra.

30. See JULIE E. COHEN, CONFIGURING THE NETWORKED SELF (2014); Julie E. Cohen, *Turning Privacy Inside Out*, 20 THEORETICAL INQUIRIES IN LAW 1 (2019); Julie E. Cohen, *What Privacy Is For*, 126 HARV. L. REV. 1904 (2013).

31. Neil M. Richards, *The Dangers of Surveillance*, 126 HARV. L. REV. 1934, 1946 (2013).

32. Sophie Kleeman, *In One Quote, Snowden Just Destroyed the Biggest Myth About Privacy*, MIC, May 29, 2015, https://www.mic.com/articles/119602/in-one-quote-edward-snowden-summed-up-why-our-privacy-is-worth-fighting-for [https://perma.cc/7GBL-8RD4].

33. Candy Thompson, *MTA Recording Bus Conversations to Eavesdrop on Trouble*, BALTIMORE SUN, Oct. 17, 2012 (buses); Emily Opio, *Baltimore Spending Board Approves Surveillance Plane Pilot Program to Capture Images From City Streets*, BALTIMORE SUN, Apr. 1, 2020 (spy planes).

34. Davey Winder, *How to Stop Your Smart Home Spying on You*, THE GUARDIAN, Mar. 8, 2020, https://www.theguardian.com/technology/2020/mar/08/how-to-stop-your-smart-home-spying-on-you-lightbulbs-doorbell-ring-google-assistant-alexa-privacy.

35. Camila Domonoske, *Vibrator Maker to Pay Millions Over Claims It Secretly Tracked Use*, NPR, Mar. 14, 2017, https://www.npr.org/sections/thetwo-way/2017/03/14/520123490/vibrator-maker-to-pay-millions-over-claims-it-secretly-tracked-use; Ashley Carman, *Sex Toy Company Admits to Recording Users' Remote Sex Sessions, Calls It a "Minor Bug,"* THE VERGE, Nov. 10, 2017, https://www.theverge.com/2017/11/10/16634442/lovense-sex-toy-spy-surveillance [https://perma.cc/8DHT-6WES]; Rose Minutaglio, *Is Your Sex Toy Spying on You?*, ELLE, Oct. 14, 2019, https://www.elle.com/culture/tech/a28846210/smart-sex-toy-dildo-butt-plug-hacking/ [https://perma.cc/VLJ4-2UBJ].

36. See Neil Richards & Woodrow Hartzog, *Taking Trust Seriously in Privacy Law*, 19 STAN. TECH. L. REV. 431, 437 (2016) (collecting examples). For workplace use of predictive analytics as "creepy," see Don Peck, *They're Watching You at Work*, THE ATLANTIC, Dec. 2013, https://www.theatlantic.com/magazine/archive/2013/12/theyre-watching-you-at-work/354681/. For Google's use of health and Gmail

data for its own purposes, see Sidney Fussell, *Google's Totally Creepy, Totally Legal Health-Data Harvesting*, THE ATLANTIC, Nov. 14, 2019, https://www.theatlantic.com/technology/archive/2019/11/google-project-nightingale-all-your-health-data/601999/ (describing as "creepy" Google's secret partnership with healthcare network Ascension, titled "Project Nightingale," which shared confidential health data between the two entities without patient knowledge or consent); James Vincent, *The Problem With Google's Health Care Ambitions Is That No One Knows Where They End*, THE VERGE, Nov. 12, 2019, https://www.theverge.com/2019/11/12/20961018/google-health-care-project-nightingale-patient-data-collection-ambitions (describing as "creepy" Google's secret "Project Nightingale" health-data sharing agreement with Ascension Health). For Zoom privacy, see Sara Morrison, *Zoom Responds to Its Privacy (and Porn) Problems*, VOX, Apr. 2, 2020, https://www.vox.com/recode/2020/3/31/21201019/zoom-coronavirus-privacy-hacks (describing certain features of Zoom, such as its attention tracking function, as "invasive, creepy and unwelcome" in many settings). For DNA database and smart speaker data used by police, see Megan Molteni, *The Creepy Genetics Behind the Golden State Killer Case*, WIRED, Apr. 27, 2018, https://www.wired.com/story/detectives-cracked-the-golden-state-killer-case-using-genetics/ (describing as "creepy" a genealogy website that was intended to be used by people looking to learn more about their families but that was used by law enforcement to track down a serial killer); Geoffrey A. Fowler, *How We Survive the Surveillance Apocalypse*, WASH. POST, Dec. 31, 2019, https://www.washingtonpost.com/technology/2019/12/31/how-we-survive-surveillance-apocalypse/ (describing as "creepy" in-home voice assistants such as Amazon's Alexa and Apple's Siri and how the recordings captured by the device are subsequently used).

37. See, e.g., Kashmir Hill, *How Target Figured Out a Teen Girl Was Pregnant Before Her Father Did*, FORBES, Feb. 16, 2012, https://www.forbes.com/sites/kashmirhill/2012/02/16/how-target-figured-out-a-teen-girl-was-pregnant-before-her-father-did/#6f9e14b06668 (reacting to Duhigg's article and positing that "what Target discovered fairly quickly is that it creeped people out that the company knew about their pregnancies in advance"); Hugh J. Watson, *Addressing the Privacy Issues of Big Data*, 19 BUS. INTELLIGENCE J. 2, 4 (2014) https://www.academia.edu/33249975/Addressing_the_Privacy_Issues_of_Big_Data ("Although Target's activities are legal, they strike some people as creepy, if not inappropriate."); Nina Golgowski, *How Target Knows When Its Shoppers Are Pregnant—and Figured Out a Teen Was Before Her Father Did*, THE DAILY MAIL, Feb. 18, 2012, https://www.dailymail.co.uk/news/article-2102859/How-Target-knows-shoppers-pregnant--figured-teen-father-did.html (describing Target's practice of mixing extremely targeted ads in with more generic ads as an effort to "avoid a creeped out, stalker-like feeling" from customers); Kelly Bourdet, *Target Knows You're Pregnant*, VICE, Feb. 18, 2012, https://www.vice.com/en_us/article/qkkepv/target-knows-you-re-pregnant [https://perma.cc/E8UK-2JT] ("It's doubtlessly unnerving to receive baby food coupons before you've even told your extended family that you're expecting. So, how does Target keep from skeeving out women? They just fake it. They take all their baby advertising and intersperse it with meaningless advertisements for things like lawnmowers and light bulbs."); Jordan Ellenberg,

What's Even Creepier Than Target Guessing That You're Pregnant?, SLATE, June 9, 2014, https://slate.com/human-interest/2014/06/big-data-whats-even-creepier-than-target-guessing-that-youre-pregnant.html (stating it is "[s]pooky to contemplate, living in a world where Google and Facebook and your phone, and, geez, even Target, know more about you than your parents do"); George Kuhn, *How Target Used Data Analytics to Predict Pregnancies*, DRIVE RESEARCH, Dec. 6, 2016, https://www.driveresearch.com/market-research-company-blog/how-target-used-data-analytics-to-predict-pregnancies/ (stating that the Target marketing department's practice of mixing normal ads with targeted ads was to minimize the "creep factor").

38. Maria Cantwell, *The State of Online Privacy and Data Security*, U.S. Sen. Comm. on Commerce, Science and Transportation, at 6, Nov. 2019 https://www.cantwell.senate.gov/imo/media/doc/The%20State%20of%20Online%20Privacy%20and%20Data%20Security.pdf.

39. Shara Tibken, *Apple's Cook Says Ads That Follow You Online Are "Creepy,"* CNET, Apr. 6, 2018, https://www.cnet.com/news/apple-tim-cook-says-facebook-ads-that-follow-you-are-creepy-daca-dreamers-privacy-taxes/.

40. Omer Tene & Jules Polonetsky, *A Theory of Creepy: Technology, Privacy, and Shifting Social Norms*, 16 YALE J. L. & TECH. 59, 61 (2013–14).

41. *Id.* at 101.

42. See MARGARET O'MARA, THE CODE: SILICON VALLEY AND THE REMAKING OF AMERICA, 366 (2019).

43. Helen Nissenbaum, *Privacy as Contextual Integrity*, 79 WASH. L. REV. 119, 155 (2004); NISSENBAUM, PRIVACY IN CONTEXT, supra.

44. NISSENBAUM, PRIVACY IN CONTEXT, *supra*, at 3.

45. *Id.*

46. Nissenbaum, *Privacy as Contextual Integrity, supra*, at 145.

47. NISSENBAUM, PRIVACY IN CONTEXT, supra, at 3, 11.

48. *Katz v. United States*, 389 U.S. 347, 360–61 (1967) (Harlan, J., concurring). Justice Harlan's concurrence has become the widely accepted test for determining when a person has a reasonable expectation of privacy under the Fourth Amendment. See *United States v. Jones*, 565 U.S. 400, 406 (2012) ("Our later cases have applied the analysis of Justice Harlan's concurrence in that case, which said that a violation occurs when government officers violate a person's 'reasonable expectation of privacy.'"). For a recent case noting Harlan's concurrence as the legal test and discussing its importance, see *Georgia v. Georgia.Public.Recource.Org*, 140 S. Ct. 1498, n. 10 (2020) (Thomas, J. dissenting) (using the Harlan concurrence as an example of famous "separate writing [that] takes on a canonical status").

49. *Katz v. United States*, 389 U.S. at 360–61; see also *United States v. Karo*, 468 U.S. 705, 726 (1984) (citing *Katz* in noting that "two people who speak face to face in a private place or on a private telephone line both may share an expectation that the conversation will remain private"); *United States v. United States Dist. Court*, 407 U.S. 297, 308 (1972) (citing *Katz* and discussing warrantless wiretaps, stating, "Nor is there any question or doubt as to the necessity of obtaining a warrant in the surveillance of crimes unrelated to the national security interest").

50. Evan Selinger, *Why Do We Love to Call New Technologies "Creepy"?*, SLATE, Aug. 22, 2012, https://perma.cc/UZ9W-DZCH.

51. Ye Diana Wang & Henry H. Emurian, *An Overview of Online Trust: Concept, Elements, and Implications*, 21 COMPUTERS IN HUMAN BEHAVIOR 105 (2005), http://citeseerx.ist.psu.edu/viewdoc/download?doi=10.1.1.90.2184&rep=rep1&type=pdf.

52. danah boyd, *Facebook's Privacy Train Wreck*, 14 CONVERGENCE 13 http://www.danah.org/papers/FacebookPrivacyTrainwreck.pdf; Tiffany A. Pempek, Yevdokiya A. Yermolayeva, & Sandra L. Calvert, *College Students' Social Networking Experiences on Facebook*, 30 J. APPLIED DEV. PSYCH. 227 (2009).

53. Sam Biddle, *Facebook's New News Feed: The Biggest Change in Years*, GIZMODO, Mar. 7, 2013, http://gizmodo.com/5989228/facebooks-new-news-feed-the-biggest-changein-years-updating-live.

54. E.g., GLENN GREENWALD, NO PLACE TO HIDE: EDWARD SNOWDEN, THE NSA, AND THE U.S. SURVEILLANCE STATE (2014) (Snowden revelations); FRANK PASQUALE, BLACK BOX SOCIETY (2015) (scoring algorithms).

55. JULIA ANGWIN, DRAGNET NATION 4–5 (2014).

56. Richards, *The Dangers of Surveillance, supra*, at 1936; ZUBOFF, THE AGE OF SURVEILLANCE CAPITALISM, supra, at 8–9, 12–14.

57. Katharina Buchholz, *How Much of the Internet Consists of Porn?*, STATISTA, Feb. 11, 2019, https://www.statista.com/chart/16959/share-of-the-internet-that-is-porn/; Alexis Kleinman, *Porn Sites Get More Visitors Each Month Than Netflix, Amazon and Twitter Combined*, HUFFINGTON POST, Dec. 6, 2017, https://www.huffpost.com/entry/internet-porn-stats_n_3187682.

58. Alexis C. Madrigal, *Deconstructing the Creepiness of the "Girls Around Me" App—and What Facebook Could Do About It*, THE ATLANTIC, Apr. 2, 2012, https://www.theatlantic.com/technology/archive/2012/04/deconstructing-the-creepiness-of-the-girls-around-me-app-151-and-what-facebook-could-do-about-it/255351/.

59. Ammar Kalia, *Newly Single? A Beginner's Guide to the Best Dating Apps*, THE GUARDIAN, Dec. 2, 2019, https://www.theguardian.com/lifeandstyle/2019/dec/02/newly-single-a-beginners-guide-to-the-best-dating-apps.

60. Marshall Kirkpatrick, *Facebook's Zuckerberg Says the Age of Privacy Is Over*, READWRITEWEB, Jan. 10. 2010.

61. Lisa A. Austin, *Why Privacy Is About Power, Not Consent or Harm*, at 150, in A WORLD WITHOUT PRIVACY? WHAT LAW CAN AND SHOULD DO (Austin Sarat ed. 2015).

62. Ryan Calo, *Digital Market Manipulation*, 82 GEO. WASH. L. REV. 995, 1015 (2014); STEFAN H. THOMKE, EXPERIMENTATION WORKS: THE SURPRISING POWER OF BUSINESS EXPERIMENTS 85 (2020).

63. E.g., Matthew Keys, *A Brief History of Facebook's Ever-Changing Privacy Settings*, MEDIUM, Mar. 21, 2017, https://medium.com/@matthewkeys/a-brief-history-of-facebooks-ever-changing-privacy-settings-8167dadd3bd0.

64. Ron Kohavi & Stephan Thomke, *The Surprising Power of Online Experiments*, HARV. BUS. REV., Sept.–Oct. 2017, at 2; Hannah Fry, *Big Tech Is Testing You*, THE NEW YORKER, Feb. 24, 2020, https://www.newyorker.com/magazine/2020/03/02/big-tech-is-testing-you [https://perma.cc/6U57-Y2DY].

65. *Id.* For other discussions of A/B testing and related forms of human experimentation at technology companies, see, e.g., MICHAEL LUCA & MAX H. BAZERMAN, THE POWER OF EXPERIMENTS: DECISION-MAKING IN A DATA-DRIVEN WORLD (2020); THOMKE, EXPERIMENTATION WORKS, *supra*; RON KOHAVI ET AL., TRUSTWORTHY ONLINE CONTROLLED EXPERIMENTS: A PRACTICAL GUIDE TO A/B TESTING (2020); Ya Xu et al., *From Infrastructure to Culture: A/B Testing Challenges in Large Scale Social Networks,* available in PROCEEDINGS OF THE 21ST ACM SIGKDD INT'L CONF. ON KNOWLEDGE DISCOVERY AND DATA MINING, Aug. 2015, at 2227–36, https://dl.acm.org/doi/abs/10.1145/2783258.2788602; Diane Tang et al., *Overlapping Experiment Infrastructure: More, Better, Faster Experimentation,* available in PROCEEDINGS OF THE 16TH ACM SIGKDD INTERNATIONAL CONFERENCE ON KNOWLEDGE DISCOVERY AND DATA MINING, July 2010, at 17–26, https://dl.acm.org/doi/10.1145/1835804.1835810.

66. ZUBOFF, THE AGE OF SURVEILLANCE CAPITALISM, supra, at 10.

67. Id. at 11.

68. Shane Richmond, *Eric Schmidt: Google Gets Close to the "Creepy Line,"* TELEGRAPH, Oct. 5, 2010, https://ubcckengaren.blogspot.com/2010/10/eric-schmidt-google-gets-close-to.html.

69. Neil Richards & Woodrow Hartzog, *The Pathologies of Digital Consent,* 96 WASH. U. L. REV. 1461, 1463 (2019).

70. JOSEPH TUROW, THE VOICE CATCHERS: HOW MARKETERS LISTEN IN TO EXPLOIT YOUR FEELINGS, YOUR PRIVACY, AND YOUR WALLET (2021).

71. STEVEN LEVY, FACEBOOK: THE INSIDE STORY 475–76 (2020); Jefferson Graham, *Is Facebook Listening to Me? Why Those Ads Appear After You Talk About Things,* USA TODAY, June 27, 2019, https://www.usatoday.com/story/tech/talkingtech/2019/06/27/does-facebook-listen-to-your-conversations/1478468001/.

72. See 18 U.S.C. § 2511 (prohibiting the interception of wire, oral, or electronic communications); 18 U.S.C. § 2520 (authorizing the recovery $10,000 per violation in civil damages for violations of ECPA).

73. LEVY, FACEBOOK, *supra*, at 476.

74. Richards & Hartzog, *Taking Trust Seriously, supra*, at 444.

75. *Written Testimony from Facebook to House Energy and Commerce Committee for Record of April 11, 2018 Hearing,* June 29, 2018, https://docs.house.gov/meetings/IF/IF00/20180411/108090/HHRG-115-IF00-Wstate-ZuckerbergM-20180411.pdf.

76. The term "privacy as control" was memorably used by Paul Schwartz in his own perceptive and farsighted critique of control talk in the late 1990s. See Paul M. Schwartz, *Privacy and Democracy in Cyberspace,* 52 VAND. L. REV. 1609, 1658 (1999). The critique of control I offer in this chapter has been undeniably shaped by Prof. Schwartz's visionary early work.

77. Samuel D. Warren & Louis D. Brandeis, *The Right to Privacy,* 4 HARV. L. REV. 193, 198 (1890).

78. WESTIN, PRIVACY AND FREEDOM, *supra*, at 7.

79. *Id.*

80. Woodrow Hartzog, Privacy's Blueprint: The Battle to Control the Design of New Technologies 58–64 (2019); U.S. Dept. of Health, Educ. and Welfare, *Records, Computers and the Rights of Citizens: Report of the Sec's Advisory Committee on Automated Personal Data Systems* xxiii–xxiv (1973).

81. See Privacy Act of 1974, Pub. L. No. 93-579, § 2(a)(4), 88 Stat. 1896 (1974) (codified as amended at 5 U.S.C. § 552a; California Consumer Privacy Act, Cal. Civ. Code § 1798.100 *et seq.* (2020).

82. EU Reg. 2016/679, pmbl. ¶ 7, 2016 O.J. (L 119) 1, 2 (GDPR Recital 7).

83. EU Regulation 2016/679, arts. 4(7), 24, 2016 O.J. (L 119) 1, 33 (definition and responsibilities of a "controller").

84. Christine Wilson, Comm'r, Fed. Trade Comm'n, *A Defining Moment for Privacy: The Time Is Ripe for Federal Privacy Legislation, Remarks at the Future of Privacy Forum*, 2, 13, Feb. 6, 2020.

85. Google. Inc., *Privacy & Terms*, https://policies.google.com/privacy#infochoices [https://perma.cc/9Q8E-WN6B] (last visited May 25, 2020).

86. Mark Zuckerberg, *A Privacy-Focused Vision for Social Networking*, Facebook, Mar. 6, 2019, https://www.facebook.com/notes/mark-zuckerberg/a-privacy-focused-vision-for-social-networking/10156700570096634/ (emphasis added).

87. Erin Egan & Dave Braser, *Now You Can See and Control the Data That Apps and Websites Share With Facebook*, Facebook, Aug. 20, 2019, https://about.fb.com/news/2019/08/off-facebook-activity/ [https://perma.cc/9J87-8WSE].

88. *Written Testimony of Rachel Welch, SVP of Policy and External Affairs Charter Communications on "Examining Safeguards for Consumer Data Privacy" Before the Senate*, Sept. 26, 2018, https://policy.charter.com/testimony/written-testimony-rachel-welch-senior-vice-president-policy-external-affairs-charter-communications-examining-safeguards-consumer-data-privacy-senate-com/.

89. Barclays, *Smart Data: Putting Consumers in Control of Their Data and Enabling Innovation*, https://home.barclays/content/dam/home-barclays/documents/citizenship/our-reporting-and-policy-positions/Barclays-submission-BEIS-Consultation-on-Smart-Data.pdf [https://perma.cc/5CCZ-HDX5].

90. Kenneth Olmstead & Michelle Atkinson, *Apps Permissions in the Google Play Store*, Pew Res. Ctr., Nov. 10, 2015, http://www.pewinternet.org/2015/11/10/apps-permissions-in-the-google-play-store/.

91. Woodrow Hartzog, *The Case Against Idealising Control*, 4 Eur. Data Pro. L. Rev. 423, 428 (2018).

92. Richards & Hartzog, *Taking Trust Seriously*, *supra*, at 444.

93. Brett Frischmann & Evan Selinger, Re-Engineering Humanity 210 (2018); Zuboff, The Age of Surveillance Capitalism, *supra*.

94. Google, *Privacy & Terms*, https://policies.google.com/privacy#infochoices [https://perma.cc/9Q8E-WN6B] (last visited May 25, 2020).

95. Amazon Privacy Notice, https://www.amazon.com/gp/help/customer/display.html?nodeId=468496 [https://perma.cc/P5LL-CZ3R] (last visited May 25, 2020).

96. *Id.*

97. Alex C. Madrigal, *Reading the Privacy Policies You Encounter in a Year Would Take 76 Work Days*, THE ATLANTIC, Mar. 1, 2012, http://www.theatlantic.com/technology/archive/2012/03/reading-the-privacy-policies-youencounter-in-a-year-would-take-76-work-days/253851; Aleecia M. McDonald & Lorrie Faith Cranor, *The Cost of Reading Privacy Policies*, 4 I/S: J. L. POL'Y INFO. SOC'Y 543 (2009).

98. NORWEGIAN CONSUMER COUNCIL, 250,000 WORDS OF APP TERMS AND CONDITIONS (2016).

99. *Id.*

100. See, e.g., Hope King, *Facebook Messenger Tracks Your Location by Default*, CNNBUSINESS, May 28, 2015, https://money.cnn.com/2015/05/28/technology/facebook-messenger-location-tracking-android/; Thomas Germain, *Facebook's New Location Settings Give Users More Control*, CONSUMER REPORTS, Feb. 20, 2019, https://www.consumerreports.org/privacy/new-facebook-location-privacy-setting/ ("In a blog post, Facebook said that users who turned on Facebook's Location History setting in the past will now see an alert notifying them about the new control. For users who have Location History on, the Background Location setting will be turned on by default."); April Glaser, *Facebook Will Tell You How to Turn Off Facial Recognition: Why Wait?*, SLATE, Sept. 3, 2019, https://slate.com/technology/2019/09/turn-off-facial-recognition-facebook-default-how-to.html. ("On Tuesday, Facebook announced an important change to its stance on face ID. Now, all facial recognition, including tagging, will be turned off by default for new users, who can choose to opt in. If you already had facial recognition turned on, you won't receive a notice to turn it off.").

101. Fry, *Big Tech Is Testing You*, *supra* ("In fact, if you've recently used Facebook, browsed Netflix, or run a Google search, you have almost certainly participated in an experiment of some kind. Google alone ran fifteen thousand of them in 2018, involving countless unsuspecting Internet users. 'We don't want high-level executives discussing whether a blue background or a yellow background will lead to more ad clicks,' Hal Varian, Google's chief economist, tells the authors. 'Why debate this point, since we can simply run an experiment to find out?' ").

102. For more information on the concept of dark patterns, see Harry Brignull's website, Dark Patterns, http://www.darkpatterns.org (last visited May 25, 2020). See also Lior Strahilevitz & Jamie Luguri, *Shining a Light on Dark Patterns*, U. Chicago Pub L. Working Paper No. 719, 2019, https://ssrn.com/abstract=3431205.

103. NORWEGIAN CONSUMER COUNCIL, DECEIVED BY DESIGN: HOW TECH COMPANIES USE DARK PATTERNS TO DISCOURAGE US FROM EXERCISING OUR RIGHTS TO PRIVACY (2018), https://fil.forbrukerradet.no/wp-content/uploads/2018/06/2018-06-27-deceived-by-design-final.pdf

104. Consider, for example, Zuckerberg's Senate testimony, in which "control" came up an astonishing sixty-five times. *Transcript of Mark Zuckerberg's Senate Hearing*, WASH. POST, Apr. 10, 2018, https://www.washingtonpost.com/news/the-switch/wp/2018/04/10/transcript-of-mark-zuckerbergs-senate-hearing/ [https://perma.cc/BE5J-KPFP] (containing Facebook CEO Mark Zuckerberg's testimony before the Senate Commerce and Judiciary Committee). ("Senator, the way I think about this is there

are two broad categories. This probably doesn't line up with whatever the—the specific report that you were seeing is. And I can make sure that we follow-up with you afterwards to get you the information you need on that. The two broad categories that I think about are content that a person [has] chosen to share and that they have complete control over, they get to control when they put into the service, when they take it down, who sees it. And then the other category are data that are connected to making the ads relevant. You have complete control over both. If you turn off the data related to ads, you can choose not to share any content or control exactly who sees it or take down the content in the former category."); Srinivas Narayanan, *An Update About Face Recognition at Facebook*, Facebook, Sept. 3, 2019, https://about. fb.com/news/2019/09/update-face-recognition/ [https://perma.cc/V5XG-P62A] (beginning with the sentence "Facebook has always given you control over whether we use face recognition technology to recognize you in photos").

105. Austin, *Why Privacy Is About Power, Not Consent or Harm*, *supra*, at 150–59.

106. Egan & Braser, *Now You Can See and Control the Data That Apps and Websites Share with Facebook*, *supra*.

107. NORWEGIAN CONSUMER COUNCIL, OUT OF CONTROL: HOW CONSUMERS ARE EXPLOITED BY THE ONLINE ADVERTISING INDUSTRY 5–6 (2020), https://fil. forbrukerradet.no/wp-content/uploads/2020/01/2020-01-14-out-of-control-final-version.pdf.

108. Cf. Alice E. Marwick, *Privacy Work*, Privacy Law Scholars' Conference, June 2020 (unpublished manuscript on file with author).

109. Laura Parker, *The World's Plastic Pollution Crisis Explained*, NAT. GEO., June 7, 2019, https://www.nationalgeographic.com/environment/habitats/plastic-pollution/.

110. Jessica Glenzer, *Trump's Decision to Allow Plastic Bottle Sales in National Parks Condemned*, THE GUARDIAN, Aug. 20, 2017, https://www.theguardian.com/us-news/2017/aug/20/trumps-decision-to-allow-plastic-bottle-sales-in-national-parks-slammed.

111. Cf. FRISCHMANN & SELINGER, RE-ENGINEERING HUMANITY, *supra*.

112. Scott R. Peppet, *Unraveling Privacy: The Personal Prospectus and the Threat of a Full-Disclosure Future*, 105 Nw. U. L. REV. 1153, 1153–54 (2015); Motor Vehicle Safety Act of 2010, S. 3302, 111th Cong. § 107 (legislation introduced by Congress in 2010 to make recording devices mandatory in new cars); Patrick R. Mueller, Comment, *Every Time You Brake, Every Turn You Make—I'll Be Watching You: Protecting Driver Privacy in Event Data Recorder Information*, 2006 WIS. L. REV. 135 (2006).

113. Sam Stanton & Ryan Lillis, *Relative's DNA From Genealogy Websites Cracked East Area Rapist Case, DA's Office Says*, SACRAMENTO BEE, Apr. 28, 2018; Megan Molteni, *The Creepy Genetics Behind the Golden State Killer Case*, WIRED, Apr. 27, 2018, https://www.wired.com/story/detectives-cracked-the-golden-state-killer-case-using-genetics/.

114. Jeena Harbison & Mark Osborne, *DNA from tissue taken out of alleged Golden State Killer's trash led to arrest, warrant shows*, ABC News, June 2, 2018, https://abcnews. go.com/US/dna-tissue-alleged-golden-state-killers-trash-led/story?id=55602892..

115. See Lisa Austin, *Rereading Westin*, 20 THEORETICAL INQUIRIES L. 53 (2019).

116. Austin, *Why Privacy Is About Power, Not Consent or Harm, supra*, at 2–3.

117. Kirkpatrick, *Facebook's Zuckerberg Says the Age of Privacy Is Over, supra*.

118. See HARTZOG, PRIVACY'S BLUEPRINT, supra, at 197 ("Virtually every design element of social media technologies is made with one goal in mind—to get you to share, baby, share."). Hartzog further explains using Facebook as an example, "New features like the 'On This Day' feature were built to nudge users to repost previously submitted photos and updates. Reminders about special occasions like Mother's Day were engineered to nudge you to stay in contact with other users. The Facebook app has even started going through the new photos and other content on your phones and asking if you'd like to post them. . . . Every little required expenditure of effort is seen as a barrier between you and the Post button. For example, the menu bar for the mobile Facebook app wasn't moved to the bottom of the screen just for aesthetics. It was to get those buttons closer to your thumbs.").

119. ZUBOFF, THE AGE OF SURVEILLANCE CAPITALISM, *supra*, at 340. Zuboff's review also found that majorities supported increased "user control over personal information." *Id*. Though I have already explained my reservations with the limits of fetishizing control as a solution for privacy, a wish for more control and less disempowerment over data practices also supports the conclusion that people do, in fact, care about privacy.

120. Brooke Auxier, *Most Americans Support Right to Have Some Personal Info Removed From Online Searches*, Pew Res. Ctr., Jan. 27, 2020, https://www.pewresearch.org/fact-tank/2020/01/27/most-americans-support-right-to-have-some-personal-info-removed-from-online-searches/?utm_source=adaptivemailer&utm_medium=email&utm_campaign=20-01-27%20right%20to%20be%20forgotten&org=982&lvl=100&ite=5321&lea=1191334&ctr=0&par=1&trk= [https://perma.cc/WEC9-VRN3]; Brooke Auxier et al., *Americans and Privacy: Concerned, Confused and Feeling Lack of Control Over Their Personal Information*, Pew Res. Ctr., Nov. 15, 2019, https://www.pewresearch.org/internet/2019/11/15/americans-and-privacy-concerned-confused-and-feeling-lack-of-control-over-their-personal-information/?utm_source=AdaptiveMailer&utm_medium=email&utm_campaign=19-11-15%20Privacy&org=982&lvl=100&ite=4962&lea=1125032&ctr=0&par=1&trk= [https://perma.cc/6UC3-5KHX].

121. See, e.g., Andrew Perrin, *Half of Americans Have Decided Not to Use a Product or Service Because of Privacy Concerns*, Pew Res. Ctr., Apr. 14, 2020, https://www.pewresearch.org/fact-tank/2020/04/14/half-of-americans-have-decided-not-to-use-a-product-or-service-because-of-privacy-concerns/; Sam Sabin, *Most Voters Say Congress Should Make Privacy Legislation a Priority Next Year*, MORNING CONSULT, Dec. 18, 2019, https://morningconsult.com/2019/12/18/most-voters-say-congress-should-make-privacy-legislation-a-priority-next-year/ (finding that 65% of American voters agreed that "data privacy is one of the biggest issues our society faces and legislation is needed to stop data breaches").

122. Glenn Greenwald, *NSA Collecting Phone Records of Millions of Verizon Customers Daily*, THE GUARDIAN, June 6, 2013, https://www.theguardian.com/world/2013/jun/06/nsa-phone-records-verizon-court-order [https://perma.cc/UC9Q-BSP9];

Barton Gellman & Laura Poitras, *U.S., British Intelligence Mining Data From Nine U.S. Internet Companies in Broad Secret Program*, WASH. POST, June 7, 2013, http://www.washingtonpost.com/investigations/us-intelligence-mining-data-from-nine-us-internet-companies-in-broad-secret-program/2013/06/06/3a0c0da8-cebf-11e2-8845-d970ccb04497_story.html?tid=a_inl_manual   [https://perma.cc/N4S6-TXCN]; Mark Mazzetti & Michael S. Schmidt, *Ex-Worker at C.I.A. Says He Leaked Data on Surveillance*, N.Y. TIMES, June 9, 2013, https://www.nytimes.com/2013/06/10/us/former-cia-worker-says-he-leaked-surveillance-data.html [https://perma.cc/4UF6-9RWQ].

123. 18 U.S.C. § 3103a.(b) (containing the relevant section of the U.S.A. Patriot Act authorizing delayed notice of search warrants if three criteria are met); Cyrus Farivar, *How a Hacker Proved Cops Used a Secret Government Phone Tracker to Find Him*, POLITICO, June 3, 2018, https://www.politico.com/magazine/story/2018/06/03/cyrus-farivar-book-excerpt-stingray-218588 [https://perma.cc/FD9Q-8RXM]; Sam Biddle, *Long-Secret Stingray Manuals Detail How Police Can Spy on Phones*, THE INTERCEPT, Sept. 12, 2016, https://theintercept.com/2016/09/12/long-secret-stingray-manuals-detail-how-police-can-spy-on-phones/ [https://perma.cc/9V8Z-5CFV].

124. George Packer, *Amazon and the Perils of Non-Disclosure*, THE NEW YORKER, Feb. 11, 2014, https://www.newyorker.com/books/page-turner/amazon-and-the-perils-of-non-disclosure [https://perma.cc/A8C8-2KHL] ("Amazon is reflexively, absurdly secretive—only giving the absolute minimum information required by law or P.R."); Spencer Woodman, *Exclusive: Amazon Makes Even Temporary Warehouse Workers Sign 18-Month Non-competes*, THE VERGE, Mar. 26, 2015, https://www.theverge.com/2015/3/26/8280309/amazon-warehouse-jobs-exclusive-noncompete-contracts [https://perma.cc/BXY5-DRD5]; Tyler Pager, *After Amazon Contest, N.Y. Lawmakers Want to Block Negotiations Done in Secret*, N.Y. TIMES, Dec. 20, 2018, https://www.nytimes.com/2018/12/20/nyregion/amazon-nda-law-nyc.html [https://perma.cc/B4VR-RHP2]; Scott Calvert, *After Amazon HQ2, Some Lawmakers Question Nondisclosure Requirements*, WALL ST. J., Nov. 26, 2018, https://www.wsj.com/articles/after-amazon-hq2-some-lawmakers-question-nondisclosure-requirements-1543228202 [https://perma.cc/3VT7-SMAQ]; Chad Livengood, *Detroit's Amazon Incentives Remain "Trade Secret,"* CRAIN'S DETROIT BUSINESS, Mar. 12, 2018, https://advance-lexis-com.libproxy.wustl.edu/api/document?collection=news&id=urn:contentItem:5RW7-F7F1-JC0G-403S-00000-00&context=1516831; Brandon Brown, *Amazon Sues After Ex-worker Takes Google Job*, SEATTLE TIMES, July 1, 2014, https://www.seattletimes.com/business/amazon-sues-after-ex-worker-takes-google-job/ [https://perma.cc/5GQT-6M44] (detailing the lawsuit by Amazon against a former AWS sales-team employee, Zoltan Szabadi, who sought to work at Google's cloud services platform); Monica Nicklesburg, *Amazon Sues Former AWS Exec for Joining Rival Google Division as Cloud Wars Escalate*, GEEK WIRE, July 31, 2019, https://www.geekwire.com/2019/amazon-sues-former-aws-exec-joining-rival-google-division-cloud-wars-escalate/   [https://perma.cc/GBK7-PVRY]; Tom Krazit, *It's Business, and It's Personal: How Amazon Web Services*

Decides to Enforce Non-compete Contracts, GEEK WIRE, June 15, 2017, https://www. geekwire.com/2017/business-personal-amazon-web-services-decides-enforce-non-compete-contracts/ [https://perma.cc/H7K4-FS98].

125. Joe Nocera, *Apple's Culture of Secrecy*, N.Y. TIMES, July 26, 2008, https://www. nytimes.com/2008/07/26/business/26nocera.html   [https://perma.cc/2BEK-HK4V]; Jeff John Roberts, *Why You Should Be Worried About Tech's Love Affair With NDAs*, FORTUNE, Apr. 29, 2019, https://fortune.com/2019/04/29/silicon-valley-nda/ ("At companies like Google, Apple, and Amazon, every low-level employee or contractor is expected to sign an NDA, and so are vendors and visitors."); Olivia Solon, *"They'll Squash You Like a Bug": How Silicon Valley Keeps a Lid on Leakers*, THE GUARDIAN, Mar. 16, 2018, https://www.theguardian.com/technology/2018/mar/16/silicon-valley-internal-work-spying-surveillance-leakers   [https://perma.cc/7CXW-DCEU]; Sharon Florentine, *NDAs Stifling Tech Workers' Voices*, CIO, Sept. 7, 2018, https://www.cio.com/article/3304297/ndas-stifling-tech-workers-voices.html [https://perma.cc/87WK-83CT].

126. Olivia Solon, *Iphone Spyware Lets Police Log Suspects' Passcodes When Cracking Doesn't Work*, NBC NEWS, May 18, 2020, https://www.nbcnews.com/tech/security/iphone-spyware-lets-cops-log-suspects-passcodes-when-cracking-doesn-n1209296.

127. See Danielle Keats Citron & Frank A. Pasquale, *Network Accountability for the Domestic Intelligence Apparatus*, 62 HASTINGS L. J. 1441 (2011).

128. Shea Bennett, *Tumblr, Facebook, Twitter, Instagram & Snapchat—How Teens Use Social Media [INFOGRAPHIC]*, All Twitter: The Unofficial Twitter Resource, Oct. 18, 2013, http://www.mediabistro.com/alltwitter/teens-social-media_b50664.

129. Emily Nussbaum, *Kids, the Internet, and the End of Privacy: The Greatest Generation Gap Since Rock and Roll*, N.Y. MAG., Feb 12, 2007, http://nymag.com/news/features/27341/.

130. Gina Keating, *Disney CEO Bullish on Direct Web Marketing to Consumers*, REUTERS, JULY 23, 2009.

131. DANAH BOYD, IT'S COMPLICATED: THE SOCIAL LIVES OF NETWORKED TEENS (2014).

132. danah boyd & Alice Marwick, *Social Privacy in Networked Publics,* A Decade in Internet Time: Symposium on the Dynamics of the Internet and Society, Sept. 2011.

133. *Id.*; see also Alice Marwick, Diego Murgia-Díaz, & John Palfrey, *Youth, Privacy and Reputation* (literature review) (2010), https://papers.ssrn.com/sol3/papers.cfm?abstract_id=1588163.

134. boyd & Marwick, *Social Privacy in Networked Publics, supra.*

135. Chris J. Hoofnagle, Jennifer King, Su Li, & Joseph Turow, *How Different Are Young Adults From Older Adults When It Comes to Information Privacy Attitudes and Policies?* (2010), http://ssrn.com/abstract=1589864.

136. MIREILLE HILDEBRANDT, SMART TECHNOLOGIES AND THE END(S) OF LAW 120 (2015); see also Alyson Leigh Young & Anabel Quan-Haase, *Privacy Protection Strategies on Facebook*, 16 INFO. COMM. & SOC. 479 (2013) (detailing these types of strategies).

137. See, e.g., *Finstagram—a Secret Instagram Account to Post Ugly Selfies*, THE GUARDIAN, FEB. 21, 2017, https://www.theguardian.com/technology/shortcuts/2017/feb/21/finstagram-secret-instagram-account-post-ugly-selfies; Marwick, Murgia-Díaz, & Palfrey, *Youth, Privacy and Reputation, supra*.

138. J. Henley, *"Are Teenagers Really Careless About Online Privacy?,"* THE GUARDIAN, OCT. 21, 2013, http://www.theguardian.com/technology/2013/oct/21/teenagers-careless-about-online-privacy.

139. boyd & Marwick, *Social Privacy in Networked Publics, supra*, at 10.

140. Jacob Kastrenakes, *Google's Chief Internet Evangelist Says "Privacy May Actually Be an Anomaly,"* THE VERGE, Nov. 20, 2013, https://www.theverge.com/2013/11/20/5125922/vint-cerf-google-internet-evangelist-says-privacy-may-be-anomaly.

141. ANTONIO García Martínez, CHAOS MONKEYS: OBSCENE FORTUNE AND RANDOM FAILURE IN SILICON VALLEY (2016).

142. Jeff Bercovici, *The Playboy Interview: A Candid Conversation With Nick Denton*, PLAYBOY, Feb. 21, 2014, https://playboysfw.kinja.com/the-playboy-interview-a-candid-conversation-with-gawke-1527302145.

143. Antonio García Martínez, *I'm an Ex-Facebook Exec: Don't Believe What They Tell You About Ads*, THE GUARDIAN, May 2, 2017, https://www.theguardian.com/technology/2017/may/02/facebook-executive-advertising-data-comment.

144. Jacob Kastrenakes, *Gawker Settles Lawsuit That Drove It Into Bankruptcy*, THE VERGE, Nov. 2, 2016, https://www.theverge.com/2016/11/2/13499530/gawker-hulk-hogan-settle-31-million [https://perma.cc/Q8N9-AVED]; Rupert Neate and Alan Yuhas, *Gawker Media Files for Bankruptcy in Wake of Costly Hulk Hogan Lawsuit*, THE GUARDIAN, June 10, 2016, https://www.theguardian.com/media/2016/jun/10/gawker-media-bankruptcy-auction-hulk-hogan-lawsuit [https://perma.cc/RR6A-W5AB].

145. Andrew Ross Sorkin, *Peter Thiel, Tech Billionaire, Reveals Secret War With Gawker*, N.Y. TIMES, May 25, 2016, https://www.nytimes.com/2016/05/26/business/dealbook/peter-thiel-tech-billionaire-reveals-secret-war-with-gawker.html [https://perma.cc/7YTA-93PU]. I should disclose here in the interests of transparency that I did some legal consulting work for Hogan's legal team in 2014, but I had no knowledge of Thiel's involvement, which came to light later.

146. *Mark Zuckerberg Testimony: Senators Question Facebook's Commitment to Privacy*, N.Y. TIMES, Apr. 10, 2019.

147. Zuckerberg, *A Privacy-Focused Vision for Social Networking, supra*.

148. *Id.*

Part 2

1. E.g., CATHARINE MACKINNON, FEMINISM UNMODIFIED 100 (1987) ("[A] right to privacy looks like an injury got up as a gift."); CATHARINE A. MACKINNON, TOWARD A FEMINIST THEORY OF THE STATE (1989); Reva B. Siegel, *"The Rule of Love": Wife*

Beating as Prerogative and Privacy, 105 YALE L. J. 2117 (1996) (documenting the ways in which nineteenth-century marital privacy rules served to legitimate husbands' abuse of their wives under the law). But see ANITA L. ALLEN, UNEASY ACCESS: PRIVACY FOR WOMEN IN A FREE SOCIETY (1988) (disagreeing with MacKinnon on whether privacy's association with patriarchal inequality makes it unredeemable by feminist theory).

2. LOUIS D. BRANDEIS, OTHER PEOPLE'S MONEY—AND HOW THE BANKERS USE IT, 62–63 (1914).

Chapter 4

1. DAVID KIRKPATRICK, THE FACEBOOK EFFECT 31 (2010); see also Sarah C. Haan, *Bad Actors: Authenticity, Inauthenticity, Speech, and Capitalism*, U. PENN. J. CONST'L L. at ms. 10 (forthcoming 2020).

2. Facebook, *Updating the Values That Inform Our Community Standards*, Sept. 12, 2019, https://about.fb.com/news/2019/09/updating-the-values-that-inform-our-community-standards/.

3. Haan, *Bad Actors, supra*, at 32.

4. Cherry Wilson, *Salman Rushdie Able to Use Own Name on Facebook After Identity Conflict*, THE GUARDIAN, Nov. 14, 2011.

5. Abby Phillip, *Online "Authenticity" and How Facebook's "Real Name" Policy Hurts Native Americans*, WASH. POST, Feb. 10, 2015.

6. Brittney McNamara, *This Person Says Facebook's "Authentic Name" Policy Is "Anti-Trans,"* TEEN VOGUE, Nov. 7, 2017; Caitlin Dewey, *Why the Debate Over "Real Names" Matters—for Drag Queens on Facebook and Everyone Else*, WASH. POST, Oct. 6, 2014; Mathew Ingram, *Facebook's Real Name Policy Cause Clashes With Some Gay and Transgender Users*, GIGAOM, Sept. 12, 2014.

7. Violet Blue, *Facebook Nymwars: Disproportionately Outing LGBT Performers, Users Furious*, ZDNET, Sept. 12, 2014, https://www.zdnet.com/article/facebook-nymwars-disproportionately-outing-lgbt-performers-users-furious/.

8. E.g., Emily Price, *Twitter and Human Rights: A Complicated Story*, Human Rights First, Mar. 26, 2014, https://www.humanrightsfirst.org/blog/twitter-and-human-rights-complicated-story; Chloe Tennant, *Russia Charges Activist for a Facebook Post*, Human Rights Watch, Mar. 22, 2019, https://www.hrw.org/news/2019/03/22/russia-charges-activist-facebook-post#.

9. Haan, *Bad Actors, supra*, at 36–37 (collecting sources).

10. *Id.*

11. Facebook, *Updating the Values That Inform Our Community Standards, supra..*

12. See NEIL RICHARDS, INTELLECTUAL PRIVACY: RETHINKING CIVIL LIBERTIES FOR THE DIGITAL AGE (2015).

13. *Id.*

14. *Id.*

15. VIRGINIA WOOLF, A ROOM OF ONE'S OWN (1929).

16. ERVING GOFFMAN, THE PRESENTATION OF SELF IN EVERYDAY LIFE 132–37 (1959).

17. *Id.* at 112.

18. Cohen's work is voluminous, but her four key works on this topic are JULIE E. COHEN, CONFIGURING THE NETWORKED SELF (2014); JULIE E. COHEN, BETWEEN TRUTH AND POWER: THE LEGAL CONSTRUCTIONS OF INFORMATIONAL CAPITALISM (2019); Julie E. Cohen, *What Privacy Is For*, 126 HARV. L. REV. 1904 (2013); Julie E. Cohen, *Turning Privacy Inside Out*, 20 THEORETICAL INQUIRIES IN LAW 1 (2019).

19. COHEN, CONFIGURING THE NETWORKED SELF, *supra*, at 149.

20. Cohen, *What Privacy Is For*, *supra*, at 1908.

21. See *id.* at 1908–9 (collecting sources).

22. *Id.* at 1909.

23. *Id.*

24. *Id.* at 1910.

25. *Id.*

26. *Id.*

27. Taylor Lorenz, *"OK Boomer" Marks the End of Friendly Generational Relations*, N.Y. TIMES, Oct. 29, 2019.

28. Chelsea Ritschel, *Millennials and Gen Z Are Feuding Over Side Parts and Skinny Jeans on Tiktok*, THE INDEPENDENT (UK), Feb. 20, 2021.

29. Arwa Mahdawi, *The Culture War Between Gen Z and Millennials Is On: The First Battle? Side Partings*, THE GUARDIAN, Feb. 10, 2021.

30. SALMAN RUSHDIE, JOSEPH ANTON: A MEMOIR (2012).

31. Facebook, *Updating the Values That Inform Our Community Standards*, *supra* (emphasis added).

32. KIRKPATRICK, THE FACEBOOK EFFECT, *supra*, at 199.

33. Oliver L. Haimson & Anna Lauren Hoffmann, *Constructing and Enforcing "Authentic" Identity Online: Facebook, Real Names, and Non-normative Identities*, FIRST MONDAY 21(6), https://doi.org/10.5210/fm.v21i6.6791. See also Oliver L. Haimson, Anne E. Bowser, Edward F. Melcer, & Elizabeth F. Churchill, *Online Inspiration and Exploration for Identity Reinvention*, CHI '15: PROCEEDINGS OF THE 33RD ANNUAL ACM CONFERENCE ON HUMAN FACTORS IN COMPUTING SYSTEMS 3809–18 (2015), http://doi.org/10.1145/2702123.2702270,

34. Mikaela Pitcan, Alice E Marwick, & danah boyd, *Performing a Vanilla Self: Respectability Politics, Social Class, and the Digital World*, 23(3) J. COMP - MEDIATED COMMS. 163 (May 2018), https://doi.org/10.1093/jcmc/zmy008.

35. WALT WHITMAN, SONG OF MYSELF (1892).

36. The classic work here is GOFFMAN, THE PRESENTATION OF SELF IN EVERYDAY LIFE, *supra*.

37. J. C. R. Licklider, *Man-Computer Symbiosis*, 1 IRE TRANSACTIONS ON HUMAN FACTORS IN ELECTRONICS 4 (Mar. 1960).

38. JARON LANIER, YOU ARE NOT A GADGET: A MANIFESTO (2010).

39. Haimson & Hoffmann, *Constructing and Enforcing "Authentic" Identity Online*, *supra*.

40. SCOTT SKINNER-THOMPSON, PRIVACY AT THE MARGINS (2021).

41. Nicholas Negroponte, Being Digital (1995).

42. See, e.g., Cass R. Sunstein, Republic.com (2001); Cass R. Sunstein, Republic.com 2.0 (2009); Cass R. Sunstein, #Republic: Divided Democracy in the Age of Social Media (2018).

43. Eli Pariser, The Filter Bubble: How the New Personalized Web Is Changing What We Read and How We Think (Reprint ed. 2012).

44. Sunstein, Republic.com 2.0, supra, at 55.

45. Zeynep Tufekci, The Real Bias Built in at Facebook, N.Y. Times, May 18, 2016, at A27.

46. Sunstein, #Republic, supra, at 259–62.

47. Cohen calls this phenomenon "semantic discontinuity." Cohen, Turning Privacy Inside Out, supra. See also Cohen, Configuring the Networked Self, supra, at 149–50.

48. Shoshana Zuboff, The Age of Surveillance Capitalism (2019).

49. Alan F. Westin, Privacy and Freedom 33 (1967).

50. Neil M. Richards, The Dangers of Surveillance, 126 Harv. L. Rev. 1934, 1946 (2013); Cohen, Configuring the Networked Self, supra.

51. Timothy Macklem, Independence of Mind 36 (2008).

52. See, e.g., Jonathon Penney, Chilling Effects: Understanding Them, and Their Harms, June 2020 (manuscript on file with author).

53. Jeremy Bentham, Panopticon, in 3 Opinions of Different Authors Upon the Punishment of Death 321, 328 (Basil Montagu ed. 1816).

54. George Orwell, Nineteen Eighty-Four (Irving Howe ed. 1982) (1949).

55. Id. at 14.

56. See, e.g., Daniel J. Solove, The Digital Person 33–35 (2004); Kevin D. Haggerty & Richard V. Ericson, The Surveillant Assemblage, 51 Brit. J. Soc. 605, 606–8 (2000).

57. Melissa Bateson et al., Cues of Being Watched Enhance Cooperation in a Real-World Setting, 2 Bio. Lett. 412, 414 (2006).

58. Steve Lohr, Unblinking Eyes Track Employees, N.Y. Times, June 21, 2014.

59. Lamar Pierce et al., Cleaning House: The Impact of Information Technology on Employee Corruption and Productivity, 61 (10) Management Science 2299 (2015).

60. Jonathon W. Penney, Chilling Effects: Online Surveillance and Wikipedia Use, 31 Berkeley Tech. L. J. 117, 125–26 (2016) (finding surveillance chilling effect, due to Snowden revelations, on Wikipedia article access); Jonathon W. Penney, Internet Surveillance, Regulation, and Chilling Effects Online: A Comparative Case Study, 6(2) Internet Policy Review 1 (2017) (finding evidence of government and corporate surveillance chilling effects on a range of online activities, including sharing and speech); Alex Marthews & Catherine Tucker, Government Surveillance and Internet Search Behavior, in Cambridge University Handbook on Surveillance Law (David Gray et al. eds. 2017) (finding surveillance chilling effect, due to Snowden revelations, on Google search results); Elizabeth Stoycheff et al., Privacy and the Panopticon: Online Mass Surveillance's Deterrence and Chilling Effects, 21(3) New Media & Society 602 (2019) (finding "spiral of silence" effect due to online social media surveillance).

61. Marthews & Tucker, Government Surveillance and Internet Search Behavior, supra, .

62. Penney, *Chilling Effects: Online Surveillance and Wikipedia Use, supra*, at 125–26.

63. See Richards, *The Dangers of Surveillance, supra*; PENNEY, CHILLING EFFECTS, *supra* (collecting studies). A sampling of the vast literature that empirically explores different aspects of chilling effects through a variety of methodologies include FDR GROUP & PEN AMERICAN CENTER, CHILLING EFFECTS: NSA SURVEILLANCE DRIVES U.S. WRITERS TO SELF-CENSOR 3–4 (2013), https://pen.org//sites/default/files/Chilling%20Effects_PEN%20American.pdf

(noting that 28% of the writers surveyed had "curtailed or avoided" certain online activities due to "fear of surveillance"); Sauvik Das & Adam Kramer, *Self-Censorship on Facebook, in* SEVENTH INTERNATIONAL AAAI CONFERENCE ON WEBLOGS AND SOCIAL MEDIA 120 (2013), https://ojs.aaai.org/index.php/ICWSM/article/view/14412;

Manya Sleeper et al., *The Post That Wasn't: Exploring Self-Censorship on Facebook*, ACM: PROCEEDINGS OF THE 2013 CONFERENCE ON COMPUTER SUPPORTED COOPERATIVE WORK 793 (2013), https://dl.acm.org/citation.cfm?id=2441865; FDR GROUP & PEN AMERICAN CENTER, GLOBAL CHILLING: THE IMPACT OF MASS SURVEILLANCE ON INTERNATIONAL WRITERS (2015), https://pen.org//sites/default/files/globalchilling_2015.pdf [https://perma .cc/GJ88-TMY2] (noting that the international community is similarly engaging in forms of self-censorship); Keith N. Hampton et al., *Social Media and the "Spiral of Silence,"* PEW Res. Ctr., 2014, at 4, https://www.pewresearch.org/internet/2014/08/26/social-media-and-the-spiral-of-silence/[-https://perma--.cc/QWP2-5QJS] (finding, for example, 86% of respondents less willing to discuss NSA surveillance revelations online than off); Judith Townend, *Online Chilling Effects in England and Wales*, 3(2) INTERNET POLICY REVIEW (2014), https://policyreview.info/articles/analysis/online-chilling-effects-england-and-wales; Lee Rainie et al., *Americans' Privacy Strategies Post-Snowden*, PEW Res. Internet Project, Mar. 16, 2015, at 4, https://www.pewresearch.org/internet/2015/03/16/americans-privacy-strategies-post-snowden/ (noting that 25% of those aware of surveillance have "changed the patterns" of their use of "technological platforms"); Elizabeth Stoycheff, *Under Surveillance: Examining Facebook's Spiral of Silence Effects in the Wake of NSA Internet Monitoring*, 93(2) JOURNALISM & MASS COMMUNICATION 296 (2016) Penney, *Chilling Effects: Online Surveillance and Wikipedia Use, supra*, at 125–26; Ben Marder, Adam Joinson, Avi Shankar, & David Houghton, *The Extended "Chilling" Effect of Facebook: The Cold Reality of Ubiquitous Social Networking*, 60 COMPUTERS IN HUMAN BEHAVIOR 582 (2016); Jonathon W. Penney, *Internet Surveillance, Regulation, and Chilling Effects Online: A Comparative Case Study*, 6(2) INTERNET POLICY REVIEW 1 (2017); Marthews & Tucker, *Government Surveillance and Internet Search Behavior, supra,*; Yoan Hermstrüwer & Stephan Dickert, *Sharing Is Daring: An Experiment on Consent, Chilling Effects and a Salient Privacy Nudge*, 51 INTERNATIONAL REVIEW OF LAW AND ECONOMICS 38 (2017); Stoycheff et al., *Privacy and the Panopticon, supra*; Jonathon W. Penney, *Privacy and Automated Legal Enforcement: The DMCA as a Case Study*, 22 STAN. TECH. L. REV. 412 (2019) (exploring chilling effects associated with the DMCA's automated removal notice system); Danielle Keats Citron & Jonathon W. Penney, *When Law Frees Us to Speak*,

87 FORDHAM L. REV. 2317, 2319–20 (2019); M. Büchi et al., *The Chilling Effects of Algorithmic Profiling: Mapping the Issues*, 36 COMPUTER LAW & SECURITY REVIEW 1 (2019). I am grateful to Jon Penney for his generosity in pointing me in the direction of many of these sources, and I encourage any reader who is this deep in the endnotes to read Jon's work immediately, if you haven't already.

Chapter 5

1. Glenn Greenwald, Ryan Grim, & Ryan Gallagher, *Top-Secret Document Reveals NSA Spied on Porn Habits as Part of Plan to Discredit "Radicalizers,"* HUFF. POST, Nov. 26, 2013, https://www.huffpost.com/entry/nsa-porn-muslims_n_4346128.
2. *Id.* (containing a photographic excerpt of the document).
3. *Id.*
4. *Id.*
5. *Id.*
6. Many of the claims that follow were ones I first made in Neil M. Richards, *The Dangers of Surveillance*, 126 HARV. L. REV. 1934 (2013). This chapter represents a substantially updated and streamlined version of many of those arguments.
7. ALAN F. WESTIN, PRIVACY AND FREEDOM 23 (1967).
8. GEORGE ORWELL, NINETEEN EIGHTY-FOUR (1949). For one contemporary critique of the "Big Brother" metaphor as a helpful way of understanding our modern surveillance society, see BERNARD E. HARCOURT, EXPOSED: DESIRE AND DISOBEDIENCE IN THE DIGITAL AGE, chapter 1 (2015).
9. Neil M. Richards, *Intellectual Privacy*, 87 TEX. L. REV. 387 (2008); NEIL RICHARDS, INTELLECTUAL PRIVACY: RETHINKING CIVIL LIBERTIES FOR THE DIGITAL AGE (2015).
10. See, e.g., *Lujan v. Defenders of Wildlife*, 504 U.S. 555 (1992); *Spokeo v. Robins*, 136 S.Ct. 1550 (2016). I explore this point in greater depth in Expert Report of Prof. Neil Richards, *Data Protection Comm'r of Ireland v. Facebook* (Irish High Court 2017) ("Schrems II"), https://papers.ssrn.com/sol3/papers.cfm?abstract_id=3120546.
11. *Clapper v. Amnesty International*, 133 S.Ct. 1138 (2013).
12. *Wikimedia Foundation v. National Security Agency*, 143 F.Supp.3d 344 (D.Md. 2015). The Fourth Circuit recently reversed the trial court on this point, 857 F.3d 193 (2017), and the litigation continues.
13. *Schrems v. Data Protection Commissioner*, Case C-362/14, Curia, Eur. Ct. of Just. (2015).
14. *Data Protection Comm'r v. Facebook Ireland Ltd., Maximillian Schrems*, Case C-311/18, Curia, Ir. H. Ct. (2020). I should disclose here that I served as an expert witness in *Schrems 2* for the Irish Data Protection Commissioner on American privacy law.
15. ORWELL, NINETEEN EIGHTY-FOUR, *supra*, at 3.
16. *Id.* at 4.

17. *Id.* at 20.
18. See DORIAN LYNSKEY, THE MINISTRY OF TRUTH: THE BIOGRAPHY OF GEORGE ORWELL'S 1984 (2019).
19. *Id.* at 3–24 (recounting Orwell's increasingly disenchanting experiences in Spain).
20. GEORGE ORWELL, HOMAGE TO CATALONIA (1938); GEORGE ORWELL, POLITICS AND THE ENGLISH LANGUAGE (1913) (Penguin Classics ed. 2013).
21. Daniel J. Solove, *Privacy and Power: Computer Databases and Metaphors for Information Privacy*, 53 STAN. L. REV. 1393 (2001); DANIEL J. SOLOVE, THE DIGITAL PERSON: TECHNOLOGY AND PRIVACY IN THE DIGITAL AGE (2004).
22. See Neil M. Richards, *The Information Privacy Law Project*, 94 GEO. L. J. 1087 (2006) (doing exactly that).
23. See Margaret Atwood, *Everybody Is Happy Now,* THE GUARDIAN, Nov. 17. 2007 (contrasting Orwell's "hard" dystopia with Huxley's "soft" one).
24. Some good points of entry into this literature are Gary T. Marx, *Surveillance Studies,* in INTERNATIONAL ENCYCLOPEDIA OF THE SOCIAL AND BEHAVIORAL SCIENCES (2nd ed. 2015); DAVID LYON, SURVEILLANCE STUDIES (2007); KEVIN D. HAGGERTY & MINAS SAMATAS, EDS., SURVEILLANCE AND DEMOCRACY (2010); and SEAN P. HIER & JOSHUA GREENBERG, EDS., THE SURVEILLANCE STUDIES READER (2007).
25. See LYON, SURVEILLANCE STUDIES, *supra,* at 18–22.
26. See *id.* at 23.
27. *Id.* at 14.
28. *Id.*
29. See *id.* at 15–16.
30. Marx, *Surveillance Studies, supra,* at 733.
31. ZYGMUNT BAUMAN & DAVID LYON, LIQUID SURVEILLANCE: A CONVERSATION (2012).
32. For an excellent description of the origins, scope, and ultimate demise of Stellar Wind, see LAURA K. DONOHUE, THE FUTURE OF FOREIGN SURVEILLANCE: PRIVACY AND SURVEILLANCE IN A DIGITAL AGE (2016).
33. E.g., AMERICAN CIVIL LIBERTIES UNION, JUSTICE-FREE ZONES: U.S. IMMIGRATION DETENTION UNDER THE TRUMP ADMINISTRATION (2020); Adrian Horton, *How Netflix's Immigration Nation Shows the True Horror of ICE Agents,* THE GUARDIAN, Aug. 19, 2020, https://www.theguardian.com/tv-and-radio/2020/aug/19/netflix-immigration-nation-ice-true-horror.
34. Kim Lyons, *ICE Just Signed a Contract With Facial Recognition Company Clearview AI,* THE VERGE, Aug. 14, 2020, https://www.theverge.com/2020/8/14/21368930/clearview-ai-ice-contract-privacy-immigration.
35. DONOHUE, THE FUTURE OF FOREIGN SURVEILLANCE, *supra,* at 54.
36. See Jennifer Valentino-DeVries et al., *Your Apps Know Where You Were Last Night, and They're Not Keeping It Secret*, N.Y. TIMES, Dec. 10, 2018, https://www.nytimes.com/interactive/2018/12/10/business/location-data-privacy-apps.html; Thorin Klosowski, *Facial Recognition Is Everywhere: Here's What We Can Do About It*, N.Y. TIMES, July 15, 2020, https://www.nytimes.com/wirecutter/blog/how-facial-recognition-works/. See also Steven Feldstein, *The Global Expansion of AI Surveillance*, Carnegie Endowment,

Sept. 17, 2019, https://carnegieendowment.org/2019/09/17/global-expansion-of-ai-surveillance-pub-79847; Darrell M. West & John R. Allen, *How Artificial Intelligence Is Transforming the World*, Brookings Institution, Apr. 24, 2018, https://www.brookings.edu/research/how-artificial-intelligence-is-transforming-the-world/.

37. See Jobie Budd et al., *Digital Technologies in the Public-Health Response to COVID-19*, 26 Nat. Med. 1183 (2020), https://doi.org/10.1038/s41591-020-1011-4; Drew Harwell, *AI Baby Monitors Attract Anxious Parents: "Fear Is the Quickest Way to Get People's Attention,"* Wash. Post, Feb. 25, 2020, https://www.washingtonpost.com/technology/2020/02/25/ai-baby-monitors/; Charise Rohm Nulsen , *10 Apps for Parents to Monitor Kids' Mobile Use*, Family Education, Mar. 18, 2021, https://www.familyeducation.com/10-apps-for-parents-to-monitor-kids-mobile-use; Shourjya Sanyal, *How Are Wearables Changing Athlete Performance Monitoring?*, Forbes, Nov. 30, 2018, https://www.forbes.com/sites/shourjyasanyal/2018/11/30/how-are-wearables-changing-athlete-performance-monitoring/#7fa0709bae09.

38. Bauman & Lyon, Liquid Surveillance, *supra*, at 2–3.

39. Scott R. Peppet, *Unraveling Privacy: The Personal Prospectus and the Threat of a Full-Disclosure Future*, 105 Nw. U. L. Rev. 1153, 1153–56 (2011).

40. *Id.* at 1156.

41. Richards, Intellectual Privacy, *supra*, at 95–108; see also Richards, *Intellectual Privacy, supra*; Neil M. Richards, *The Perils of Social Reading*, 101 Geo. L. J. 689 (2013).

42. See John Inazu, Liberty's Refuge: The Forgotten Freedom of Assembly (2012).

43. See Richards, Intellectual Privacy, *supra*.

44. *Whitney v. California*, 274 U.S. 357, 375 (1927) (Brandeis, J., concurring). For additional context on Brandeis and the First Amendment, see, e.g., Bradley C. Bobertz, *The Brandeis Gambit: The Making of America's First Freedom, 1909–1931*, 40 Wm. & Mary L. Rev. 557, 607–11 (1999); Vincent Blasi, *The First Amendment and the Ideal of Civic Courage: The Brandeis Opinion in Whitney v. California*, 29 Wm. & Mary L. Rev. 653 (1988); Richards, Intellectual Privacy, *supra*, chapter 2.

45. Julie E. Cohen, *What Privacy Is for*, 126 Harv. L. Rev. 1904, 1913 (2013).

46. Samuel D. Warren & Louis D. Brandeis, *The Right to Privacy*, 4 Harv. L. Rev. 193, 196 (1890).

47. Cohen, *What Privacy Is For, supra*, at 1916.

48. Harcourt, Exposed, *supra*, at 52–53.

49. Cass. R. Sunstein, #Republic: Divided Democracy in the Age of Social Media (2017).

50. See Lyon, Surveillance Studies, *supra*, at 14.

51. David J. Garrow, The FBI and Martin Luther King, Jr.: From "Solo" to Memphis (1981).

52. S. Rep. No. 94-755, at 81 (1976) (quoting Memorandum from Frederick Baumgardner to William Sullivan (Jan. 28, 1964)).

53. See Andrew G. McCabe, The Threat: How the FBI Protects America in the Age of Terror and Trump (2020).

54. Wiretap Act, 18 U.S.C. § 2510-22 (1968), codified as amended and expanded by the Electronic Communications Privacy Act of 1986.

55. See McCABE, THE THREAT, *supra*, at 20–21.

56. Jessica Bennett, *The Complicated Case of Katie Hill*, N.Y. TIMES, Nov. 1, 2019.

57. Danielle Citron, *Sexual Privacy*, 128 YALE L. J. 1870, 1915–17 (2019). See also Sebastian Anthony, *Reported Cases of Webcam Blackmail Double Are Linked to Four Suicides*, ARS TECHNICA, Nov. 30, 2016, https://arstechnica.com/tech-policy/2016/11/webcam-blackmail-cases-double-uk-suicides/; Benjamin Wittes et al., *Sextortion: Cybersecurity, Teenagers and Remote Sexual Assault*, Brookings Institution, May 11, 2016, https://www.brookings.edu/research/sextortion-cybersecurity-teenagers-and-remote-sexual-assault/.

58. David Smith, *Ex-Congresswoman Katie Hill Is "Still Here"—and She Wants the World to Know It*, THE GUARDIAN, Aug. 22, 2020. The quoted language is Smith's, but it summarizes the sentiments Hill discloses in the interview.

59. See, e.g., Maria Los, *A Trans-Systemic Surveillance: The Legacy of Communist Surveillance in the Digital Age* 176–77, in SURVEILLANCE AND DEMOCRACY (Kevin D. Haggerty & Minas Samatas eds. 2010).

60. *Id.* at 180.

61. E.g., Anupam Chander, *Jasmine Revolutions*, 97 CORNELL L. REV. 1505, 1516–17, 1525–28 (2012).

62. Matthieu Aikins, *Jamming Tripoli*, WIRED, June 2012, at 146, 176.

63. *Id.*

64. See Richards, *The Dangers of Surveillance*, , *supra*, at 1954. For a journalist's account of how this unfolded in the latter days of Gadhafi's Libya, see Aikins, *Jamming Tripoli*, supra.

65. *See* Stephan Faris, *The Hackers of Damascus*, BLOOMBERG BUSINESSWEEK, Nov. 15, 2012, http://www.businessweek.com/articles/2012-11-15/the-hackers-of-damascus.

66. See JULIE COHEN, CONFIGURING THE NETWORKED SELF: LAW, CODE, AND THE PLAY OF EVERYDAY PRACTICE (2012); JULIE COHEN, BETWEEN TRUTH AND POWER: THE LEGAL CONSTRUCTIONS OF INFORMATIONAL CAPITALISM (2019); Lisa M. Austin, *Enough About Me: Why Privacy Is About Power, Not Consent (or Harm)* in A WORLD WITHOUT PRIVACY? WHAT LAW CAN AND SHOULD DO (Austin Sarat ed. 2014).

67. *United States v. Isa*, 923 F.2d 1300, 1302 (8th Cir. 1991).

68. Heather A. Conley, *Successfully Countering Russian Electoral Interference*, Ctr. for Strategic & Int. Studs., June 21, 2018, https://www.csis.org/analysis/successfully-countering-russian-electoral-interference; Andrew Higgins, *It's France's Turn to Worry About Election Meddling by Russia*, N.Y. TIMES, Apr. 17, 2017; Laura Daniels, *How Russia Hacked the French Election*, POLITICO, Apr. 23, 2017, https://www.politico.eu/article/france-election-2017-russia-hacked-cyberattacks/.

69. See MARY BEARD, SPQR: A HISTORY OF ANCIENT ROME 391–94 (2015).

70. *Id.* at 392.

71. Spencer Ackerman, *CIA Admits to Spying on Senate Staffers*, THE GUARDIAN, July 31, 2014.

72. See *id.* See also Letter from Sen. Bernie Sanders to Gen. Keith Alexander, Director, NSA dated Jan. 2, 2014, https://www.sanders.senate.gov/download/letter-to-nsa?id=EEE1F3B1-9DD4-4CDB-96FC-D2A145709A9C&download=1&inline=file.

73. See *id.* See also Charlie Savage & Sharon LaFraniere, *Republicans Claim Surveillance Power Abuses in Russia Inquiry*, N.Y. TIMES, Jan. 19, 2018, https://www.nytimes.com/2018/01/19/us/politics/republicans-surveillance-trump-russia-inquiry.html.

74. See, e.g., LYON, SURVEILLANCE STUDIES, *supra*, at 107–8.

75. See, e.g., ROY COLEMAN, RECLAIMING THE STREETS 226–28 (2004); LYON, SURVEILLANCE STUDIES, *supra*, at 107–8; Roy Coleman, *Surveillance in the City: Primary Definition and Urban Spatial Order*, in THE SURVEILLANCE STUDIES READER (Sean P. Hier & Joshua Greenberg eds. 2007) at 231, 234–35.

76. LYNNE CHENEY, JAMES MADISON: A LIFE RECONSIDERED 65 (2015).

77. For an expanded version of this argument, see Neil M. Richards & Jonathan H. King, *Big Data Ethics*, 49 WAKE FOREST L. REV. 393, 428 (2014).

78. Nicholas Confessore, *The Unlikely Activists Who Took On Silicon Valley—and Won*, N.Y. TIMES MAG., Aug. 14, 2018.

79. See Sasha Issenberg, *How President Obama's Campaign Used Big Data to Rally Individual Voters*, MIT TECH. REV., Dec. 19, 2012, https://www.technologyreview.com/2012/12/19/114510/how-obamas-team-used-big-data-to-rally-voters/.

80. Although it made global news in 2018, the *Guardian* first broke the story about the work of Cambridge Analytica in 2015. See Harry Davies, *Ted Cruz Using Firm That Harvested Data on Millions of Unwitting Facebook Users*, THE GUARDIAN, Dec. 11, 2015, https://www.theguardian.com/us-news/2015/dec/11/senator-ted-cruz-president-campaign-facebook-user-data; Carol Cadwalladr, *The Great British Brexit Robbery: How Our Democracy Was Hijacked*, THE GUARDIAN, May 7, 2017, https://www.theguardian.com/technology/2017/may/07/the-great-british-brexit-robbery-hijacked-democracy.

81. Richards & King, *Big Data Ethics, supra*, at 428.

82. ROGER McMANEE, ZUCKED: WAKING UP TO THE FACEBOOK CATASTROPHE, 237–38 (2019).

83. *Revealed: Trump Campaign Strategy to Deter Millions of Black Americans From Voting in 2016*, Channel 4 (UK) News Investigations, Sept. 28, 2020, https://www.channel4.com/news/revealed-trump-campaign-strategy-to-deter-millions-of-black-americans-from-voting-in-2016; Dan Sabbagh, *Trump 2016 Campaign "Targeted 3.5m Black Americans to Deter Them From Voting,"* THE GUARDIAN, Sept. 28, 2020.

84. Justin McCurry, *South Korea Spy Agency Admits Trying to Rig 2012 Presidential Election*, THE GUARDIAN, Aug. 4 2017, https://www.theguardian.com/world/2017/aug/04/south-koreas-spy-agency-admits-trying-rig-election-national-intelligence-service-2012.

85. *Id.*

86. E.g., LYON, SURVEILLANCE STUDIES, *supra*, at 30–32.

87. E.g., STEVEN LEVY, IN THE PLEX 336–41 (2011) (Google); STEVEN LEVY, FACEBOOK: THE INSIDE STORY 207 (2020).

88. See Jon D. Michaels, *All the President's Spies: Private-Public Intelligence Partnerships in the War on Terror*, 96 CALIF. L. REV. 901, 917–18 (2008).

89. OSCAR H. GANDY JR., THE PANOPTIC SORT 15 (1993).

90. SHOSHANA ZUBOFF, THE AGE OF SURVEILLANCE CAPITALISM 509–10 (2019).

91. Julia Angwin et al., *Facebook Enabled Advertisers to Reach "Jew Haters,"* PROPUBLICA, Sept. 14, 2017.

92. Alex Kantrowitz, *Google Allowed Advertisers to Target People Searching Racist Phrases*, BUZZFEED NEWS, Sept. 15, 2017.

93. Julia Angwin & Terry Parris Jr., *Facebook Lets Advertisers Exclude Users by Race*, PROPUBLICA, Oct. 28, 2016.

94. See generally JOHN GILLIOM, OVERSEERS OF THE POOR (2006); DAVID LYON, SURVEILLANCE AFTER SEPTEMBER 11 (2003); KEVIN D. HAGGERTY & RICHARD V. ERICSON, EDS., THE NEW POLITICS OF SURVEILLANCE AND VISIBILITY (2006); DAVID LYON, ED., SURVEILLANCE AS SOCIAL SORTING (2003).

95. Danielle Keats Citron, *Technological Due Process*, 85 WASH. U. L. REV. 1249, 1258 (2008).

96. Marianne Bertrand & Sendhil Mullainathan, *Are Emily and Greg More Employable Than Lakisha and Jamal? A Field Experiment on Labor Market Discrimination* 94(4) AM. ECON. REV. 991 (2004).

97. Gideon Mann & Cathy O'Neil, *Hiring Algorithms Are Not Neutral*, HARV. BUS. REV., Dec. 9, 2016, https://hbr.org/2016/12/hiring-algorithms-are-not-neutral.

98. CATHY O'NEIL, WEAPONS OF MATH DESTRUCTION: HOW BIG DATA INCREASES INEQUALITY AND THREATENS DEMOCRACY 21 (2016).

99. No, really: "Top 11 Fake Clickbait Headlines: You Won't Believe Number 4," PRIMOWEB COLLECTION, Mar. 7, 2017.

100. Pema Levy, *Trump and Zuckerberg Both Want You to Believe Facebook, a Private Company, Is the Public Square*, MOTHER JONES, May 29, 2020. The U.S. Supreme Court has repeatedly referred to the internet in similar terms. See *Reno v. ACLU*, 521 U.S. 844 (1997) ("Through the use of chat rooms, any person with a phone line can become a town crier with a voice that resonates farther than it could from any soapbox. Through the use of Web pages, mail exploders, and newsgroups, the same individual can become a pamphleteer."); *Packingham v. N.C.*, 137 S.Ct. 1730, 1737 (2017) ("modern public square"). See also Danielle Keats Citron & Neil M. Richards, *Four Principles for Digital Expression (You Won't Believe #3!)*, 95 WASH. U. L. Rev. 1353 (2018) (identifying and critiquing this practice).

101. SUNSTEIN, #REPUBLIC, *supra*, at 215–17.

102. See Mann & O'Neil, *Hiring Algorithms Are Not Neutral*, *supra*.

103. SARAH IGO, THE KNOWN CITIZEN: A HISTORY OF PRIVACY IN MODERN AMERICA 3 (2018).

104. E.g., *Id.*, 9, 49 (African Americans); 21–24 (chaperones and gender in the Gilded Age); 49–50 (aliens); 294–303 (sexual privacy).

105. See Rose Hackman, *Is the Online Surveillance of Black Teenagers the New Stop-and-Frisk*, THE GUARDIAN, Apr. 23, 2015, https://www.theguardian.com/us-news/2015/apr/23/online-surveillance-black-teenagers-new-stop-and-frisk.

106. See Diala Shamas & Nermeen Arastu, Mapping Muslims: NYPD Spying and Its Impact on American Muslims (2013).

107. See John Gilliom, Overseers of the Poor: Surveillance, Resistance, and the Limits of Privacy (2001); Nathalie Maréchal, *First They Came for the Poor: Surveillance of Welfare Recipients as an Uncontested Practice*, 3 Media & Comm. 56 (2015), https://doi.org/10.17645/mac.v3i3.268.

108. See Kevin R. Johnson, *Trump's Latinx Repatriation*, 66 UCLA L. Rev. 1442 (2019); Rachel E. Rosenbloom, *Policing Sex, Policing Immigrants: What Crimmigration's Past Can Tell Us About Its Present and Its Future*, 104 Calif. L. Rev. 149, 164–97 (2016). See also Lily H. Newman, *A "Smart Wall" Could Spark a New Kind of Border Crisis*, Wired, Feb. 21, 2019, https://www.wired.com/story/border-smart-wall-privacy-surveillance/ (for a discussion on border surveillance in a digital world).

109. See Kashmir Hill, *The Secretive Company That Might End Privacy as We Know It*, N.Y. Times, Feb. 10, 2020, https://www.nytimes.com/2020/01/18/technology/clearview-privacy-facial-recognition.html; Nathan F. Wessler, *We're Taking Clearview AI to Court to End Its Privacy-Destroying Face Surveillance Activities*, ACLU, May 28, 2020, https://www.aclu.org/news/privacy-technology/were-taking-clearview-ai-to-court-to-end-its-privacy-destroying-face-surveillance-activities/.

110. *Carpenter v. United States*, 138 S. Ct. 2206 (2017); *Whalen v. Roe*, 429 U.S. 589 (1977). See also Paul Ohm, *The Many Revolutions of Carpenter*, 32 Harv. J. L. & Tech. 357 (2019); Richards, *The Information Privacy Law Project, supra*.

Chapter 6

1. For an engaging description of the ways in which the term "Luddite" has evolved over time, see Jeffrey Wasserstrom, *"Civilization" and Its Discontents: The Boxers and Luddites as Heroes and Villains*, 16:5 Theory & Society 675 (1987). The classic treatment of the political consequences of new technologies is Langdon Winner, *Do Artifacts Have Politics?*, 109:1 Dædalus 121 (1980).

2. Arjen E. van't Hof et al., *The Industrial Melanism Mutation in British Peppered Moths Is a Transposable Element*, 534 Nature 102 (June 2, 2016), http://ow.ly/IPnt30bA8Tt; Jonathan Webb, *Famous Peppered Moth's Dark Secret Revealed*, BBC News, June 1, 2016, http://www.bbc.com/news/science-environment-36424768; *Moth Turns From Black to White as Britain's Polluted Skies Change Colour*, The Telegraph, June 19, 2009, http://www.telegraph.co.uk/news/earth/wildlife/5577724/Moth-turns-from-black-to-white-as-Britains-polluted-skies-change-colour.html.

3. *United States v. E. C. Knight Co.*, 156 U.S. 1 (1895); *Hammer v. Dagenhart*, 247 U.S. 251 (1918), overruled by *United States v. Darby*, 312 U.S. 100 (1941); *Carter v. Carter Coal Co.*, 298 U.S. 238 (1936).

4. *Lochner v. New York*, 198 U.S. 45 (1905).

5. See *United States v. Butler*, 297 U.S. 1 (1936); *Railroad Retirement Bd. v. Alton R. Co.*, 295 U.S. 330 (1935). See also *Panama Refining Co. v. Ryan*, 293 U.S. 388 (1935); *A. L. A. Schechter Poultry Corp. v. United States*, 295 U.S. 495 (1935).

6. See G. E. WHITE, THE CONSTITUTION AND THE NEW DEAL (2002).

7. See National Traffic Motor Vehicle Safety Act of 1966, PUB. L. No. 89-563, 80 STAT. 718 (1966); Occupational Safety and Health Act, 29 U.S.C. §§ 651–78 (1976); FTC, Bureau of Consumer Protection, Dietary Supplements: An Advertising Guide for Industry, Apr. 2001, https://www.ftc.gov/system/files/documents/plain-language/bus09-dietary-supplements-advertising-guide-industry.pdf; 21 U.S.C. § 301 et seq. (1938), as amended. See also Section 5 of the Federal Trade Commission Act (FTC Act), 15 U.S.C. § 45(a) (1914), amended by Wheeler-Lea Act, Pub. L. No. 75-447, 52 Stat. 111 (1938). See also 42 U.S.C. § 7401 et seq. (1970); 33 U.S.C. §1251 et seq. (1972).

8. For the classic discussions of the ways in which law responded to the Industrial Revolution, whether by facilitation, a "protective countermovement," or both, see KARL POLANYI, THE GREAT TRANSFORMATION: THE POLITICAL AND ECONOMIC ORIGINS OF OUR TIME (1957); MORTON J. HORWITZ, THE TRANSFORMATION OF AMERICAN LAW 1780–1860 (1977); MORTON J. HORWITZ, THE TRANSFORMATION OF AMERICAN LAW 1870–1960 (1992). For an analogous discussion of the transformation of law in the information revolution, see JULIE E. COHEN, BETWEEN TRUTH AND POWER: THE LEGAL CONSTRUCTIONS OF INFORMATIONAL CAPITALISM (2019).

9. FRANK PASQUALE, BLACK BOX SOCIETY (2015).

10. See Neil Richards & Woodrow Hartzog, *Taking Trust Seriously in Privacy Law*, 19 STAN. J. L. & TECH. 431 (2016); Neil Richards & Woodrow Hartzog, *Privacy's Trust Gap*, 126 YALE L. J. 1180 (2017).

11. For an argument in favor of open rather than closed technologies, see JONATHAN ZITTRAIN, THE FUTURE OF THE INTERNET AND HOW TO STOP IT (2008).

12. 15 U.S.C. §45(a).

13. For detailed examinations of how the FTC has struggled with these information-age problems, see Daniel J. Solove & Woodrow Hartzog, *The FTC and the New Common Law of Privacy*, 114 COLUM. L. REV. 583 (2014); CHRISTOPHER JAY HOOFNAGLE, FEDERAL TRADE COMMISSION PRIVACY LAW AND POLICY (2016). For a call for reform from these three scholars, see Chris Jay Hoofnagle, Woodrow Hartzog, and Daniel J. Solove, *The FTC Can Rise to the Privacy Challenge, but Not Without Help from Congress*, Brookings, Aug. 8, 2019, https://www.brookings.edu/blog/techtank/2019/08/08/the-ftc-can-rise-to-the-privacy-challenge-but-not-without-help-from-congress/. They conclude, "[I]f the FTC is to be a successful regulator of tech platforms, it needs more resources, more tools, a greater shield from political pressure, and a clear Congressional mandate. Only then can it develop and give effect to a broader vision of privacy, power, and human flourishing for a safe and sustainable information society." *Id.*

14. JOHN MILTON, AREOPAGITICA (1644).

15. *Abrams v. United States*, 250 U.S. 616, 630 (Holmes, J., dissenting).

16. *Schenck v. United States*, 249 U.S. 47, 52 (1919). For a fascinating intellectual history of the origins and evolution of Holmes's aphorism, see Carlton F. W. Larson, *"Shouting 'Fire' in a Theater": The Life and Times of Constitutional Law's Most Enduring Analogy*, 24 WM. & MARY BILL RTS. J. 181 (2015).

17. See *Twitter Terms of Service*, Twitter, June 8, 2020, https://twitter.com/en/tos; *Terms of Use*, Instagram, Apr. 19, 2018, https://help.instagram.com/478745558852511/?helpref=hc_fnav.

18. E.g., Uber, *Opportunity Is Everywhere*, July 15, 2020, https://www.uber.com/us/en/drive/.

19. Ryan Calo & Alex Rosenblat, *The Taking Economy: Uber, Information, and Power*, 117 COLUM. L. REV. 1623 (2017).

20. For an example of one UX engineer at Microsoft pushing back against the "user" trend, see Geof Miller, *We Have Customers, Not Users*, MEDIUM, June 17, 2019, https://medium.com/microsoft-design/we-have-customers-not-users-1f208f16ad3a.

21. ARI EZRA WALDMAN, INDUSTRY UNBOUND: PRIVACY, PRACTICE, AND CORPORATE POWER (2021).

22. TIM WU, THE ATTENTION MERCHANTS (2016).

23. Nicholas Carr, *Digital Sharecropping*, in UTOPIA IS CREEPY AND OTHER PROVOCATIONS, at 30 (2016).

24. *Id.*

25. The novelist Philip Pullman makes a similar point in his essay "Let's Write It in Red: The Practice of Writing." See PHILIP PULLMAN, DÆMON VOICES: ON STORIES AND STORYTELLING 149–50 (2017).

26. Amazon.com, Inc., Annual Report (Form 10-K), at 3 (Feb. 1, 2019).

27. BERNARD E. HARCOURT, EXPOSED: DESIRE AND DISOBEDIENCE IN THE DIGITAL AGE (2015).

28. Neil Richards & Woodrow Hartzog, *The Pathologies of Digital Consent*, 96 WASH. U. L. REV. 1461 (2019).

29. For more on the "control illusion," see Richards & Hartzog, *Taking Trust Seriously in Privacy Law*, *supra*, at 445.

30. Charles Duhigg, *How Companies Learn Your Secrets*, N.Y. TIMES, Feb. 16, 2012.

31. *Id.*

32. WOODROW HARTZOG, PRIVACY'S BLUEPRINT: THE BATTLE TO CONTROL THE DESIGN OF NEW TECHNOLOGIES (2018); Calo & Rosenblat, *The Taking Economy*, *supra*, at 1670 (exploring how "access to information coupled with control of design permits . . . firms . . . to manipulate their users).

33. THE WHITE HOUSE, CONSUMER DATA PRIVACY IN A NETWORKED WORLD: A FRAMEWORK FOR PROTECTING PRIVACY AND PROMOTING INNOVATION IN THE GLOBAL DIGITAL ECONOMY (2012), https://obamawhitehouse.archives.gov/sites/default/files/privacy-final.pdf.

34. See Natasha Singer, *Why a Push for Online Privacy Is Bogged Down in Washington*, N.Y. TIMES, Feb. 28, 2016.

35. *Id.* at iii. (emphasis added).

36. *Transcript of Mark Zuckerberg's Senate Hearing,* Wash. Post, Apr. 10, 2018 (emphasis added).

37. Evgeny Morozov, To Save Everything Click Here (2013).

38. See, e.g., Daniel A. Farber, The First Amendment 23–40, 51–55 (5th ed. 2019).

39. E.g., Adam Thierer, Permissionless Innovation: the Continuing Case for Comprehensive Technological Freedom (2014).

40. See Steven Levy, Facebook: The Inside Story 240–43 (2020); Margaret O'Mara, The Code: Silicon Valley and the Remaking of America 370 (2019).

41. I am grateful to Woody Hartzog for expressing this point in this way. For an example of this phenomenon at Facebook, see Levy, Facebook, *supra,* at 370.

42. 2010 O.J. (C83) 389. Proclaimed by the Commission, Dec. 7, 2000. Proclamation and text at 2000 O.J. (C364) 1. See also *Katz v. United States,* 389 U.S. 347; *Carpenter v. United States,* 138 S. Ct. 2206 (2018); Privacy Act of 1974, Pub. L. No. 93-579, § 88 Stat. 1896, *amended by* 5 U.S.C. § 552(a); *Whalen v. Roe,* 429 U.S. 589 (1977).

43. See The White House, Consumer Data Privacy in a Networked World, *supra.* See also *Microsoft Privacy Report,* https://privacy.microsoft.com/en-US/privacy-report.

44. E.g., Google, First Amendment Protection for Search Engine Search Results (2012) (search results); *Sorrell v. IMS Health,* 131 S. Ct. 2652 (2011) (rejecting the algorithm argument); Ellen Nakashima & Mark Berman, *Apple Says FBI Seeks "Dangerous Power," Files Motion Opposing Court Order to Help Unlock iPhone,* Wash. Post, Feb. 25, 2016 ("Code = speech").

45. See Neil M. Richards, *Why Data Privacy Law Is (Mostly) Constitutional,* 56 Wm. & Mary L. Rev. 1501 (2015).

46. See *id.*; Neil M. Richards, *Reconciling Data Privacy and the First Amendment,* 52 UCLA L. Rev. 1149 (2005); Daniel J. Solove & Neil M. Richards, *Rethinking Free Speech and Civil Liberty,* 109 Colum. L. Rev. 1650 (2009).

47. *Sorrell,* 131 S. Ct. at 2685 (Breyer, J., dissenting).

48. See Richards, *Why Data Privacy Law Is (Mostly) Constitutional, supra,* at 1519. As I explain in that paper, the principal constitutional problem with the privacy law in *Sorrell* was that it discriminated against certain kinds of speakers (drug reps) engaging in protected speech (in-person commercial solicitation of doctors) on the basis of their viewpoint ("Doctor, please prescribe our drugs and not those of other companies"). The law burdened this expression by barring only drug reps from using analytics to deliver their message but did not burden other people speaking about drug policy. For this reason, it was a viewpoint-based restriction on protected commercial speech, and it was unconstitutional because it did not survive strict scrutiny. But it did not hold that the use of analytics itself was protected expression. Indeed, viewpoint-based restrictions on expression are so disfavored in First Amendment law that even laws singling out unprotected expression (like KKK cross burnings) for viewpoint-based restrictions are unconstitutional. See *R.A.V. v. City of St. Paul,* 505 U.S. 377, 391 (1992).

49. Paul Ohm, *The Myth of the Superuser: Fear, Risk, and Harm Online,* 41 U.C. Davis L. Rev. 1327, 1330 (2008). To be clear, Ohm was making this point in the slightly

different context of cybersecurity law, but I believe that the broader claim I use his idea for here remains valid.

50. HARCOURT, EXPOSED, *supra*.

51. *Id.* at 19.

52. ANNE HELEN PETERSEN, CAN'T EVEN: HOW MILLENNIALS BECAME THE BURNOUT GENERATION (2020). Petersen's book is as expansion of a viral article that first appeared (appropriately enough) on *BuzzFeed*. See Anne Helen Petersen, *How Millennials Became the Burnout Generation*, BUZZFEED NEWS, Jan. 5, 2019, https://www.buzzfeednews.com/article/annehelenpetersen/millennials-burnout-generation-debt-work.

53. DANIEL KAHNEMAN, THINKING, FAST AND SLOW 43 (2011).

54. Richards & Hartzog, *The Pathologies of Digital Consent, supra*, at 1492–94; Woodrow Hartzog, *The Case Against Idealising Control*, 4 EUR. DATA PROTECT. L. REV. 423, 429 (2018); AM. PSYCHOL. ASSOC., WHAT YOU NEED TO KNOW ABOUT WILLPOWER: THE PSYCHOLOGICAL SCIENCE OF SELF-CONTROL (2012), https://www.apa.org/topics/willpower; John Tierney, *Do You Suffer From Decision Fatigue?*, N.Y. TIMES, Aug. 17, 2011.

55. The phrase, of course, is Pollan's. See MICHAEL POLLAN, THE OMNIVORE'S DILEMMA (2007).

56. Walton H. Hamilton, *The Ancient Maxim Caveat Emptor*, 40 YALE L. J. 1133 (1931).

57. See Calo & Rosenblat, *The Taking Economy, supra*, at 1671–75; see also HOOFNAGLE, FEDERAL TRADE COMMISSION PRIVACY LAW AND POLICY, *supra*, at 4–5.

58. 15 U.S.C. §45(a); Wheeler-Lea Act, Pub. L. No. 75-447, 52 Stat. 111 (codified as amended at 15 U.S.C. § 45(a)(1) (1938)).

59. See Danielle Keats Citron, *The Privacy Policymaking of State Attorneys General*, 92 NOTRE DAME L. REV. 747, 754 (2016).

60. Ryan Calo & Alex Rosenblatt, *The Taking Economy: Uber, Information, and Power*, 117 Colum. L. Rev. 1623, 1675 (2017).

61. See Directive 95/46/EC of the European Parliament and of the Council of Oct. 24, 1995, on the protection of individuals with regard to the processing of personal data and on the free movement of such data, 1995 O.J. (L 281/31); Regulation (EU) 2016/679 of the European Parliament and of the Council of Apr. 27, 2016, on the protection of natural persons with regard to the processing of personal data and on the free movement of such data, and repealing Directive 95/46/EC (General Data Protection Regulation), 2016 O.J. 2016 (L 119/1).

62. Daniel J. Solove, *Privacy Self-Management and the Consent Dilemma*, 126 HARV. L. REV. 1879 (2013).

63. For an extended argument along these lines (that does get into the specifics of law reform), see Woodrow Hartzog & Neil Richards, *Privacy's Constitutional Moment and the Limits of Data Protection*, 61 B.C. L. REV. 1687 (2020).

64. Kristine Phillips, *"Nobody's Got to Use the Internet": A GOP Lawmaker's Response to Concerns About Web privacy*, WASH. POST, Apr. 15, 2017, https://www.washingtonpost.com/news/powerpost/wp/2017/04/15/nobodys-got-to-use-the-internet-a-gop-lawmakers-response-to-concerns-about-web-privacy/?utm_term=.0eee3d4f6000.

65. See Hoofnagle, Federal Trade Commission Privacy Law and Policy, *supra*, at 28 (dating the FTC's pursuit of false advertising claims to the early 1920s).

66. Solove & Hartzog, *The FTC and the New Common Law of Privacy*, *supra*, at 595–97, 620–25; Hoofnagle, Federal Trade Commission Privacy Law and Policy, *supra*. See also *In re JetBlue Airways Corp. Privacy Litig.*, 379 F. Supp. 2d 299; *Dyer v. Nw. Airlines Corps.*, 334 F. Supp. 2d 1196; *In re Nw. Airlines Privacy Litig.*, 2004 WL 1278459 (D. Minn. 2004).

67. Hoofnagle, Federal Trade Commission Privacy Law and Policy, *supra*, at 157.

68. Federal Trade Commission, *FTC Imposes $5 Billion Penalty and Sweeping New Privacy Restrictions on Facebook,* press release, July 24, 2019, https://www.ftc.gov/news-events/press-releases/2019/07/ftc-imposes-5-billion-penalty-sweeping-new-privacy-restrictions.

69. Hoofnagle, Federal Trade Commission Privacy Law and Policy, *supra*, at 154–57; Solove & Hartzog, *supra*, at 593–94. See also Stephen Hetcher, *The FTC as Internet Privacy Norm Entrepreneur*, 53 Vand. L. Rev. 2041 (2000).

70. Allyson W. Haynes, *Online Privacy Policies: Contracting Away Control Over Personal Information?*, 111 Penn St. L. Rev. 587, 593–94 (2007).

71. *Cf.* Solove & Hartzog, *The FTC and the New Common Law of Privacy*, *supra*, at 628–30 (discussing FTC "broken promises" cases).

72. The phrase "broken promises of privacy" was popularized by Paul Ohm, though in a slightly different context. See Paul Ohm, *Broken Promises of Privacy: Responding to the Surprising Failure of Anonymization*, 57 UCLA L. Rev. 1701 (2010).

73. See 21 C.F.R. § 101.1–101.108. See also Corey A. Ciocchetti, *The Future of Privacy Policies: A Privacy Nutrition Label Filled With Fair Information Practices*, 26 J. Marshall J. Computer & Info. L. 1 (2008); Patrick Gage Kelley et al., *A "Nutrition Label" for Privacy*, Proc. 5th Symp. on Usable Privacy & Security (SOUPS) no. 4 (2009).

74. Ryan Calo, *Against Notice Skepticism in Privacy (and Elsewhere)*, 87 Notre Dame L. Rev. 1027, 1030 (2012) (defining "visceral notice" as "leverag[ing] a consumer's very experience of a product or service to warn or inform" rather than "describing practices in language or symbols"); Richards & Hartzog, *Taking Trust Seriously in Privacy Law*, *supra*, at 462–65; Richards & Hartzog, *Privacy's Trust Gap*, *supra*, at 1213–23.

75. Solove & Hartzog, *The FTC and the New Common Law of Privacy*, *supra*, at 667–69.

76. See *id.* (making a similar argument).

77. 15 U.S.C. § 45(n).

78. See Solove & Hartzog, *The FTC and the New Common Law of Privacy*, *supra*, at 640–42 (collecting examples).

79. *Id.* at 643.

80. William A. McGeveran, *The Duty of Data Security*, 103 Minn. L. Rev. 1135, 1137 (2019).

81. *FTC v. Wyndham Worldwide Corp.*, 799 F.3d 236, 240–42 (3d Cir. 2015) (describing the FTC allegations about Wyndham's practices). The judgment that they were "atrocious" is McGeveran's. See McGeveran, *The Duty of Data Security*, *supra*, at 1194.

82. *Wyndham*, 799 F.3d at 245.

83. *Id.* at 246 (quoting Wyndham Reply Brief at 6).

84. *Id.* at 247.

85. See McGeveran, *The Duty of Data Security, supra.* See also *LabMD v. FTC*, 894 F.3d 1221, 1237 (11th Cir. 2018) (vacating an FTC order that required "reasonable" data security practices as saying "precious little about how this is to be accomplished").

86. Richards & Hartzog, *The Pathologies of Digital Consent, supra.*

87. *Olmstead v. United States*, 277 U.S. 438, 472–73 (1928) (Brandeis, J., dissenting) (quoting *Weems v. United States*, 217 U.S. 349 (1910)). Brandeis was quoting *Weems*, but the passage also evokes the famous introduction to "The Right to Privacy," the landmark article that represented a modern starting point for privacy law in America. See Samuel D. Warren & Louis D. Brandeis, *The Right to Privacy*, 4 HARV. L. REV. 193, 193 (1890) ("Political, social, and economic changes entail the recognition of new rights, and the common law, in its eternal youth, grows to meet the demands of society.").

88. See, e.g., NATASHA DOW SCHÜLL, ADDICTION BY DESIGN: MACHINE GAMBLING IN LAS VEGAS (2014) (study of the use of design, surveillance, and behavioral psychology to make casinos addictive to gamblers); JOSEPH TUROW, THE AISLES HAVE EYES: HOW RETAILERS TRACK YOUR SHOPPING, STRIP YOUR PRIVACY, AND DEFINE YOUR POWER (2018); Kimi Yoshino & Dave McKibben, *A Park With a Powerful Spell*, L.A. TIMES, Mar. 15, 2019 (Disneyland).

89. HARTZOG, PRIVACY'S BLUEPRINT, *supra*, at 145.

90. Joshua Bote, *Facebook Tweaks Homepage, No Longer Says It Is "Free and Always Will Be*," USA TODAY, Aug. 27, 2019.

91. David Adam Friedman, *Free Offers: A New Look*, 38 N.M. L. REV. 49, 68–69 (2008) (arguing that "free" is deceptive in many contexts).

92. SHOSHANNA ZUBOFF, THE AGE OF SURVEILLANCE CAPITALISM 63–70 (2019).

93. *Id.* at 127.

94. Kristina Shampanier et al., *Zero as a Special Price: The True Value of Free Products*, 26:6 MARKETING SCIENCE, 742 (Nov.–Dec. 2007).

95. Mary Ellen Gordon, *The History of App Pricing, and Why Most Apps Are Free*, Flurry.com, July 18, 2018, https://www.flurry.com/post/115189750715/the-history-of-app-pricing-and-why-most-apps-are.

96. Chris Jay Hoofnagle & Jan Whittington, *Free: Accounting for the Costs of the Internet's Most Popular Price*, 61 UCLA L. REV. 606, 608 (2014).

97. *Id.* at 610–11.

98. See *id.* at 657–65 (considering these and other options).

99. Sheera Frenkel & Kevin Roose, *Zuckerberg, Facing Facebook's Worst Crisis Yet, Pledges Better Privacy*, N.Y. TIMES, Mar. 21, 2018, https://www.nytimes.com/2018/03/21/technology/facebook-zuckerberg-data-privacy.html.

100. Nicholas Thompson, *Mark Zuckerberg Talks to Wired About Facebook's Privacy Problem*, WIRED, Mar. 21, 2018, https://www.wired.com/story/mark-zuckerberg-talks-to-wired-about-facebooks-privacy-problem/.

101. Marshall Kirkpatrick, *Facebook's Zuckerberg Says the Age of Privacy Is Over*, READWRITE, Jan. 2, 2010, http://readwrite.com/2010/01/09/facebooks_zuckerberg_ says_the_age_of_privacy_is_ ov#awesm=~oo2UUoqssyO3eq.

102. See Richards & Hartzog, *Taking Trust Seriously in Privacy Law*, *supra*; Neil Richards & Woodrow Hartzog, *Trusting Big Data Research*, 65 DEPAUL L. REV. 579 (2017); Richards & Hartzog, *Privacy's Trust Gap*, *supra*; Neil Richards & Woodrow Hartzog, *A Duty of Loyalty for Privacy Law*, 99 WASH. U. L. REV. (forthcoming), https://papers.ssrn.com/sol3/papers.cfm?abstract_id=3642217.

103. Jack M. Balkin, *Information Fiduciaries and the First Amendment*, 49 U.C. DAVIS L. REV. 1183 (2016); Kiel Brennan-Marquez, *Fourth Amendment Fiduciaries*, 84 FORD. L. REV. 611, (2015); Dennis D. Hirsch, *Privacy, Public Goods, and the Tragedy of the Trust Commons: A Response to Professors Fairfield and Engel*, 65 DUKE L. J. ONLINE 67 (2016); Ari Ezra Waldman, *Privacy as Trust: Sharing Personal Information in a Networked World*, 69 U. MIAMI L. REV. 559, 561 (2015); Kirsten Martin, *Transaction Costs, Privacy, and Trust: The Laudable Goals and Ultimate Failure of Notice and Choice to Respect Privacy Online*, 18 FIRST MONDAY (Dec. 2013),http://firstmonday.org/ojs/index.php/fm/article/view/4838/3802.

104. See Richards & Hartzog, *A Duty of Loyalty for Privacy Law*, *supra*.

105. Robert Booth, *Facebook Reveals News Feed Experiment to Control Emotions*, THE GUARDIAN, June 29, 2014.

106. Jonathan Zittrain, *Facebook Could Decide an Election Without Anyone Ever Finding Out*, THE NEW REPUBLIC, June 1, 2014, https://newrepublic.com/article/117878/ information-fiduciary-solution-facebook-digital-gerrymandering.

107. JARON LANIER, YOU ARE NOT A GADGET: A MANIFESTO (2011); BRETT FRISCHMANN & EVAN SELINGER, RE-ENGINEERING HUMANITY (2018); Evan Selinger & Brett Frischmann, *Will the Internet of Things Result in Predictable People?*, THE GUARDIAN, Aug. 10, 2015, https://www.theguardian.com/technology/2015/ aug/10/internet-of-things-predictable-people.

108. Neil Richards, *The iPhone Case and the Future of Civil Liberties*, BOSTON REVIEW, Feb. 25, 2016, http://www.bostonreview.net/us/neil-richards-apple-iphone-privacy [http://perma.cc/RNC6-QXDA].

109. Neil Richards & Jonathan Heusel, *We Will Work Out the Commercial, Clinical, Ethical and Legal Issues Around Genome Sequencing*, THE WIRED WORLD IN 2018, WIRED MAGAZINE (UK) (2017).

Conclusion

1. See HELEN NISSENBAUM, PRIVACY IN CONTEXT: TECHNOLOGY, PRIVACY, AND THE INTEGRITY OF SOCIAL LIFE 3 (2010).

2. Julie E. Cohen, *What Privacy Is For*, 126 HARV. L. REV. 1904, 1904 (2013).

3. See NEIL RICHARDS, INTELLECTUAL PRIVACY: RETHINKING CIVIL LIBERTIES IN A DIGITAL AGE (2015).

4. See Nissenbaum, Privacy in Context, *supra*.

5. Eur. Conv. Fund. Rts. Art 8; Eur. Charter of Fund. Rts. & Freedoms Arts 7 & 8.

6. See Commission Regulation 2016/679, 2016 O.J. (L 119) 1 (EU) (providing the new GDPR).

7. Pub. L. 93-579 § 2 (1974).

8. See Lawrence Cappello, None of Your Damn Business: Privacy in the United States From the Gilded Age to the Digital Age 200–203 (2020).

9. Danielle Keats Citron, *The Privacy Policymaking of State Attorneys General*, 92 Notre Dame L. Rev. 747, 748–51 (2016).

10. See California Reader Privacy Act of 2012, Cal. Civ. Code § 1798.90 (Deering Supp. 2012); Illinois Biometric Information Privacy Act, 740 Ill. Comp. Stat. Ann. 14/15.

11. See Scott Skinner-Thompson, Privacy at the Margins (2021).

12. Julie E. Cohen, *Turning Privacy Inside Out*, 20 Theo. Inq. in L. 1 (2019).

13. Ari Ezra Waldman, Industry Unbound: Privacy, Practice, and Corporate Power (2021).

Index

For the benefit of digital readers, indexed terms that span two pages (e.g., 52–53) may, on occasion, appear on only one of those pages.